WORK
AND
HUMAN
BEHAVIOR

Third Edition

WORK
AND
HUMAN
BEHAVIOR

Third Edition

Walter S. Neff

Aldine de Gruyter
New York

ABOUT THE AUTHOR

Walter S. Neff is Professor Emeritus, New York University and Professor of Psychiatry (Psychology) at the School of Medicine, SUNY/Stony Brook. He received his PhD in experimental psychology from Cornell University. His early work was in the area of the social psychology of mental disorder. He was one of the pioneers in the developing and controversial field of psychiatric rehabilitation. Dr. Neff has taught at several universities and was, for 12 years, Director of Research of the Chicago Jewish Vocational Service. His chief research focus has been on the psychological problems of work adjustment and in the use of work as a therapeutic medium for the emotionally disturbed. He is a Fellow of the American Psychological Association and Past-President of the Division on the Psychological Aspects of Disability of the APA.

Aldine de Gruyter
A Division of Walter de Gruyter, Inc.
200 Saw Mill River Road
Hawthorne NY 10532

Library of Congress Cataloging in Publication Data

Neff, Walter Scott, 1910–
      Work and human behavior.

      Bibliography: p.
      Includes indexes.
      1. Work—Psychological aspects. 2. Labor and
laboring classes—Mental health. I. Title.
BF481.N34   1985   158.7   85-1219
ISBN 0-202-30319-5
ISBN 0-202-30320-9 (pbk.)

Printed in the United States of America
10 9 8 7 6 5 4 3

To Mary, Rick, and Alan

CONTENTS

3. The Study of Work Behavior

4. Work as a Sphere of Individual Behavior

5. Psychoanalytic Theories of Work Behavior

6. Psychological Theories of Work Behavior

10. The Techniques of Work Adjustment

III • WORK AND MENTAL HEALTH

11. Psychopathology and Work: Some Conceptual Issues

12. Work and the Psychoses

PREFACE TO THE THIRD EDITION

In the first edition of *Work and Human Behavior,* the author examined work from the points of view of social psychology and social psychiatry. Work was seen as a uniquely human activity, which has decisively differentiated the human being from other living organisms. While other animals are compelled to live in the world largely as they find it, the unique biological equipment of *Homo sapiens*—the hyperdeveloped brain, upright posture, the prehensile hand with an opposing thumb, binocular vision—have enabled him to *alter* aspects of the physical world in order to live in it more certainly and more easily. This process of alteration—ranging from the chipping of stones to make tools and weapons, at one extreme, to the complexities of modern industry, at the other—comprises the process we call *human work.* Work also has its social aspects as it both generates and is enmeshed by a very wide variety of social relationships. Finally, work was examined as an issue in individual psychology, leading to formation of a general theory of work behavior. All this comprised Parts I and II of the first edition. The book concluded with two additional sections: Part III dealt with some clinical issues—the assessment of work potential, the techniques of work adjustment, and the problems of maladaptation to work and Part IV examined some contemporary problems—the handicapped worker and the consequences of technological innovation.

The second edition of this book was prompted by two considerations: first, the need to update after a lapse of some years and, second, the appearance in the 1970s of two new kinds of problems. The first of these had to do with work alienation and the second with the problems and dilemmas of the work of women and minorities.

A third edition now seems appropriate. In addition to updating the material of the second edition, new issues have arisen that are currently leading to a certain amount of public clamor. The first issue concerns the sources of worker productivity prompted by the current decline of preeminence of United States industry both in the world market and in certain aspects of our internal market. The second issue involves the complex relations between work and mental health, with work being viewed, on one hand, as a factor in the generation of insecurity and mental illness and, from another, as a factor in the treatment of the severe mental disorders. While much of the current published material on these two issues is characterized more by heat than by enlightenment, the third edition includes new chapters in these widely debated areas.

Part I brings together what we know and can guess about the nature of human work. Chapters 2–3 examine the role of work in various human societies, including, of course, our own. We next turn to a consideration of how work behavior develops in the individual, from infancy to adulthood, with particular attention to its transactional character. In the course of doing so, we review some contemporary theories of work behavior and assemble one of our own. Part II is concerned with the assessment and treatment of inappropriate work behavior. Part III is entirely new and deals with the complex relations of work and mental health. Part IV updates the materials on women and minorities, considers the affects of technology and poverty, and includes a new section on productivity.

Walter S. Neff

ACKNOWLEDGMENTS

Much of the research and experience background that made this book possible was supported by the Social and Rehabilitation Service of the U.S. Department of Health, Education and Welfare. I am particularly grateful to Drs. James F. Garrett, William A. Usdane, and Joan Criswell of the SRS Division of Research, who gave me continual encouragement. I am also in the debt of Dr. William Gellman, Executive Director of the Jewish Vocational Service of Chicago, whose stimulating and creative leadership of this pioneering agency made my 12-year association with it a continuous intellectual challenge. Many other people have contributed, since research is a social enterprise.

I am also grateful to New York University, whose grant of sabbatical leave during the first half of 1968 gave me the needed time for the bulk of the actual writing of the first edition.

1 | THE SCOPE OF THE PROBLEM

It is desirable at the outset to specify those aspects of the work of human beings that are the primary concern of the present writer. Work is so pervasive a human activity that it has engaged the attention of an extremely wide variety of writers, commentators, and thinkers. Work is also so many-sided a human enterprise that it has been written about from a great many different points of view, representing almost every field of knowledge and almost every level of our social structure. Merely to identify these points of view is an impressive task. Work has been written about by theologians and philosophers, by poets and novelists, by historians, economists, and sociologists, by biologists and naturalists, by politicians, by essayists and journalists. It has been described as both a blessing and a curse, as the chief means through which man has developed a high culture, and as a ravager of our natural environment. Entire theories of society have been built on it, and it has been the subject matter of extremely bitter social struggles, ranging from relatively localized labor strife to major wars and revolutions. Clearly, man's ability to work, including the complex and variegated social relations that have developed around man-as-worker, constitutes one of those great domains of human activity that—in one way or another—shape the lives of almost all of us. It is equally clear that one cannot enter into all the aspects of the world of work with equal competence and authority. Each of us has his own vantage point—his own particular axe to grind.

THE SOCIAL PSYCHOLOGY OF WORK

It will be helpful at the outset if the writer describes his *own* vantage point, so that his sins of omission and commission will become more intelligible. We wish to approach the problems of human work from the standpoint of a psychologist—more exactly, a social psychologist. We see the ability to work as one of those major human competencies that our species has developed as a function of our biological structure, our evolutionary and cultural history, the complex and varied pressure of social norms

1

and social conventions, and the accidents and idiosyncracies of our individual biographical pasts. From this point of view, work is a problem in social behavior. Like other great domains of social behavior—the ability to speak a language, the ability to enter into enormously varying sets of sexual and familial relationships—the human ability to work is a dauntingly complex function of biology and culture. One of our interests is to work out the relationships between the basic biological equipment we bring to our work and the great array of cultural norms, demands, and traditions that we internalize with varying degress of effectiveness during the long process of growth from infancy to adulthood. In this connection, we need to distinguish between the *necessary* conditions of the human ability to work and its *sufficient* conditions. From one standpoint, the individual human being is not born with the ability to work effectively any more than he is born with the ability to make a successful marriage. It is true that certain built-in *biological* features of *Homo sapiens* must be regarded as conditions without which our ability to work would not be possible: upright posture, binocular vision, the prehensile hand, a hyperdeveloped cerebrum. It is also true that the adult ability to work is a product of a long series of individually experienced events and circumstances that occur within an elaborate matrix of sociocultural demands, expectations, structures, and traditions. One of our major concerns will be to consider the manner in which the nonworking child becomes a working adult.

Continuing our specification of the vantage point of this volume, we should add that we have a strong interest in the psychopathology of work. Given that the adult ability to work is not simply a function of our anatomical structure, given that it is an outcome of a long process of personal and interpersonal development, it is important to know something about the various ways in which this process can go wrong. It does not take much observation of human work behavior to discover that people work with greatly varying degrees of effectiveness and commitment. There are people who appear unable to work at all, even though they possess at least the minimal physical equipment. There are others who find it psychologically necessary to work even in the presence of major handicapping conditions and who perform their work at very considerable personal cost. There are compulsive workers who are driven to work by imperative internal demands, and there are others who are driven to work only by external necessity or by social forces that they cannot resist. And, of course, there are a great many people who simply take work for granted as one of the given conditions of human existence. However, we will be concerned here primarily with the problems of individuals for whom work presents some kind of major adaptive difficulty, either because of a physical or mental handicap or because of one or another kind of failure in the socialization process.

The problems of maladaptation to work are many and complex. Current study has revealed a fairly large number of people in our society who find it very difficult or impossible to work and a still larger number whose work history is so unstable or erratic that the maintenance of gainful employment can be considered a major life problem. Speaking more broadly, most of us, at some time in our lives, encounter a variety of difficulties in deriving a maximal degree of satisfaction from our work or cannot avoid some measure of irritation, anxiety, anger, or feelings of decreased personal worth. Under these circumstances, it may seem surprising that the vast literature of psychiatry and clinical psychology includes little concerning the human problems of working.[1]

Before we can focus on the psychopathology of work, however, we will have to examine the importance of work to the human condition, and we will have to examine the process through which the nonworking child becomes a working adult. Some conceptual matters are necessary preliminaries. First, because our attitudes to work are not something that each of us needs to invent *de novo* but are in large measure set for us by the special and peculiar history of particular societies, we shall have to consider the various social and cultural contexts within which human work has been, and is, performed. Societies and cultures have assigned very different values to work, many of which tend to be reflected in inconsistent ways in its contemporary evaluation. Second, we shall have to deal with the difficult task of defining work and relating its meanings and functions to those of other human activities. Third, we shall have to describe the formal and informal structure of work-situations, since the manner in which we work is at least as much a function of the work setting as it is of the particular psychological baggage we bring to the workplace. Fourth, we shall try to develop a general

---

[1]A persistent but untraceable story has it that when Sigmund Freud was once asked to specify the main activities of human existence, he answered: *Lieben und Arbeiten*—to love and to work. It remains true, however, that Freud and his followers have written a great deal abut love but very little about work. Of the thousands of titles listed in a comprehensive index of psychoanalytical writings (Grinstein, 1960), fewer than a dozen papers relate to work or labor. None of the major psychiatric texts, whether psychoanalytic or not in their basic persuasion, makes more than a passing reference to this issue, and a great many do not mention it all. This is despite the fact that disruption of the ability to work is seen as a significant diagnostic criterion of severe mental disorder. It seems likely that this situation is traceable to a generalized presumption that impairment of the ability to work is a consequence of a "deeper" set of problems, and it is the latter that should receive primary attention. A corollary of this presumption is a belief that if the more "basic" emotional problems are solved, the work problems will fall into place. We shall be at some pains to question this assumption in a later chapter.

We should note that this comparative neglect is in process of being rectified. A new subspecialty focused on mental health problems in the workplace (McLean, 1974, 1979; Cooper and Payne, 1978) is in process of development in the name of Occupational Psychiatry. Further, renewed interest in the problem is attested to by the convening in March 1982 of the first national conference on Work and Mental Health (see footnote 4, Chapter 12).

theory of the work personality; general personality theory has tended to neglect this particular facet of human behavior. Finally, we shall attempt to describe the various ways in which the development of an adequate work personality may be impeded, thus producing a taxonomy of work pathology.

WORK AS A PSYCHOLOGICAL PROBLEM

We have said that work is a social phenomenon that must be understood in the context of social institutions and structures. But work is performed by individual human beings, not societies. Although virtually all human beings in all societies must somehow come to terms with the demand to work, the manner in which each person meets this demand is a problem in individual psychology. The conditions that influence how we work, and whether we work at all, are not only social and historical but also individual and personal. We shall have to consider the latter set of conditions and examine how they interact with the first set.

Within the general discipline of psychology, two subspecialties have developed that take different aspects of human work as a primary focus: industrial psychology and vocational psychology. Although we shall have to come to terms with both these fields, the content of this volume does not fall neatly into either.

Industrial psychology has concerned itself largely with the factors that militate for and against work *efficiency*. The essential ability to work at all is taken as given, and the focus of study is on other questions: What abilities are required by different kinds of work? What types of work are preferred by people of different education and background? What is the effect of variation of working conditions on productivity and morale? How can we improve the efficiency of the supervisor and executive? What are the effects on work of various patterns of organization in the workplace? Some industrial psychologists have carried out extensive studies of mental health problems encountered in the workplace, although these have been generally looked on as factors influencing productivity. The overriding interest is in work efficiency.

The main interest of vocational psychology has been in the variables that influence occupational choice. What is it that impels individuals to become doctors, engineers, teachers, mechanics, laborers? Can we develop assessment systems that will enable us to identify the capabilities required by this or that occupation? Can we develop early warning systems in order to spot career potentialities, and can we influence the process through which young people make occupational choices? In the course of attempting to answer these questions, vocational psychologists have carried out valuable studies of the development of vocational attitudes. We will incorporate the results of these studies when we attempt to generate our own theory of work behavior (cf. Chapters 7 and 8).

These are matters of considerable interest in themselves and of considerable importance for the majority of people who work. We are interested here, however, in what might be called a prior set of questions. Why are some people unable to adjust to work under even the best of working conditions? What are the life experiences that facilitate or impede a satisfactory adjustment to work? Is there a specialized set of demands and pressures, conventions and rituals, with which each person must cope, constituting a *subculture of work*? Does it make any sense to speak of the *work personality*, a sector of human behavior that may be distinct from other aspects of the human personality? Does work involve the possibility of conflicts and dilemmas that are sufficiently different from those in other life-spheres that relatively specialized kinds of *psychopathological work behavior* make their appearance?

What we will formulate here, then, is a general theory of *work adjustment*, which will account for the tremendous range of variation in behavior among people confronted with the demand to work. In this sense, the perspective of the writer is that of the general social psychologist interested in the analysis of human behavior in social settings. From this perspective, work is a two-sided process. On the one hand, it is a human activity that takes place in highly socialized settings, and many of its characteristics are only intelligible if they are understood as responses to the demand characteristic of work situations. On the other hand, the ability to work is a consequence of a prolonged period of socialization, during which the individual has internalized (with greater or less effectiveness and with much idiosyncratic variation) a long series of instructions, traditions, customs, and rituals, which together make up the experience background for the motivation to work and produce what can be called the individual work-style.

We should add that we have no intention of limiting ourselves in this volume to purely theoretical issues. An extensive field of practice already exists, designed to help disabled, handicapped, or otherwise maladapted people to improve their vocational adjustment. By this time in the United States, thousands of professionals are providing services to hundreds of thousands of clients who have problems bearing upon work.[2] During the past few decades, we have accumulated a considerable body of information. We know a good deal about many of the broad social factors affecting

---

[2]Two large federal agencies—the Department of Labor and the Social and Rehabilitation Service (SRS) of the Department of Health, Education, and Welfare (now the Department of Health and Human Services)—spend millions of dollars annually to help people with their vocational problems. Every state of the Union maintains public agencies devoted to this interest, which in turn have developed relations to a network of private agencies. Most local systems of education now employ specially trained teachers for vocational guidance, and many universities maintain vocational guidance services. A large number of institutions of higher education now present specialized courses of instruction designed to produce

employment and unemployment—the vagaries of the business cycle, the consequences of technological change, the effects of racial and religious discrimination, the roles and functions of education, socioeconomic status, and similar societal variables. We have some knowledge concerning methods of guidance and counseling. Much of the latter technology, however, is simply borrowed from the more general field of psychotherapy, and there are some questions the writer will raise later concerning the appropriateness of these techniques for certain important issues related to work. What is largely lacking, however, in this new field of practice is systematic consideration of how any individual develops those attitudes, feelings, reactions, and behaviors that we subsume under the general heading of the *work personality*. Particularly serious, for a field that is committed to remedy the problems of the vocationally disadvantaged, is the fact that we lack readily available information on the varieties of *work psychopathology*.

WORK AND MENTAL HEALTH

In Chapters, 11, 12, and 13, we shall examine the relations among work, mental disorder, and mental health in some detail, but at the outset we want to point to some matters of general interest. There is a two-sided character to the connections between work and mental health. That is to say, there are both positives and negatives. The question of which set predominates for any given individual is a complex affair.

Experts in the helping professions have pointed to a number of positive sides to working. First, work is "reality-bound," that is, the working person is confronted with a range of largely impersonal and objective activities that may have the effect of diminishing his preoccupation with the personal and subjective. Second, to be able to work in a work-oriented society is to be "like" others and thus to ameliorate the terrible feelings of isolation and pathological uniqueness that plague many emotionally disturbed persons. Third, in a culture that places great stress on independence and competence, chronic unemployment can only exacerbate feelings of worthlessness and low self-esteem which may already be troublesome for other

---

trained professionals oriented to the various problems of adjustment to work. This field of practice is quite new (largely dating from the mid-1950s), struggling still for a professional identity and attempting to find its way through the morass of the helping services. During the 1960s, there was a vast expansion of both training and service facilities, largely as a consequence of the commitment of a series of federal administrations to full employment as a matter of social policy. The launching by the Johnson administration of an official "war on poverty," disclosures of serious underemployment among many (especially black) minority groups, increasing concern about the consequences of the mechanization and automation of work, demands for change in work opportunities made by various special interest groups (youth, women, the aged)—all these have been factors in bringing the problems of work and work adjustment to the level of national importance.

reasons. Fourth, people in recovery from an episode of severe mental disorder may find that it is only some form of gainful employment that will keep them from living the rest of their lives in a mental hospital or nursing home. All this is quite beside the obvious advantages of a guaranteed income from gainful employment.

Of course, there are many negatives as well, with some authorities arguing that the negatives outweigh the positives. A great many people in modern society are limited to work tasks that are both boring and meaningless, leading to weakened motivation to work and an unwillingness to commit a great deal of energy to perform it. There are also people who cannot easily bear the competitive pressures inherent in many work situations, for whom success is a dangerous risk and failure a catastrophe. For others, to work means to subordinate themselves to a capricious and unfeeling authority, a limit on personal freedom. As we shall have occasion to note in a later chapter, most work situations are highly *social* in nature. Working requires not only that one must perform certain tasks but also that one must somehow deal with a variety of people carrying out a range of social roles: supervisors, peers, subordinates, customers, consumers. People whose relationships with others tend to be precarious may find it difficult to adapt to work because they cannot handle its social aspects, even though they may be quite able to perform a given work task.

Thus, work is both a condition of mental health and a condition of mental disorder. Like the family, work seems to be something we cannot do without, but it has its share of problems and difficulties. In examining the relations between work and mental health, we must be careful to avoid being one-sided. For most people, work is neither an unalloyed blessing nor a total curse. There are, of course, individual representatives of either extreme, but they appear to be small minorities. Most of us appear to muddle along in the domain of work without so much strain that we fall apart, but without a great deal of gratification either. But *some* important elements of gratification are provided by working, and we shall have to tease them out. Other sides of working are less pleasant, and we should not ignore them. The gratification a person derives from working, as well as whatever anguish he may also receive, is an exceedingly complex outcome of an *interaction* between the cultural, psychological, and social baggage the individual brings to his job and the physical and social demands of the work situation itself. Adjustment to work is neither wholly a matter of ideology, attitude, and motivation— claims for the force of the Judeo–Christian ethic notwithstanding—nor wholly a matter of the conditions of work. Facilitation of a given individual's adaptation to work may involve tinkering with both terms of this equation.

We cannot, of course, deal with this complex set of issues in one fell swoop. The bulk of the book to follow examines necessary aspects of the relations of work and mental health: changes in the conceptualization of work throughout human history, views as to the genesis of our individual attitudes to work, the kinds of demands made by typical work situations—all this culminating in a theory of work behavior. Only then are we prepared to confront directly the relations of work and mental health generally, a task we undertake later in Part III.

PRODUCTIVITY

One of the great public outcries of the present decade is based on the claim that the productivity of the American worker is in a state of sharp decline. The occasion for the outcry has been the successful penetration of the huge American domestic market by industrial products from abroad. The most obvious example is the successful penetration of the American home market by the Japanese-produced automobile, which now claims some 25% of our domestic market. The result has been what looks like a permanent state of crisis in the American automotive industry, with mass unemployment among auto workers and the closing or underutilization of major factories. Since the production of automobiles is a centerpiece of American industry, there has also been a pronounced ripple effect, involving production losses in other vital industrial sectors: steel, nonferrous metals, production machinery, machine tools, and the like. The foreign car, whether Japanese, West German, French, or Italian, is not the only invader of the American home market. There is an increasingly long list of successful industrial imports: textiles, clothing, electronic goods, cameras and optical equipment, medical equipment, etc. While such an eventuality seems still far from realization, some authorities are currently arguing that the United States is in danger of being reduced to some kind of semicolonial status: a producer and exporter of food and raw materials and an importer of manufactured goods. Of course, the consequences for our political and economic influence and for our standard of living are almost too awesome to contemplate.

The factors governing the productivity of labor are exceedingly intricate, and some lie quite beyond the purview of this volume. However, work is still performed by human beings, even if their labors now take the form of service of ever more complex and powerful machines. It is legitimate to ask, therefore, to what degree the current production crisis can be attributed to factors on the human side, whether the particular human beings we are concerned with are laborers or managers, engineers or scientists, planners or politicians. Since many of the human players in the productive process have competing, even antagonistic, interests, we should not be surprised to encounter much blame-avoidance and mutual scapegoating. It has been charged, for example, that our current economic problems are traceable to a decline in the power of the traditional work ethic, so that workers are no longer willing or able to deliver a "fair day's work for a fair day's pay." On the other hand, it has been charged that our problems arise from an excessive preoccupation on the part of American management with short-term profits, so that they are unwilling or unable to forego immediate for long-term gains. Self-indulgent laziness at one pole, blind greed at the other!

All of this seems too simple! In this volume, our objective is to analyze the origin and development of the human ability to work. In doing so, we shall also have to examine the conditions of work: the social, environmental, and ecological factors that influence the manner in which work is performed. Once we have done so, we are then in a better position to consider the human factors involved in productivity. In the concluding section of the book, we shall return to the tangled problems of the roles of human beings in the process of industrial production.

A TRANSACTIONAL APPROACH

I think it is a service to the reader for an introductory chapter to specify the writer's theoretical vantage point. The writer is a psychologist—but there are many psychological specialties. As a discipline, psychology straddles a very wide array of disparate problems, ranging from those of interest to physiology, at one extreme, and to sociology, at the other. Psychology is both a life science and a social science and is variably listed as one or the other (or both) in university catalogues. It will be obvious that the writer finds the problems of social science more congenial and of greater personal interest, but it is also true that he could not ignore certain characteristics of *Homo sapiens* as a biological species. The writer is also largely an environmentalist, although he is fully aware that the ability of the human animal to maintain and generate culture is itself a consequence of a long process of biological evolution.

We have used the term *behavior* in the title of this volume, although we know that this term has always been an ambiguous one for psychologists, who assign many meanings to it. We shall attempt to specify what *we* mean by it. It would be a mistake, however, to believe that our use of the term implies commitment to any particular "school" of psychological theorizing. In particular, it implies no commitment to the theoretical position identified as *behaviorism,* a theoretical standpoint very prominent in psychology from the early writings of John B. Watson to the contemporary work of B. F. Skinner. As a theoretical position, behaviorism encompasses two basic ideas: First, that all (or virtually all) human psychological activity is a function of learning; second, that our investigative methodologies should avoid any effort to determine what is going on inside the "black box" of the human head (thoughts, feelings, ideas, wishes, etc.) but instead confine themselves to an objective description of what organisms actually *do*. We accept certain aspects of the former notion (plasticity, modifiability, adaptability *are* prime characteristics of the human organism) but reject the second idea as an intolerable restriction of the scope of the psychological enterprise. We believe it is both possible and necessary to make valid inferences concerning those psychological processes that lie behind our actions: feeling states, affects, attitudes, beliefs, and motivations.

Why, then, do we use the word *behavior* at all? In part because, through usage, it has come to be a synonym for general psychological activity. In part because, by connotation, it helps us to avoid the mind–body problem. But we still need to specify our definition. We will take the position that human psychological activity—behavior—is essentially *transactional;* that is, we are always dealing with a highly complex interrelationship between certain characteristics of the organism and certain characteristics of its surround. The exact nature of this interrelationship is very difficult to penetrate, but we agree with Dewey and Bentley (1949) that it has the nature of a transaction. Since this term is familiar to us chiefly from business practice, where it is used to define a contract or agreement between two or more parties to an economic event, we will need to indicate its relevance for the theory of behavior.

The use of the term for us implies that the organism is neither merely a passive recipient or registrar of environmental stimuli nor is it wholly an independent initiator of its psychological behavior. In its natural form—as human beings behave *in vivo,* so to speak—psychological behavior is *activity-in-an-environment,* with the two terms of this expression scarcely separable. From earliest infancy, the human organism is engaged in active efforts to know and master its environment, in the service of an increasingly tangled network of needs and aims. The human being thus develops, for example, an entire repertory of perceptual habits and skills, which enable him to deal with objects in terms of size, distance, shape, color, and an array of identifying meanings and characteristics. It is true that we can set up laboratory situations in which the organism is reduced to a near-passive state (the trained and instructed subject) and thus attempt to study the range of stimuli to which he can respond under these circumstances. But this operation is full of theoretical hazards, as research in the perceptual constancies has amply demonstrated. In their ordinary activity in the world, human beings do not merely *sense;* they *perceive.* Perceived objects do not merely have sensory qualities; they have meanings, values, uses. The child is not merely handed these identifying characteristics of his surround by his physical constitution or by the nature of the physical world. He learns how and what to perceive through a complex process of seeing, hearing, touching, grasping, tasting, moving, throwing, and the like. Moreover, the process of knowing is motivated by needs and accompanied by feeling and emotion. Thus, the behavioral modes develop through *action* on and through the environment, in the service of needs.

Our examination of human work will be made from this kind of understanding, which has come to be known as the *transactional approach.* From this standpoint, adult work behavior may be considered the complex product of a long series of events, through which the individual learns to assign certain meanings to a wide range of environmental phenomena and, simultaneously, attempts to cope with certain environmental demands. To use engineering language, we can look upon the process as a complicated input–output analysis.

In terms of input, we are all, to a significant extent, selective perceivers. Each of us can attend, at any given moment, to only a portion of the vast array of physical stimuli that continuously bombard our receptors, and each of us has learned to place different interpretations on what is "out there." Two persons at work may both "see" the same thing—for example, the foreman walking into the room. One person may register this event as a sign of danger, because he has learned to be fearful of authority, while the other individual perceives the same objective event as a stimulating challenge, because *he* has learned that authority figures dispense rewards as well as punishments. From this point of view, we experience environmental stimuli and act on them as if we are living in what Cantril (1957) called an "assumptive world"; the assumptive world consists of an individualized set of expectancies and attitudes about the surround that each of us develops as a consequence of a series of transactions with it.

Output also varies idiosyncratically, and not only because of variations in native ability.[3] Our actions, including our behaviors at work, are a function of two sets of conditions: the demand characteristics and structure of the immediate setting with which we are interacting, and the entire set of psychological baggage that we bring with us into the setting. From this, it follows that there are two kinds of distinctions to consider. First, we will want to explore the possibility that work behavior differs from other broad kinds of human behavior because work settings make different demands from those of other kinds of settings. Second, we will need to examine how work behavior differs from person to person, based on different sets of life experiences.

How does the transactional viewpoint influence our conceptualization of human work? First, we will take the position that work behavior is a complex series of interactions manifested by persons (working individuals) when they

[3]We cannot here enter into the difficult issue of heredity and environment, since it is a topic of such complexity and controversy that it would divert us from our main task. Suffice it to say, however, that the science of psychology does not yet have the tools to make a determination of how inheritance and experience interrelate to influence the ability to work. We are currently passing through a period of intense argument concerning the degree to which "intelligence" is a function of innate capacities, and we are a long way from developing the methodologies with which to settle the argument. It is plausible to observe that infants appear to differ at birth in sensitivity, motility, responsiveness, and the like, but the relationships between these observations and adult work behavior are still obscure. Whatever the ultimate outcome of the IQ controversy, we will concern ourselves here entirely with postnatal events.

are imbedded in or confronted with certain characteristic environments (work situations). Second, we will assume that these interactions (transactions) are *adaptive behaviors,* that they reflect how each person has learned to cope with certain environmental demands and pressures since early childhood. Third, we will assume that we can account for most significant aspects of human work behavior without invoking primary drives or instincts as explanatory variables. We adopt this assumption partly because we believe that the human animal is far less dependent upon such built-in trigger-like mechanisms than are other animal species, and partly because, in the present state of knowledge, invocation of instincts is simply a confession of ignorance. Finally, a necessary prerequisite for this task will be an effort to develop a phenomenology of the demand characteristics of work situations, if we are to understand work behavior as a series of rather specialized transactions that the individual develops in dealing with the pressures of his surround.

Thus, in succeeding chapters, we will focus on two broad sets of variables: (1) the variables that describe the demand characteristics of work situations, and (2) the variables that influence the origins and forms of the selective perceptions and differential coping behaviors displayed by individuals who are confronted with the demand to work. In dealing with the first problem, we will lean heavily on the disciplines of history, anthropology, and sociology. The second problem brings us more squarely into the region of social psychology.

To be true to our aim of looking at work from the transactional standpoint, we will have to avoid two errors: that kind of analysis that focuses on the individual in disregard of the surround and that which focuses on the surround in disregard of the individual. Although the requirements of discourse will force us to deal separately with the working person and the work situation, we will try to be continually aware that we are merely making temporary abstractions of the features of a unitary process.

PEOPLE WHO ARE "APPARENTLY UNEMPLOYABLE"

So far we have concerned ourselves largely with matters of general theory. We believe, however, that our views have been strongly influenced by the kinds of practical issues we have been compelled to consider. It is necessary to say something, therefore, about the experience that has provided the setting in which the writer's ideas have evolved. This seems all the more pertinent since much of the material to be presented derives from observations made on rather special kinds of people in unique work situations.

For some 30 years, the writer observed the work behavior of individuals whom society has regarded as unemployable. These persons had not been able to adjust to work, although they were physically capable of doing so.

More exactly, they displayed physical, mental, and/or emotional disabilities, but their impairments were not so severe that work was out of the question. Although the range of kinds of disability was very wide, their severity could best be described as mild to moderate. An illustration is afforded by a client with relatively mild mental retardation (tested IQ in the range 50–70), who is capable of performing many simple work tasks but has never been in a position to acquire the many and varied social skills that he needs to deal acceptably with work as a social situation. A second example is an individual with a history of epilepsy, now under reasonably good medical control, who is not able to cope with the social consequences of his occasional seizures and who is so psychologically traumatized that his habitual defense may be to withdraw from social contact altogether. A third kind of case, very frequent in the population we are considering, is a person with a long-term emotional disorder, who can carry out a variety of work tasks but who cannot tolerate the interpersonal demands that are inseparable components of most work situations.

These people all appear to be potentially capable of working, but something stands in the way. To explain this statement, we will have to distinguish between the *necessary* and *sufficient* conditions of work. By the former set of conditions, we are referring to the fact that most work situations present us with an irreducible aggregate of requirements, which we must meet in order to be able to work at all. Some degree of motility, a measure of manual dexterity, the ability to comprehend and follow instructions, the ability to perform a task—all of these can be described as the necessary requirements of work. On the other hand, the ability to meet these requirements may not be *sufficient* to make us workers. We cannot be so fearful of authority, for example, that the mere presence of a supervisor reduces us to a state of apparent paralysis. We cannot (usually) decide for ourselves how long we shall work, when we shall begin, or at what pace we shall proceed. Work situations are *social* situations, characterized by very complex sets of norms, rituals, customs, and social demands. It is thus possible for an individual to be able to meet the necessary conditions of work without being able to meet the sufficient conditions.

Of course, some individuals are unable to meet either set of conditions of work—the very young and the very old, the severely mentally deficient, the bedridden, some psychotics. The term *unemployable* should probably be reserved for people who can meet *neither* the necessary *nor* the sufficient conditions of work. The client population that has been of interest to the writer should perhaps be described as "apparently unemployable." In the abstract, or under special conditions, they can meet the formal requirements of work. In practice and in reality, they appear to be unemployable.

Another way of characterizing the apparently unemployable client is to distinguish between the intellectual and motor requirements of work and its affective and social requirements. Work not only demands some quantum of cognitive–motor capacity but it also engages the feelings and emotions, and it is most often carried on in a fairly complex social situation. Work is not a "natural" activity, like breathing, digesting, or even perceiving. Typically, one works for a reason! Work is essentially a *social* activity, carried through because of a great array of social expectations and demands, both conscious and unconscious, overt and covert. The world of work is a kind of subculture, complete with traditions, customs, laws, rituals, compulsions, rewards, and sanctions. We work at certain times, in certain places, and in certain prescribed ways. Training in certain work habits is one of the kinds of training that every organized society, no matter how primitive and undeveloped, imposes on its children. All societies have developed more or less formal means for achieving this objective. Similarly, there is a very widespread social expectation, cutting across most societies and cultures, that the healthy members of the society will perform some kind of useful work, granting the existence of exemptions for the very young, the very old, the very sick, or the very powerful. In Chapter 7 we shall describe work as an aspect of culture. Suffice it to say, at this point, that the "apparently unemployable" client is a person who has been unable to adapt to the work subculture. In the language of sociology, he is unable or unwilling to play the role of a worker, although he may have the physical and cognitive capacity to do so.

We have not been particularly concerned with the *kinds* of work that people do (or wish to do). Our primary interest is focused on the ability to work per se, with less regard to what is done or what level of training or skill is essential to its execution. The existence of differential work preferences, varied work interests, and all sorts of levels of skill are not unimportant features of the entire work process. They relate, however, to the individual differences among people who can work, while we are concerned with people who *cannot* work at all or who require specialized assistance in order to become employable. At the same time, our study of the psychopathology of work should tell us a good deal about the entire work process, just as our knowledge of human neurology has largely been acquired through the study of people who have suffered some impairment or damage of neural tissue.

Until a few years ago, the kind of vocationally disadvantaged individual we have been describing was not considered feasible for any directed process of vocational training or job placement. Public or private vocational agencies generally tended to dismiss this kind of client as "unmotivated" and busied themselves with the more rewarding categories of people who were responsive to the traditional techniques of psychological testing and vocational counseling. The developing rehabilitation movement, in the period prior to the 1950s, was almost exclusively preoccupied with the physically disabled client who was strongly motivated to work and merely needed to be provided with a concrete and specific service—a prosthetic device, a hearing aid, a prescribed series of sessions of physical therapy, a trade training course—in order to be able to reembark on gainful employment.

After World War II, however, concern for the health and welfare problems of the entire citizenry was greatly heightened and widened, and it was not long before the "apparently unemployable" client became one of its foci. Unfortunately, the problems posed were stubborn and would not easily yield to the most persistent application of the techniques then available. The kind of client we have been discussing proved to be particularly resistant to traditional diagnostic and therapeutic techniques. One of the major problems, therefore, that had to be faced and solved by the rehabilitation movement in the postwar period was how to provide a useful vocational service for the client who could not be adequately tested, who was able to express no particular preferences for or interests in any kind of employment, who had such meager capabilities for verbal communication that he could not be engaged in any meaningful kind of counseling process, and whose work-history was so scanty or nonexistent that it was quite impossible for the professional worker to have any clear idea of whether the client was capable of working at all.

In the early 1950s, I became involved in what turned out to be a pioneering effort to develop a new vocational technique designed to render meaningful assistance to the "apparently unemployable" client.[4] The core of this technique involved the development of a simulated work situation in which a professionally trained staff could observe the work behavior of the apparently unemployable client. The essential rationale of this procedure was that which lies at the basis of the "experimental mock-up," that is, a testing procedure that takes place in a contrived environment that mirrors as closely as possible the real environment that it is desired to predict or control. Thus, if it is desired to predict the behavior of an individual in an actual work situation or if it is desired to identify and modify work behavior that is now inappropriate, it would seem logical to confront such an individual with customary working conditions.

Observation of the behavior of the apparently unemployable client in such a contrived work setting provided much of the information that follows. The simulated work situation provided us with an unparalleled opportunity to observe what goes on in actual work and at the same time to get underneath the process to the variables that were influencing what we saw. While it might be argued that everything we could see was available daily in any actual factory setting, it should be remembered that we were interested in the psychopathology of work, that is, we were interested in the kinds of

[4]This program, which became known as the Vocational Adjustment Center (VAC), was developed by the Jewish Vocational Service of Chicago and will be described in detail in Chapter 10.

work behavior that would lead to a worker being dismissed within a few hours or days of his placement on a job. Actually, it was possible to "see" more than is customarily visible in the ordinary factory setting, since the workshop staff were not passive observers; they were actually engaged in supervising the work process at the same time as they were observing client behavior. From this complex mix of action and observation, our theory of work behavior has gradually developed.

It should be noted that in composing this volume and, in particular, in drafting a third edition, the writer was confronted with a number of difficult choices relating to the inclusion and exclusion of a wide range of material. He wanted to analyze human work as a problem in social psychology and, from this vantage point, provide some insights on the relations between work and mental health, and between work and productivity. He found, however, that he could not stay neatly within his own field of professional expertise—psychology—but was compelled to examine the writings of a wide array of humanists and medical and social scholars, including historians, economists, sociologists, theologians, psychiatrists, as well as developmental, industrial, and vocational psychologists. In not all instances was his academic and professional training suitable for so varied a task. In addition, although his primary interest was in achieving a coherent theory of work behavior, he certainly could not ignore the empirical insights and observations of a varied horde of practitioners, including what he learned from his own practice.

It is hoped that the result is a contribution to the social and behavioral sciences in general in a particular field that yet lacks a precise name. Perhaps the best way to describe this volume is that, on the one hand, it brings together what we know about the sociology and psychology of work and, on the other, it presents an introduction to the new field of psychiatric rehabilitation.

I | THE NATURE OF HUMAN WORK

2 | WORK AND HUMAN HISTORY

We know very little about the beginnings of work. The historians of the ancient world give us little information about how people worked or what they thought about the work they did. Similarly, the other great fields of knowledge that provide us with both direct and analogical information about man's past—archeology and anthropology—have largely concerned themselves with other things. Yet, even the meager and fragmentary evidence available leads to the inference that work has been construed in different ways at different times and in different types of societies.

A historical study of the meaning of work is not merely of abstract interest. Individuals in modern society attach quite different meanings to work, in general, and to different kinds of work, in particular. Are these meanings intrinsic to the work-process itself, or have they merely become associated with work? Like all other aspects of human activity, work behavior is in part a function of the work-process itself and in part a function of how people regard the process. We are all, to some degree at least, creatures of our past. Human thoughts and feelings are not wholly determined by contemporary conditions. The ideas that surround human work are, in part, archaic survivals of periods of human history when very different conditions of work prevailed.

Most of what we know or can guess about changes in the conception of the meaning of work must be inferred from quite indirect and fragmentary evidence. Unfortunately, it is unlikely that further research will greatly improve our knowledge. The records of the more distant past are almost entirely concerned with political events—the rise and decline of ruling families and dynasties, wars and conquests, the outcomes of great social struggles. Something can be gleaned, however, from accounts of prevailing codes of law and from the testamentary documents of the great religions. Philosophers also have written occasionally about the role and meaning of human labor. What is entirely missing from sources of the past are accounts of how human workers, as individuals, thought and felt about their work. The rather meager historical observations that exist tend either to be quite abstract reflections on work as an aspect of the human condition or laws and ordinances that regulate the control and disposal of human labor.

An effort to write a history of human work would have to rely on rather indirect evidence, although data are not wholly lacking. Indirect evidence, however, needs to be interpreted, and we cannot be certain whether we are dealing with fact or merely with opinion. Before we sketch historical meanings attached to work for our purposes, we will need to confront two perplexing problems of historical interpretation, both of which bear directly on this particular subject. The first concerns what is most often called the economic interpretation of history as exemplified by the writings of Karl Marx; the second concerns various theories of cultural evolution.

THE ECONOMIC INTERPRETATION OF HISTORY

The basic Marxist doctrine (cf. Marx, 1887; particularly Chapters XV–XXXIII) is that the manner in which the bulk of the members of any society make their living is the primary determinant of everything else—its systems of religious belief, social systems and social structure, political philosophy, and even critical aspects of its literature and art. The economic relations of any given society are regarded as its base; everything else is superstructure. Therefore, as the base changes, so in the long run does everything else. Thus, the human worker is the key figure in history. The kinds of work he performs, as well as the manner in which the fruits of his labor are distributed, constitute the essence of human history. According to this view, the non-Marxist historian studies only the effects of the historical process, while the Marxist studies the causes. The most revolutionary force in human history is technological change in the manner in which men wrest their livings from nature. Social institutions are merely more or less appropriate mirrors of given levels of technological development. When prevailing social forms become outmoded by changes in the base, they must give way to new ones, although the process is marked by great social struggles and upheavals and may be slowed down or speeded up by human political action.

It is relatively easy to see the motivations and objectives of this view of human history, although determination of its validity has turned out to be a far more difficult matter. Whatever Marx was, he was certainly a radical critic of capitalist society. He was also a product of the mid-nineteenth century, when the initial triumphs of physical and biological science appeared to be sweeping everything before them. Although Marx was by no means the only intellectual of the nineteenth century to dream of applying the new methods of science to the study of human history, he was one of the first to attempt to combine radical social criticism with the scientific world outlook. Marxism has always presented itself as a *scientific* theory, based on discovery of the "laws of motion of history," which were thought to be as rigorous as any laws that governed the movements of physical objects or the generation of species. History was not simply a record of the thoughts and actions of great men, although this was how it appeared on the surface. The actions and thoughts of men were conceived of as consequences of the social relations into which men entered in producing the goods and necessities of material existence. What Marx hoped to be able to prove— and what his many followers believe he *did* prove—is that contemporary capitalism is simply a temporary and transient set of social institutions which arose in response to certain advances in the technology and organization of human labor and which has become obsolescent as technology advances.

Marx was by no means the originator of many of his ideas. Marx himself acknowledges his debt to many other writers: the English classical econo- mists, particularly Adam Smith and Ricardo; the French encyclopedists and utopians such as Saint-Simon and Fourier; and, above all, the German phi- losopher Hegel. He could have extended the list of credits. The industrial revolution and the great democratic revolutions that took place in England, France, and the United States, created widespread interest in the role and dignity of human labor. The American Constitution and Bill of Rights were the first major political documents to deal specifically with the rights of labor, and Jefferson and Franklin had a good deal to say on labor as the source of human wealth and welfare. Marx was also profoundly influenced by the ideas of Darwin and rushed to apply the principles of biological evolution to the development of human society. In this also he has not been alone, since such social philosophers as Haekel and Spencer made similar attempts. But, like many of his contemporaries, Marx was a great synthesizer and system-builder. He was able to bring together the ideas of many others, invent some of his own, and integrate them in a coherent theory of radical social change. That he was not only able to profit by the intellectual currents of his period but was also the prisoner of them is attested to by the failure of some of his most cherished prognostications. Capitalist democracy has proved to be far more resilient and flexible than Marx predicted. The great social revolutions of the twentieth century have taken place in under- developed countries like Russia and China, where Marx thought they were least likely.

Most damaging to the Marxist viewpoint is the evident failure of Marx's prediction that the proletarian revolution would smash the restraining "fet- ters" of capitalist social relations and bring about full development of both worker productivity and of political, social, and cultural liberty. Regrettably, the revolutions of the present century, which have taken place under the banner of Marxism–Leninism, are hardly characterized by the appearance of states that feature expansion in worker productivity and enhanced civil rights. There is certainly no sign of the famous "withering away" of state power, which was one of Marx's more utopian prognostications. We cannot, however, here enter into a general discussion of the merits and demerits of Marxism, per se. Such an enterprise would lead us far beyond the primary objectives of this book.

For our purposes, the chief significance of Marxism is that it focused attention on the human worker as a prominent actor on the social stage.[1] It need not be inferred, as Marx did, that work is the sole, or even chief, determinant of human history. In fact, to the degree that this view is an essential element of Marxism, then it must be affirmed that the entire theory remains unproved. Human behavior is too complex to be reduced to a single set of causes, and Marxism must be seen as one of the varieties of reductionism that have been so seductively attractive to many social theorists. The laws of history that Marx thought he discovered are simply hypotheses. The data of social interactions remain very difficult both to analyze and interpret, and the social scientist still faces many observational and methodological problems. Many modern sociologists and social scientists properly regard Marx as a great innovator and pioneer, but no more.

While others called attention to the importance of human work in human affairs, Marx's work heightened interest in it. In a sense, the student of human history was confronted with a variable, which had hitherto been overlooked. As a consequence, a number of historians, archeologists, sociologists, and anthropologists began a search for data that would confirm or disconfirm some of Marx's ideas about the role and significance of human labor. We are neither in a position to argue for or against the economic interpretation of history. We are in some position to profit from the search for data that this controversy stirred up. Marx may not convince us that the laborer is the chief actor in the drama of human history, but we have been made acutely aware that he is on the stage.

WORK AND THEORIES OF SOCIAL EVOLUTION

Another factor impeding a rational account of the role of work in human history has been the controversy around various theories of social evolution. One of the unlooked-for consequences of the publication of Darwin's *Origin of Species,* in 1859, was the avidity with which the idea of evolution was seized upon to account for the rise and decline of human societies. During the following half century, a great many social historians and ethnographers began to use the idea of evolution as an organizing principle in their studies of human history. Although the various schemas differ in detail, the general idea was that human beings have progressed through a series of evolutionary social and cultural stages. The notion of human progress was central, the

---

[1]In common with a number of contemporary social scientists, De Grazia (1962) has called attention to the impetus given by Marx to studies of work behavior. See also Friedmann (1955) and Hughes (1958).

general movement being from the simple to the complex, from the primitive to the sophisticated.

One such set of evolutionary stages was that proposed by Lewis Henry Morgan, an American ethnographer who carried through extensive studies of the Iroquois in western New York (Morgan, 1887). Morgan sees mankind developing through three evolutionary stages: Savagery, Barbarism, and Civilization. Morgan's ideas greatly influenced the Marxists, particularly Friedrich Engels, who elaborated Morgan's system to five stages (cf. Engels, 1884/1902): Tribal Society, Slave Society (e.g., classical Greece and Rome), Feudal Society, Capitalist Society, and Socialist Society (the next evolutionary stage). Alternative models of cultural evolution were proposed by Westermarck (1889), Lubbock (1870), and Tyler (1887), among a great many others.

The general theory of cultural evolution has been subjected to harsh criticism from a number of vantage points. First, it has been attacked simply as an unscientific metaphor, a criticism based on the quite correct argument that nothing in the theory of biological evolution is applicable to human culture, which is the unique product of a single species. Second, many social theorists disliked its strong implication of human progress and were not prepared to see contemporary societies as somehow "better" or "higher" than older societies. Third, the theory was rejected by the influential school of British Diffusionists, who were committed to the idea that cultural forms were invented by particularly influential peoples and spread to others through borrowing and conquest. Fourth, the theory was attacked as gratuitously metaphysical by an increasing number of empirically minded anthropologists who felt that the entire question was meaningless. Finally, commitment to intensive analysis of single societies, under the influence of such influential figures as Malinowski and Boas, tended to make this entire issue irrelevant. Very recently, however, there has been something of a renewed interest in the factors that govern cultural change, although the focus of study is far from being the entire canvas of human history (cf. Steward, 1955; Service, 1962).

Many of the models of cultural evolution are based on the technology of human labor, that is, on the different ways in which men have learned to extract their livelihood from nature. Morgan, for example, subdivides each of his three chief evolutionary stages into three levels: lower, middle, and higher. He associates each successive stage with "enlargement of the sources of subsistence" (Morgan, 1887). As an example, he distinguishes the higher stage of Savagery from lower stages through the development of the technology of hunting. Similarly, Barbarism is associated with settled agriculture and the large-scale domestication of animals. Change in the technology of human labor is seen as the prime force that regulates the evolution of human culture.

We are again faced with the risk that a single, albeit important, factor in a complex network of determinants has been elevated to the status of the sole or chief determinant. Evidence by now indicates that the cultural character- istics of human groups are influenced by a great many other variables: climate, geography, local features of the physical environment, relative pop- ulation size, contacts with other peoples, the consequences of war, conqu- est and social struggles, the rise and decline of systems of belief, and even the influence of particularly charismatic personalities. There are abundant examples in history of the destruction of technologically advanced societies by more "primitive" peoples, for instance, the conquest of the technically advanced Roman Empire by Germanic tribesmen or the more recent dep- redations of the Mongolian horse-archer, who turned quite advanced Asiatic societies into heaps of ruins. The labor technology of a particular human society is apparently neither the chief determinant of its viability nor of its many other characteristics.

What is of interest to us here is a narrower question, which needs to be considered in its own right and quite apart from its possible bearing on theories of cultural evolution. These phenomena involve possible associa- tions between the kinds of work that predominate in particular societies and the ideas *about* that work. To anticipate our conclusions, these ideas are not only a function of the type of work performed but also of a wide range of historical and cultural conditions. Nothing in these data is evidence for any particular theory of cultural evolution, since they may be obtained by look- ing at cultures cross-sectionally, as well as sequentially. Although the plan of this chapter is to elicit the meaning of work in societies of different degrees of technological complexity, there are no necessary implications that these degrees are organized in any rigid historical sequence. In considering the issues that arise from the relations between work and culture, we need not and will not take any position with regard to the pros and cons of theories of cultural evolution.

WORK AND SOCIAL ORGANIZATION

Whether we accept a developmental paradigm of human history of the type suggested by V. Gordon Childe (1936, 1946), or if we merely look at human societies cross-sectionally at the same point in time, it is evident that men have entered into an immense variety of forms of social organization. At the same time, it is also evident that human societies differ greatly in their internal complexity. At least one of the aspects may be observed in the means by which its members predominantly make their living. If we attempt to order societies in terms of levels or degrees of complexity (whether or not we can find a historical order in these levels), we can find at one extreme the relatively small tribal band that gains its subsistence by hunting and by the gathering of natural food products. At the other extreme, we can place the very large, heavily urbanized and industrialized societies of present-day

Europe and North America. It is evident that the hunting and gathering forms of social organization are very ancient. They apparently prevailed during most of the 1–3 million or so years that constitute the geological lifetime of the various hominid species and of the 50–100 millennia that make up the span of *Homo sapiens*. At the other historical extreme, the industrialized society is very recent, having been in existence in its developed form hardly more than a few centuries. Between these extremes, and starting with what Childe calls the Neolithic Revolution (circa 8000–6000 B.C. in Southwest Asia; cf. Anderson, 1952), there have existed a wide variety of forms of social organization based on agriculture and the domestication of food-producing animals as the primary means of life. These latter societies vary enormously in development and complexity of structure, but the basic labor force in each is the agricultural and/or pastoral producer.

In the sections to follow, we shall characterize the kinds of work performed in various societies, with the objective of indicating the manner in which the meanings attached to work are, in a certain measure, reflections of culture. We may then begin to have some glimmerings of the reasons why human work, as we currently regard it, seems to have many meanings and implications, some of them contradictory, which contribute to many individuals' ambivalent and conflicting attitudes toward it.

HUNTING AND GATHERING SOCIETIES

It is, of course, impossible to know anything of the attitudes toward work of our Paleolithic forebears. They left nothing behind them except the stones they worked, occasional skeletons, heaps of refuse, and a few cave drawings and primitive inscriptions. The very little we know is a tribute to the patience and ingenuity of two or three generations of paleoarcheologists. We know something of the tools and weapons they fashioned and of their use of fire (Watson, 1950). We can infer that they lived in very small bands and in a continuously migratory form of existence, following the wild game and bound to the seasonal distribution of wild vegetables, cereals, fruits, and berries. We can even guess something about the early development of religious and spiritual beliefs from the examination of burials. But everything else is lost.

In order to learn something of the nature of work behavior in human groupings that are limited to hunting and gathering, we are forced to turn to what can be learned from the small remnants of hunter–gatherers who still exist in certain remote corners of the earth. Of course, there is a danger in this expedient, as anthropologists have frequently warned. We cannot tell if a contemporary hunting–gathering people constitutes a deteriorated and degraded remnant of what was once a more developed and complex culture or if they are, in reality, Stone Age survivals. Typically, they continue to exist only because they occupy the most intractable and undesired habitats, where more developed subsistence technologies are not easily applicable—the frozen tundras of the Arctic Circle, the almost totally barren deserts of Southwest Africa and Central Australia, the dense and virtually impenetrable rain forests of South America, Africa, and tropical Asia. Whether they have been forced into these intractable areas or simply could not escape from them is impossible to determine.

Contemporary examples of the hunting-gathering society are afforded by the more unacculturated aboriginal peoples of Central Australia, by the surviving Bushmen of the Kalahari Desert in Southwest Africa, and by the forest Pigmies of Central Africa. Illustrations of hunting–gathering peoples who are undergoing rapid acculturation or are already virtually culturally extinct are the Eskimo of the Far North, certain Amerindian tribes of the high, western plateaus adjacent to the Rockies (e.g., the Paiutes of the Great Basin), and certain tribal groupings in the high rain forests of the Malayan Peninsula (cf. Forde, 1934). What appears to be common to these people is that the exigencies of securing the means of existence are so pressing and the resources available so limited that everyone in the tribal grouping is expected to "work," even comparatively small children. These peoples live an extremely marginal existence, in highly inimical and impoverished environments. That they manage to exist at all in such hostile surroundings is a tribute to human ingenuity. Within the limits of Stone Age technology and with no motive power available other than human muscle, most of these isolated groupings have managed to develop techniques of living that are remarkably adaptive to their environments.[2] Nevertheless, these environments are so terribly inadequate that the maintenance of life is extremely precarious. Compared to the physical size of the habitat, populations remain very small. Deaths from starvation and thirst are almost commonplace.

Under these conditions, it seems highly unlikely that the concept of work as a distinctive sphere of behavior was able to acquire any separate meaning at all. Where the labors of procuring the means of existence are so all-pervasive that everyone must participate and where need is so pressing that such labors may be virtually continuous, they may not be perceived as separate activities at all. Typically (cf. Forde, 1934; Buxton, 1924), the hunting–gathering tribe displays almost nothing resembling a division of labor, except between men and women. Males are more heavily engaged in activities related to hunting and fishing and are, of course, the sole developers of the arts of warfare. Women are primarily engaged in the gathering of

---

[2]Many writers have commented on the highly appropriate kinds of clothing, shelter, and weapons developed by the Eskimo tribes of the Far North; others have observed the intricate techniques for finding and storing water that the Bushmen have developed in the Kalahari Desert. These techniques are so impressive that many of them have been at once adopted by Europeans who have penetrated these areas in modern times (cf. Forde, 1934; Herskovits, 1952).

natural products, the fabrication of clothing and "household" implements, and the processing of foods for consumption. On the other hand, the manufacture of tools, weapons, and equipment is not otherwise a specialized function. Hunters make their own weapons and snares; women, their own implements. No one is exempt from some kind of labor, except very young children. There are no men who are specialized solely as weapons-makers or canoe-builders; everyone is a "jack-of-all-trades" (Herskovits, 1952). Similarly, to the degree that there are priests, chieftains, or other forms of political or social leaders, the activities attendant on these offices are carried out extra-curricularly, so to speak. Like their fellow tribesmen, even the shamans and war-leaders are *primarily* hunter–gatherers.

Language provides an indirect but impressive bit of evidence of the diffuseness of work in these societies. Their spoken languages do not have a distinctive term for "work," although there are usually extremely elaborate vocabularies for the various kinds of activities and objects involved in hunting, gathering, and the fabrication of implements. Boas has pointed out (Boas, 1911) that the Eskimoes have over a score of distinctively different words for "snow." Correspondingly, there are many different words for the same animal, depending on its usefulness, potential for danger, sleeping or waking state, etc. Many preliterate tongues are extraordinarily rich in words to convey detailed information, and equally rich in terms implying social, spiritual, and religious abstractions (Elkin, 1938). However, work appears to be such a natural activity, akin to breathing or existing, that it does not require a distinctive term to describe it.

If contemporary hunting–gathering societies provide any clue to man's distant past, it is that the earliest meaning attached to work is hardly a distinctive meaning at all. It also seems likely that no distinction existed between work and nonwork, between labor and leisure. Herskovits (1952) carefully points out that the labors of primitive man are very arduous and virtually continuous. Even when the hunt has been successful and the men are presumably merely "sitting about the campfire," they are usually occupied with something—making an arrow, chipping an arrow-head, shaping a scraper, etc. The women are continually busy. In one form or another, this implicit meaning of work—that work is a "natural" activity—persists to the present day. As we shall see, what was once conceived of as something that all men do became in time something that is only "natural" for certain men.

WORK IN EARLY AGRICULTURAL AND PASTORAL SOCIETIES

A more elaborate division of labor cannot appear until the techniques of food production become sufficiently advanced so that they are capable of producing a considerable surplus over the immediate needs of the primary producer. This advance in technique occurred at different times in different parts of the world and has not yet appeared in some places. However, it has been associated with a certain stage of development of the arts of agriculture and the taming of animals for food and labor. The earliest complex social organizations first appeared naturally enough, within the fertile valleys of the great rivers of the Near East, China, India, and North Africa. These areas were marked by specially fortunate combinations of favorable climate as well as the regular fertilization of soils through annual flooding, which made it possible for comparatively dense agricultural populations to develop. Similarly, the steppe and savannah areas of Central Asia and Africa proved to be ideal conditions for the development of powerful cultures based on pastoralism, once men learned to tame and breed animals for food and transport. Whether the particular form of society that gradually arose was predominantly based on cultivation, was primarily pastoral, or was mixed in type, what was clearly common to all of them was the provision of a relatively stable and ample supply of food and raw materials, a condition that is virtually unknown to the hunting–gathering society.

Under the conditions of an ample and stable supply of food, it was possible for some men to be free from the necessity of full-time—or even part-time—production of the necessities of life. The society becomes productive enough not only to supply the needs of the primary producer and his immediate blood family or kinship group but also to supply the needs of men who become entirely specialized for other occupations—craftsman, priest, political leader. Only at this point does work begin to acquire all sorts of distinctions and qualifications as well as an increasingly complicated infrastructure of evaluative meanings. The hunting–gathering society is perfectly capable of distinguishing between men's and women's work. In fact, men of the hunting–gathering society will endure the most extreme privations rather than perform the kind of labor that is traditionally associated with the work of women; similarly, women never hunt (the male *berdache*, in Plains Indian societies, performed women's work and was often homosexual and transvestite as well). With the development of herding and agriculture, however, we not only find different kinds of work (with different evaluative meanings attached to each) but also distinctions between workers and nonworkers, again with different evaluations related to a developing power structure.

According to Linton (1955), the beginnings of systematic cultivation of cereals (barley, wheat, rice, etc.) and the domestication of food-producing and laboring animals (cows, sheep, goats, water-buffaloes, etc.) probably took place as more or less associated activities in the same areas of the world. It appears likely that the first form of transition from the hunting–gathering society was the so-called Neolithic village (Childe, 1936), the earliest known signs of which date back some 8,000–10,000 years in the general region of Southwestern Asia. This is the region roughly bounded by the Mediterranean on the west, the high central Asian mountains on the east, the Black and Caspian Seas on the north, and the belt of deserts ranging from

Sinai to India on the south. In this area of a more or less uniform continental climate (hot summers and cold winters), the principal wild grasses that came under cultivation were barley and wheat, while the principal animals available for domestication were sheep, goats, cattle, and (for transport) the ass and the donkey. The early village economy was apparently a mixed economy, with the clear demarcation of agricultural and pastoral peoples being a later development (Clarke, 1946; Curwen and Hatt, 1953). Whatever the actual course of development, which undoubtedly depended on variations in climate and habitat, the relatively sparse groups of hunter–gatherers gradually were replaced by numerically much more populous aggregates of village farmers. It is not even certain that the earliest cultivators were initially sedentary, although settled habitation was one of the ultimate consequences of cultivation. The final establishment of settled habitation was the precondition for everything else that followed: increasing density of population, a rapid development of technology, the consequent appearance of a division of labor, the rise of the early urban civilizations. As Neolithic farming spread into areas not quite suitable for it, adaptations and alterations took place. One of the most important of these differentiations was into cultures that were predominantly based on agriculture and those based on pastoralism. The semiarid steppe and savannah areas of Asia and Africa were poorly adapted for primitive cultivation but were immensely suitable for large-scale pastoral economies. Pastoral societies developed in just such areas in the late Neolithic, but their dependence upon a grazing animal made such new groupings quite the opposite of sedentary. Thus, the Neolithic Revolution gradually produced two quite different groupings of "farmers": the sedentary villager and the migratory pastoralist.

The consequences of the emergence of Neolithic farming were profound, although our brief sketch can hardly do justice to the complexities of the process. For our purposes, we are interested not merely in the fact that improved food production permitted relatively enormous population increases, but that it created new kinds of men: not only people who specialized in quite different kinds of labor but also people who became specialized not to work at all, at least in the sense of physical work.

Undoubtedly, populations had to grow considerably and villages had to join together in more or less stable confederations before the need for such men became obvious. But, sooner or later, they appeared. It seems reasonable to suppose that one of the new divisions of labor that eventually arose, in addition to the ancient division between the sexes, was a division between the laborer and nonlaborer. Along with the gradual development of the material technology of food procurement, there must also have been a gradual development of knowledge. The ancient farmer not only had to know where to plant his seeds, he also had to know *when* to plant them. Apparently, the earliest efforts to acquire and maintain systematic knowledge of nature had to do with the succession of seasons—when major annual changes in temperature take place, when increases and decreases in rainfall are to be expected, when the flooding of rivers will occur. It is no accident that astronomy is the oldest of the exact sciences, since the apparent movements of the visible stars and planets are the most stable clues to the succession of the seasons. Men who became unusually expert in this kind of knowledge must early have been thought to possess the most magical of powers, since the entire welfare of the cultivating community depended on their decisions.

Since the borders between magic and knowledge were hardly distinguishable, it seems logical that the possessors and developers of early astronomical observation and calculation would be priests. Thus, the shaman or medicine man—who is only a part-time diviner and controller of nature in the hunting–gathering society—eventually becomes a full-time priestly intellectual, as the agricultural economies develop. The earliest religions of which we have any record appear to be heavily tied to astronomical observation and the control of cultivation; the earliest evidence of centralized government appears to point to essentially theocratic forms of organization and control (Wooley, 1928; Frankfort, 1951).

The second kind of nonworker who gradually evolved from the mass of agricultural producers might have been the war-chief, who gradually moved into full-time political leadership as the regulation and control of society became more complex. As we have seen, such functions were part-time and temporary in the hunting–gathering societies. Among the predatory tribes of the American Plains, the war-chief was simply a more able and experienced warrier who was temporaily appointed as a leader for particular raids or actions (Swanton, 1952; Opler, 1941). When conflict was not the order of the day, he was a hunter and food-collector like his fellows. However, as the Neolithic village grew in productive skills and population and as villages began to band together for defense or conquest, the need for continuous military leadership must have gradually become a necessity. What probably began as a system of gifts and the lion's share of the loot must eventually have evolved into more or less formal systems of taxation: a fixed share of the social surplus is systematically drained off to maintain the growing institutions of priestly and military leadership which a denser and more productive population both produces and requires. Around these two functions, also, there arises an increasing network of attendant technicians: scribes, surveyors, clerks, weapon-makers, builders of public buildings and fortifications, tax-collectors, police and household-warriors, etc. The advantages of being freed from the exigencies of agricultural labor must soon have become intertwined with issues of social power, and an early differentiation begins to take place between the noble—whose sole functions are the arts of government and war—and the commoner who functions as the primary producer of goods and services.

So far, we have been discussing consequences that have the character of a developing distinction between mental and manual labor, although we should emphasize that the former was not considered work at all until comparatively modern times. However, within the sphere of work itself, other differentiations were taking place—the full-time craftsman, the full-time trader, the peasant, and the herdsman. Whereas the Paleolithic hunter and the early Neolithic villager was a jack-of-all-trades, the gradual development of population and technology made it possible for people to become specialists. It is probable that the early development of work specialization was on a tribal or village basis, with entire tribes or villages becoming specialists in certain occupations. In Bedouin Arabia and many parts of Africa today, special tribes, whose sole occupation is fabrication of weapons and implements, wander among the sedentary villagers and migratory herdsmen as the tinkers and metal-workers of the area (Glueck, 1940). Similarly, strategically situated villagers might have become specialized as merchants and seamen, giving up virtually all concern with food production to make their living by trade. As villages grew into towns and larger and more stable markets were provided, the migratory craftsmen and traders began to settle in the towns. The craftsmen and merchants who lived in the early urban centers of Asia Minor were most often depicted as outlanders—foreigners—who were not citizens of the community and were subjected to special taxes and exemptions. As time went on, however, the craftsman and the merchant eventually become indistinguishable parts of the general community but are recognizable as distinct occupations.

We have briefly outlined the development of a division of labor because it bears upon the many meanings that have become associated with work. One of these meanings, which apparently made its appearance very early, distinguishes between occupations that are ignoble and degrading and those that are acceptable or even noble. Not always connected with the heaviness or monotony involved, the meaning has very particularized cultural origins. For example, the contemporary nomadic Bedouin in Central Arabia and North Africa are willing to labor very arduously in breeding and training the camels that are their primary source of wealth and power, but they will not soil their hands with agriculture or the fabrication of weapons and equipment. To procure these necessities, they use slaves or serfs, secure the needed products by raids on sedentary villagers, or engage in trade.

This particular pattern of culturally derived attitudes toward different kinds of work is found—and appears to have existed for thousands of years—among many human groupings who have specialized in the domestication of food-producing or transport animals (Musil, 1928). Contemporary accounts of the Masai and Watutsi of Central East Africa (Forde, 1934) or the Fulana of the Western Sudan (Stenning, 1959) make one imagine that the same general pattern must have prevailed among such ancient peoples as the Aryan invaders of the Indian subcontinent or the pre-Classical Greeks who came down with their herds of cattle on the Aegean.

Among many pastoral peoples, the successfully domesticated animal becomes not only the chief basis of wealth and power but a religious and cultural symbol as well—so much so that the breeding and care of the animal becomes the only acceptable occupation for the adult male. Where such pastoral people have conquered or subjugated more sedentary, agricultural peoples, they have either exterminated the latter or transformed them into servile food-producers. Witness the recent bloody struggles between the cattle-breeding Watutsi and the agricultural Bahutu of Central Africa. Apparently, following upon their conquest of the cultivating Bahutu a few centuries ago, the pastoral Watutsi were able to impose a feudal regime in which, as the master-tribe, they could spend all their time on the arts of war and government while remaining passionately devoted to their cattle; the semiservile Bahutu supplied everything else. We can speculate that the same sort of events might have taken place on an immense scale when the cattle-breeding Aryans subjugated the apparently agricultural Dravidian-speakers of ancient India.

However, many societies have existed—and still exist—where the land-holding tiller of the soil is the primary "citizen" of the society. Recall the Greek city–states of the early period, in which the land-holding farmer was the only free citizen of the tribe and where other occupations—those of the craftsman, merchant, or even teacher—were relegated to the slave or outlander. But one of the early consequences of the massive division of labor into cultivating and pastoral peoples was a great initial advantage to the latter in the arts of war. Buxton (1924) points out that among early pastoral peoples the relatively great increases in population due to a guaranteed food supply, the comparative lightness of the work involved, the continuous need to defend the herds against animal and human enemies, their great mobility compared to the sedentary cultivator, and the continuous pressure to find more fertile grazing lands, have combined to make some pastoral nomads the most warlike peoples in history. Many times in Africa, during comparatively modern times, the cattle nomad has conquered sedentary cultivators.

Of course, the classical example of the power of horse nomadism (a later development than domestication of the cow) is afforded by the Mongol conquests of all of Asia and parts of Europe just a few centuries ago. Whereas the hunting–gathering society simply exterminated its human enemies or used their bodies for food, when cultivation and pastoralism became successful ways of life, the military societies of the ancient world fairly quickly must have discovered new uses for subjugated peoples. While the original objective of the military raid simply might have been loot, it eventually became evident that the conquered sedentary cultivator can be disciplined or compelled to be a continuous source of food and labor. Thus, the institutions of slavery or other forms of forced labor became one of the early consequences of the large-scale development of agriculture, especially where successful cultivation of the soil or domestication of animals led to great spurts in population and consequent military power. Since the peasant farmer was the chief labor force of the ancient world, and since the pastoral conqueror did not regard the care of animals as work but rather as the noble occupation of the free warrior, it is easy to see how work began to take on a generally servile or degraded meaning wherever the pastoral nomad managed to subjugate the sedentary cultivator.

THE GRECIAN EXAMPLE

The Proto-Grecian peoples who invaded the Aegean Peninsula in a series of waves during the third and second millennia B.C., were apparently largely pastoral peoples, like the Aryan invaders of India. They might have developed a considerable culture in the steppe areas of Hither Asia and Eastern Europe, but it was a culture based largely on domestication of animals rather than settled agriculture. Like many other pastoral and seminomadic peoples, the early Greek invaders must have had a developed and relatively efficient military organization, since we have seen that reliance on large-scale domestication appears generally congenial to the development of warriors.

Whatever the case, once the early Greek invaders reduced the indigenous population and divided the land and power among themselves, a new division of labor began to make its appearance. Even in the Homeric legends, it is perfectly appropriate for the Greek hero to care directly for his cattle and for his wife to perform certain household duties (the weaving of cloth, for example). All heavy agricultural pursuits were relegated to helots or slaves, who were often the conquered native peoples, sedentary cultivators of the soil. By the time the Greek city–states were fully established, the free Greek citizen had managed to divest himself of all need to labor. This trend reached its apogee among the Spartans, but the Athenian did not lag far behind. The Classical Greek writings make it clear that all useful work in the Greek city–states—even the occupations related to trade and education—was performed by slaves, serfs, or outlander noncitizens. Under these circumstances, it is easy to see how Greek thought developed the conception that work is inherently servile and degrading.

Hannah Arendt (1958) presents us with an extremely interesting discussion of the concepts of labor and work in the classical world. She appears to turn things on their heads, however, when she argues that slaves become degraded because they perform labor, rather than that ancient labor became degraded when it was generally relegated to slaves to perform. A conquering people always manages to convince itself that the activities of the conquered are contemptible. The warlike Bedouin use slaves or client peoples to cultivate the soil in the oases under their control and regard camel-breeding and trade as the only noble occupations for the free warrior. The mixed cattle–cultivation economies of Bantu Africa are characterized by a pattern where the sole occupation of the males is to care for the herds; cultivation is entirely relegated to their women or slaves. So it must have been in Classical Greece, where gradually all kinds of work became the forced labor of the unfree, so that to work at all was to be akin to a slave.

Arendt, however, interprets the writings on labor in Classical Greece as an indication that there is something inherently degrading about labor. To be compelled to labor is equivalent to being subhuman. She draws her arguments from the comments of Plato and Aristotle on slavery and from the legal institutions governing slave and free labor in the Greek and Roman worlds. She cites Aristotle's opinion of slavery to the effect that "without the necessaries, life, as well as the good life, is impossible" (Aristotle's *Politics*) and reports his conclusion that to be a master of slaves is the human way to master necessity and thus is not against nature. From this, Arendt infers that the degradation of the slave does not arise merely from his unfree condition but from the fact that he is forced to labor, that he is metamorphosed into something "akin to a tame animal," like a bullock or an ox. She goes on to assert that "the institution of slavery in antiquity, though not in later times, was not a device for cheap labor or an instrument of exploitation for profit, but rather the attempt to exclude labor from the condition of man's life" (Arendt, 1958, p. 84). She adds that Plato and Aristotle appear to regard the free peasant as almost as ignoble as the slave, because the exigencies of life compel him to labor. Arendt thus defines labor itself as ignoble, because it is hardly distinguishable from the activities through which animals go in maintaining life.

Arendt also argues that men have always distinguished between "labor" and "work" and have used different terms for these activities in most developed languages. She uses the term *animal laborens* to describe the kinds of work which must be done over and over again to produce the essentially transitory products (food, water, firewood, etc.) necessary for the maintenance of life. On the other hand, the term *Homo faber* is reserved for the craftsman or artisan, the fabricator of tools and semidurable products. She regards the latter as less degraded than the former because he leaves some impress upon the world and because the products of his use of energy have some degree of permanence. Nevertheless, Arendt regards both forms of work as less than human because both imply the necessity of man to provide himself with the necessaries of life "as animals do." The truly human condition, as Arendt sees it, is supplied by the example of the free Athenian citizen, who was able to divest himself of all need to labor by the possession of slaves and could thus devote all of his time to the *vita activa:* the activities of politics, the management of human relations, persuasion, and war.

Now, while Arendt's views are stimulating and provocative, we believe that she mistakes certain culturally derived meanings for the inherent nature of work itself. There would appear to be little doubt that she correctly reflects the thought of Classical Greece and Rome. It appears to the writer, however, that labor begins to take on a servile cast in history only when one group of people manages to subjugate another and forces them to labor. Under these conditions, if one is a member of the dominant group, it may indeed be degrading to perform certain kinds of work, since to do so is to be akin to a slave or an alien.

Until a division of labor occurs between workers and nonworkers, with the former condition being associated with some kind of subjugation or dependent state, labor itself cannot be a "bad" thing. Once large-scale slavery or forced labor makes its appearance, then the work that conquered or dependent peoples are forced to perform takes on a servile cast. Correspondingly, it then becomes noble to be freed from the necessity to labor. Gradually, new equations begin to arise (labor is equal to servility, freedom from labor equals nobility). Gradually, also, all sorts of institutions and cultural norms arise to support the equations. Thus, in modern times, the slaveowner of the pre-Civil War American South justified the "peculiar institution" by the fact that it freed the slaveowner from the necessity to labor, so that he could pursue knowledge, culture, and the full development of democratic institutions. Similarly, under quite different historical conditions, the Chinese mandarin grew his fingernails very long and bound the feet of his women. We can find the same origins in the contempt held for any kind of work by the feudal aristocrat of medieval Europe, who felt degraded by any kind of work, even the labors of management and trade. It is interesting that quite similar attitudes still prevail among many cattle-breeding tribes of Africa, who have either been able to compel sedentary cultivators to perform labor for them or who relegate such tasks to their women (Marshall, 1965). Generally a militarily dominant people—who can force others to work for them—can develop the conviction that labor is servile.

The Grecian example provides us with the clearest case of the conditions under which work acquires totally negative meanings. Contrary to Arendt, we believe that it is not work itself that is degrading but the power relationships and social structures that surround it. Since the relationships of power and status differ greatly from society to society, we will expect the meanings ascribed to work also to differ.

THE RISE OF NEW MEANINGS

The meanings ascribed to work cannot be derived directly from the nature of the activity but have many complex social and cultural determinants. Some further insight into these determinants can be gained by exploring how the meanings ascribed to work have changed since the Classical period of Greece and Rome.

If we restrict our study of work and human history to the European tradition, we find two apparently contradictory trends. On the one hand, the decline of cities after the fall of the Roman Empire, and the parallel con-solidation of agrarian feudalism, greatly reinforced the conception of the landholding aristocracy that every kind of work was ignoble. On the other hand, new ideas about work began to appear in connection with the con-temporary development of the great monastic brotherhoods, which gradual-ly became great productive enterprises in their own right. In his rules for the behavior of monks, St. Benedict declared that both manual and intellectual labor was a religious duty. Rule XLVIII of the Benedictine Order reads as follows: "Idleness is the enemy of the soul and therefore, at fixed times, the brothers ought to be occupied in manual labor, and, again at fixed times, in sacred reading" (Bettenson, 1947). While the primary duties of the monk were directly religious, work was increasingly seen in the monastic orders as a way of serving the Lord. Idleness was condemned as opening the door to licentiousness. The function of work was not to secure material wealth, but to discipline the soul. Thus, work began to be conceived of as ennobling rather than degrading, as a way of serving God.

While it is customary to attribute these positive ideas about work to the rise of the Protestant Ethic, it is worth noting that they became current as early as the sixth century A.D. and can be considered an essential element in Roman Catholic doctrine. The difference is that initially these new ideas were confined to the members of the monastic brotherhoods and tended to lose their force as the monastic orders became rich and powerful. Luther declared that the monks had become idle and parasitic, living off the labor of the peasant just as the landlord did. By his time, however, the agrarian feudalism of the early Middle Ages had already undergone marked changes. Cities were in the process of reestablishing their sway over the countryside as centers for trade and fabrication. While power and prestige were still largely in the hands of the landholding nobles and the high church dignitar-ies, the merchants and the master artisans were becoming increasingly wealthier and more numerous. The idea that work was ennobling began to pass from the monastic orders to these new men of the late Middle Ages—merchants, artisans, and traders—who wanted to find merit in their own pursuits. And, of course, the path to wealth and power for these new group-ings in society was through work.

Although the Protestant Reformation did not itself invent the idea that work was ennobling, it was a very powerful force in spreading these new meanings of work. Historians of the rise of modern capitalism have offered different reasons for these changes. While Weber (1930) finds the source of the new ideas about work in the religious controversy itself, Tawney (1926) argues that the Protestant Reformation was an expression of the aspirations of the rising groups of merchants and craftsmen in the later period of medieval society. However, both of these historical interpretations tend to be one-sided. The idea that work was both ennobling and a path to salvation had its roots in the religious controversies, but it also was congenial to the new citizens of the growing towns and cities. These were essentially landless people—many were runaway serfs and former feudal retainers—who could sustain themselves only through labor and had no reason to continue to consider it disgraceful. Compared to the hands of the landholding aristocrat, their hands were dirty, whether actually sullied through manual labor or metaphorically sullied through the mental operations of writing, reckoning, calculating, trading, or handling money.

What had formerly been largely a rule for monks, along with chastity and obedience, now began to acquire religious sanction as a way of life for the laity as well. The ideas of monastic Christianity, however, suffered something of a sea-change when they were taken over by their new advocates. The monks were ordered to work because Benedict believed that they could thereby better serve God. The merchants and artisans who became enthusiastic supporters of the Protestant reforms saw work as the path to *individual* salvation, both here on earth and in the afterlife to come. These new attitudes toward work and toward life became most clear in the adherents of the sterner and more puritanical Protestant sects (e.g., Calvinism).

It is worth noting, however, that the religious content of the new ideas about work and their secular application were somewhat contradictory. Calvinist doctrine, for example, nowhere explicitly states that an industrious life is a prerequisite for salvation. In fact, the concepts of original sin and predestination imply that salvation is a matter of God's will, and the elect are chosen in advance of their lives on earth. For the Protestant theologian as well as his Catholic opponent, it was the afterlife that counted. Devotion to God was still the only important aspect of man's life on earth. But what impressed the Protestant laity was the widespread belief that idleness was a path to damnation and work the path to salvation. In the Protestant countries, the moral ideal became that of the sober, prudent, and industrious Christian, who could pile up credit with the Lord by hard labor and "good works" in the world below.

Whether the sources of the Protestant Reformation were economic or ideological, or both, it seems clear that its outcome was the consolidation of new ideas about work. While labor was earlier considered simply as God's punishment for man's sins, or as a brutal necessity forced on the powerless by the powerful, it now acquired moral dignity in its own right. Thus, the countries in which the Protestant Reformation was most successful also became predominantly work-oriented societies, in which the general atmosphere was most conducive to the rapid breakup of agrarian feudalism and the most thoroughgoing industrial progress.

No sooner had the work concept acquired this "good' meaning than the rapidly developing division of labor in a manufacturing society began to invent additional subtleties of meaning. Distinctions began to arise between "mental" and "manual" labor, between skilled and unskilled work, and between the labor of the manager of an enterprise and the labor of "hands" or "operatives." While all labor was now seen as "good," there were degrees of goodness. Mental work was better than manual work; skilled work better than unskilled work. Thus, within the framework of the new "positive" meaning of work, a hierarchy of evaluations of work reflected a status hierarchy in society. The outcome of the process is that today we assign social values to people not so much in terms of their religious beliefs or their genealogical descent (these factors still have force, but not exclusively so) but in terms of what kind of work they perform. Whatever the meanings assigned to positions in this evaluative hierarchy, common to all its levels is the assumption that work is a necessary, even desirable, aspect of the human condition. However, this concept is essentially modern and would have been wholly alien to the citizen of Classical Athens or the feudal noble of Medieval Europe.

WORK IN THE UNITED STATES

The conceptions of work that have so strongly influenced the history of the United States are, perhaps, the classical example of the change in its meaning. From the beginnings of colonial America, work has been persistently glorified as something intrinsically good in itself. The reasons appear fairly obvious in the special history of the settlement of North America. First, the bulk of the original white settlers of North America were already convinced advocates of the Protestant Ethic. Second, the conditions they encountered were highly uncongenial to the establishment of any kind of agrarian feudalism, except under the special circumstances of black slavery in the South. Unlike the situation in parts of Central and South America, there were no dense populations of agricultural Indians who could be relatively easily enslaved or enserfed. The aboriginals of Northern and Eastern North America were relatively small in numbers and still largely at the hunting–gathering level of technical development. It was far easier to exterminate them or to drive them away than to transform them into servile laborers. Although attempts were made to introduce the manorial system, based on white indentured labor, they could not succeed. The abundance of open land, the extreme scarcity of labor, the early preoccupation with manufacturing and trade, combined with the general antiaristocratic opinion that many settlers brought with them—all these factors very early established North America as the land where the path to success and security was through hard work.

Except for the slave-owning areas of the American South, no country has been so work-oriented as the United States. Although the idea that work is a virtue was brought to the New World from Europe, the special conditions of life in the United States greatly accentuated it and gave it a special quality. Even in the industrialized countries of Europe, there remained strong aristocratic traditions that maintained a very sharp distinction between intellectual and manual work. The professional or manager never worked with his hands, and the manual worker was never expected to use his head. In America, however, this strong distinction between mental and manual work was never so sharp, in part because of the frontier tradition and in part because mechanical invention and tinkering with machinery were early seen both as a path to individual success and a contribution to the common good. The "rags to riches" success story became a great American theme and has been much more than merely a legend. The American of all classes was expected to be "good with his hands," even though manual work was understood to be a just a sideline and a hobby for the educated elite. In no country has the inventive mechanic and the practical engineer reached so high a status as in the United States and, in instances, so much monetary reward. In no country also has there been so much deliberate glorification of the "school of hard knocks" as compared to the university education. The other side of the coin, of course, was a tendency until comparatively recently to depreciate theoretical education as compared to practical experience on the job. In contrast to Europe, in America it was not degrading to start out life as a laborer, although there was certainly no advantage in remaining one.

Although these traditions have somewhat weakened in present-day America and changed their internal character, they are still strong. The idler tends to be derogated as a drone or parasite. If he is very poor, he is regarded with contempt as someone who doesn't *want* to work; if he is very rich, he is, at best, merely tolerated, but not really respected. Even the multi-millionaire is expected to perform some kind of work, although it is no longer anticipated that he will work with his hands. The enormous pace of industrialization in the United States, however, has brought about something of a major shift in the evaluation placed on different *kinds* or work. While it is still more virtuous to work than to be idle, people are now evaluated in accordance with a very elaborate occupational hierarchy. Work is "good" but certain kinds of work are "better" than others. White-collar work is valued more than blue-collar work, and the executive has higher status than the subordinate. However, even the most exalted occupations in the United States are still looked upon as *work,* and it is even believed that the top leaders of industry, government, and science work harder than anyone else. Heavy manual labor has been stripped of whatever value it once might have had by the great advances in technology, but a man who puts in many hours at his desk or in his office is respected. The meaning of work in the contemporary United States is, therefore, in the sharpest possible contrast to its negative evaluation in Classical Greece and Rome.

It is, however, impossible to ignore the fact that counteracting trends are at work. The runaway pace of industrial technology has, for many blue-collar workers, the consequence of beginning to undermine some of the intrinsic human values attached to work. The 1960s, marked by the involvement of the United States in an increasingly unpopular and unsuccessful war, was also marked by the disaffection of some of our most highly educated young people from the traditional values of hard work and success. For a brief period, it seemed that the more prestigious the university, the more certain it was to be a center for the systematic undermining of values traditionally associated with work. Much of the force of this movement became dissipated with the withdrawal of the United States from further involvement in the Vietnam imbroglio, but some of the echos of this widespread attack on the American work-ethic still remain. We shall examine these issues in more detail in later chapters.

SUMMARY

Since this chapter is itself a summary of an extensive historical and anthropological literature, it may seem senseless to write a summary of its contents. There is, however, a point to be made. What is the overall impression to be derived from this brief tour through the history of human work? We believe that the tour was desirable because it suggests that the meanings attached to work are very much a matter of particular sets of prevailing cultural norms. It is also evident that the evaluation placed on work and the hierarchy of values attached to different *kinds* of work varies sharply from society to society. These differences are not so much a reflection of the intrinsic nature of the work performed—its difficulty or danger—but rather appear to be determined by complex sets of social, political, and even religious beliefs and events.

From this point of view, work is a cultural transaction. What people think and feel about it, the degree to which it is gratifying, frustrating, or merely endurable, apparently depends on the particular society in which they live. Since cultural ideas are rarely wholly lost, even though the societies that produced them have disappeared, some of our current ideas about work have the aspect of cultural survivals. But with respect to individuals, *the main thing we will have to know about the ability to work is the manner in which a particular person internalizes a prevailing set of social and cultural norms.*

3 | THE STUDY OF WORK BEHAVIOR

Despite the varied roles of work in human history and the pervasiveness of the need to perform it, serious study of work behavior is a comparatively recent phenomenon. During most of the period of human existence on earth, the ability to work, including the problems faced in performing it, has largely been taken for granted. A number of massive social changes had to take place before the realization began to develop that work was not simply a God-given natural resource, like air and water, but a complex and variable human activity. For thousands of years, the worker was largely invisible—at least, for those whose task it was to write about human affairs. The great theologians, philosophers, and historians of the past, who concerned themselves with almost every aspect of human life, have had very little to say about work. This was because, until comparatively recently, work, as essentially a private activity, was carried out by "silent" members of society under various forms of compulsion: slaves, serfs, peasants, and guild craftsmen. It was not until the eighteenth and nineteenth centuries that a series of technological innovations took place that have thoroughly transformed the nature of work and have brought work and the worker into the public arena. These technological changes were so far-reaching in their consequences that we now speak of them as revolutionary: the *Industrial Revolution*.

CONSEQUENCES OF THE INDUSTRIAL REVOLUTION

During the nineteenth century in England, three great sets of inventions radically transformed the nature of human work, namely, the development of the technology to use coal instead of charcoal for the production of iron; the invention and development of power-driven machinery for the production of cotton cloth; the invention and development of the steam engine. Together, these technological breakthroughs laid the basis of the factory system of production, which transformed work from a largely private activity to a predominantly public one. The factory system and all its supporting enterprises—large-scale transportation, warehousing, merchandising, and

41

so on—not only brought about enormous improvements in the material standards of life but also created a host of new problems in its wake. Millions of people, who hitherto spent their entire working lives in relative obscurity as farmers, hunters, pastoralists, or individual craftsmen, were brought together in increasingly large aggregates, where their work behavior was under almost continuous observation and control.

Another major consequence of the Industrial Revolution was the undermining of the various forms of forced labor that characterized most essentially agricultural societies. The development of the factory system and a money economy required a kind of worker who was no longer tied to a plot of land and was neither bound nor protected by the half-secret regulations of the craft guild. The factory system required a relatively free and mobile worker who was, in effect, the sole owner and disposer of his ability to work and who was free to sell this ability in an open labor market. An inevitable sequel was the series of democratic revolutions of the eighteenth and nineteenth centuries, which radically transformed the conditions of work. It is, of course, not within the scope of this volume to enter into the manifold aspects of democratic rule, except to indicate that the establishment of the freeworker created a new problem: the sources of the individual motivation to work. This kind of question could arise only as a function of a widespread conviction that the individual is free to dispose of his labor, *or not,* as he pleases.

Although work had to become both relatively public and relatively free before it could be thought of as a problem worth studying, not all aspects of work behavior at once became issues for systematic investigation. The excessive rigors and deprivations of the early factory system, the dislocations attendant on the collapse of feudal arrangements, the unbounded prospects of freedom implied in the democratic revolutions, the increasingly fierce conflicts between capital and labor—all of these riveted the attention of the writers of the nineteenth century upon the political and social implications of industrialization. The radical reformers and social revolutionaries of this period were not so much concerned with the problems of the individual worker as they were with the social position of the entire class of workers. Nevertheless, as the great social struggles of the past 100 years began to gather force, all sides of the conflicts began to perceive that the worker was a new kind of actor on the social scene. Inevitably, interest began to arise in him as an individual.

It was not merely the rise of the factory system that focused attention on the problems of human work. The overriding quality of the twentieth century has been the enormously increasing acceleration of the rate of technological change. This rate of change is so swift that obsolescence has become a major problem not only for machines but also for people. The past 70 years have seen such rapid technological development that entire industries have virtually disappeared and millions of people have been forced to confront a situation in which their old ways of working are no longer available. These vast dislocations have taken place chiefly in the industrially developed countries of the world—and particularly in the United States—but the effects of these changes have also been profound in less developed countries. It is not too much to say that we are currently in the throes of a *second Industrial Revolution,* the effects of which on work may be as thoroughgoing as those of its predecessor.

Although we cannot here go into the detail that this problem merits, we can note four phenomena that deeply influence the nature of work and labor. First, the technical revolution in agriculture has brought about the virtual disappearance of individual farming as a way of life and labor in the United States. Second, a direct consequence of the first, is the vast process of urbanization in which millions of people have been forced to move from the farms to the cities in search of employment. Third, the past few decades have seen a fundamental change in the make-up of the industrial labor force. The rapid development of semiautomatic and fully automatic machinery has contracted the labor force at its two extremes: sharply lowering the demand for unskilled labor at one end and for the highly skilled craftsman at the other. Finally, an outcome of enormously increased man-hour productivity has been a major shift in the occupational composition of the American labor force: from commodity production to the delivery of various types of service.

What has happened in American agriculture illustrates the breathtaking onrush of technology. As recently as 1900, the United States was still predominantly an agrarian country. Almost one-half of our entire labor force still worked on farms, and the bulk of the energy resources expended on farming was still "natural" in origin: the muscle power of human beings and draught animals and the forces of wind and water. The American population was still largely rural, living on farms and in agriculturally based small towns. Considerable farm machinery was utilized, but it was still subordinate to the labor and experience of the farmer and his family. The basic industrial revolution in agriculture did not take place until the 1920s and was an outcome of the gasoline-driven motor. Once this process began, hardly 60 years ago, the application of motor-driven machinery and artificial fertilizer to farming has been so widespread that agriculture has been transformed into something akin to the factory system (i.e., production based on hired labor which tends increasingly toward automatic machinery). The result has been such gigantic increases in productivity that the traditional farm labor force—the farmer and his family—is approaching the vanishing point. Whereas roughly 40% of the American labor force lived and worked on farms in 1900, farm employment had dropped to less than 6% of a vastly increased labor force by 1970 (Allee, 1967; Burch, 1970).

The consequences of this great technical revolution in agriculture are so profound that we are still in the process of digesting them. Within a single generation, millions of people have been forced to give up a settled way of life and labor, which they and their forebears have enjoyed (or endured) for thousands of years, and have been physically displaced to the cities. The magnitude of this dislocation becomes comprehensible only when we remember that the bulk of mankind has labored with the forces of nature for 8000–10,000 years and that almost everything we currently experience as culture arose on the basis of the largely unassisted labor of the peasant–farmer. In what we now think of as "backward" countries, this situation still prevails. It is only in the most technically developed nations, and only in the past generation or two, that we are witnessing the rapid death of individual farming—with all of its implications for styles of work and the relations of the worker to nature and to machines.

One result of the mechanization of agriculture has been the general urbanization of the American population. According to the 1970 census, three-quarters of over 200 million living Americans resided in urban areas, over one-third of whom lived in the 10 largest metropolitan areas (World Almanac, 1972). We need not look much further than the technical revolution in agriculture to account for some of the problems of the city in mid-century America. The bulk of these displaced millions have been Southern blacks (once employed as sharecroppers and tenant farmers in what was a labor-exhaustive cotton-producing agriculture) and Southern and Midwestern white farmers, whose small farms—some owned, some rented—have been absorbed into large-scale factory farming (Bagdikian, 1964). Most of the people who have made up this huge migration from the countryside to the city are poorly educated, possess very little in the way of easily marketable work skills, and are accustomed to a work-style more adjusted to the rhythms of nature than to the requirements of modern industry. The resulting pressures on current urban educational systems and housing resources are too well known to require comment.

The problems raised by this vast internal migration are aggravated by the effects of technological change on the basic makeup of the modern labor force. For most of its early period of rapid development, American industry was able to make great advances on the basis of the largely unskilled, ex-peasant laborer: the European immigrant. During the roughly 50 years from the end of the Civil War to our entry into World War I, almost 30 million European immigrants came to the United States; most of them went to work in the mines and factories which could then use vast quantities of unskilled labor. It was the heavy, relatively poorly paid, unskilled labor of the first-generation immigrants—combined with the potentialities inherent in American public education—that enabled their second and third generation descendants to escape into the skilled and white-collar occupations. This traditional path to upward mobility in the United States, however, is currently being undermined by the greatly reduced demand for unskilled labor. Hand labor is increasingly redundant, and much of American industry is now engaged in "mass" production, a situation in which a smaller and smaller, semiskilled labor force tends and maintains increasingly automatic machinery. The result has been unemployment for an increasing portion of the displaced agricultural migrants.

The final effect of the second Industrial Revolution on which we wish to comment has been the current shift from industrial production to the delivery of services. For some 20 years, the direct production of tangible goods has employed considerably less than one-half the labor force. It is expected by 1980 (Flanders, 1970; Johnson, 1968) that almost three-quarters of all workers will be employed in the so-called service industries: recreation, health services, clerical, sales and managerial occupations, communications, and transportation. The important point here is that the bulk of the jobs involved will require considerable formal education. As an illustration of the increase in educational demands and requirements, the average number of years of education of the American soldier during World War I was fewer than 8 years; during World War II, the average number of years of education reported was approaching 12. It is now estimated that more than one-third of the American labor force in 1980s will have had some years of education beyond high school. In other words, work in the United States during the present and future decades will demand levels of technical expertise that were not required two or three generations ago.

If the first Industrial Revolution made labor a public enterprise and led to the serious study of the motivation to work, the second Industrial Revolution has brought a host of new problems in its wake. First, there has been the virtual collapse of an ancient tradition of work: the seasonally determined and "natural" labor of the individual peasant–farmer and his family. The displacement of millions of people from the farms to the cities has brought about a situation in which sons can no longer follow the furrows in their fathers' footsteps. The footsteps themselves have vanished! Second, the very rapid development of entire new technologies has caused entire industries to decay and has brought about great reductions in traditional occupations and work-styles (the railroads and deep-shaft mining are cases in point). Third, the unrelenting spread of fully and partially automated machinery has brought about a kind of leveling and contraction of the spectrum of work-skills, sharply reducing the demand both for the unskilled manual laborer, at one extreme, and for the highly skilled independent artisan, at the other.

In later chapters, we shall deal with some of the consequences of technological change for the worker. There is the tangled issue of work alienation, thought by many to be a result of the repetitive and monotonous character of highly mechanized labor. There is the problem of the greatly prolonged education now required for entry into many occupations. There is the very serious problem of training and retraining, faced annually by masses of people who have been employed in industries that suddenly become obsolescent. Finaly, we shall have to concern ourselves with the fact that the shift from primary production to the service, maintenance, and managerial occupations requires the development of social skills that hitherto were relatively foreign to the requirements of work.

One of the side effects of this massive set of interrelated and complex problems has been the rise and expansion of a new kind of professional: the *vocational counselor*. Entry into the labor force is no longer the relatively simple matter of working on the family farm or presenting one's unskilled labor power to the factory gate. Also, the breakdown of the apprenticeship–journeyman system has meant that the path to some level of work skill is through a system of formal education rather than the result of on-the-job training. Further, there are the vast problems of retraining faced by people who can no longer find employment in traditional industries, in which they might have worked for a considerable portion of their adult lives. In this book, we shall deal with some of the issues that this new profession must face. But first, since any field of expertise is always influenced by its past, we need to know something of how the whole thing began.

THE TECHNOLOGY OF WORK

The first efforts to carry on a scientific study of work behavior were focused exclusively on work simply as a technical factor in the process of production. These investigations began at about the turn of this century and were designed entirely to serve the interests of efficient factory management. They were in no sense humanitarian, except perhaps in relation to an overall aim of increasing the available flow of goods and services. Frederick W. Taylor (1911) is the recognized pioneer in what has come to be known as time-and-motion study, a type of analysis of task performance that is still a primary feature of modern industrial planning. Another early investigator was Frank B. Gilbreth (1909, 1911), who coined the term *therblig* for what he believed were the irreducible time–motion units of any work task. This entire system of work analysis came to be called "Taylorism" after its innovator and was widely heralded during the first two or three decades of the century as the great panacea for all the ills of industry.

From one point of view, the central aim of these early studies was to make the worker as much like a machine as possible. This process, in technical terms the "rationalization of work," involved the analysis of any work-task into a series of maximally efficient and uniform body movements. Taylor carefully observed laborers performing rather simple, repetitive tasks and was struck by the enormous variability in their movements. He also detected what he believed were wasteful expenditures of energy, so that less was produced in a given unit of time at the cost of increased fatigue. While Taylor and his many followers and imitators were not terribly concerned with the discomforts of fatigue, they were aware that a tired worker was an inefficient producer. Thus, a by-product of Taylorism has been some reduction in the discomforts entailed in manual labor—a gain for the worker as well as his employer. However, the worker has never taken very kindly to the figure of the efficiency engineer standing behind him, stopwatch in hand, and organized labor has always tended to look askance at the various schemes for scientific work-analysis.

The reasons are obvious. In a situation in which the fruits of increased productivity were by no means automatically shared with the worker, he was understandably suspicious of attempts to speed up his efforts. But there were also more subtle considerations involved in these early studies of human work. The central aim of the entire process was to reduce human variability, to make the work process as machinelike as possible; but this aim runs counter to some very powerful human motives and aspirations, about which we shall have more to say in Chapter 8. One of Taylor's more naive but strongly held beliefs was that if workers could be made to understand that the new systems entailed less total expenditure of energy and also entailed somewhat greater monetary rewards, they would eagerly accept them. Perhaps Taylor also shared that particular management viewpoint that regards workers merely as so many units of potential labor-power. The mistake here is analogous to the fiction of the "economic man," a favorite abstraction of certain classical economists. Just as people do not function uniformly to maximize their incomes and minimize their expenditures, so also workers tend to resist the conception that they are simply interchangeable units of production. The massive social changes that created the free worker also created a widespread concern for human individuality. The modern worker brought his own particular ways with him to the job and was not inclined to give them up easily. Gradually, later investigators learned that the monetary incentive is not the *sole* motive for work, although it is certainly one of the chief reasons.

Despite the misconceptions of these early studies of work behavior, they were the forerunners of what is today a fairly widespread field of scientific investigation. The modern specialty of industrial engineering is largely concerned with the most efficient deployment and organization of the relations between man and machines. There is now almost as much interest in adapting the machine to particular characteristics of the human machine-tender as in adapting the human being to the machine. A good part of the subspecialty of industrial psychology is concerned with these issues, although the so-called efficiency expert is more frequently a person with a background of training in industrial engineering and business management. As we shall see, the psychologist in industry has increasingly been called upon to solve other kinds of problems. By this time, a very large research literature exists on the technical conditions of work. Both organized labor and industry, as well as government, spend millions annually in seeking out the most efficient and humane uses of human labor.

It is not our intention here to enter into the technology of the work-process or to summarize the many studies that have been reported (cf. Dubin, 1958; Cottrell, 1955; Chapanis, 1959; Handy and Trumbo, 1980). The primitive time-and-motion studies of Taylor and Gilbreth have been justly criticized for their heavy bias toward atomism, their systematic ignoring of individual differences in work methods, and their tendency to substitute an abstract geometry of motion for the natural give-and-take of man and his environment. But, despite the evident weaknesses of the earlier studies, the malady lingers on. The very size and complexity of modern industry and the evident advantages of mass production favor a continued search for the maximal degree of uniformity in work behavior. The difference now is that, although the basic investigatory motive probably remains the same (the efficient use of human labor), there is now far more attention to the well-being and state of mind of the worker and the degree to which any system of work must take into account the wide variations displayed by workers in physical and mental characteristics. A fundamental misconception of the early studies was that there was thought to be only "one best way" to perform each job. The modern industrial engineer knows that he must design his machinery and organize his plan of work to fit not merely the "best" or "most adaptable" worker but a very motley collection of workers who vary in age, size, strength, adaptability, and a host of personal and temperamental factors.

Although the technology of work is not our primary concern, it should be noted that this field of investigation has expanded to include studies of the physical environments in which work takes place and, most recently, highly sophisticated examinations of the complex interrelationships between man and machine. There have been, for example, intensive studies of the effects on work of various kinds of illumination (e.g., Ferree and Rand, 1936), of the effects of ventilation and various atmospheric conditions (cf. the highly informative reports of the Industrial Fatigue Research Board of Great Britain), and of the effects of noise on performance (Berrien, 1946; McCormick, 1957). The needs of the equipment-design industry and of military technology have now led to heavy emphasis on what are being called the "human factors" in industrial engineering, in which the objective is to adapt machines to the sensory and motor capacities of the human beings who will use them (McCormick, 1957; Woodson, 1954). Finally, with the ushering in of the electronic age, we are now witnessing the development of elaborate theories and programs for "man–machine systems" (cf. Gagné, 1962).

What can we learn from this entire technology concerning the problems of human work? First, we are reminded that work, like many other human activities, is highly responsive to the environment in which it takes place, although we will be more concerned with the social and interpersonal characteristics of work environments (see Chapter 7) than with their physical features. Second, the very mistakes made by many of the investigators and the subtle shifts in emphasis that have taken place are indications that the working human being is an extremely complex entity, who varies not only in physical and mental capacity but also in feelings, emotions, attitudes, beliefs, aspirations, and ideals. Third, the detailed job analyses written by industrial engineers are very useful in giving us concrete insights into exactly what it is that people are required to do. Finally, the enormous number of variables and factors that have been shown to influence work behavior presents us with a salutary warning that one of the greatest threats to an understanding of work behavior is oversimplification. Human work is an extremely intricate affair, and easy conclusions should be avoided.

THE "HUMAN" ASPECTS OF WORK

One of the important, although unintended, outcomes of industrial engineering has been the recognition that human work cannot be easily reduced to so many quanta of mental and muscular energy. Work, after all, is performed by human beings, who bring into the workplace not only their intellectual and motor skills but also their individualities. The intelligent reader may complain that this should have been obvious from the beginning and that Taylor and all his followers should have had common sense enough to realize that they were chasing a chimera. For a number of reasons, however, an appeal to common sense would not have been heeded. Most of the students of work technology were trained as scientists, and the scientific enterprise, at least in its initial stages, attempts to isolate its phenomena of interest and to reduce them to manageable proportions. Another source of bias (which may have been more or less unconscious) is that they approached their studies of work from the general vantage point of the employers and users of labor. Industrial management was keenly aware of the economic triumphs brought about through the establishment of units of near-identical machines and the mass production of highly uniform and interchangeable commodities. It is understandable that they could be easily convinced of the advantages of a labor force composed of so many uniform and interchangeable units, capable of exact measurement as factors in production. Unlike machines, however, human workers come in many sizes, shapes, and packages. Worse, they do not shed their individualities, as they do their street clothing, in the factory locker room.

However disturbing this brutal fact of life might have been to the students of work technology, they deserve some credit for facing up to it, once it was perceived as a reality. Not until the early 1930s was it recognized that the attitudes, motivations, and personality of the worker might be quite as important conditions of work as the manner in which work was organized or the particular conditions of illumination and ventilation. Since that time, however, the study of work behavior has shifted rather sharply toward an emphasis on what could be called the "human" sides of work. The modern industrial engineer is now called upon to learn something about human

psychology, although he has not always been, perhaps, a particularly interested and effective student. More to the point, the trained psychologist
has been recruited by industry, bringing with him, of course, his own special
viewpoints and expertise. Much of what we know now about human work
has become available only during the last two or three decades as a result of
this shift in emphasis.

THE HAWTHORNE STUDIES

This series of ground-breaking investigations derives its name from the
industrial site in which it was carried out, the Hawthorne Works of the
Western Electric Company in Chicago. The studies provide an almost
hilarious example of the manner in which important discoveries can arise
from glaring mistakes. The Hawthorne studies are very widely cited, however, because they are the initial case history of the consequences of
forgetting—and then remembering—that workers are also human beings.

In 1924 when the studies were launched, the Hawthorne Works of Western Electric was the primary producer of telephonic equipment and employed thousands of both male and female workers. Because of the standard
nature of the basic commodity (the telephone), work was organized on a
mass production basis, and a large part of the labor force was deployed in
assembly of the many telephone components. No special skills were required, but the most desired qualities of the labor force were dexterity and
speed in carrying out rather simple, repetitive tasks. The workers were not
organized into labor unions, and the general posture of management tended
to be paternalistic. In this setting, a series of studies was designed to investigate the effects of a wide range of working conditions on productivity.
The objective was to discover how rates of production would be influenced
by varying such factors as illumination, rest pauses, length of working day,
pay rates, the provision by the company of hot lunches, etc. Precautions
were taken both to improve the quality of such conditions and to worsen
them at various stages of the experiments. So far, they were straightforward
studies of some of the conditions of work, which had been similarly studied
in other industries and other parts of the world.

The striking and incongruous result of certain of these studies was that
productivity continued to *rise*, whether relevant working conditions were
improved or worsened. This was a facer, and it is to the credit of the Hawthorne investigators that they did not quietly suppress their results and turn
to more fruitful matters. On the contrary, they began to investigate the
reasons for these incongruities. In order to secure the full cooperation of
their experimental subjects (which management had decided should be on a
voluntary basis), the investigators had inadvertently made participation in
the experiments very attractive. The participating workers had been freed
from the close supervision prevailing in their ordinary work departments;

they worked in a small group of workers of their own choice; they were assigned to a more cheerful and comfortable workroom; they could talk more freely during work; they were given explanations about the purpose of their work and were consulted about what they did. In short, they not only were receiving an extraordinary amount of attention from important plant personnel but were able to develop an *esprit de corps* that had hitherto apparently not marked the general labor force at Hawthorne. They came to feel that they had been singled out by management for their special qualities as persons and, in return, worked to full capacity even under unfavorable conditions. The conclusion of the Hawthorne investigators was that attitude and morale were more effective determinants of increased output than the more familiar work conditions they had been attempting to study.

These findings then led the Hawthorne investigators to a further series of researches that was now directly focused on the human sides of work. Intensive interviews were carried out with over 21,000 workers, in which it was noted that giving the employee an opportunity to express his opinions about work tended to improve his attitude to it. Systematic observations were carried out, through which it was discovered, among other things, that the apparently disorganized work force was actually composed of many informal groupings that exerted considerable pressures on individual work performance. Gradually, the impression arose that the workers at Hawthorne were participants in a kind of semisecret subculture, which had its own unformulated but powerful traditions and customs, which was largely unknown to management, and which was sometimes wholly at cross-purposes with stated management objectives. These findings, as well as those of the earlier Hawthorne studies, were reported in two very interesting and influential books (Roethlisberger and Dickson, 1939; Mayo, 1933).

The net effect of the Hawthorne studies was the launching of what was later called the "human-relations" movement in industrial management. Its central theme consists of the belief that quite remote personal problems and personal characteristics of the worker as a human being may have profound effects on his "style" of work, the quality and quantity of his work-output, and even whether he is willing to work at all. Unfortunately, in the hands of some of its more enthusiastic and less critical practitioners, "human-relations" in industry became another kind of panacea and has been somewhat discredited as a result. After all, the primary purpose of industry is to produce and distribute a larger flow of goods and services at reduced costs to itself. To the degree that a more well-informed, happier, and better adjusted worker is a better producer—well and good! But industrial organizations are neither welfare institutions nor hospitals, and there are obvious limits to the degree that they can concern themselves with the psychological well-being of their employees. There are, of course, many other characteristics of the setting that sharply restrict the effectiveness of any human-relations program—limits on occupational mobility, the intrinsic monotony and meaninglessness of many kinds of work, the built-in differentials of reward related to status, etc. Carefully controlled later studies of the relations between morale and productivity have yielded inconsistent results (Brayfield and Crockett, 1955; Haire, 1959; Herzberg, Mausner, Paterson, and Capwell, 1957), considerably dampening earlier enthusiasms.

It should be noted that the Hawthorne research has, during the intervening years, acquired certain mythical qualities and has not been free from attack. It is not generally known that only five worker–subjects participated in the crucial research (cf. Argyle, 1953) and that no efforts were made to replicate the results with other groups of workers. Many investigators today would, of course, regard the number of subjects to be laughably small for reliable statistical inference. Moreover, it does not seem to be noticed or commented on that all the workers involved in the study were women (the investigators and supervisors were all men)—a circumstance which, 50 years ago, could make for considerable sex-bias, unconscious domination, and lack of generalizability. It seems likely that more rigorous research standards might have created a research situation where the famous Hawthorne effect would not have made its appearance.

From a quite different standpoint, the Hawthorne studies have come under attack through criticism of the ideological stance of the chief investigators. As early as the 1960s, it was argued (Carey, 1967) that the research was dominated by promanagement biases, which influenced both the selection and retention of the worker–subjects. More recently, an elaborate critical analysis of the Hawthorne data from an admittedly Marxist viewpoint has appeared (Bramel and Friend, 1981). The latter writers make the claim that the apparent upward trend of the Hawthorne productivity data is an illusion and is based on the dismissal of unsatisfactory subjects and their replacement with "rate-busters." In a subsequent issue of the same journal in which this criticism appeared, a reply to the Bramel–Friend paper (Sonnenfeld, 1982) reports interviews with three of the five original worker–subjects, since retired, which support the inference that the abusive supervision characteristic of the main factory floor was absent from the Test room and that the workers were encouraged to develop considerable camaraderie. This defender of the Hawthorne research makes what I believe to be a proper inference that "individual work behavior is rarely a pure consequence of simply cause and effect relationships but rather is determined by a complex set of factors . . ." and further that "the work-place must be seen as a social system and not merely a production system" (Sonnenfeld, 1982, 1398–1399).

The significance of the Hawthorne studies is that they laid the basis for a needed breakthrough into an entirely new conception of human work. Their actual findings are often cited simply as an example of poor experimental design. Professors are still fond of warning their students against the "Hawthorne effect" (the influence that sheer participation in an experiment may have upon the subject's behavior). The Hawthorne studies are far from being merely convenient illustrations of the pitfalls in experimental design. They have made an entire generation of behavioral scientists aware that human work is far more than merely a particular kind of cognitive–motor performance but engages and is influenced by a great many other psychological processes and factors. It is, after all, the entire human being who works. The Hawthorne studies have served the purpose of calling it to our attention that the worker brings far more to his task than a variable ability to follow instructions and carry out a prescribed series of movements. He also brings his momentary moods, as well as more enduring emotions and feelings, his social beliefs and attitudes, his entire personality. Although they have been less studied, these aspects of human work are now believed to be of crucial importance.[1]

THE SOCIOLOGY OF WORK

During the past few decades, a number of books and research papers have signaled the establishment of a major subspecialty within the field of sociology. This area of interest is concerned with examining the social structures and institutions that modern society has developed to cope with the problems of human work. The focus of attention is not so much on the individual worker as on workers in the mass, although the term *mass* may refer to aggregates ranging in size from small work-groups to entire occupations. This new field of investigation has a variety of names: industrial sociology (Miller and Form, 1957; Schneider, 1957); the sociology of industrial relations (Knox, 1956); the world of work (Dubin, 1958); occupational sociology (Smigel, Monane, Wood, and Nye, 1963); work and society (Gross, 1958). Perhaps the simplest and most descriptive title is simply the sociology of work (Caplow, 1954). A number of important problems have been brought under study: the social roles and statuses that characterize

[1]In passing, it is also of interest that the management methods and insights into work behavior characteristic of the Human Relations movement comprise the core of contemporary Japanese industrial management. It is hardly a secret that the American market is currently suffering successful invasion by high quality products of Japanese manufacture (cars are the best, but not the only, example). Many commentators are calling attention to what they think of as the unique qualities of Japanese labor management cooperation, which are presented as the secret of high quality and efficient production. On the other hand, Japanese writers have made it clear that the vaunted Japanese methods were largely imported from the United States and were pioneered in the Hawthorne studies and the subsequent Human Relations movement. It is ironic that certain of the Japanese methods of industrial management, which we are now frantically trying to imitate, were originated here but not widely applied. It would be a matter of some interest to comparative anthropology to know why these methods of management were easily adaptable in Japan but not in their country of origin.

different occupations and professions, the effects of work-groups on work behavior, the structure and dynamics of work organizations, the relations of industry to the community at large, and the value systems of the different components of an industrialized society. While this field is still relatively young and is struggling with many difficult problems of methodology and interpretation, there is already a considerable body of fact and theory.

It is not our intention here to comment on the many kinds of problems that have been studied by industrial sociologists, although they are all interesting and informative in their own right. Our primary concern is with the ability to work per se, and most of these studies take the sheer ability to work for granted. However, certain central themes have been of special interest to the sociologist of work and contribute to our understanding of how work is perceived by the people who perform it. The first of these themes has to do with work as a social role, while the second deals with work alienation.

WORK AS A SOCIAL ROLE

One of the major analytic tools of modern sociology is the concept of *social role* (cf. Parsons, 1951; Merton, 1957). Although definitions of this term differ in detail, the basic concept is that certain kinds of behavior are expected and demanded from people who are recognized as having prescribed functions within a social system. Roles are regulated by social norms which, in turn, are components of culture. According to Parsons, the term *role* is used to describe those aspects of behavior that are normatively regulated, that is, the ways in which people *ought* to behave in terms of whatever social function they are supposed to be carrying out. It is clear that roles are based on a certain mutuality of expectation among two or more people and that they are heavily tinged with evaluative considerations. People are constantly judged by others in terms of how well or poorly they play their respective role. From this point of view, the primary unit of social behavior is the social role. The whole of society can be analyzed by describing the variety of roles that people are expected to play and the manner in which these roles interact.

Given the importance of the concept of *social role* to contemporary sociology, sociologists of work have naturally paid considerable attention to the role of the worker. Because these studies have isolated those behavioral characteristics that serve to differentiate certain *particular* occupations from others, they are somewhat lacking in generality. Gross (1964) has commented that some occupations have received a great deal of attention and many others none at all. Occupations at the two extremes of the occupational hierarchy have been studied in detail: physicians, professionals, and executives, at one extreme (cf. Hughes, 1960; Dalton, 1959; Janowitz, 1960), and migratory laborers, prostitutes, and waitresses, at the other (Anderson,

1923; Cressey, 1932; Whyte, 1948). Despite the selective specificity and concreteness of most of these studies, their value to the student of work is considerable. They comprise, so to speak, the case-history material that allows us to formulate a number of general concepts.

These studies suggest that work in modern society is overwhelmingly a *public* and *social* activity. Different occupations require not only certain combinations of physical and intellectual capabilities but also a set of social behaviors that, on the surface at least, may appear to be quite unrelated to the particular job. These social behaviors include details of dress and grooming, the style and content of speech, the ability to relate in certain standardized ways to peers, to subordinates, and to superiors in complex social hierarchies, and even the necessity of accepting (or at least appearing to accept) various systems of opinion and belief. To become a worker, therefore, one must not only be willing and able to learn the job, but one must also be willing and able to learn the "rules of the game." The former are certainly the necessary conditions of work, but the latter comprise the *sufficient* conditions, which must be met if the work role is to be played at all. The industrial engineer has focused his attention primarily on the skills of the job, but the occupational sociologist has provided us with rich data suggesting that *both* sets of conditions are essential to human work.

The sociological term for these sets of required social behaviors is *occupational colleagueship* (Gross, 1958). Its components arise in part from the technical requirements of different kinds of work and in part from considerations related to protective solidarity. Of importance to the members of almost all occupations is a series of implicit and explicit definitions of who is a marginal and who is a full colleague. This sort of distinction is most clearly marked and explicitly formulated in the professional occupations and in the highly skilled crafts, but it pervades all kinds of work to a greater or lesser extent. At stake here are not only the obvious economic considerations but also many subtleties relating to prestige, social status, and personal identity. Even among unskilled laborers, invidious distinctions are made between the veteran and the tyro, so that the new worker may be the object of all sorts of horseplay and misdirection until he has absorbed enough protective coloration to be accepted as a full member of the work group.

Occupational colleagueship appears to involve a number of components. First, and perhaps most important, is the exercise of control over the entry of new members. The medieval guilds are often cited as the supreme examples of the elaboration of rules governing occupational entry, but the modern professions and crafts are not far behind. The difference is that the regulations of the guilds were predominantly secret, whereas the rules of entry into the modern professions and crafts are largely regulated by public law and openly recognized practice. The current preoccupation with the formulation of state licensing regulations is a reflection not only of the purpose of regulating standards of competence but also of desires to restrict entry, limit competition, and establish an occupational identity. In the more unskilled occupations, these latter objectives are obviously much more difficult to achieve but are striven for, in part, through labor union membership and in part through a variety of more informal kinds of social pressure.

A second, more subtle, aspect of colleagueship concerns what can be called the work-style; in other words, distinctive patterns of dress, speech, and deportment that are essentially marks of identity. They serve to differentiate who is "in" from who is "out" and therefore contribute to feelings of solidarity. One of the more important components of the work-style is the development of specialized occupational languages, which sometimes reach the proportions of a semisecret lingo or argot. Not just technical terminology, with which the outsider is simply not expected to be familiar ("shop-talk"), this jargon also includes certain qualitative aspects of ordinary speech. Thus, the factory worker and the soldier consider it both necessary and desirable to talk "tough" and to use obscenities with abandon (Elkin, 1946); the college professor must sound both erudite and precise; the white-collar officer worker genteel and polite. Almost equally important are styles of dress, which vary in the rigidity of requirements from the official uniform of the soldier or policeman to the less standardized but equally compulsory business suit of the white-collar worker. Similarly, the marks of occupational identity are enhanced by forms of greeting, the use or misuse of honorific titles, and the degree to which formal or casual conversation is permitted or encouraged.

Third, occupational colleagueship is both policed and maintained by the establishment of both formal and informal associations and organizations. The professional association not only exists to formulate and enforce the "rules of the game" but is also a public forum and an arena for social intercourse. The members of one's own occupational association can be better counted on even than one's own blood relatives to "know" what it means to be a physician, a plumber, or an auto worker. It is even possible to enhance one's feelings of status and identity by achieving some sort of leadership role in one's occupational association or labor union. Many of the same considerations apply to the many forms of informal association that arise whenever groups of workers are brought together.

While the considerations of colleagueship do not exhaust the many aspects of the work role, they give some idea why the process of becoming a worker is far more complicated than it appears at first glance. In addition to possessing the required basic skills and talents, one is also required to "act" like a worker and "look" like a worker. These additional requirements vary greatly from occupation to occupation. A great many people "fail" in particular occupational endeavors because they cannot or will not meet the social requirements of particular work roles. The skills of work are as much social and interpersonal as they are physical and intellectual.

THE PROBLEM OF WORK ALIENATION

Just as the concept of *social role* is one of the major analytical tools of modern sociology, the concept of *alienation* is one of its major themes. The great social and political philosophers of the nineteenth century—such men as De Tocqueville, Marx, Weber, Durkheim, Simmel—were social critics as well as social observers. All of them were preoccupied with different aspects of the consequences of industrialization and urbanization in Western Europe and the breakup of feudal institutions. As Nisbet argues, in his book on the sources of sociological theory (1966), the writers of the nineteenth century were deeply concerned with certain massive changes in the human condition that had been brought about by two centuries of technical, social, and political revolutions. Basically, these writers tried to explain five phenomena: changes in the conditions of labor, changes in property relations, the increasing sway of the city over the countryside, the irresistible force of technological progress, and the spread of the factory system.

In observing these phenomena, all these writers were intent on the negative, as well as the positive influences, and of technical and social change, although they drew quite different conclusions. One of the great negative influences is summed up in the term *alienation.*'' For most of these writers, the negative side of technical and social progress has been the increasing isolation of the individual from his fellow human beings. Replacing the closely knit farming village is the huge, impersonal city, an aggregate of strangers. Replacing the semipatriarchical feudal estate is the modern factory, in which the only nexus between worker and employer is monetary. Replacing a personal God and an omnipresent religion is increasing secularism and the decay of absolute moral and ethical codes. Thus, the enormous gains achieved by the triumphs of individualism were balanced by the loss of a thousand ties that contributed to personal security. The alienation of the worker from his work, of the communicant from his religion, of the clan member from his kinfolk, of the members of families from each other—all these are seen as some of the more unpleasant fruits of industrial and social progress.

The central theme of the alienation theorists regarding work is that industrialization and the factory system have made work increasingly meaningless to the individuals who are required to perform it. This idea dates from the rise of the factory system. De Tocqueville, for example, believed that the human worker was being degraded into an automaton through economic specialization and the division of labor. He wrote:

> When a worker is unceasingly and exclusively engaged in the fabrication on one thing, he ultimately does his work with singular dexterity; but at the same time he loses the general faculty of applying his mind to the direction of his work. He every day becomes more adroit and less industrious; so that it may be said of him that in proportion as the workman improves, the man is de-

graded. What can be expected of a man who has spent twenty years of his life in making the heads for pins? . . . In proportion as the principle of the division of labor is more extensively applied, the workman becomes more weak, more narrow-minded, and more dependent (De Tocqueville, 1835).

It is clear that De Tocqueville believed that work is meaningful only when the worker has full control over the entire productive process and is able to express in the final product his individuality, creativity, and pride in workmanship. For De Tocqueville, and for many sociologists since his day, industrialization transformed the creative artisan or individual farmer into a simple cog in an increasingly gigantic and complex machine.

The phrase "alienation of work" is not derived from De Tocqueville, who never used it, but from the writings of Karl Marx, who wrote with even greater fervor on the deadening consequences of the factory system. Unlike De Tocqueville, however, Marx saw work losing its positive meaning not because of technology itself but because of the property relations characteristic of capitalist society. For Marx, work alienation meant the separation of the worker from *ownership* either of the means of production or of the final product:

In what does this alienation consist? First, that work is external to the worker, that it is not part of his nature, that consequently he does not fulfill himself in his work but denies himself, has a feeling of misery not well-being, does not develop freely a physical and mental energy, but is physically exhausted and mentally debased. . . . His work is not voluntary but imposed, *forced* labor. . . . Finally, the alienated character of work for the worker appears in the fact that it is not his work but work for someone else, that in work he does not belong to himself but to another person (Marx, cited in Bottomore and Rubel, 1964).

The results are the same as those that were seen by De Tocqueville: the loss of all pride in labor and the degradation of the worker into a mere appendage to a machine.

While Marx's conception of alienation has been strongly influential, it is highly specialized and has persisted chiefly in the writings of his committed followers. Non-Marxist sociologists, however, view alienation more in the spirit of De Tocqueville, particularly as these themes become elaborated in the writings of Max Weber and Émile Durkheim. Weber believed that the chief difficulties of modern society lay in the increasing bureaucratization and secularization of all aspects of life—including work. Durkheim believed that a consequence of industrialization and large-scale urbanism was increasing erosion of all the traditional means by which the individual identifies himself as a person; he coined the term *anomie* to describe this increasing feeling of lack of identity which, in extreme cases, may lead to crime, all forms of social deviancy, and even suicide. For these writers, the price that mankind has been forced to pay for technological and social progress has been an increasing alienation of human beings from each other, from established systems of ethical and social values, and from their work.

So far, we have been dealing with views of alienation that reflected the early *rise* of the factory system, the first Industrial Revolution. The great social philosophers of the nineteenth century were commenting on what they perceived as the undermining and collapse of an ancient established order, the traditional agrarian societies that had persisted for thousands of years. In these societies, the bulk of mankind lived their entire lives in small, self-contained, rural villages. Whatever the defects of village life—and in retrospect, we can see that there were many—there were also certain virtues: a closeness to nature and to the other human beings who made up the village population, a high degree of stability, and an inbuilt sense of identity. People knew who they were; it was what they always had been and what they expected to be for future generations. They were the primary producers of virtually everything necessary for their lives: their food, their habitations, their clothing, their tools and instruments. Work was regulated by tradition and sanctified by religion. Its meaning was simple and direct; its products were concrete and realized objects that could be used and enjoyed by the person who produced them. Work seemed as inevitable as the seasons—and as natural.

Whether village life and the work of the peasant–farmer were ever really so idyllic an afair is a moot question. But, whatever the case, the rise and spread of industry had virtually caused this way of life and labor to disappear. The major defect of nineteenth-century social criticism is that it was nostalgic. It looked back on a way of life that was already passing out of existence and could not be restored. Millions of people have been forced to leave the farms for the cities, and they cannot return. Millions more have appeared quite ready to give up the certainties and easy identifications of village life for the promise of a higher material standard of life through wage labor. For better or worse, the overwhelming majority of people in the technically developed countries must find their work in one of thousands of new occupations made available by modern industry.

This great social transformation has not brought about the disappearance of concern about work alienation, but the character of that concern has certainly changed. If anything, concern about the meaning of work itself has become very widespread in the present decades (the 1960s and 1970s). The older social criticism was aimed chiefly at the *conditions* of work: the length of the working day, the levels of wages and compensation, the inability of the new factory worker to resist the demands and exploitation of the employer, the worker's vulnerability to the horrors of cyclical unemployment, the lack of safety precautions, the general absence of job security. The great social struggles of the late nineteenth and early twentieth centuries established a hitherto nonexistent set of rights: the right of the new wage-earning class to organize and bargain collectively with the employer. The battle over the legitimacy of such rights in the United States was very sharply fought, but by the 1950s, the basic issue at stake was largely resolved. In the mass production industries, at least, the trade union is now a legal fact of life, buttressed and legitimized by both tradition and public law. Such fundamental issues as working hours, compensation, seniority rules, and job security are now matters of public negotiation, supported by a wide network of labor legislation.

It has become fashionable in certain quarters to criticize the established trade unions for what is felt to be a loss of the militancy and idealism with which their early struggles were conducted. Labor union officials are described as "fat cats" interested only in raising the wages of their immediate constituents and insensitive and indifferent to the plight of large groups who are relatively new entrants to the labor force: racial minorities, women, youth. While we are very far from a labor millenium, it seems to me that these criticisms express a certain lack of historical perspective. The early labor struggles were fought with a crusading fervor because they concerned elementary human rights: the right to organize and bargain collectively, the right to strike, the demand for union recognition. The issues being fought about were also basic. Was the individual laborer to have any say about how long he works, his level of compensation, the circumstances of his promotion or dismissal? Were the organizations formed by workers to obtain these new rights, their trade unions, to be "recognized" by employers and legitimized by the state? It is hardly a matter of insignificance that, by the middle of the twentieth century, these basic rights were largely won and are now virtually taken for granted. But the victories have brought new problems in their wake.

It can hardly be doubted that the successful trade union organization of the mass production industries has brought to millions of workers real economic benefits and even a certain measure of independence and power. Working hours are fixed by law, real wages have risen sharply, the procedures of hiring and dismissal are regulated strictly, and some vital conditions of work are subject to contractual negotiation. If the worker is laid off, he has the cushion of unemployment insurance; if he is too old to work or if he reaches the age of formal retirement, he can draw on Social Security; if he is injured on the job, he can receive workman's compensation. All these are real achievements of the trade unions and of the social legislation that the activity of organized labor largely brought into being. If the trade union is conceived of as an organization of wageworkers designed to secure such basic rights, if the crusading militancy of the early unionists was fired by the general denial of these rights, if the long and bitter struggles of the earlier years have resulted in a general victory for collective bargaining—then it is easy to see that a certain complacency and a reduced level of idealism might be a natural result.

Why, then, the present level of concern about work, since it is clear that the conditions of work, in the advanced countries at least, have improved greatly? That there is a present high level of concern can hardly be doubted. We can choose three publishing events in the early 1970s that attest to this new worry about work and indicate something about its character. First, there is the release of a special report by the U.S. Department of Health, Education and Welfare, titled *Work in America*. Second, there is the unexpected success of the runaway best-seller *Working*, which consists of interviews with people on what they do on the job and what they feel about their work (Terkel, 1974). Finally, there is the general tone of many of the studies reported in an important new collection of monographs on work commisssioned by the National Vocational Guidance Association (Herr, 1974). We shall deal briefly with certain of the ideas brought forward in these three quite different volumes.

In certain respects, the report of the federal Department of Health, Education, and Welfare is the most remarkable. It was commissioned by a leading cabinet member of a federal administration firmly committed to the traditional work ethic, a person considered by many to be politically and socially conservative. *Work in America* is a compilation based on 40 commissioned studies carried out by an impressive array of social scientists. Its purpose was to produce an assessment of the attitude of workers to their work and to suggest what might be done to improve the quality of work for most of those who are required to perform it. What is most amazing about *Work in America*—amazing when one considers that it is an official document of a business-oriented administration—is the grimness of the picture it paints. The chief theme of the book is that work has lost—or it losing—its chief meanings, its central values, for a large portion of the American labor force. *Work in America* is not concerned with the ancient grievances that brought the labor movement into being. It takes for granted that the most flagrant abuses of the worker are now largely ameliorated, that compensation is more reasonable, hours of work fixed and regulated, unions recognized, employment and dismissal no longer arbitrary affairs. It concentrates instead on a new and widespread malaise: Workers increasingly complain that their work is meaningless, boring, repetitive, and dull. As the writers of *Work in America* put it:

What most workers want, as more than 100 studies in the past 20 years show, is to become masters of their immediate environments and to feel that their work and they themselves are important—the twin ingredients of self-esteem. Workers recognize that some of the dirty jobs can be transformed only into the merely tolerable, but the most oppressive features of work are felt to be avoidable: constant supervision and coercion, lack of variety, monotony, meaningless tasks, and isolation. An increasing number of workers want more autonomy in tackling their tasks, greater opportunity for increasing their skills, rewards that are directly connected to the intrinsic aspects of their work, and greater participation in the design of work and the formulation of their tasks (1973; p. 13).

The writers of this monograph document their assertion that it is not only the factory-based blue-collar worker who is a victim of the feeling that his work is meaningless but that this feeling is shared by a substantial proportion of people in the clerical and white-collar occupations. By and large, it is only the highly skilled and independent professional who finds his work interesting, personally rewarding, and would choose his occupation again if he had his life to live over. In this connection, a recent survey is referred to, one undertaken by the Survey Research Center of the University of Michigan, with support from the Department of Labor (uncited). This study, described by the writers of the report as "unique and monumental," asked a representative sample of 1533 American workers how they would rank 25 aspects of work. The following is reported as the preferred order, by workers of all occupational levels:

1. Interesting work
2. Enough help and equipment to get the job done
3. Enough information to get the job done
4. Enough authority to get the job done
5. Good pay
6. Opportunity to develop special abilities
7. Job security
8. Seeing the results of one's work

Continuing this theme, answers are reported to the question: "What type of work would you try to get into if you could start all over again?" According to the study, "of a cross-section of white-collar workers (including professionals), only 43% would voluntarily choose the same work that they are doing, and only 24% of a cross-section of blue-collar workers would choose the same kind of work if given another chance." By occupation, the results are summarized in the following table:

Table 3.1. Percentages in Occupational Groups Who Would Choose Similar Work Again[a,b]

Professional and lower white-collar occupations	Percentage	Working-class occupations	Percentage
Urban university professors	93	Skilled printers	52
Mathematicians	91	Paper workers	42
Physicists	89	Skilled autoworkers	41
Biologists	89	Skilled steelworkers	41
Chemists	86	Textile workers	31
Firm lawyers	85	Blue-collar	24
Lawyers	83	(cross-section)	
Journalists (Washington correspondents)	82	Unskilled steelworkers	21
		Unskilled autoworkers	16
Church university professors	77		
Solo lawyers	75		
White-collar workers (cross-section)	43		

[a]Reprinted from Work in America by the Special Task Force of the Department of Health, Education and Welfare by permission of the MIT Press, Cambridge, Massachusetts.
[b]Data attributed to a study by Robert L. Kahn, 1972.

The writers of Work in America point to a number of sources for the widespread dissatisfaction with work that they find to be characteristic of the contemporary American labor force. First, they blame Taylorism (see Chapter 3) and what they characterize as a "misplaced" conception of work efficiency. Second, they present data to show that the dream of becoming "one's own boss" through hard work and suitable training is rapidly becoming a myth. Third, they show that the predominant trend of the twentieth century is toward the large-scale corporation and the bureaucratic institution—a trend that "minimize[s] the independence of the workers and maximize[s] control and predictability for the organization." They approvingly cite the following definition of alienation:

> Alienation exists when workers are unable to control their immediate work processes, to develop a sense of purpose and function which connects their jobs to the over-all organization of production, to belong to integrated industrial communities, and when they fail to become involved in the activity of work as a mode of personal self-expression. (Blauner, 1964)

Not the least surprising aspect of Work in America are the conclusions drawn by its writers. In effect, they level a direct attack on some of the most cherished tenets and procedures of large-scale industry. They contrast "industrial efficiency" with "social efficiency." The former is defined in its usual economic sense: maximum output at lowest direct cost; labor is simply a cost of production, to be minimized as much as possible. In contrast, the writers call for a national policy that stresses "social efficiency," a policy that "recognizes that the production of goods or services by a firm may result in costs or benefits that occur in society and which are not accounted for in the internal audit of any firm or all firms together" (*Work in America*, p. 24). Among social costs discussed are the consequent mental and physical health of the labor force and the effects of work on the family, on rates of crime, delinquency, and psychosis, and on feelings of reduced psychological well-being and personal satisfaction.[2]

After reviewing the relatively meager efforts of corporate business to take such costs into account, the writers of *Work in America* conclude as follows:

> For society, the main benefits from an increase in the quantity and quality of jobs will be in avoiding some of the very large costs now incurred by the present way in which we do business. These costs are not fully tallied in the annual costs of our corporations and bureacracies; they are the costs of such job-related pathologies as political alienation, violent aggression against others, alcoholism and drug abuse, mental depression, an assortment of physical diseases, inadequate performance in schools and a larger number of welfare families than there need be. These costs are born by the citizen and by society; they must be included in any systematic accounting of the costs and benefits of work in America. A precedent for this has been established in environmental policy; the precedent needs to be extended to social policy (p. 28).

The phenomena reported by *Work in America*,[3] presented in the abstract language of social science, are made dramatic and personal in a recent book by Studs Terkel: *Working: People Talk About What They Do All Day and*

[2]The opinions expressed in *Work in America* have not gone unchallenged. A number of criticisms are to be found in a special issue of the *Journal of Occupational Medicine* (vol. 16, 1974). O'Toole (1974) presents data showing that the alleged connection between "dull, routine and meaningless jobs" and job dissatisfaction is less close than is argued by the writers of *Work in America*. Strauss (1974), among others, has questioned whether work-role and the meaning of work are of salient importance among blue-collar workers.

[3]Ten years have elapsed since the publication of *Work in America*. Although the report has been described as "very influential" (Cooper and Payne, 1978, p. 5), it might well be asked whether the aforementioned influence has actually changed the practices of American industrial management. The answer is that, as of 1984, virtually no changes have taken place in American production practice, or is it anticipated that any notable change is to be expected in the immediate future, despite the current furor about "Japanese" methods of management. Deeply entrenched cultural and economic practices are difficult to alter except by outright military conquest and prolonged political domination. It is to be feared that *Work in America* has been more influential among a narrow circle of industrial sociologists and academicians than among the industrial managers who were its primary target.

How They Feel About What They Do. Terkel is a writer and radio and television talk-show interviewer working out of Chicago, who has specialized for some years in presenting the problems and interest of the "common man." To prepare the present volume, Terkel roamed the country with a tape recorder, interviewing a wide collection of people about what they did on their jobs, what they liked or disliked about them, what were their hopes and dreams. The hundreds of interviews reported in *Working* are not, of course, any kind of representative or randomly selected sampling. But Terkel has been clever in reporting the language and opinions of people in a wide variety of occupations: from assembly-line worker to plant manager; from waitress to proprietor; from taxi driver to dentist. Of course, these interviews were edited for publication, and one must assume that the respondents were not chosen at random. One can assume that the materials presented reflect the interviewer's biases and interests, and it would appear that some obvious axes are being ground. But, taken for what they are, the interviews supply fascinating insights into what some people think their jobs actually are like. Like the material presented in *Work in America,* the overall tone is dysphoric. For the majority of informants, work is dull, demeaning, meaningless, and is being performed only because the consequences of unemployment are more terrible than the work available. But, to return to a point made earlier, the bulk of complaints are not about the level of compensation, the hours of work, or the circumstances of hiring and dismissal. The general improvement of these working conditions has apparently permitted other complaints to surface. This is very well expressed in a long interview with the young president of the Lordstown local of the auto workers union. Consider this interview with the knowledge that the General Motors assembly plant in Lordstown, Ohio, is reputed to be "the most automated, fastest line in the world" for the mass production of automobiles. The labor force is mostly young, and the labor leader talking is only 29:

> Fathers used to show their manliness by being able to work hard and have big, strong muscles. . . . The young guy, now, he doesn't get a kick out of saying how hard he can work. I think his kick would be just the opposite: 'You said I had to do that much, and I only have to do *that* much. I'm man enough to stand up and fight for what I say I have to do.' It isn't being manly to do more than you should. That's the difference between the son and the dad. Father felt patriotic about it. They felt obligated to that guy that gave him a job. . . . Whereas the young guy believes that he has something to say about what he does. He doesn't believe that when the foreman says it's right that it's right. Hell, he may be ten times more intelligent as this foreman. . . . The almighty dollar is not the only thing in my estimation. There's more to it—how I'm treated. What I have to say about what I do, how I do it. It's more important than the almighty dollar. *The reason might be that the dollar's here now.* It wasn't in my father's young days. I can concentrate on the social aspects, my rights (Terkel, 1974, pp. 187–194; italics added).

It may be noted that this young labor leader is not complaining about the level of wages, about hours of work and arbitrary dismissal, about the historical problems that brought the trade union into being. As he says, "the dollar's here now." His litany of dissatisfaction reflects what is apparently a widespread feeling that the worker has been reduced to a dispensable cog in a giant machine, that the worker is now concerned over his autonomy in deciding *how* he should work.

Our third illustration of current writing on modern work alienation is to be found in an important collection of studies published in 1974 as a basic text for vocational guidance and career counseling. *Vocational Guidance and Human Development* (Herr, 1974) is a publication of the National Vocational Guidance Association, a second decennial volume designed to update an earlier and equally important publication (Borow, 1964). Like *Work in America* which reflects the views of officialdom and the highly personal comments found in Terkel's interviews, the problem of work alienation is prominent in this new text. The tone of the volume is set by its opening chapter ("Apathy, Unrest and Change: The Psychology of the 1960s"), written by Henry Borow, who was the editor of the first publication in this series. The quality of Borow's concerns can be gleaned by a few excerpts from this chapter:

> While work in its generic sense continues to be valued, it seems clear that many Americans, youth and adults alike, no longer embrace the axiom that work for its own sake is rewarding and ennobling. The Puritan spirit . . . had at one time furnished an atmosphere which engendered and fortified a belief in the intrinsic merits of labor. But work has lost its religious meaning for most citizens and even the valuing of work as a social duty is gravely challenged. In an earlier age economic scarcity and privation supplied the motive force for a work-or-perish ethos. Few today recall the Depression of the 1930s. . . . Many young adults may now be too well-educated and too antiauthoritarian to submit to dull, routine jobs which fail to serve personal values and, in particular, the need for self-esteem. During the 1960s, absenteeism in business and industry rose sharply, and job turnover, early retirement, and the reluctance of employees to work overtime, even at extra pay, were common problems. . . . An intractable form of alienation is bred by work which denies the individual any opportunity for expression of autonomy, which excludes him from decision-making processes that affect his welfare, which binds him to the job and company through an unrewarding relationship with impersonal supervision. . . . It is ironic that improvements in fundamental economic and physical conditions of employment have, over the years, elavated the job expectations of workers and led them to demand even greater returns from their work in the form of self-regard and a sense of meaningful effort (Borow, 1974, pp. 21–22).

Given the high degree of similarity in the assertions found in these quite different but illustrative publications, what can we say about current attitudes to work? First, it seems clear that amelioration of the worst horrors of the early factory system—killingly long hours of labor, starvation wages, the unrestricted power of the employer—has brought new problems to the surface. Perhaps some basic questions had to be solved first in order to permit attention to the *quality* of work—attention that, in the earlier days of what amounted to a fundamental struggle for existence, would have been something of a luxury. Second, the current criticism of work appears to be lacking in the nostalgic quality of much of the criticism of the nineteenth-century critics. The alleged golden age of the independent farmer and the apprentice–journeyman system has vanished so completely that it is now only imperfectly remembered. The processes of secularization, urbanization, and industrialization have now gone so far that they are generally accepted as irreversible. The question now is whether work *itself* can continue to be the central life value that it clearly was for so long a period. The core of the contemporary work alienation may not express a longing for a different *kind* of work, but a nagging worry that *any* kind of work is a meaningless and pointless activity from which mankind should be relieved as soon as possible.

The widespread nature of these complaints is attested to by a number of recent studies. Among the more important are those of Wilensky and Kornhauser.

Wilensky developed an index of work alienation based on a study of the relations between work and leisure (Wilensky, 1964) and then attempted to measure the amount of alienation characteristic of different kinds of work. His procedure was first to attempt to establish what people thought were desirable (or desired) qualities of themselves as persons and then to ask whether the work they did was congruent or discordant with this prized self-image. He was able to determine that work was evaluated positively or negatively along six dimensions: (1) the degree to which it permitted ordinary social contacts with others; (2) the degree to which there was opportunity to exercise one's own judgment and intelligence; (3) the chance to be recognized for doing work well; (4) the chance to use one's own skills; (5) relative freedom from close supervision; and (6) opportunity for promotion and advancement.

Using self-report scales based on these criteria, Wilensky reports a number of interesting findings. His first general finding is that severe alienation appears less widespread than the general theory of alienation would seem to imply. Second, although there is a somewhat higher frequency of disaffection among blue-collar than white-collar workers, occupational stratification and social class are by no means the only determinants of work alienation. At least equally important are the relative degrees of constraint, freedom, and mobility that characterize particular work situations. In some instances, executives and engineers were more discontented with their work than were manual workers in the same firms, because the former expected more freedom and mobility than their particular jobs provided.

Kornhauser investigated the mental health of factory workers, particularly in giant automotive plants (Kornhauser, 1965) and paints a much darker picture than we get from Wilensky's studies. Kornhauser presents convincing evidence that the assembly-line worker, although comparatively well-paid since the advent of unionism, tends to regard both his job and himself with contempt. He sees his work both as monotonous and meaningless, its sole value being the money it brings. He wants to escape from the plant or at least to have his children escape. He feels trapped in a dead-end occupation, which involves doing the same thing over and over again. He dreams of being "his own boss" in a small business or trade, but very few succeed in breaking out. To the degree that workers report life-satisfactions, they are almost entirely attributed to off-the-job experiences: family activities, relations with friends, recreation. These workers find their work a negative and meaningless activity that they must perform to earn money.

While the differences between these two studies appear considerable it should be stressed that the investigators were directing their attention to quite different aspects of the problem. Wilensky was interested in alienation in its *relative* aspects, that is, the differences between different occupations and different strata within the same occupation. Kornhauser, on the other hand, confined his attention to a single occupation, probably the archetype of the modern rationalization and routinization of human work. Wilensky admits that his measures probably underestimate the actual degree of alienation, both because his measures depend on self-report and because the very directness of his questions might have discouraged expressions of discontent. Wilensky also feels that the "vast majority" of his subjects were indifferent to their work in the sense that their "jobs neither confirm their prized self-image nor deny it." (p. 146).

That negative or indifferent work attitudes have an influence on other aspects of the worker's private and public life is shown by a recent study of blue-collar union members (Sheppard and Herrick, 1972). It is reported here that when ordinary aspirations concerning work are frustrated, a mood of bitterness and cynicism arises that reflects itself in reduced levels of political participation and social involvement. The alienated worker tends not to attend union meetings, to vote with lower frequency both in union and general elections, and, when he does vote, to favor candidates described as extremist, displaying a kind of right-wing populism. These workers are also described as more authoritarian in their outlook, more frequently given to racial and minority prejudice ("Archie Bunker"), and taking a dim view of social progress. It is significant that these views are expressed with greater frequency by workers who are required to perform the dullest and most routinized jobs. In the same plants, those blue-collar workers whose jobs afford some degree of variety and autonomy were found to score lower on the utilized measures of political and social alienation.

In his book, Dahl (1970), after summarizing a number of current studies of the relation of work to political participation, concludes with the following observation: that if workers were to be permitted to participate in the affairs of the enterprise, then their current lassitude and indifference might change into interest and concern.

Obviously, a great deal more research is needed to determine the precise scope and extent of work alienation. Enough has been done so far, however, to indicate that work alienation is a social problem of some dimensions. It is clear that some workers have highly negative feelings about their work, although it is equally clear that this phenomenon is not universal. The alienation of the worker from his work seems to vary with the degree to which it is repetitive, closely supervised, deals with part-processes only, gives meager opportunity for sociability with others, and is seen as dead-end employment. Of course, as the rationalization and mechanization of more and more kinds of work proceed apace, the areas of discontent with work (cf. Bell, 1956) may appreciably widen. This is feared as one of the consequences of automation, which we shall discuss more fully in Chapter 5.

SUMMARY

The Industrial Revolution and its successor movements have brought about a radical transformation in the nature of human work. The rise and spread of the factory system brought work into the public arena and, in effect, made it a problem for study. The individual peasant–farmer or peasant–craftsman was largely the manager of his own labor and, not infrequently, the owner of his own tools of production. If he worked poorly, he might suffer for it, risking starvation or the loss of his means of livelihood. But this was as far as it went. When tens, hundreds, and thousands of people were brought together into one place—the factory, the railroad, the mine— to serve and maintain increasingly complex and costly machinery, it became possible to begin to think of ways of controlling *everything* about the process of production—including the worker himself.

The early studies of work behavior were a logical outgrowth of the victories of the machine system. The great virtue of the industrial machine is that a given action—whether joining, grinding, shaping, or turning—can be repeated in a highly uniform manner. If machines are so marvelous, why not make people as machine-like as possible? The result was the advent of Taylorism, the time-and-motion study, the minute subdivision of labor, the assembly line; in a word, mass-production. The efforts to "rationalize" the nature of work brought about enormous increases in productivity but also revealed or created a set of new problems. Whereas different units of the same machine can be fabricated to be virtually identical and uniform in performance, workers appear to come in all sorts of packages. The workers who enter the factory gate not only vary widely in cognitive and motor abilities, they also vary in a host of other human qualities: aspirations, feelings, attitudes, opinions, beliefs. The famous Hawthorne studies made some of these sources of work behavior manifest and laid the basis for increasingly intricate studies of work motivation. The early studies of work motivation were largely failures, proceeding as they did on the naive assumption that workers were akin to automatic machines; but they were instructive failures. Subsequent studies of work motivation have become increasingly sophisticated, drawing upon influences that reside in the general society of which workers are a part and even entering the domains of national and cultural differences (see Chapters 7 and 8).

The aggregation of masses of people into single work-sites also brought into existence a new scholarly subspecialty: the sociology of work. We have commented here on two themes that have become prominent in work sociology: work conceived of as a *social role* and the problems of *work alienation*.

Sociologists have provided very useful information bearing upon the role of the worker, particularly on the behaviors people are expected to display in particular occupations. Adaptation to work requires not only a certain stated set of cognitive and motor skills but also the ability to conform to a rather elaborate set of social expectations. In many occupations, these expectations are quite demanding, covering such apparently irrelevant details as kind of clothing, manner of speech, and prescribed ways of relating to others. Most of the requirements are enforced by a variety of informal social pressures, but some are actually maintained and policed by formal organizations: trade unions and professional associations. In effect, to be a worker, one is required to "act" and "look" like a worker. These demands have been seen to be particularly forceful in certain occupations selected for study, but some conformity to the "rules of the game" is an important condition for adjustment to almost any kind of work in modern society. The studies of the occupational sociologists are important to our own theory of work behavior because they indicate the degree to which work skills are at least as much social and interpersonal as they are physical and intellectual.

The second problem that we have examined in this chapter concerns work alienation. Here again the bulk of the studies have been carried out by social scientists. Alienation and anomie have been major sociological themes since Durkheim, and the discontent of workers with their work has been a very important stimulus for the rise of great social and political movements. In this connection, we distinguished between two views concerning work alienation. The first of these is an earlier position, characteristic of the great social thinkers of the nineteenth century, which criticized certain consequences of the first Industrial Revolution: the rise of the factory system. The second set of concerns about work alienation is decidedly contemporary. It does not deplore the rise of industrial technology per se. Instead, it calls for a new technology, a technology that would display as much concern for human relations in industry as is now displayed for productive efficiency. The specter is now being raised that work itself is in danger of losing its meaning as a central value in human life. Nevertheless, contemporary students of work alienation are not merely looking back to a supposed golden age when work was a valuable means of relating to nature. Rather, they are calling for radical revision of the *organization* of work, to counter apparent feelings of many workers that they are merely cogs in a gigantic industrial machine.

In short, the new specialty calling itself the sociology of work has begun to reveal something about the nature of work that the student of work behavior cannot ignore. Whatever the sources of the human ability to work, however people vary in their reactions to the demand to work, people work in complex social situations. From the social scientist, we are beginning to learn a number of things about the stimulus dimensions of work behavior, without which our perceptions of how people act at work would be largely unintelligible.

4 | WORK AS A SPHERE OF INDIVIDUAL BEHAVIOR

In Chapter 1, it was argued that work behavior—indeed, all behavior—has something of the character of a transaction. The common meaning of the term *transaction* involves an exchange, an interchange, between two sets of events or phenomena. In the case of work, the two terms of the transaction are the working individual and the sociocultural milieu in which work takes place. So far, we have sketched some of the more important features of the *second* term of the transaction: the sociocultural milieu. While historians and social scientists have not paid a great deal of attention to human work, they have not been entirely indifferent to it. Enough has been written to suggest that we cannot understand work behavior without grasping some of the essential features of the kinds of human societies in which work takes place. Much of the motivation for work, the kinds of work that people are required to do, the meanings they attach to it, the conditions under which they perform it—all these crucial issues clearly involve the internalization of various sets of social and cultural norms. Exposure to the writings of historians and anthropologists diminishes the force of a dangerously fallacious mode of thought—that mode of thought that attempts to explain anything important about human behavior by simply invoking the concept of *human nature*. Man is not only a social animal, he is also the only animal with a *culture* (Dobzhansky, 1962). So far, we have attempted to show that many characteristics of work behavior are functions of social and cultural structures; more exactly, to give some picture of the *demand* side of work behavior: the working environments with which the working individual is required to transact. The picture we have presented is global and societal. In Chapter 7, we will specify the concrete features of typical work situations that, in effect, comprise the current subculture of work.

But what of the other term of the transaction? As we have said earlier, work is performed by individuals, not societies. The sociology of work can give us some idea of the structure and characteristics of work environments, but we have still to consider how individuals interact with the work environments they enter. We shall also have to be concerned with the psychological baggage that the individual brings with him as he confronts the demand to work. If, in our earlier chapters, we were concerned with the sources of certain *uniformities* in work behavior across persons—uniformities that had their source in prevailing sociocultural norms—we are now interested in the sources of *variations* in work behavior from person to person.

In shifting our attention from society to the individual, we must continue to keep in mind our belief that the human personality is, to a considerable extent, a social product. A person is as he is, in part at least, because of the thousands of messages and demands with which he has been bombarded since early infancy by all sorts of "culture bearers": parents, teachers, age peers, role models. But this is not the whole story! Each person receives slightly different messages, depending upon the personal make-up and the social character of the messenger. Each person responds differently to what is superficially the same message because of subtle differences in his own emotional and social makeup. Personality is a problem in individual psychology as well as social psychology. In attempting to answer the question of why one person works as he does, or why another person experiences certain major difficulties in adapting to work, it is not enough to invoke broad social and cultural factors. These cannot be ignored, as we have been at some pains to point out. There are, however, idiosyncratic factors: issues reflecting the unique qualities of every individual life. Work is not *only* a social phenomenon; it is also a problem in individual psychology.

An effort to write an individual psychology of work is, I believe, long overdue, but it is not easy to formulate. The problems of interest to most psychologists are, at the same time, too general and too specific for our purpose. The bulk of psychological research and theorizing is focused on basic psychological processes: perception, sensory process, learning, and the like. Specialists are interested in such issues as the development and structure of human personality and the problems and treatment of mental disorder. The difficulty faced by the present writer is that everything about the human being is somehow involved in the process of working: perceptual, cognitive, and motor skills, personality development, behavioral and mental abnormalities and deviations, interpersonal and social reactions—virtually all the fields and subdivisions of psychology. Workers use the full range of psychological equipment on the job. They perceive and learn; they display emotional responsiveness; they enter into social interactions; they display all types of personality structures and formations; their work is influenced by a wide range of behavioral disorders including some peculiar to work itself. In what sense is it possible to say anything about the psychology of work that is not already to be found somewhere in any good textbook of psychology?

We believe that it *is* possible to formulate an individual psychology of work. However, we will not need to review what passes for established knowledge about basic psychological process. Undoubtedly, perception and learning at work are not essentially different from perception and learning in any situation. Similarly, personality development and emotional responsiveness obey the same laws at work as they do in any human interaction. There are only a limited number of ways in which behavior can go wrong, and it is not likely that we will find any new psychiatric syndromes in relation to work that are not already described in the psychiatric literature. The working individual brings to his task the same general psychological baggage that he brings with him to any other situation.

There is a sense, however, in which the psychology of work differs from the psychological aspects of other life situations. This becomes evident if we think of work as a rather specialized set of demands with which the individual is required to cope. The important factor is the *coping* required. The operative word here is *coping*. We will show, therefore, that work requires a different set of behaviors from those elicited, for example, by such other broad life domains as love and play. We shall also argue that what one must learn in order to adapt to work differs both in kind and quantity from the requirements of other life spheres.

In the present chapter, we shall examine how the demand to work differs from other major life demands. Before we do so, however, we shall have to define what we are talking about.

DEFINITIONS OF WORK

Webster's International Dictionary (second and third editions) includes 20 different definitions of the noun "work" and over 30 separate meanings of the verb. Common to all of these references is the allusion of some kind of activity, although the activity described is not always one that is carried on by human beings, or even by living beings at all. For example, in the branch of physics called mechanics, the term *work* is used to describe the transference of force or energy from one body or system to another. Similarly, cider is described to be "working" when it is engaged in the process of fermentation. In the same way, the term *work* is used to describe the act or product of any mechanical power and also the object on which that power is "working." It is even used (although usually in the plural) to designate the place where work is done or as the collective term for the moving parts of a mechanism. However, at least some of the definitions refer to the activities of human beings, and it is in this sense that we shall use the word here.

Work, then, is to be seen as activity of living beings. But what kind of activity? The initial definition Webster offers for the noun is:

> Exertion of strength or faculties for the accomplishment of something; physical or mental effort directed to an end.

The first of 11 definitions of the intransitive verb is:

> To exert oneself physically or mentally for a purpose, esp., in common speech, to exert oneself thus in doing something undertaken for gain, for improvement in one's material, intellectual or physical condition, or under compulsion of any kind, as distinct from something undertaken for pleasure, sport, or immediate gratification. . . .

At least in English usage, human work is obviously conceived of as an instrumental activity. Assuming that the dictionary is correct, people do not perform work for its own sake but as a means for the procurement of other ends. To work, therefore, is not merely to "do something"; it is to do something "for a purpose." It is interesting to note, in passing, that the writer of the above definition appears to find something debasing in the notion that work is undertaken for gain, since he attributes this allusion to "common speech." As in the case, however, with the usage of many words that are ancient in the language, common speech may tell us more about the psychological connotations of the word than what is written down in the dictionary. It is probably fair to say that the most widespread connotation of the term *work* is that it is designed to get something for the person who performs it. If we ask what is the "something" that work is designed to get, then common speech also tells us that work is the means by which man makes his living. Despite Webster's curious reluctance to admit it, there appears to be a very close association between work as a human activity and the complex structure of procedures man has elaborated to procure his means of subsistence.

If we have arrived at a supposition that work is an instrumental or goal-directed activity designed to procure the means of subsistence, are we prepared also to agree that *all* animals work, or is work a peculiarly *human* activity? In seeking a reasonably clear distinction between human behavior and the behavior of other animals, we are confronted with impressive semantic difficulties. After all, man is an animal, in some respects like any other animal, in the sense that he follows certain fundamental biological laws like the inevitability of death and the need to eat. However, man has managed to erect upon these biological needs such an immense structure of social and cultural phenomena that the basic biological substratum sinks under the weight and almost vanishes.

Consider, for example, the act of eating! Like any other living organism, man must continuously find certain chemical substances in his environment, incorporate them into his body, and transform them chemically into a form that his tissues can use. If he stops this process, he cannot arrest the continuous breakdown of the cells that make up his body, and he ceases to live. So long as we restrict an examination of food ingestion to the investigational methods of comparative biology and physiology, we find the minutiae of the process in man are very similar to those that take place in any of the higher mammals. A given digestive enzyme in *Macacus rhesus*, for example, functions in an identical manner in the stomach of *Homo sapiens*. Of all the animals, however, only man has been capable of developing a mystique, a philosophy, a social system, and a science about even his most naturally compelling activities as a living organism. Monkeys do not concern themselves with table manners nor have they erected taboos against the eating of certain foods. Man has developed entire industries devoted to nothing else but the processing of food, industries that include such apparently irrelevant features (irrelevant to monkeys, at any rate) as attractive packaging. Man has converted the act of eating, which in all other animals retains a direct and almost automatic aspect, into a set of exceedingly complex social arts. Thus, while many animals display certain food preferences, only man has managed to convert this rather straightforward biological fact into an elaborate maze of customs, traditions, rituals, and even quasi-scientific and scientific theoretical systems.

Turning to work, even a skimpy acquaintance with comparative biology is enough to tell us that all animals expend energy to secure their means of subsistence. In the higher and more complex animals, this expenditure of energy seems organized, purposive, and goal-directed. The food-getting activities of many infrahuman animals seem very much like work, if work is defined as a goal-directed activity designed to secure the means of subsistence for the living orgainsm. Volumes have been written upon what looks like an elaborate organization of the food-getting process among the so-called social insects. There are also somewhat less well-documented studies of foresight, learning, and teamwork among the higher predatory mammals.

Despite these instances, we are prepared to maintain here that *Homo sapiens* is the working animal and that this is one of the great qualitative distinctions between man and the infrahuman animals. The key issue is *planned* alteration of the physical environment. While many animals make certain changes in the world about them—the nest-building activities of certain insects and birds, the dam-building of beavers—animals other than man generally tend to live in the world as they find it. Only man by virtue of certain physical assets not available to the other species—a hyperdeveloped central nervous system, upright posture, opposing thumbs, binocular vision—massively intervenes to change the structure and relationships of the physical world about him. Archeologists appear to accept this distinction when, in trying to decide whether a particular fossilized bone is hominoid or anthropoid, they are happy to find accompanying artifacts (worked stones) which are perceived as exclusively human products. The very early instances of primitive man are distinguished from merely anthropoid varieties not only by a larger brain capacity and a more upright posture but also by the presence or absence of stone tools.

To highlight this distinction, let us examine the food-getting activity more closely. Like the carnivores, *Homo sapiens* is a predatory animal. From the early dawn of his existence as a species, he must have been in competition with other predatory animals for edible game. But the nails, teeth, and general physical strength and speed of the hominoid organism are relatively poor instrumentalities with which to seize the kill. Very early in his career on earth, during the many thousands of years during which man was essentially a hunting–gathering animal and long before the earliest beginnings of primitive agriculture or animal husbandry, man must have learned to alter nature in order to supplement his meager bodily resources. He learned to make snares and traps, to dig pits, to trim a branch into a club, to sharpen stones. It may be argued fairly that the earlier instances of the development of a human technology have the character of prosthetic devices, that is, instruments devised to make up for man's relative physical weakness and lack of bodily specialization. Thus, what man could not run down or seize by sheer excess of speed or agility, he learned to trap or snare; what he could not kill by sheer strength or by the sharpness of teeth and claw, he learned to club or spear.

According to this view, the lion or tiger who stalks and seizes his prey may be acting in a goal-directed manner to procure the means of subsistence, but he is not working because he is not altering the physical environment to serve his uses. Man, on the other hand, who digs a pit or chips a stone in order to kill an animal for food, has been able to achieve his objective by altering something in the world about him to meet his needs. It is therefore in some effort to master the environment rather than merely live in it that we find an important essential of the process we call work.

Let us review some of the elements that make up our conception of the meaning of work. First, work is an essentially *human* activity; other animals may expend a great deal of directed energy in staying alive, but only men work. Second, work is an *instrumental* activity; it is performed in order to procure the means of subsistence. Third, work is *self-preservative* activity; it is carried out in order to maintain life. Fourth, work is an *alternative* activity; its objective is to alter or change some aspect of man's environment so that staying alive will be made more certain and more efficient. The specification of these four primary characteristics does not, of course, exhaust the various meanings assigned to work, but we believe these are its basic features. We shall see how the human talent for building a host of secondary functions upon primary ones tends to make the primary characteristics lose significance. *Work, then, is an instrumental activity carried out by human beings, the object of which is to preserve and maintain life, which is directed at a planned alteration of certain features of man's environment.*

THE FORMS OF WORK BEHAVIOR

We have not as yet discussed work in its generic sense, as a major sphere of life behavior, which we will distinguish from other life spheres. Both common and learned speech distinguish many kinds of work, to which usage has assigned somewhat differing meanings and connotations.

The first distinction is that our language contains a number of synonyms for "work," all of which appear to bear somewhat different connotations. The most frequently encountered synonym for work is "labor," or in the British spelling, "labour." Webster also tells us that *labour* is Old French in origin, presumably from the Latin *labor*. Since the term *work* presumably derives from the Anglo–Saxon word *werc* or *weorc*, we can speculate that the term *labour* came into the English language later than the term *work*, perhaps being an importation of the Norman conquerors.[1]

Whatever their difference in origin, the two words have somewhat differing connotations. Although very often used simply as a synonym for "work," the term *labor* tends to imply activities that are heavier, more arduous, less skilled, and often lower in status. In the same sense, we tend to think of "creative work" as being something very different from "manual labor." "Work" appears to imply some desirable combination of intellectual and motor skill, while "labor" may often suggest the mere application of brute muscular power to some menial task. This distinction is sharpened when we use such words as *travail, toil,* and *drudgery*.[2]

These five terms, all more or less synonymous, appear to reflect in turn greater expenditure of energy, less admixture of intellectual and cognitive components, more pain and less pleasure. Also, as we move from "work" to "drudgery," we appear to move down in status. Webster explicitly recognizes these differences in connotation by offering as one of the definitions of labor:

> The service rendered or part played by the laborer, operative and artisan in the production of wealth, as distinguished from the service rendered by capitalists or by those whose exertion is primarily or almost entirely mental.

In addition to using four or five synonyms for work, we distinguish various forms of work through the use of appropriate descriptive adjectives. We

---

[1]The Oxford English Dictionary derives the word *work* from Old English, Old High German, and Old Frisian and finds its earliest usages in manuscripts dating from the ninth century (ca. 850). On the other hand, the derivation of "labour" is from Old French, and its earliest usage in English manuscripts dates from around 1300.

[2]*Travail* is also Old French in origin and appears in English usage toward the end of the thirteenth century. It is defined in the Oxford English Dictionary as "labour or toil of a painful or oppressive nature." *Toil* is similar in origin and usage and is defined as "severe and continuous labour . . . [and] also implies struggling, tiring and fatiguing work." The term *drudgery* is of uncertain origin (the Oxford speculates that it may be Norse in origin) and implies slavish or mindless labor: "to perform mean or servile tasks; to work hard or slavishly; to toil at laborious or distasteful work."

contrast, for example, mental work and manual work and, somewhat more colloquially, white-collar work and blue-collar work. We also distinguish kinds of work by level of skill, although more often in connection with manual work than in discussing various kinds of professional, intellectual, and white-collar occupations. The U.S. Department of Labor has developed an elaborate tenfold classification of occupations (U.S. Department of Labor, U.S. Employment Service, 1949) with many subdivisions, which is based on distinctions within work similar to those we have just mentioned.

Obviously, the kind of work one does or is expected to do may be an important determinant of the personal evaluation one places upon it. A considerable literature has developed on the conditions that influence occupational choice and the degree to which work satisfaction is dependent upon the kind of work that is performed. While we will consider certain facets of this problem at a later stage, our first concern is with the meaning of work in general, regardless of its subdivisions. There is good reason to believe that the basic components of the work personality have some degree of independence from the particular kind of work that is being performed. Our evidence for this belief will be presented in Chapter 8.

The definition of work at which we have arrived is tentative and merely formal. We have so far been considering the meaning of work as if it were a wholly isolated sphere of behavior, to be described entirely in its own terms. Actually, we can isolate one sphere of human activity from all others only with some peril. We will learn more about work if we consider it in relation to other major spheres of human behavior. We shall first consider work in relation to its antonym—play.

WORK AND PLAY

On the surface, it should be relatively easy to distinguish between work and play. On the other hand, ordinary speech suggests that the distinctions we are seeking are not always clearly kept in mind. Very wealthy men may "work" very hard in situations where there is no prospect of material gain, and football players "work" hard in spring practice. Children play at working and sometimes adults work at playing. The term *play* has almost as many ascribed meanings in the language as its antonym, and an exclusively semantic exercise will not be rewarding. More can be learned about the relationships between work and play by an attempt to examine exactly what human beings do when they play.

Perhaps the most thoroughgoing effort to examine play as a global activity is found in the work of Johan Huizinga (1955). Although Huizinga's approach is that of the social philosopher or cultural historian rather than that of the behavioral scientist, he makes a number of instructive points about play. Huizinga finds play to be such an important area of human activity that he believes it to be intrinsic to such dispersed domains as religion, law, war, art, and literature. He goes so far as to coin a new label (*Homo ludens:* man as player), to place alongside the more familiar terms: *Homo sapiens* and *Homo faber.*

The first major characteristic of play that Huizinga finds is that it is a *free* activity. There is nothing forced or compelled about it, either by biological nature or social necessity. As he puts it, "for the adult and responsible human being play is a function which he could equally well leave alone." Play is superfluous. It can be deferred or suspended at any time. It is never a task but is performed at leisure during "free time." Only when play begins to be bound up with obligation and duty does it begin to turn into something else. Thus, when a salesman plays golf with a prospect in order to sell him something, his play begins to look suspiciously like work.

A second characteristic of play that Huizinga regards as closely bound up with the first is that it is not "real life." There is a strong element of "pretending" in play, which suggests close simulation of other important life activities. But the objectives and outcomes always remain clearly different. Many of the games of children consist of elaborate efforts to simulate the nonplay activities of grownups, but of course we are all aware, as are the children, that they are "only pretending." Even where these games of children are learnedly described as important preparatory activities for adult life, they are still regarded as play, not work. Similarly, in the organized play of adults we find many of the characteristics of competition, combat, and even war, but it is obvious that we are dealing with a simulation, not an identity. The terminology of chess is military in its origin, but the outcome of the game does not decide the fate of nations. This "unreal" aspect of play does not appear to militate against its seriousness or the degree of emotional commitment that play may entail. It can be absorbing in the sense that everything else pales into insignificance. It can arouse the most intense feelings and even passions. At the same time, there are always clearly understood limits and "rules" that cannot be transcended, which are intended to maintain the "unreal" character of what is taking place. When a violently competitive contact sport spills over into a free fight among the players, the game is stopped. Similarly, a "war-game" is perceived as only a simulation of the real thing, although it may be played out with the utmost seriousness.

A third characteristic of play that Huizinga finds important has to do with the manner in which it is limited by time, place, and its structural organization. The temporal features of play are more obvious in its adult forms, in which the game is over after a specified number of minutes or as soon as a certain score is achieved. Even less organized forms of play, however, are related to time, in the sense that the day or week is divided into "play time" and "work time." Similarly, one plays in a "place," whether it is a playroom, a playground, an arena, a club, or the like. Most important are the "rules" of play, in which Huizinga finds its peculiar structural organization. He argues that all play has its rules and that their purpose is to determine what "holds" in the temporary world in which play is performed. When the rules are broken, the play-world collapses. Thus, the role of the umpire is to maintain the distinction between play-world and the real-world. To the degree that the world of the young child is entirely a world of play, such a distinction may not appear to be needed; yet, as Piaget has repeatedly emphasized, children appear to regard the learning of the rules of play as one of the most serious obligations of their lives (Piaget, 1951). As play becomes more organized and more adult, the rules extend themselves to include many matters of ritual, including dress (the uniform), forms of social organization (the team, the club), and tends to incorporate many aspects of society at large.

Thus, for Huizinga (1955), play is a

> free activity standing quite consciously outside "ordinary" life as being "not serious," but at the same time absorbing the player intensely and utterly. It is an activity connected with no material interest and no profit can be gained from it. It proceeds within its own proper boundaries of time and space according to fixed rules and in an orderly manner. It promotes the formation of social groupings which tend to surround themselves with secrecy and to stress their difference form the common world by disguise or other means (p. 13).

If we examine Huizinga's conceptions of the nature of play, we see that not all of these characteristics serve to distinguish work from play. Work also tends to be carried on within specific temporal limits, in certain assigned places and according to certain rules. It can be argued that work also promotes the formation of "social groupings," in language and in many other identifying characteristics. On the other hand, the first part of his summary statement is the crux. Play is not "real," it is simulative and symbolic. Whatever else work is, it is certainly "real." In play, we attempt to master the environment for the sheer pleasure of doing so; in work, we struggle with the environment for compelling material reasons. Play is not really an instrumental activity at all; it is performed for its own sake.

In this basic fact—that people and animals appear to perform play as an end in itself—lies the chief distinction between play and work. It is, of course, possible to draw very different inferences from this simple conclusion. While it influences Huizinga to establish play as the most important component of all human culture, it leads Freud (1908) to rather different observations. For Freud, play is for children and work is for adults. Play is an activity that is infantile and primitive; it is ruled by the pleasure principle rather than the reality principle; it is something that the developing individual has to learn to give up as he moves toward maturity. Play in adults is regressive; it is the product of impulse rather than reason; its determinants are unconscious rather than conscious. The pleasures of play are opposed by Freud to the pains of work, but only the latter is worthwhile for the serious adult. Even the highest achievements of creative art were, for Freud, basically similar in their dynamics to the play of children: In both cases, the aim is pleasure, and in both cases the product is achieved through impulse and gratification.

Given that play is aimless, or rather that the aim of play is the play activity itself, given also that work is phylogenetically and ontogenetically later than play, how is the playing child transformed into the working adult? Somewhere hidden in the vicissitudes of this transformation are the factors that distinguish the person for whom working is a severe problem from other people who appear to be able to work effectively without any apparent difficulty or pain. We will describe the dynamics of the transformation from play to work in Chapter 8.

WORK AND LOVE

It is not, perhaps, customary to counterpose the terms *work* and *love* or even to examine their relationships. For most of us, these two spheres of life activity are so different in kind, process, and object that it would belabor the obvious to attempt to set down a series of conceptual distinctions. Unlike our observations on work and play, we will be concerned here not so much with the differences between work and love but with certain similarities in their dynamics and in their respective roles in human behavior.

One of Freud's great contributions to our understanding of human behavior was his abundant instruction to us that human love is very complex. It is true that Freud's preoccupation with psychopathology led to concern principally with the darker aspects of these relationships, but Freud also turned our attention to those aspects of our relationships to others that are irrational and infantile, hidden and alien. It is not our intention here to debate the degree to which we might regard certain of Freud's contentions as one-sided or even the degree to which he appears to ignore or underestimate the role of certain social forces in bringing about the human dilemmas that he reports. Rather, we are interested in Freud's ideas concerning unconscious motivation, his concern with developmental stages, and his primary contention that adult behavior is heavily influenced by the experiences and events of early childhood, which the adult might have long forgotten or, indeed, repressed. It is in these respects that we believe it is possible to draw certain analogies (as well as distinctions) between love and work.

Like adult love, adult work appears to be the outcome of a long process of individual development, starting in childhood and passing through many vicissitudes and stages, setbacks and advances. An adult's ability to work is related to experiences and events encountered in certain formative periods of development. Of course, it is necessary to specify, as we shall in detail later on, that these early experiences and events are by no means identical with those that influence our ability to love, but the manner in which we cope as children with certain demands is important nonetheless. These developmental aspects of work will be a matter of some concern to us, since we are interested in the psychopathology of work as Freud was interested in the psychopathology of love.

Another aspect of the analogy we are drawing between love and work is the degree to which the latter may be influenced by all sorts of hidden motives, of which the individual worker may not be aware or which he does not acknowledge. It is true that we have just defined work as an instrumental activity designed to procure the means of subsistence. It is probably also true that if we asked people why they worked, the most ready reply would be that they worked for money. But, man appears able to sustain diverse motivations in what look like very simple activities.

What other motives appear to be served by working, granting that their force will vary from case to case? One important set of unconscious motives for working is related to our needs for self-esteem. Other important motives may reflect our needs to identify ourselves, to assign ourselves certain recognized roles in society. Still others may be related simply to the need for activity, to avoid boredom. For some, work may gratify certain needs for creativity. This list of motives for work is far from exhaustive. There may be many others in particular people, some of which may be hidden or relatively inaccessible.

Another aspect of the analogy is that, like love but perhaps less conspicuously so, work involves human emotions, the affective side of behavior. It is now almost a commonplace that the factory is a small society and that work may engage almost any human passion. Much of the concern of the industrial psychologist is with *differential* productivity. Our own concern will be with the manner in which work arouses both negative and positive affects: fear, guilt, anxiety, and hostility in some, restlessness and uneasiness in others, satisfaction and enthusiasm in still others. We cannot understand human work merely from an examination of its perceptual, cognitive, and motor components, although these undoubtedly play important roles. Work also engages the affects. Our objective will be to examine the kinds of emotions with which work is enmeshed in particular individuals and to relate these entanglements to particular forms of work pathology.

Of course, the analogy between work and love cannot be pressed too far. The differences between these spheres of human activity are at least as impressive as the similarities. Like play, love is not easy to conceive of as an instrumental activity, which work certainly is. Also, it would appear that more pitfalls lie in the way of the development of adequacy at love than confront the development of adequacy at work. Our purpose in presenting the analogy, however, is to call attention to aspects of work that have tended to be overlooked or taken for granted: the developmental aspects of work, the complexity of work motivations, the degree to which work involves the emotions.

In setting a framework for later detailed discussion, it is useful to point to one important difference between love and work that has far-reaching methodological and therapeutic implications. We are referring to a critical distinction in the developmental histories of work and love as general spheres of human behavior. Although we have said that adult work and adult love are similar in the sense that both pass through a prolonged period of development in the individual human being, we might deceive the reader if we did not also point to important differences in the manner in which the development takes place. It is likely that the emotional habits that make up the content of adult love find their origins fairly early in the individual's life, perhaps in the first few months of infancy. Whether we follow Freud's biologically tinged notions of the stages of libidinal fixation or whether we accept more culturally oriented ideas, it is probable that some of the emotional patterns that play a part in adult love are formed during very early interactions between the child and the mother. Even the most behavioristically oriented psychologist might accept the proposition that we begin to learn certain habitual modes of emotional response very early in infancy. On the other hand, the habitual modes of response that later coalesce into the adult pattern of working do not appear in infancy but in a much later period of childhood, probably not until the child (in modern civilizations, at least) is first confronted with formal schooling. This distinction in time of onset will turn out to be very useful for us when we later define the work personality as a semiautonomous sphere of the general personality, autonomous in the sense that the conditions that influence work behavior are by no means identical with those that influence the behaviors associated with love.

The vicissitudes of love also appear to be much more closely related to events and experiences within the family setting than the vicissitudes of work. The instrumental roles of the father and mother—as well as those of other family members—are important in the development of the individual's attitudes to work. But the latter appear subject to a wider array of influences—the school, the peer group, the society generally. We shall specify these extrafamilial conditions of work in Chapter 8.

Thus, as general spheres of human behavior, work and love display certain fundamental similarities and certain fundamental differences as well. We have stressed the similarities because we think it is critical to state at the outset that work, like love, engages the emotions, that it is made up of irrational as well as rational components, that it is formed by conditions of which we may be individually unaware, as well as by others of which we are fully conscious. On the other hand, it is equally important to indicate that the conditions that form the ability to love are not identical with those that form the ability to work and that disturbances in either sphere are not traceable to the same causes. The latter issue will become particularly relevant when we consider the possibilities of giving therapeutic assistance to people who find themselves unable to work. We will encounter many instances in which it turns out to be quite inappropriate to attempt to treat the inability to work by giving "deeper" therapy in the areas of the inability to love.

TOWARD AN INDIVIDUAL PSYCHOLOGY OF WORK

In developing an outline for a model of the individual psychology of work, we must start with the proposition that the basic psychological equipment the worker brings to his job is not different from what he brings to any other life situation. To what degree does it make sense, therefore, to speak of a special psychology of work behavior. Our answer, insofar as we can find it, lies in the distinctive character of work as a unique sphere or domain of life activity, different in its demands, its structure, and its objectives from such other major life spheres as love and play.

There appear to be three important differences between work and the two other major life domains: love and play. The first of these, as we have seen, is that work is perceived by most as a clearly *instrumental* activity. Work is not merely a spontaneous expenditure of energy to stay alive or even (metaphorically) to ensure the perpetuation of the species. It is something that human beings carry through in order to obtain other *desiderata*. Whatever complexities displayed by love and play (human beings have a confusing tendency at times to make even love and play look like work), these domains of human behavior are essentially ends in themselves. It is this indirect nature of work behavior—its instrumental character—that makes it necessary to understand its motivation.

The second difference between work, play, and love concerns differences in the developmental process through which our attitudes to love and play, on the one hand, and out attitudes to work, on the other, are formed. As we shall show, our attitudes to love and play are basically formed within the family setting, during the very early years of infancy and childhood. On the other hand, our attitudes to work appear to find their origins in extrafamilial settings and at a later period of life (adolescence and early adulthood). A third set of differences arises from the fact that the conditions that produce difficulties in adapting to work are by no means identical with those that produce problems in the areas of love and play. We shall be at some pains to describe these conditions in Part III, below.

We cannot afford to ignore, however, the many similarities that also exist in the apparently separate domains of work, play, and love. In its effort to stay alive, the human animal has massively intervened in its environment, has invented extremely complex and varied social relations, has, in effect, made himself. So also in the worlds of play and love! The play of animals other than man and of very young children appears to be basically spontaneous. The growing child, however, quickly discovers that there is also something very serious about play. He must master increasingly elaborate sets of rules, he must learn how to use bewilderingly varied tools and instruments, he must fit himself into complicated social networks. Play also begins to serve purposes other than the mere joyful expenditure of energy and, when it becomes professionalized, tends to be virtually indistinguishable from work. Nevertheless, the world of play and the world of work are basically distinct life domains, and one of our problems is to understand how the playing child is transformed into the working adult.

5 | PSYCHOANALYTIC THEORIES OF WORK BEHAVIOR

Human beings work with varying degrees of ease, comfort, and efficiency. Some people work quite well, some poorly, some cannot work at all. Looking only at the negative aspects, work appears to be one of the major life-arenas in which behavior pathology would be studied. Contrary to expectations, however, such disciplines as psychiatry and clinical psychology have paid little attention to the adaptive and maladaptive mechanisms implicated in work. The literature on the psychodynamics and psychopathology of work is in fact disappointingly meager.[1] Obviously, the student of psychopathology has been interested in problems other than those that bear directly upon the ability to work. One of the many reasons for this situation lies in the very powerful influence of psychoanalytic theory, which has generally focused the attention of students of pathology on the ability of people to love or be loved. As a result, other spheres of behavior have either been ignored or it has been assumed that pathology in them can be directly derived from disturbances of the ability to love. Nevertheless, the psychiatric and psychoanalytic literature has made some references to human work, which we must review in attempting to develop our own theory of work behavior (cf. Neff, 1965).

---

[1]This statement remains true for the bulk of the literature emanating from the fields of clinical psychiatry and clinical psychology, but as of the publication of this third edition, some exceptions must be noted. As of 1984, there is a fairly large and rapidly developing literature on work stress (cf. Cooper and Payne, 1978; Cooper, 1982). Although the chief concerns of this research are in the medical and physical signs of stressed reactions to work, mental health issues are not wholly ignored (Cooper and Marshall, 1978). Second, during the past 2 or 3 years, there are signs of a renewed interest in the relations of work and mental health, particularly on the use of work as a modality in the treatment of mental illness. We shall deal with these issues in Part III, below. It remains true, however, that the relations of work and psychopathology appear to be of interest only to a tiny minority of psychiatrists and psychologists, who are essentially mavericks within their chosen fields.

FREUD ON WORK

Freud's remarks on work are scattered very sparsely through his writings and are typically encountered as incidental observations. His evaluation of the importance of work in man's psychological economy is ambivalent. On the one hand, he argues that work is one of the two great spheres of human activity, without which human society cannot be understood. Freud (1953, vol. 21, p. 101) says: "The communal life of human beings had . . . a two-fold foundation: the compulsion to work, which was created by external necessity, and the power of love. . . . *Eros* and *Ananke* have become the parents of human civilization. . . . In this sense, work is one of the forces that binds men to each other and thus lays the basis for human society. Thus, he writes:

> After primal man had discovered that it lay in his own hands, literally, to improve his lot on earth by working, it cannot have been a matter of indifference to him whether another man worked with him or against him. The other man acquired the value for him of a fellow-worker, with whom it was useful to live together (1953, vol. 21, p. 99).

On the other hand, Freud obviously saw work not as a pleasurable activity to be sought but as a painful burden to be endured. He states that "human beings exhibit an inborn tendency to carelessness, irregularity and unreliability in their work and . . . a laborious training is needed before they learn to follow the example of their celestial models" (Freud, 1953, vol. 21, p. 93). Work, for Freud—like all other aspects of adult life—involves a "renunciation of the instincts," entails giving up the pleasures of childhood, and means a life ruled by the *reality principle* rather than the *pleasure principle*. The only pleasures that can be involved in work are libidinous in origin, are modifications of Eros. Thus, he concludes that "collections of men are to be libidinally bound to one another. Necessity alone, the advantages of work in common, will not hold them together. But Man's natural aggressive instinct, the hostility of each against all and of all against each, opposes this programme of civilization" (1953, vol. 21, p. 122). Elsewhere, he points out how the instinctual love that forms the nuclear family is modified and blunted in society to "aim-inhibited affection," which binds men and women together "in a more intensive fashion than can be effected through the interest of work in common" (1953, vol. 21, p. 102).

The role Freud assigns to work is consistent with his general views of adult human functioning. Freud sees adult human behavior as the outcome of a long struggle between, on the parents' side, the objective of socializing an asocial and amoral animal, and, on the child's side, the objective of finding those modes of behavior that have the double aspects of meeting the demands of the parents and retaining some vestige of forbidden pleasures. Of course, neither party to the struggle plans its operations rationally or with full consciousness. But the process of child development is a process of active, even oppressive, socialization in which the parents direct against the libidinal and aggressive instincts of the child all the massive force of their overwhelming authority and their greatly superior intelligence and maneuverability. In this unequal struggle, the child, faced by the terrible consequences of the loss of parental love and support, must succumb. Successful surrender involves the discovery of modes of behavior that satisfy the demands of the parents and, with good fortune, will retain some portion of the pleasures of unrestricted instinctual gratification. Had Freud written directly on this issue, he presumably would have said that work is one of the activities the human being develops as a means of coping with the inner and outer demands made upon him. The *manner* in which he works—or the guilt he may feel over not working—is a function of a complex set of feelings, attitudes, and ideas that develop as the child perceives, reacts to, and incorporates the parental models of behavior.

Freud's voluminous writings include very little more that bear upon work than the few remarks cited above. He was interested in the play of children and in artistic and creative work (Freud, 1953, vol. 9, pp. 143–153 and vol. 12, pp. 218–226). He apparently did not find it necessary to record his observations on common, everyday work, assuming he ever bothered to reflect deeply upon it, perhaps partly because he was struggling to solve problems that were far more painful to his patients than work incapacity or inefficiency, and partly because work was not perceived as a serious economic problem by his patients.

OTHER PSYCHOANALYTIC CONCEPTIONS

The concern of many neo-Freudians with ego development and the process of adaptation has turned attention to somewhat different problems from those that preoccupied the classical Freudians. Erikson, for example, has tried to work out a theory of ego growth that includes crucial stages of development well beyond the crises of early childhood in which Freud was primarily interested (Erikson, 1959, 1963). Where Freud leaves his readers with the impression that the most important aspects of personality development are concluded by the time the child is 5 or 6 years old, with the resolution of the third stage of psychosexual development (the phallic stage), Erikson discerns later important stages of development through what Freud called the latency period (from the Oedipal period to the onset of puberty) and through early and late adolescence as well.

It is of particular interest to note here that one of Erikson's crucial later stages (he places it in the latency period) is the "industry stage," in which the young person first begins to develop his attitudes toward work and achievement. Freud seems to imply the attitudes toward work and toward important persons encountered while working (peers, subordinates, supervisors, employers) are substantially determined by the events of early childhood—the manner in which the person works out his relationships to the nuclear parents during the early childhood crises of oral, anal, and phallic development. For Erikson, it would appear that the early childhood stages are *necessary* but not *sufficient* to account for adaptation to the demands of work. In extending the scope of the experiences that play a formative role in personality development, Erikson by no means discounts the importance of early childhood. Certainly, the growing child must first meet and resolve the problems of weaning, sphincter-training, and early jealousy before he can begin to work out his relationships to schoolmates, teachers, and employers. It is certainly also true that an epigenetic view of development—to which Erikson subscribes—demands conceiving of the older child as meeting later experience with abilities and emotions already heavily infuenced by earlier experience. But whereas Freud's early view has led various followers to conclude that the events of early childhood are sufficient to account for adult emotional life, Erikson seems to be saying that the affective stages of later childhood and adolescence are an essential part of development.

Ives Hendrick has attempted to take account of human work in a manner that appears to stand midway between classical Freudian theory and modern ego theory. One of the questions he raises is concerned with the sources of the enormous amount of energy man has displayed in subduing and changing his natural environment.[2] Hendrick became convinced that Freud's two principles of mental functioning (the pleasure principle and the reality principle) were insufficient to account for the psychosocial activities of the total organism. Hendrick interprets Freud as saying that pleasure is available to the human organism in only two ways—either through direct gratification of the primary instinctual drives or through an indirect and attenuated gratification achieved by the defense mechanisms that reality forces the ego to develop. For Hendrick, this conceptual structure is insufficient to explain the continuous and persistent efforts of the human animal to explore the world, understand it, and alter it to suit his convenience. Hendrick believes that, in addition to the primary pleasures achieved through gratification of the sexual and aggressive instincts, and the derivatives and transformations of these instincts that reality imposes during

[2]This interest in the executive aspects of human behavior is reflected in David McClelland's work on the "achievement motive" (McClelland, Atkinson, Clark, and Lowell, 1953). It is also emphasized in a major paper by White which marshals evidence against those theories of motivation that rely upon a drive reduction model. White includes both Freud and Hull among proponents of the latter kind of theorizing (see White, 1959). For a criticism of White's remarks on Freud, see David Rapaport (1950). White has elaborated his ideas in an important monograph, "Ego and Reality in Psychoanalytic Theory" (1963). We shall examine this issue at greater length in Chapter 10.

child development, there is a third source of primary pleasure: "that . . . sought by efficient use of the central nervous system for the performance of well-integrated ego functions which enable the individual to control or alter his environment" (Hendrick, 1943b). He calls these ego functions the executant functions and feels that psychoanalysis has overlooked them or taken them for granted.

Thus, Hendrick puts forward the thesis that there is a *work principle* that governs the operation of the executant functions. Following Freud's theorem that the source of all mental energy lies in the instincts, Hendrick posits a "mastery instinct" as the source of energy of the executant functions (Hendrick, 1943a). The pleasure in work, then, is a consequence of gratification of the instinct to master the environment. Hendrick sees his work principle as more than the set of defense mechanisms that comprise the reality principle. Sublimation, displacement, rationalization, and similar defenses may manifest themselves in work, but cannot fully account for work pleasure. Similarly, the repetition compulsion cannot account for many aspects of work activity but appears only when the ego is inadequate. However, Hendrick does not apply this interpretation to the infantile compulsion to practice, over and over again, certain sensory and motor integrations—a compulsion that disappears once mastery is achieved.

Barbara Lantos, a psychoanalyst who has been strongly influenced by Hartmann, Kriss, and Loewenstein, has written two papers specifically on work (Lantos, 1943, 1952). She reminds her colleagues that, in clinical practice, disturbances of working capacity are second in importance only to disturbances of sexuality, but that very little attention has been paid to work in the psychoanalytic literature. In the earlier paper, she begins her observations on the dynamics of work by commenting on the play of children. Noting that children do not work, she speculates that children's play involves two distinct kinds of pleasure. One she defines as pleasure in the function itself, which finds its source in pregenital autoerotic gratification. The second is pleasure in achievement, which, she says, "lies outside the activity itself." In the play of either children or adults, the first kind of pleasure is dominant; the second kind, if it has any part at all, is subordinate. Lantos believes that work is principally related to the second kind of pleasure. She contrasts work and play as follows:

> The principle of playing means that what is done, is done for its own sake; gratification lies in the activity itself. The principle of working means that an action is not undertaken for its own sake, but for some other purpose, serving the ends of self-preservation: gratification lies not in the action as such, but in obtaining something by means of it (Lantos, 1943, p. 118).

Thus, play and work are distinguished not by their content but by their purpose. Mountaineering may be a very arduous activity, but it is play for the tourist and work for the guide.

Like Erikson, Lantos feels that the transition from pleasure in activity to pleasure in achievement takes place during the latency period, which is observed only in human beings—here she cites Freud's remark that animals reach adulthood without passing through a latency period. The association of the latency period with learning and education suggests that the educational process has as one of its aims the transformation of pleasure in activity to pleasure in achievement, although, of course, the former need not be wholly given up in acquiring the latter.

Finally, Lantos asks why feelings of independence, freedom, and security are pleasurable and points to their connection in most people with the ability to guarantee one's own existence by one's own achievements. She speculates that a child finds it natural to have his needs for self-preservation served by parents (or parental surrogates), but that an adult who is deprived of his work loses the essential condition of being an adult. Lantos relates the anxieties experienced by those who cannot or need not work to the feelings of fear arising from the fact that "the instinct of self-preservation is not transformed into life-supporting work" (Lantos, 1943, p. 118).[3]

In her later paper, Lantos notes that Hendrick and Oberndorf agree with her chief contention—that work is a dynamically important activity for human beings. Lantos feels, however, that Hendrick goes too far in assuming a "work instinct." She returns to her earlier argument that work is related to the self-preservative instincts and then elaborates this argument in terminology familiar to psychoanalytic ego psychology, redefining work as a "highly integrated ego activity serving self-preservation" (Lantos, 1952). Work is specifically human and is related to the fact that the instinctual series is broken in man, with the interposition of mental activity between the instinctual need and the gratifying act. She sees pleasure in work achievement as an *ego* reaction, as distinct from libidinal pleasure, which is an *id* reaction. Since, in man, most of the objects of adult gratification are not obtainable *directly* (as in the instinctual sequence in animals) but must be worked for, the original energy available for instinctual acts "floats" into the ego. There it becomes desexualized and deaggressivized ("neutralized," according to Hartmann, 1958). In childhood, the energies that arise in the course of "breaking" the instinctual sequence are available for controlling and manipulating the environment.

In close similarity to Freud, however, Lantos feels that men do not work spontaneously. The work-related motive is self-preservation, "mediated by intelligence, reinforced by conscience" (Lantos, 1952). In a final extension

---

[3]In this connection, Kutner has observed that workers who are disemployed because of aging may often experience severe anxieties related to feelings of dependency and insecurity that they have not had since they were children. In speaking of the reactions of male workers, Kutner adds that for some of them the demand that they give up their work is equivalent to a demand that they change their sex (Kutner, Fanshell, Togo, and Langner, 1956).

of her analysis, Lantos argues that two different forces impel men to work. One is an outer force—necessity—the initial origin of Freud's *reality principle*. The other is inner: "Internalized aggression is the ultimate guarantee of the maintenance of work, and, therefore, of self-preservation. To quote Freud: 'The ego has set itself the task of self-preservation'" (Lantos, 1952:442). The source of this internalized aggression is the superego, and it is directed against the *id* impulses to be ruled by the pleasure principle.

Karl Menninger and C. P. Oberndorf have written papers on work that appear to hew more closely to orthodox psychoanalytic views. Both men regard adult work as best understood in relation to the defensive activity of *sublimation,* through which the human adult may gratify his sexual and aggressive impulses in altered and socially acceptable forms. For Menninger, work is a sublimated mix of the strivings of the life and death instincts:

> Of all the methods available for absorbing the aggressive energies of mankind, work takes first place. . . . The essential point is that in work, as contrasted with purposeless destruction, the aggressive impulses are molded and guided in a constructive direction by the influence of the creative (erotic) instinct (Menninger, 1942).

Reflecting on the meager attention psychoanalysts have paid to the problems of work, Menninger states flatly that "three-fourths of the patients who come to psychiatrists are suffering from an incapacity of their satisfaction in work or their inability to work. In many it is their chief complaint" (Menninger, 1942). He then asks why it is that work becomes dissociated from pleasure, finding the answer in insufficient eroticization of the aggressive element. Following Freud, he finds no reason to believe that work is pleasurable in itself, only that there are certain circumstances in which pleasure can become associated with work. As *external* conditions of work pleasure, he lists: (1) a minimum of compulsion; (2) positive group feelings among co-workers; (3) an absence of excessive discomfort or fatigue; (4) some pride in the product; and (5) some conviction that the work is useful and appreciated. He also cites two *internal* conditions: relative freedom from guilt associated with pleasure, and relative freedom from neurotic compulsions to work or not to work. Menninger regards the two internal conditions of work pleasure as relating to solutions of the instinctual vicissitudes of early childhood, particularly those concerned with basic parent–child relationships.

Like Menninger, Oberndorf (1951)[4] invokes the mechanism of sublimation to account for both the activity of work and associated pleasure. Oberndorf specifically criticizes Hendrick's notion of the "mastery instinct" and also does not agree with Lantos' idea that work is related to self-preservation

[4]Oberndorf's paper was presented at a staff forum of the Menninger Foundation, and it appears to serve the purpose of supplying clinical material in support of Menninger's views.

alone because of "the close inclusion of many, perhaps all of the libidinal drives in work." Oberndorf's main interest, however, is in clinical material, and he cites a number of instances in his own practice where work pathologies (over- or underinvestment in work) are directly related to relationships with the parents. As an example, he describes a case in which a driving and aggressive mother with an ineffectual husband made such excessive demands for achievement upon her son that work as an ego-ideal took on a strong feminine quality, which made it incompatible with his normal masculine strivings. He completes his case presentations with the following summary:

> Persons who constantly regard work as something difficult and unpleasant are those who have not emerged from the necessity of immediate reward and who are reluctant to assume responsibility (self-support) inherent in maturity. The protraction of infantile pleasure or the necessity for its denial as one matures determines the overinvestment or underinvestment of libido in work. This interrelationship is a close and continuous one, and it seems futile to attempt to distinguish whether such libido is predominantly sexual or ego (Oberndorf, 1951).

Both Menninger's general theory of work and Oberndorf's clinical applications derive quite logically from Freud's view of the overwhelming importance of the infancy and early-childhood determiners of adult behavior.

COMMON THEMES OF INSTINCT AND EARLY PSYCHOSEXUAL DEVELOPMENT

Despite the differences in these points of view, there are common themes. First, there is a heavy preoccupation with the instincts, both as a source of motivation and as a primary locus of the "psychic energy" available for human behavior. This stress is perhaps less characteristic of Erikson, who is anxious to build a bridge between psychoanalysis and modern social theory, which, as he is aware, is reluctant to place explicit reliance upon instinct as an explanatory hypothesis. Second, it is generally supposed that the vicissitudes of work behavior in the adult may be entirely, or almost entirely, accounted for by the manner in which the affective processes are shaped by the early crises of interaction between the parents and the child. Again, Erikson is something of an exception but, as a consistent epigeneticist, he continuously emphasizes the powerful influence of earlier on later experiences. Third, these writings include only meager references to the differential effects of society and culture on individual patterns of development. Here Freud is the outstanding exception, but there is some reason to believe that Freud's view of culture is unduly restrictive and one-sided. In commenting on these common themes, we shall suggest certain alternative hypotheses that, while retaining the valuable core of psychoanalytic thinking, may have the effect of preparing the way for a more comprehensive theory.

On the Instincts

It is well known, of course, that the later writings of Freud, and certainly those of many of his more contemporary followers (the ego analysts), have tended to move away from major concern with the instincts and their transformations. Nevertheless, it is fair to maintain that psychoanalytic motivation theory is largely based on the model of drive-reduction. According to this model, the positive affects, such as pleasure or joy, are the consequences of drive-satiation, while negative affects such as pain or displeasure are experienced as a consequence of drive-arousal. In the nineteenth century and the early part of the twentieth, when it was customary to seek wholly biological explanations of human behavior, the drives in question were thought to be largely innate, and many investigators constructed long lists of human instincts (McDougall, 1923). But during the last few decades, the classical instinct theory has come to be regarded as naive, and drive theorists now consider only one or two drives as primary—for example, sex and aggression—with all other drives being increasingly regarded as "secondary," "derived," or "learned." Nevertheless, a consistent drive theorist infers the existence of some kind of drive, whether primary or secondary, whenever an affect is observed.

This sort of reasoning leads Freud, Menninger, and Oberndorf to infer than any pleasure to be derived from working must flow from libidinal components in work behavior, and Lantos utilized the same mode of thought in deriving the pleasures of work from gratification of the self-preservative instincts. Similarly, Hendrick's dissatisfaction with an account of work motivation in terms only of sex and aggression merely leads him to invent a "work instinct" or an "instinct of mastery" to account for the human animal's determined activities directed toward knowledge and control of his material and social environments. The moot point here is whether there are equally plausible alternatives to the drive-reduction model. In recent years, a number of writers have attempted to construct theories of motivation and learning that explicitly depart from the drive-reduction paradigm, for example, the views of White.[5] The current efforts to reject drive

[5]White greatly elaborated his ideas of what he calls *effectance* in a monograph (1963), written as a contribution to psychoanalytic theory. His chief point is that the active efforts that human beings put forth to influence the environment and the "feelings of efficacy" that are the psychological accompaniments of such efforts are not derivable from the basic drives that Freud conceptualized as the sexual and aggressive instincts. Rather, he attempts to marshal evidence that effectance is an "independent ego energy" which is operative at least from the moment of birth and

theory appear to arise from a belief that the bulk of human behavior can better be understood in social and cultural terms and that the drive model is at best a kind of mechanical or biological analogy. In its extreme form, this newer viewpoint occasionally falls into the pitfall of cultural relativism,[6] which tends to deny any commonalities at all in the human condition. In most cases, however, the partisans of this position simply insist that man is so largely a socialized and acculturated animal that human motivation is essentially or chiefly sociocultural rather than biological. According to this view, even sexual behavior in the human being should be regarded as drive-determined only in part, with a large share of its motivation attributable to social mores and cultural forces.

It must be admitted that the state of knowledge concerning human motivation is still so meager that neither of these differing positions can be supported with decisive evidence. Under these circumstances, individuals will adhere to one or the other, or be dissatisfied with both, largely on the basis of idiosyncratic experience and personal preference. However, it should be noted that the psychosocial theory is at least as plausible as the drive theory, although it has less authoritative spokesmen and lacks a strong tradition. In any event, it is necessary to investigate the degree to which the pleasures and pains that given people associate with various kinds of work—and even the entire structure of the motivation to work—are derivable from cultural forces rather than from subtle transformations of primary biological drives. Following such investigations, the relationship between cultural influences and biological drives can better be assayed. As we have seen (cf. Chapters 2 and 3, above), work has meant very different things to people in different societies and means very different things to people in different sectors of contemporary society. One has only to recall the prevailing attitudes toward work in Classical Greece or feudal Europe, in which the conception prevailed that many kinds of work were ignoble and degrading activities, fit only for the slave, the serf, or the outlander. Notions that work is ennobling, and even ethically and morally necessary, are only a few hundred years old and began to come into currency with the breakup of feudalism. We should recall also that there are current impressions that the present pace of technological development is again threatening to make work a meaningless activity for a great many people, and that this aspect of the Protestant Ethic is beginning to lose its force. Whatever the case, it seems regrettable that the brilliant and sensitive insights contributed by psychoanalytic theory are married to a single and rather restrictive model of human motivation.

---

which prompts the organism to explore the properties of the environment. He thus departs somewhat further from the classical Freudian position than does Hartmann, who merely wished to make a case for ego activities that reflect neutralized instinctual energy ("desexualized" and "deaggressivized"). See Chapter 10.

[6]See, for example, Ruth Benedict (1934).

On the Role of Early Psychosexual Development

The general tendency of psychoanalytic theory is to place heavy emphasis on the vicissitudes of the first few years of life, the period in which the child works out his basic relationships to the parents. In Freud's early formulation, the basic components of the emotional life are laid down by the time the child is 5 or 6 years old and constitute the overwhelmingly powerful, if unconscious, influences on later behavior. Thus, the adult reactions to authority figures—the teacher, the employer, the political leader—may be interpreted in terms of the responses of the young child to parental discipline. Various neo-Freudians have softened this principle somewhat, arguing that the early experiences are the *necessary* but not necessarily the *sufficient* determiners of adult behavior, but, by and large, the weight given to the early determiners is a distinguishing feature of psychoanalytic theory.

While the principle of early determination may contribute greatly to an understanding of certain other phenomena of adult life, its usefulness appears to become more limited when applied to work. In different ways, Lantos and Erikson assign great importance to experiences encountered in later childhood, and Hendrick goes so far as to argue that work behavior is not derivable from early libidinal and aggressive experiences at all but has a different instinctual source. The clinical literature does not support such ideas unequivocally. Certainly there are cases, as Oberndorf indicated, in which the work attitudes of the adult seem wholly or largely determined by the child's relations with his parents. There are, however, numerous instances of frank psychotics, with symptoms clearly related to early crises, but also with relatively unimpaired work capacity (Neff, 1962), and, of course, there are severe neurotics who are maladapted in many life areas but not necessarily in the area of work. Thus, it seems useful to inquire whether the variables that influence behaviors vis-à-vis work are necessarily identical with, or even derivable from, the variables that influence the ability to love, to marry, to make friends. The affective reactions mobilized by work need not be the same as those mobilized by other important life demands.

The chief point suggested by Erikson and Lantos is that the older child is confronted by a new set of life demands, quite different in quality from those that confronted him in his early years. It is true that the prelatency child must incorporate many instrumental activities: He must learn to feed himself, to put on his own clothing, to control and order his urinary and defecatory processes, and even to help in the management of the household. But it is during what Freud called the latency period that quite new tasks appear. He must begin to work out his relationships to nonfamilial figures and accept the authority of strangers. He must reduce his dependence on loved ones and begin to deal with the impersonal. Despite the influence of relationships within the family on extrafamilial relationships, to a qualitatively different extent his life is organized around achievement rather than affection. He begins the long progression that society demands from him, the development from the dependent, playing child to the independent, working adult.[7] Thus, it may well be possible that certain important factors that influence the adult adjustment to work originate at later times and in other settings than those that characterize the earlier experiences in the nuclear family.

SUMMARY

Even if one grants the possibility of certain of the theoretical alternatives, the psychoanalytic observations on work are both stimulating and suggestive. Freud's conception of the uneasy and conflicted balance of work and love cannot be ignored by a comprehensive theory of work. Erikson is most illuminating in pointing out that not only does each phase of development have something of a unique central task to solve, but also that the coping processes of any given phase are influenced by the affects, cognitions, and response-patterns evolved in connection with prior phases. Again, while it seems gratuitous to assume a special work instinct, as Hendrick does, one can agree with him that work behavior appears to be too complex to be satisfactorily accounted for within the framework of psychosexual development. Similarly, while Lantos' speculations on the role of the self-preservative instincts are questionable, we are impressed by many of her comments on the distinctions between play and work and on the importance of the latency period. Finally, the clinical observations of Menninger and Oberndorf serve as reminders that the domains of work and love are not entirely separable but vary in their interconnectedness from person to person.

On balance, however, the sparseness of the psychoanalytic writings on work has permitted only a meager penetration into the complexities of the

---

[7] It can be argued that the distinctions suggested here are too sharp, that childhood play anticipates many of the features of adult work, that the instrumental activities of early childhood are not really different in kind from those of later childhood, and the social interactions outside the family setting are largely similar to those within. To a certain extent, this argument has merit, since all life-activities display unity as well as diversity. But we are arguing here that the differences between demands and activities at different life periods will repay closer examination. Too much has been made, for example, of certain gross similarities between work and play. It was pointed out earlier (Chapter 4), that both require adherence to certain rules, that both involve competition and cooperation, and that both require certain levels of environmental mastery. But these two spheres draw on very different motivations and have quite disparate goals. Even very young children are quite capable of distinguishing play from work and use the language of "make-believe." The salesman who plays golf with a prospect largely for economic reasons is not really playing, as much of his subsequent behavior attests.

problem, leaving most questions unanswered.[8] What are the social and cultural forces that interact with familial experiences to form the adult work personality? What is the relative weight of the later determiners compared to that of the earlier experiences? Can a comprehensive theory be developed that will account for the fact that many people are almost wholly alienated from the work subculture yet appear to be reasonably adequate in other areas of ego functioning? Will such a theory equally well account for the converse? What is the treatment of choice for severe vocational maladaptation? Can amelioration of the inability to work best be achieved by reconstruction of the entire personality, or can a constructive and direct attack be made upon this particular life-sphere without necessarily attempting to solve the problems of other vital areas of adaptation? Finally, can the work personality be conceived of as possessing something of a semi-autonomous character, not only independent to a degree of the motives that play upon other areas of the personality but also possessing its own motivational structure?

While these questions are not easy to answer, they should be raised. In Chapters 7 and 8 we shall construct a more comprehensive theory of work behavior than the relatively restricted interests of the psychoanalysts permitted them to develop.

[8]The words were initially written over 20 years ago (Neff, 1965), but the situation, as described, is essentially unchanged. Psychoanalysts write voluminously on almost every subject except the domain of worker behavior and its vicissitudes. During the past decade (1975–1984), the writer has come across only one paper on work by a psychoanalyst (Pruyser, 1980). This article, written by a clinical professor at the Menninger Clinic, appeared in the house organ of the Menninger Clinic and was apparently written for a staff meeting with the objective of making practitioners aware that psychoanalytic conceptions could be applied to work. The writer's approach is uncritical and supplies us with nothing that could not have been inferred from the concepts of classical psychoanalytic theory.

6 PSYCHOLOGICAL THEORIES OF WORK BEHAVIOR

Although the psychoanalytic and psychiatric writings on work are quite meager, there is a very large literature on the *psychology* of work, the content of which, however, has tended to be rather specialized. By and large, the psychological studies of human work have tended to take it for granted that human beings can work and have focused their attention on the detection, measurement, and description of *individual differences* in occupational behavior.

Psychologists have been responsive to pressures emanating from two major fields: industry and education. The needs of industry have brought into existence a large body of research, concerning such issues as personnel selection, the factors that influence industrial morale, the psychological characteristics that differentiate successful and unsuccessful workers at various levels, and the like. The needs of education have made themselves manifest in the many studies of career planning, occupational preference, and vocational counseling. Although the industrial psychologist and the vocational psychologist tend to work in different areas of society—the former being interested in people who are already employed and the latter typically concentrating his attention on youngsters who are still in school—their researches frequently overlap. What we have is not so much a psychology of work as a psychology of *occupations:* the differential capacities, interests, and attitudes that may serve to mark off the workers in one type of occupation from those in another.

In a survey of the field of occupational psychology, one of its more authoritative spokesmen (Miller, 1974) has called attention to a marked shift in its theoretical orientation. It is perhaps more accurate to say that, prior to the 1960s, the vocational guidance expert was not interested in theory formation. The founders of the field saw themselves as social engineers; their mission was to match people and jobs. By the turn of the century, American industry had become almost bewilderingly complex. How was the new entrant to the labor market, especially the young person leaving school, to choose that job that best fitted his particular set of talents and abilities? In fact, how was the new entrant able to know just what his talents and abilities were, vis-à-vis work? The initial search for answers led to the "trait-factor" approach, which dominated vocational guidance until the middle of the century. Miller describes this conception of vocational guidance "as persuasively simple, if not actually simplistic" (Miller, 1974, p. 238). The task of the vocational guidance expert was seen as twofold: psychometric assessment and occupational information.

This highly pragmatic approach was not without underlying assumptions about vocational behavior. As Miller summarizes them, they are as follows:

> 1. Vocational behavior is largely a cognitive process; decisions are to be reached by reasoning.
> 2. Occupational choice is a single event. . . . Choice is stressed greatly and development very little.
> 3. There is a single "right" goal for everyone in the choice of vocation. There is no recognition that a worker might fit well into a number of vocations.
> 4. A single type of person works in each job. This is the corollary of the third assumption. Taken together, these two notions amount to a one-man, one-job relationship—a concept congenial to the trait-factor approach.
> 5. There is an occupational choice available to each individual . . . (Miller, 1974, pp. 238–239).

Recently, each of these tacit assumptions has been challenged. First, it has become increasingly clear to contemporary vocational psychologists that vocational choice is by no means an exclusively cognitive enterprise. There is now general recognition of the fact that the individual brings to his or her job not only particular skills and abilities but also feelings, emotions, social outlook, and an entire personality. Second, a number of current vocational psychologists have become interested in certain aspects of psychoanalytic and psychodynamic theories of behavior, particularly concerning the possible relationships between personality type and occupation. As Osipow correctly points out, the personality theorist is far more interested in such issues as impulse gratification and the management of anxiety than in such matters as skill and ability (Osipow, 1968). The third major criticism of the trait-factor approach has been from the point of view of students of human development. Occupational choice is increasingly viewed as a developmental matter, during which the individual passes through a number of developmental stages. Current research is less focused on trait-analysis than it is on the manner that individuals acquire the particular life-style that is now looked on as the primary determinant of occupational choice. Finally, there is much more current concern for the socioeconomic framework within which work behavior takes place than was ever allowed for in the trait-factor approach. It has become evident that certain social factors are powerful determinants of occupational behavior; for example, the father's occupation, the social status of the family of origin, the individual's religious, ethnic, and racial identity, and the like.

It is not our purpose here to attempt a general survey of the field of vocational psychology. For those interested, a comprehensive overview can be found in a recent publication of the National Vocational Guidance Association (Herr, 1974). Other useful works are by Crites (1969), Zaccaria (1970), Herr (1970), and Super and Bohn (1970). Rather, we will select those findings and ideas that, in our opinion, can contribute to a general theory of work behavior. Here the chief contributions may be found in the writings of Super, Ginzberg, Roe, Holland, Tiedeman, and Lofquist-Dawis.

We shall also have to take account of a prolonged effort to develop adequate instrumentation for the measurement of work adjustment. Starting in 1959, the Industrial Relations Center of the University of Minnesota has issued a long series of technical monographs and two books. In the course of their researches, the chief investigators (Lloyd Lofquist and René Dawis) have evolved a theory of work behavior. The Minnesota approach will be examined in a later section of this chapter.[1]

SUPER'S THEORY OF VOCATIONAL DEVELOPMENT

The work of Donald Super and his collaborators at Teachers College, Columbia University, represents one of the most sustained and determined efforts to evolve a theory of career patterns. Super is a vocational psychologist, whose attention has been fixed on the individual who is still in school. For some four decades, Teachers College has been one of the chief centers for the training of school psychologists and vocational counselors. During this period. Super has also directed an influential program of research concerned with the process of occupational choice. While initially Super's interests were more directly centered on the uses of aptitude and interest testing in vocational counseling (cf. Super, 1949), during the past three decades he has been heavily committed to an effort to work out a general theory of vocational development (Super, 1953, 1957, 1960; Super and Overstreet, 1960; Super, Starishevsky, Matlin, and Jordaan, 1963, Jordaan and Heyde, 1979).

Super's chief criticism of current practice in vocational counseling is that it tends to have a static, rather than dynamic, character. Its objective has been to match a set of personal attributes with another set of occupational requirements. Its traditional procedures have involved a two-sided operation: (1) the development of a classification of jobs in terms of the abilities, aptitudes, and skills required to perform them; (2) the elaboration of a battery of tests and assessment techniques, which will enable the counselor to determine if the particular pattern of traits exhibited by a given client are

[1]I wish to express my gratitude to Dr. Dawis, who has provided me with numerous reprints and some unpublished material and helped me to grasp the complexities of the Minnesota studies.

more congruent with one kind of career than with another. Of course, Super is quite aware that more is involved in vocational counseling than the mere fitting of an x-shaped peg into an x-shaped hole. The counselor is also committed to shaping the form of the peg so that it will make a better fit. But the guiding principle is that the peg must already have a certain potential shape, which the counselor then helps to strengthen and sharpen. The tacit assumption is that the counselee is already in possession of a relatively stable pattern of occupational traits, because the counselor has a very strong stake in *prediction*. He wants to be able to tell the young person who aspires to be a physicist, a teacher, or a salesman that he has a good or a poor chance of realizing his aspiration. The vocational counselor is at his best when the counselee exhibits a sharply marked pattern of abilities, aptitudes, and interests; he faces a much more difficult task when the abilities–aptitudes–interests pattern is quite ill-defined. Unfortunately, these cases occur all too frequently. What can be done to reduce their number? An obvious tactic has been to attempt to push back in time the point at which the youngster begins to be exposed to vocational guidance. In doing so, the counselor shifts his role from being merely a relatively static sorter of persons and jobs. He now takes on the character of an active agent, who sees it as his task to help bring into existence the phenomenon (a career pattern) that will be the ultimate grist for his mill.

It is to the problems of this shift in counselor role that Super has devoted the bulk of his attention in recent years. Proceeding from the well-established scientific principle that in order to control a phenomenon one must first understand it, Super has set himself the task of trying to discover the crucial factors and stages in occupational development.

In the early 1950s, Super launched an extremely ambitious follow-up study of the development of occupational patterns in a sample of approximately 300 14-year-old boys, then in the eighth or ninth grades. Titled the *Career Pattern Study* (CPS), the research was initially projected to cover a 10-year period and was later extended to cover a 20-year period. The plan was to study the subjects intensively at critical periods: ages 15, 18, 25, and 36. A large amount of data was collected, covering demographic, personal, and social variables, attitudes and interests, school and work experience, and achievement. Using elaborately structured interviews and a wide battery of achievement and interest tests—many constructed for the research—Super's focus has been on such variables as the following: concern with occupational choice; use and specificity of occupational information; extent and degree of planning; consistency of occupational preferences, taking into account both fields and levels; patterning and development of interests; work experience; liking for work; acceptance of responsibility; agreement between interests and preference, between interests and fantasy. The resulting masses of data have been subjected to a number of statistical treatments, including factor-analytic studies designed to reduce the many variables to a manageable number of common factors. Several interim reports have been issued and the most recent appeared in 1979 (Jordaan and Heyde, 1979).[2]

To make sense of his findings, Super approached his task with a theory of vocational development that he has refined and elaborated over the years. The theory was inspired by the ideas of Buehler (1933) and Havighurst (1968) but also has been strongly influenced by Ginzberg's work (Ginzberg, 1951; see next section). Generally, vocational development is thought of as a lifelong process that originates somewhere in middle childhood and continues throughout adult life. The individual is believed to pass through a series of stages, defined as growth, exploration, establishment, maintenance, and decline. These stages are roughly tied to chronological periods, although Super emphasizes that individuals pass through these stages at very different rates and may reach a terminal point without passing through all of them. Some of these developmental stages are further analyzed into substages. For example, the exploratory stage is further subdivided into three substages: (1) a "tentative" substage in early and middle adolescence, when there is the beginning of identification of a number of possible fields and levels of work but without, as yet, much specification; (2) a "transition" substage in later adolescence and early adulthood, when the person struggles with a transition from school to work or from intermediate to advanced schooling, during which choices are becoming more specific; (3) a "trial" substage in early adulthood, when the person actually enters an occupation but without a great deal of commitment and with many changes still to be anticipated. Super also makes use of such concepts as *floundering, stabilization,* and *consolidation,* which may characterize a person's behavior at various of these life-stages.

It has not been a simple matter for Super and his co-workers to coordinate their empirical findings with a general theory of vocational development. Part of these difficulties may arise from the manner in which Super has structured his theory of vocational development. The key idea in Super's

[2]The Jordaan–Heyde publication is described by Super, in an editorial forward, as the third monograph produced by the Career Pattern Study; this report focuses on a comparison of the vocational attitudes and behaviors of ninth and twelfth grade boys, or the changes that occurred between the first and last years of high school. The primary objective of the study was to determine if and how vocational attitudes have matured during the high school years. In the preface by Jordaan and Heyde, it is further stated that additional monographs are in preparation: A fourth monograph in the series (Super and Jordaan, in preparation) will focus on predictive validity, studying the relationships between the ninth and twelfth grade measures and both internal and external criteria of achievement at age 25; a fifth and "final" monograph will compare all these data to the subjects' achievements at age 36. It is also projected that a series of case studies will be prepared of careers in progress from ages 15 to 36. Should all these studies become public, we will have a very comprehensive and exhaustive picture of the patterns of work-careers in a certain segment of the American male population.

theory is the self-concept.[3] He believes that a person will make those occupational choices that are maximally consistent with his picture of himself. There is thus a fairly heavy commitment to rationalism and voluntarism. The vocational self-concept is formulated as a pattern of attitudes, interests, and aspirations that develops in the individual over time, that passes through many stages of initiation, differentiation, and articulation, and is ultimately translated into occupational choice. The basic research strategy Super has adopted is to find means of assessing the components of the self-concept in different individuals at different points in time and then to examine the relationships between these components and the career patterns that eventually make their appearance. In practice, this task has turned out to be formidable in its difficulties.

Part of these difficulties may arise from certain problems inherent in self-concept theory. This theory has a long and complex history in psychological and psychiatric literature but has eluded any very precise definition and description (cf. Wylie, 1961). The self-concept has played an important role in many influential theories of personality (Sullivan, 1953; Rogers, 1959; Bordin, 1943). There is, however, little consensus regarding its components and even less grasp of how to render these components operational for research. Super and his collaborators have had to devote a very considerable portion of their research time to the derivation of testable hypotheses and to the working out of standardized techniques of measurement. It is apparent that they have encountered many technical problems, and their very laudable and ambitious research enterprise has been slowed down and hampered by efforts to solve these problems while the research is in course.

But even if the self-concept had proved more amenable to experimental analysis, is it likely that precise description of its components would help us to predict vocational development? To support Super's theory, two general conditions would have to prevail in the real world. First, young people would have to enjoy almost unrestricted freedom in making occupational choices and in shifting from one sort of training to another as circumstances dictate. Second, these young people would have to operate at least as rationally as an electronic computer, in the sense that they would have to be more or less continually involved in matching whatever data they have about themselves to whatever data they have about occupations. Should either or both of these conditions fail to hold, then there is little reason to expect that there will be any generally detectable relationship between the pictures people have of themselves and the occupations they ultimately enter.

The theory of a strong linkage between the self-concept and occupational choice appears both too simple and too one-sided. It cannot be denied that

[3]Super's ideas on the self-concept, as related to vocational development, are to be found in Super et al. (1967).

it has a ring of plausibility and may even describe what takes place in a few individual cases. The real world of occupational behavior, however, is far more complex. Given the modern industrial society affords its youngsters far more degrees of freedom than, say, the world of agrarian feudalism, a host of factors must be considered as having some influence on occupational behavior quite apart from the self-concept. Constraints arising from socioeconomic status, the particular aspirations, biases, and predilections prevailing in individual families, barriers posed by ethnic and demographic factors, differences in the relative ease of entry into the different occupations, prevailing stereotypes concerning differential occupational prestige, the various frictions and rigidities that characterize the system of formal education, the influence of prestigious peers or adults, sheer inertia—these are only *some* of the variables that, more often in combination than singly, may serve to determine choice of occupation. Of course, many of these factors also influence the development of the vocational self-concept, and it is legitimate to ask whether the latter is not a somewhat gratuitous and redundant construct. Occupational activity is too molar as a sphere of behavior to be easily linked to a single kind of determinant. An adequate theory of vocational behavior will have to be truly multivariate in nature, in a position to draw its variables of interest from the entire domain of the social and behavioral sciences.

In one sense, then, Super is too much of a psychologist and not enough of a general social scientist. Although it seems unfair, he can be charged with committing what William James called the "psychologist's fallacy." His general approach is to attempt to identify a hypothetical psychological property (in his case, the self-concept), to attempt to analyze and measure this property, and then try to relate it to choice of occupation. But what if the self-concept is only *one* of a great many interlocking determinants of vocational behavior and not an overwhelmingly decisive one at that? Regardless of technical difficulties, the entire research enterprise is endangered by too exclusive a focus. In reply, Super might argue that, if all other conditions are held constant, the self-concept will determine occupational choice, which is all that he is attempting to demonstrate. In the real world, however, conditions are *never* constant, and the real world is the locus of Super's research enterprise. Too many things are operative to permit *any* set of purely personal attributes, no matter how construed, to bear any very close relation to the kinds of work people are actually found to perform.

Although we find Super's theory of vocational behavior both too restrictive and strategically inappropriate, his general theoretical posture is of considerable importance. His interest in development and dynamics has added a badly needed dimension to vocational counseling, a field that can too easily degenerate into a species of practical social engineering. His emphasis on longitudinal research has already revealed a number of interesting things about the process through which the nonworking child is gradually transformed into a working adult. We have learned, for example, that before the eighth or ninth grade the schoolchild is hardly aware of occupational matters. It is interesting, also, that the high school years appear to be marked by very considerable floundering. Above all, the crucial events that cause the person to move in one or another occupational direction appear to take place during the school years.

What is most important is Super's research approach. It is only through intensive and extensive longitudinal studies—in which Super and his collaborators are pioneers—that we can begin to know something about the complex determinants of vocational behavior. If we have taken exception to Super's theory of vocational development, it is because we are afraid it is too restrictive an instrument. On the other hand, he can only be praised for his insistence that vocational behavior will be understood only when the secrets of individual development are revealed.

GINZBERG ON OCCUPATIONAL CHOICE

One of the most stimulating and suggestive studies in this field (Ginzberg, Ginsburg, Axelrod, and Herma, 1951) has been produced by an extremely broad-gauged economist, who swims very expertly in interdisciplinary seas. As an economist, Ginzberg's initial starting-point was an interest in the availability, development, and conservation of human resources as a factor in production. Unlike his colleagues, however, Ginzberg has apparently rejected the option of trying to solve these problems within the framework of the usual "economic" conceptions (e.g., the price system, supply and demand). On the contrary, Ginzberg conceptualizes occupational choice as a very general kind of human behavior, which must be approached with the concepts made available by all of the chief behavioral sciences. His collaborators were, respectively, a psychiatrist, a sociologist, and a psychologist. That this was a genuine, not a titular, collaboration is attested to by the fact that the resulting product is more easily identifiable as an essay in social–psychological theory than as a contribution to economic thought.

Ginzberg's chief interest was in theory. He interviewed 91 young people, predominantly males ranging in age from 11 to 24. No claim is made that the sample was either adequate or representative of young people in general, and, in fact, no data are advanced in support of any of the ideas that Ginzberg presents. *Occupational Choice* is a book without tables and, apparently by choice, without statistics. Indeed, statistical treatment would have been gratuitous in the extreme, since the sample of persons studied was both quite small and highly selective in its characteristics. The bulk of the sample consisted of children and young adults who were attending various schools and colleges maintained by Columbia University. Being aware that this group was, as he says, "a highly favored group having a maximal degree of freedom of choice" (1951, p. 46), Ginzberg also interviewed 17 boys from more deprived environments, who were active in a nearby neighborhood community center. Only 10 of the 91 cases were girls, all of whom attended Barnard College of Columbia University. It is perfectly clear, from the restricted and specialized character of the research sample, that the Ginzberg study must be considered on its merits as an exploratory essay rather than as a set of empirical findings.

Within these limitations, and with the *caveat* that virtually everything remains to be confirmed, Ginzberg makes a number of interesting remarks about vocational behavior. On the basis of the interview materials, Ginzberg and his collaborators have evolved a theory of occupational choice that has three components. First, occupational choice is not an event but a *process,* which takes place over a period of some 8–10 years and which passes through a number of well-marked developmental stages. Second, this process is largely *irreversible,* that is, earlier decisions tend to reduce the degrees of freedom available for later decisions. Third, *compromise* is an essential feature of every choice. Significantly, Ginzberg is aware that occupational choice involves the interplay of two sets of relatively independent factors. On the one hand, at each point, we have a given set of *intra*individual determinants: abilities, interests, and aptitudes. On the other hand, we have a set of *extra*individual determinants: environmental demands, pressures, and constraints. Any given occupational choice is a function of *both* sets acting together. It is therefore fruitless to suppose (as Super apparently does) that occupational choice can be predicted from knowledge of personal attributes alone. Even apart from the problem that any given set of personal attributes is, in part at least, a function of environmental conditions, the individual does not make his choice purely in terms of the picture he has of himself. To an indeterminate extent, the individual's "choices" are made for him, by the particular environment in which he happens to be embedded.

Ginzberg envisages the process of occupational decision making in terms of three periods—*fantasy, tentative,* and *realistic.* He believes that the first of these periods is operative in the child roughly between the years of 10 and 12; the second is characteristic of the years of puberty and early adolescence, from 12 to 17; the third period runs through later adolescence and early adulthood. These temporal limits are regarded merely as approximations, obviously permitting a great deal of individual variation. During the fantasy period, to the degree that the child thinks about occupation at all, it is largely in terms of his wishes to be an adult. The child has no conception of his own capacities or of occupational opportunities and limitations. As Ginzberg puts it, "he believes he can be whatever he wants to be." During the tentative period, it begins to be impressed upon the child that he will ultimately face the problem of selecting among occupations. He begins to draw closer to reality, both in terms of his own abilities and interests and the degree to which they can express themselves in future work. During these years of early adolescence, however, Ginzberg believes the child is still concerned largely with subjective factors: his own interests, capacities, and values. Gradually, during later adolescence and early adulthood, the individual becomes increasingly concerned with the realistic opportunities and limitations of available work environments and makes those compromises that result in a final occupational choice.

In the course of describing these three developmental stages, Ginzberg also suggests a number of substages within each. He thinks, for example, that during the tentative stage there is a gradual shift from an earlier phase where the sole preoccupation is with interests ("what would I like to be?") to a later phase in which there begins to be concern with capacities ("what kind of job am I best suited for"). During the tentative period, the child also begins to be aware of values related to social status and social class. Similarly, the realistic period is subdivided into an earlier exploratory stage and later phases of crystallization and specification. Apparently, Ginzberg believes that these periods and stages are ordered in a sequential pattern and tend to take the same general course in most children.

Ginzberg's notion of irreversibility is one of his most important theoretical ideas. The chief variable here is time. The later we cut into the developmental process, the fewer are the real options for freedom of choice. The chief determinants of the increasing restriction of freedom are the frictions and rigidities inherent in the institutional environment. Earlier decisions to take or drop a given school subject can exert a powerful influence on later educational options. Not only does the educational system itself display increasing rigidity with time, but it is psychologically easier to continue on a given course of action than to abandon it and start all over in something else. The result, for almost everyone, is a series of increasingly restricted compromises between what one wants to do and what is actually available. The picture that Ginzberg presents of occupational choice is like that of a complex maze, in which successive choice-points result in a progressive narrowing of the terrain that the individual is permitted to enter. Thus, an individual may wind up in an occupation that is relatively incongruent with his actual personal attributes, largely because early and irrevocable choices were made—whether accidentally, impulsively, or simply mistakenly.

While neither Ginzberg nor Super has been able as yet to present us with very much in the way of hard evidence, Ginzberg's views seem more plausible than Super's. Super's search for the self-concept seems to ignore environmental constraints, which Ginzberg certainly does not do. Another important feature of Ginzberg's theory is that he treats the environment as "dynamically" as Super wishes to treat individuals. In other words, Ginzberg conceives of environmental determinants as playing different roles at different stages of vocational development, with the constraint that these extraindividual variables become more decisive with the passage of time. Ginzberg's theory is both more complex and more sophisticated than

Super's. Nevertheless, both of these theorists have made important contributions to our understanding of work behavior. Their empirical observations indicate that an individual's attitudes to work pass through a number of transformations; work behavior is a function of a prolonged developmental process that starts in rather late childhood and takes a number of years to crystallize. Both men appear to agree that the experiences of later childhood and adolescence are more crucial than those of infancy and early childhood (in some contrast to psychoanalytic theories), although they do so for different reasons. These are important ideas and merit detailed further investigation.

ANNE ROE AND THE ORIGIN OF
OCCUPATIONAL INTERESTS

In many respects, the work of Anne Roe is unique. Unlike most of her professional colleagues, Roe is a clinical psychologist, who has approached the problems of career development from the general vantage point of psychoanalytic theory. Her research focus has been almost exclusively on the highly professional and intellectual occupations (artists, biologists, psychologists, physicists, engineers, social workers, etc.). Over some two decades, she has produced a series of studies "in depth" of the personalities of adults who have achieved a professional identity in these occupations and has been almost alone in her utilization of clinical assessment techniques (e.g., Rorschach Test). Apart from a number of detailed research monographs, her findings have been summarized in three books (Roe, 1953, 1956; Roe and Siegelman, 1964).

In contrast to Super and Ginzberg, who tend to agree that nothing very serious takes place in vocational development until the child is 11 or 12 years old, Roe's interest has been in the events of early childhood. Her over-all research strategy is guided by a conception that occupational identity is formed through the influence of a given set of early parent-child relationships. Like the psychoanalysts, Roe's primary working hypothesis is that the basic elements of the personality are laid down in the very early interactions between parents and children, and she has tried to demonstrate that these early structures determine later occupational choice. It should be stressed, however, that Roe is not a very "orthodox" psychoanalyst. Unlike Freud and some of his followers, she makes no attempt to relate occupational identity to specific phases of psychosexual development. Her theory of occupational choice can be described as "psychoanalytic" in the sense that its focus of interest is on early childhood, and its chief concern is the affective quality of the relationships that develop between parents and children.

Roe's approach to occupational behavior has two major components. The first consists of an effort to evolve a typological classification of occupations according to the degree to which a given occupation demands dealing with people or with objects. An example of the first type is the profession of social work, while engineering typifies the second. The second component of the theory involves a classification of types of early parent–child relationships. The basic conception is that a warm and accepting parent–child relationship predisposes the child to enter "person-directed" occupations, while a cold and rejecting family atmosphere leads to choice of "non-person-directed" occupations. In its general form, this can be characterized as a kind of "approach–avoidance" theory. Children whose early experiences with people (their parents) have been pleasurable and rewarding will want to continue a close relationship to people in their working lives and thus will choose "people-directed" occupations. On the other hand, children who have experienced the parent–child relationship as basically unrewarding and unpleasant will unconsciously avoid continuation of such experiences and will preoccupy themselves with things rather than persons.

During the past decade, Roe and her students have published a number of provocative studies designed to confirm these hypotheses, but their efforts have not been marked by very much empirical success. The difficulties encountered have turned out to be as severe in the area of methodology as in theoretical formulation. Roe's research strategy has been to study relatively small groups of subjects who are in a stage of advanced training for a particular profession or who are already employed in it. She has not been able to mount truly longitudinal studies, in which the individual is followed closely from early childhood to adulthood. As a result, she has been compelled to settle for retrospective accounts by her subjects of the quality of their early child-rearing. By their very nature, data of this sort are not likely to be highly valid. Not only do adults lack a standard with which to compare the quality of the early childhood experience, but they can very easily distort it to accord with their present outlook. Roe is certainly aware of these research limitations, but she cannot escape from them. The best that can be said about this series of studies is that failure to confirm the presented hypotheses cannot, in the nature of the case, provide evidence that they are untrue.

Despite these research limitations, Roe has been able to report some significant findings, but the disclosed relationships are very weak and are often in a direction counter to her basic theory. Contrary to expectation, the social workers in her sample reported that their early parent–child experience was less warm and more stressful than was the case for her sample of engineers. At the same time, the *present* orientation of both groups was in line with the theory, that is, the adult social worker was more concerned with people and the adult engineer more concerned with things. The strongest antecedent variable turned out to be a measure of the sheer quantity of remembered social interactions, whether within the family or without. Quite obviously, findings like these, however fragmentary, suggest the need for some revision of the initial theory. In her most recent review of her work

(Roe, 1964), Roe concedes that "the choice of occupation is not nearly so direct an indication of childhood experience as had been supposed." She goes on to say that an adequate theory of vocational development will have to be much more complex than she had initially presumed.

At the conclusion of the 1964 paper, Roe makes a series of points that are sufficiently penetrating so that they deserve quotation in full. Roe states her current viewpoint on vocational development as follows (Roe, 1964, pp. 211–212):

> 1. Differentiations have been shown, but the typical personality pattern is never a universal one for the members of any group. All predictions of occupational choice are necessarily probabilistic. If predictions are made on the basis of personality alone, *the probabilities must be small.* . . . [emphasis added]
>
> 2. Personality is only one broad factor in the decisions made at any occupational choice point; how decisive a factor it is varies from instance to instance. . . . Any predictions must take external variables—the openness of society, the immediate economic situation, the changing industrial technology—into account. Beyond these are the factors of abilities, education and experience. . . . (a) For those persons who fall in the middle ranges of the population in all of most relevant personality characteristics, occupational choice will depend chiefly upon the relevant sex stereotypes and the possession of appropriate abilities. Personality factors may have little differentiating effect. . . . (b) Sex-typed occupations which require no special or extreme personality or ability factors will not generally attract people with marked deviations: e.g., populations of salesgirls, stenographers, and beauty operators should show minimal intergroup differences.
>
> 3. There is sparse evidence that both specific and general early experiences may be related to later vocational choices, but research in this field has barely begun and has not thus far touched upon the mediating mechanisms in the determination of choice.
>
> 4. The occupational life history is never dependent upon one choice alone. Vocational development is lifelong, and there are many choice points along the way. At any one of these, the weight given to any factor may differ from the weight appropriate to it at preceding or subsequent choice points. . . .
>
> 5. Because vocational life histories of women are characteristically different from those of men, and because even from women who follow an uninterrupted career line there are considerations not relevant to men, studies of occupational histories for men and women may require different concepts. It may well be that occupational classifications, too, should be different for the two sexes.
>
> 6. Practical career predictions at our present state of knowledge may not go further than from one choice point to the next. The most appropriate predictive model is a multivariate one in which all of the appropriate factors can be combined in various weightings.

I find Roe's summary of the current state of knowledge to be both quite accurate and highly persuasive. It serves as a badly needed corrective both for Super's one-sided preoccupation with intraindividual variables and for Roe's own early commitment to the importance of early experience. Above all, her present views are marked by recognition of the great complexity of the problem, a situation of which we shall have to take due account in presenting our own theory of work behavior. That Roe's present conceptions are more complex than they were initially reflects her genuine commitment to the scientific method. It is generally characteristic of the scientific enterprise that its initial attack on a problem is made with highly simplifying assumptions. It is equally characteristic of the empirical scientist that he ultimately observes that things are more complex than he had initially supposed. Roe can hardly be faulted for what may seem like a belated recognition that her initial theory was too simple. On the contrary, she deserves praise for virtually abandoning a viewpoint to which she had committed a lifetime of research. Despite what she must have strongly felt to be an inherently plausible notion, the case for a clear relation between early determiners and later behavior remains unproved.

HOLLAND AND A THEORY OF TYPES

John L. Holland, formerly of the National Merit Scholarship Corporation and more recently at Johns Hopkins University, is a maverick among American vocational psychologists. Although his research methodology is avowedly empirical and psychometric, as is typical of most American psychologists, his theoretical stance is more European than American. His primary concern has been with the *classification* of vocational behavior, and to serve this interest he has drawn heavily on the typology theories of Adler, Fromm, Jung, and Spranger. As Holland notes, however (1973), he believes that his efforts differ from the predominantly nonempirical European tradition in the following respects: (1) *his* typology is responsive to research data and has undergone revisions in relation to data; (2) it is a typology of *environments* as well as persons; (3) he is preoccupied with statistical techniques to determine degrees and patterns of resemblance to a set of models, rather than being content with an all-or-none set of personality types; (4) he has tried to connect his model with development and learning theory.

Holland's theory of vocational adjustment is essentially interactional. Four assumptions underlie his theory of vocational behavior:

> 1. Most people in our society can be classified as one of six types: realistic, investigative, artistic, social, enterprising, or conventional. Persons can also be classified by their profiles *across* the six types, in terms of a pattern of highs and lows. Holland calls this cross-type profile the *personality pattern.*
> 2. Most work environments can be classified according to the same six labels: realistic, investigative, etc. For Holland, the central characteristics of an environment are those of the people who inhabit it. Thus, in "realistic" environments, it is found that most people who inhabit them are realistic types. Like personalities, environments also have profiles, described by the relative proportions of person-types found in them.

3. There is pressure toward congruence, both on the side of people and on the side of environments. People will attempt to enter work-environments that fit their personality type; environments also select people through friendship and recruiting devices. Like tends to huddle with like.

4. A person's behavior is influenced by the interaction between his personality type and the characteristics of the environment that he has entered.

In his most recent work, Holland is also concerned with additional assumptions that serve as modifiers and bring him closer to his empirical data. These secondary assumptions are:

a. *Consistency*. Research shows that within a person or an environment, some pairs of types are more closely related than others. It is more usual, for example, to find a person or an environment that can best be described as realistic–investigative than a pairing characterized as conventional–artistic. Some person-types or environment-types are further apart than others.

b. *Differentiation*. Persons and environments can run the gamut from being sharply marked (a single high peak in a type-profile) to poor differentiation (a profile showing approximately equal scores across the six types). Prediction and counseling are obviously easier in the first case.

c. *Congruence*. Different types flourish in different environments.

Much of the data reported by Holland in support of the theory has been obtained through a series of studies of bright, upwardly mobile high school students (National Merit finalists). The primary psychometric device utilized is what he calls the Vocational Preference Inventory (VPI). The VPI is a list of 160 occupations; the subject is asked to choose those occupations he likes, or which appeal to him, to mark those he dislikes or finds uninteresting, and to ignore those about which he is undecided. Prior research had characterized each of the listed occupations as predominantly realistic, investigative, and the like. An individual's score, then, is simply enough determined by the numbers of specific occupations he selects or rejects. By and large, the research of Holland and his collaborators lend some support to the theory.

What contribution does Holland make to the general theory of work behavior? In the writer's opinion, his most important contribution lies in his effort to integrate personality theory with the theory of work behavior. We should be aware, however, that Holland conceives of personality in a rather specialized way. Personality, for Holland, is a kind of global life-way, a distinctive style of coping with any presented problem. He is only incidentally interested in the problem of concern to most clinical psychologists and psychiatrists, that is, the relations between the cognitive and emotional sides of the person or the manifold ways in which these relationships can go wrong. Maladaptation for Holland is a measure of *incongruence* between the person-type and the environment-type. Holland's approach is phenomenological and descriptive, rather than developmental.

He is aware that his personality-types have their sources in each individual's biographical history (he thinks that there may be genetic factors as well, but this possibility is simply stated, not described). His major concern, however, is the *present* fit between the person and his environment. Unhappiness arises from a poor fit: happiness is congruence!

One might raise a question or two about the manner in which Holland conceptualizes the work environment. Environments are typed rather straightforwardly and simply by counting the frequencies of the person-types who are found in them. The tacit assumption is that people are drawn to certain kinds of work-environments by the needs of their own particular personality type, and they then proceed to recruit others who are like themselves and extrude those who are different. Like seeks like! But there is something circular and unsatisfactory about Holland's environmental types. Little is said about the demand-characteristics of a particular environment-type, the sorts of tasks people are required to carry out, and the like. Furthermore, Holland does not appear to take account of the fact that a particular occupation (doctor, teacher, social worker, etc.) may provide a very wide range of environments and work-roles. Medicine, for example, is an extremely complex occupation, in which an individual physician may either serve individual patients, do research work, function as an administrator of a medical facility, operate as a consultant, write books, or teach others. The complexities of modern society are such that most occupations now require a wide variety of work roles. If this is true, then the matter of chief interest to Holland—the relationships between person-type and environment-type—will be increasingly difficult to establish.

Despite these manifest difficulties, Holland's approach to occupational psychology is both interesting and useful. At least two important ideas flow from it. First, we are reminded that work behavior is a complex transaction between working individuals and the environments they encounter. Second, we are made aware that work behavior is, in some sense, an aspect of personality. Just what aspects of personality are involved remains unclear, but this is certainly an issue with which we shall have to cope.

TIEDEMAN AND THE TECHNOLOGY OF CHOICE

Like Super and Ginzberg, David V. Tiedeman is a developmental theorist, but his chief commitment is to methodology. Formerly at Harvard, he is now associated with the American Institute for Research at Palo Alto, where he is working on the application of computer systems to vocational guidance. Tiedeman is not so much interested in the long-run development of work attitudes as he is in the specific process through which people make occupational choices. He and his students have produced a number of empirical studies of vocational decision making, which have helped to clarify some of the tangled issues involved. He has shown, for example, that sex-role and family status are at least as important determiners of choice as is the self-concept. Similarly, Tiedeman has produced data indicating that interest and personality tests are better predictors of occupational choice than are aptitude tests. He has also provided confirmation for certain of Ginzberg's observations, especially the latter's belief that the vocational self-concept in boys begins to take shape as they pass through the ninth through the twelfth grades, and that a work-values-stage (beginning around the twelfth grade) is preceded by an interests-stage (tenth grade).

Tiedeman has evolved his own version of a theory of vocational development that has its closest affinities to the psychogenic ideas of Erik Erikson (Erikson, 1963). In a work published in the 1960s (Tiedeman, O'Hara, and Baruch, 1963), he stressed the need for a broad psychosocial theory that will permit the study of how people acquire a "vocational identity." In addition to defining the problem as the individual seeking an identity, Tiedeman also follows Erikson in conceiving of development as an "epigenetic" process, one in which development proceeds by "successive differentiation from an originally undifferentiated structure" (Tiedeman et al., 1963, p. 24). He sees the process of vocational development as marked by two major phases: anticipation and implementation. The former is divided into the substages of exploration, crystallization, choice, and exploration; the latter into the substages of induction, transition, and maintenance.

In recent years, Tiedeman has become greatly interested in the development of computer-assisted self-guidance systems (cf. Tiedeman and Willis, 1972; Tiedeman and Miller, 1974). He believes that the relatively leisurely process through which people are accustomed to making vocational decisions are now being rendered obsolete by the pace of technological change. People must now be prepared for multiple careers in very rapidly changing work environments. Tiedeman appears to believe that people are now being faced with a situation in which decision making is not simply a one-time goal but a continuous process. Whatever one's particular set of skills and talents, the environment will determine how, when, and *if*, they will be used.

LOFQUIST AND DAWIS: THE PSYCHOMETRY OF WORK ADJUSTMENT

Since 1959, a long series of research studies titled the *Work Adjustment Project* has been issued by the Industrial Relations Center of the University of Minnesota under the leadership of Lloyd H. Lofquist and René V. Dawis. The Lofquist–Dawis partnership has been extremely productive, accounting for upward of 30 technical monographs (the *Minnesota Studies in Vocational Rehabilitation*), many published papers, and two books (Lofquist and Dawis, 1969; Dawis and Lofquist, 1984). This prolonged investigatory effort has been supported by the rehabilitation division of the U.S. Department of Health, Education and Welfare.

The basic aim of these researches is to develop a reliable and valid set of paper-and-pencil tests of work adjustment, tests that will be useful both to the counseling psychologists working in vocational guidance and to rehabilitation psychologists who are trying to choose appropriate training programs for disabled workers. Their methodology is determinedly empirical, very much in line with the multifactorial, trait-based approach that has produced the better known Minnesota Multiphasic test of personality, an approach that has been described jokingly as that of "Dust-Bowl empiricism." Lofquist and Dawis, however, start with a specific theory of work adjustment; their research studies have the double function of providing corroboration for the theory and the development of test instruments that can be used to measure its components. In the course of providing us with measures of the components of work adjustment, they also provide us with a theory of work behavior.

The Lofquist–Dawis theory is essentially a balance theory. We are concerned here with the degree of correspondence between the "work personality" and the "work environment." The former is made up of vocational abilities and vocational needs; the latter (the job) is described in terms of ability requirements and "need-reinforcer" characteristics. Given, first, a reasonable correspondence between a person's job skills (vocational abilities) and the task demands of a particular job (ability requirements) and given, second, a reasonable correspondence between the individual's work needs (e.g., ability utilization, adequacy of compensation, need for recognition, desired co-worker relations, character of supervision) and the degree to which the job satisfies these needs (the "need-reinforcer" system), an individual can be described as having a measurable degree of *work satisfaction*. On the work environment side, the degree to which the individual worker's abilities jibe with the specified work requirement (output, quality, etc.) and the degree to which available need-reinforcers inherent in the particular work-situation (wages, working conditions, etc.) are acceptable to the employee, together provide measures of *satisfactoriness* (the employer finds the employee useful and wants to continue his employment). Together, satisfaction and satisfactoriness should predict *tenure* (continuation of employment by the particular firm involved).

All this seems simple enough in theory but has been extremely difficult to put into operation in practice. The procedure of the Minnesota investigators involves a series of steps. First, they conceptually analyzed a given domain (e.g., work needs) into a series of components or traits. Two sets of items are then written for each component. The first set consists of items that describe what it is that the worker wants from his job (pay, recognition, flexibility, autonomy, security, working conditions, etc.). The second set consists of paired statements by job supervisors that describe the job in terms of the degree to which it meets the above desired characteristics. The resulting items were then assembled into draft tests that were administered to a large group of male subjects (aged from 18 to 65 + , occupations from blue-collar to professional, employment experience from 0 years to 31 + years) and studied for internal consistency and statistical differentiation. Once the statistical tests were deemed satisfactory, the final sets of test items were used to run correlations with the chosen outcome criteria of *satisfaction, satisfactoriness,* and *tenure.* The final outcome would be standardized tests of known reliability and measurable validity.

What is one to say of the product of this enormous and highly complex research project? The final correlations reported, as between need requirements and work tenure, for example, are all significantly different from chance but tend to be rather low, ranging from .18 to .40. While these results are quite comparable to those of other psychometric studies, they leave a great deal of the variance unexplained. More seriously, the chief investigators appear to subscribe to a rather abstract theoretical position, which does not accord very well with the disorder of the real world. Lofquist and Dawis appear to be saying that if we can only increase an individual's satisfaction with his job and, correspondingly, increase the degree to which the employer finds the worker satisfactory, then job tenure will increase. But this seems to be a quite inadequate account of the real complexities involved in maintenance of employment. Individual workers may stay on jobs that they detest because they have no reasonable alternative, and employers may keep workers on for long periods becaue *they* have no reasonable alternative. We should emphasize that these are only two of the many social and psychological conditions that are not accounted for in the Lofquist–Dawis approach.

The chief reason advanced by the Lofquist–Dawis team to support this ambitious and elaborate research effort is that the field of rehabilitation badly needs objective instruments that can measure the utility of training programs designed to help handicapped people enter (or reenter) the labor market. At present, many rehabilitation programs exist that appear merely to have the virtue of plausibility. Where outcome criteria exist, they tend to rely on actual performance data, for example (a) actual placement on a paid job in unprotected industry and (b) a given period of maintenance of employment. While such hard and objective criteria are desirable in themselves, they tell us nothing of the attitudinal and behavioral changes that make such outcomes possible, nor do they allow us to know what features of a training program made these outcomes possible in particular individuals. The Minnesota group is correct in claiming that it would be nice to have convenient measures of vocational potential. This would enable rehabilitation authorities to select the more promising candidates, to compare the effectiveness of given treatments, and to know why it is that a given treatment succeeded (or failed) when administered to a given subject. Certainly, the efficiency of rehabilitation procedures could be enormously improved if such measures were available. Unfortunately, the Minnesota data so far available suggest only rather modest success in devising such measurement instruments, with large realms of probable error left unaccounted for. In the end, one may ask whether the mental testing approach, no matter how sophisticated, is useful in assessing the vocational potential of seriously disabled people (cf. Chapter 9).

On the positive side, the student of work behavior can learn a great deal by studying the Lofquist–Dawis research reports. The initial notion that work behavior, at least in part, is determined by the interaction of a set of variables on the side of the individual (the work personality) and another set of variables describing the work environment (the demands of work), seems quite sound and is at the core of the writer's own theory of work behavior (see later Chapters 7 and 8).

CONCLUSIONS

In contrast to their psychiatric colleagues, the psychologists who have studied work behavior appear far more practical and "down-to-earth." As we have seen, psychiatry has largely ignored the problems of the world of work; where they have been considered at all, they have been looked upon chiefly as one of the consequences of a distorted or inadequate psychosexual development in very early childhood. The psychologists who have studied human work have tended to approach it quite differently. In the first place, vocational behavior is apparently assumed to be a relatively autonomous area of life activity, which not only merits intensive study in its own right but also may not be easily derivable from the experiences of infancy and early childhood. In this connection, Anne Roe has been an outstanding exception in her preoccupation with early parent-child relations, but apparently her own research has convinced her that things are not so simple as she once had thought. If we are to include Roe in terms of her latest theoretical position, all the investigators appear to agree that vocational behavior develops largely independently of the particular experiences of early childhood, is responsive to events that take place rather late in what Freud called the "latency period," and passes through a number of discernible stages throughout adolescence and early adulthood. Embedded in this view is the possibility that vocational behavior is at least as much a function of the demands of the environment as it is of intrapsychic needs and desires.

Three important suggestions appear to arise from the reviewed studies. The first has to do with the manner in which we can conceptualize the relations between work and personality. If some relationship may exist between these terms, what is it? Our ability to move toward a solution may depend in part on how we conceptualize the human personality. If personality is viewed as a kind of monolithic entity, largely fixed in its basic patterns by the events of early childhood, then there may be, in fact, no relationship at all. On the other hand, it is possible to conceive of the personality as a series or arrangement of levels and areas, each standing in some relationship to the others but each having some measure of independence as well. In this sense, it may be possible to detect certain areas of the general personality that bear closer relations to work than other areas. This raises a further interesting possibility. If the personality is made up of a set of more or less autonomous areas of functioning, then it becomes possible to be disturbed or inadequate in one area but not necessarily in another.

The second suggestion has to do with the stages through which the child is ultimately transformed into the adult worker. The available evidence indicates that the child is not much of a vocational animal until he is around 12 years old. Prior to this age, work has the meaning only of something that grown-ups do and is desired only to the extent that he wishes to be an adult. As Ginzberg puts it (the other writers tend to agree), the ideas held about work by younger children are exclusively in the realm of fantasy and have little or no relation either to their abilities or their actual interests. The child simply wants to be like his adult heroes of the moment (famous athletes, movie stars, astronauts, etc.). However, the empirical findings here may be somewhat misleading. Investigators may be mistaking the responses that children make to certain kinds of questions ("what do you want to be when you grow up?") with the actual manner in which children are coping with certain developmental tasks. I believe the grade school years have considerable importance in shaping certain behaviors that lay the basis for a future adaptation to work. The pre-high school child may not, as yet, be really *thinking* about work, but his grade school experiences are important determiners of what he will think about, when the time comes to do the thinking. We shall examine this issue at length in Chapter 8.

The third suggestion has to do with the effects of the total environment with which the child is in continuous transaction. As we have indicated, one of the virtues of many of these empirical studies is that they have forced attention on the role of extraindividual determinants. It is evident that most of these investigators have been confronted with the hard fact that it is not enough to know about personal attributes and that one must also have a great deal of information about the complexities of social environments. This problem has not always been anticipated, but it has asserted itself nonetheless. Of course, by training and inclination, the psychologist finds it easier to fix his attention on personal attributes rather than on the characteristics of environments. The bias is understandable, but it will have to be transcended if we are to gain any real understanding of the complex relations between men and their work.

7 THE CHARACTERISTICS OF WORK ENVIRONMENTS

TOWARD A GENERAL THEORY

In its over-all sense, work behavior can be regarded as the product of the interaction of two sets of variables. One set is made up of certain more or less enduring characteristics of the working individual—his abilities, skills, and aptitudes—and certain habitual patterns of cognitive and emotional responsiveness—his attitudes, opinions, and beliefs. The other set arises from certain characteristics of the work situation, as a particular kind of environment. The work situation may be seen as a special variety of *subculture*, marked by certain traditions, customs, and rules, peopled by individuals who play certain prescribed social roles, requiring from those who participate in it certain specified kinds of behavior. Like culture in general, the work subculture may be looked on as a social environment that makes a set of demands on its participants, demands that elicit certain behaviors deemed "appropriate" and that penalize others deemed "inappropriate."

Obviously, there are many different kinds of work environments, which place quite different demands on those who participate in them. The scope of these differences is implied in the common usage of such terms as *white-collar work, blue-collar work, common labor*, etc. Nevertheless, we want to inquire into the degree to which work environments have common features, while recognizing their differences. We shall also have to be aware of the general culture of which particular work environments are subordinate parts. A tribal society makes work demands on its members very different from those that workers encounter in the highly industrialized cultures of Europe and North America. Similarly, urban work differs greatly from rural work. At present, however, we will concern ourselves with the demand characteristics of work in the largely urbanized, largely industrialized societies, of which the United States is a prime example.

We should emphasize that we are considering here only one side of what is always a two-sided transaction: between the individual and his surround.

Living organisms not only live "in" an environment; they are in a continuous state of interaction with environmental forces. Human behavior is not only a function of the kind of individual the person happens to be but is also a function of what is happening to him. In the ordinary stream of events, these two sets of conditions of behavior are intertwined. We are, therefore, performing something of an abstraction when we propose an analysis of the work environment, since environmental factors are effective only to the degree that they are "perceived" [1] by the individuals exposed to them. The same physical environment may be "perceived" quite differently by different people and different physical environments may be "perceived" as identical. In the material to follow, however, we are not so much concerned with the different reactions of different persons to work as we are with the general features of the work environment. From one point of view, we will be examining a series of "pressures" and "constraints," that is, features of the environment that promote the selection of certain behaviors and the suppression of others (cf. Murray, 1938). From another point of view, we will be laying the basis for a conceptualization of the "modal work personality" (Kardiner, 1939; Inkeles and Levinson, 1954): the set of behaviors that best fits the demands of work. Just as we are looking for those features of work that are common to differing work environments, so also we will wish to find those aspects of the general work situation that tend to make the same demands on everyone, whether or not everyone is capable of meeting these demands in the same way or to the same degree.

STRUCTURAL FEATURES

The Setting

The first and most obvious thing one notes about work in modern society is that it takes place in a particular physical locale: the office, the factory, the construction site, the theater, the library, the school. One must go to work; it is not generally the sort of activity one carries out where one lives. Of course, a few occupations are exempt from this feature. For many writers and artists, their home is their only workplace. There are also a disappearing number of house servants who "live-in," and paid homework still plays a tiny part in the economy. But, by and large, we work in special places designated for this purpose, which are separate from our homes and to which we have to travel.

The Necessity for Travel. This physical separation of the workplace from the home has a number of consequences. First, one must be *able* to

---

[1] We have written the word *perceived* in quotation marks merely because we want to include the possibility that individual behavior may be influenced by events of which the person may not be fully aware.

travel, to use public or private transportation, in order to get to work. While for most of us, this is a relatively trivial demand, for some it is very stringent. Travel to work is a major problem for certain categories of the physically disabled, the severely mentally retarded, some of the emotionally disturbed. The urban explosion is increasingly making getting to work something of a full-time job in itself. It has been pointed out (De Grazia, 1962) that the problems of urban sprawl are adding approximately 2 hours to the working day of the typical worker in the major metropolitan areas. To the degree that choices are possible among jobs, the location of the workplace is becoming almost as much of a distinguishing characteristic as its nature.

The Public Character of Work. The general fact that work is carried on in a specialized locale has more subtle consequences than the travel problem. The physical setting is designated for work, not for love or for play. Thus, it is a *public* place, with stringent limitations on privacy. Most kinds of work are carried out under conditions in which the worker must be prepared to be under more or less continuous observation by both supervisors and peers. This, perhaps, reaches its ultimate extreme in the modern banking institution, in which even leading executives are expected to sit at desks that are in the full view of anyone who passes by. In most instance, however, there is something of a gradation of privacy: The more subordinate the employee, the more public is his work. Certain occupations are relatively exempt from this requirement, either by their nature or by tradition: the physician, the lawyer, the research worker, the higher business executive, and certain other categories of the higher professions. However, even these privileged categories are not exempt from observation while at work, since they are expected to be available to the eyes of their clients and at times, their colleagues.

The public character of work implies that the worker must be prepared to meet a number of quite rigid standards for dress, deportment, and social custom. Even where a special uniform is not required—as it is in the cases of police, mailmen, hospital nurses, and so on—there are many other constraints on the kinds of clothing it is considered desirable or customary to wear. The bank teller will not remain employed very long if he comes to work in slacks and a T-shirt; the bench-worker will be seen as bizarre, at the least, if he works in a suit, shirt, and tie. For both men and women, there are all sorts of rules—written and unwritten—about appropriate grooming and general physical appearance, which differ by occupations. Similarly, a great many customs and traditions regulate forms of greeting, habits of speech, styles of communication, and general deportment. All these expectations combine to form what the theorist of social roles calls the *persona*—in this case, the *work persona*. In other words, the worker must look and act in certain ways that fit certain culturally formed conceptions of the role of a worker. These role conceptions differ sharply between broad occupational groupings (blue-collar work, white-collar work, the professional, the executive, etc.) and also differ somewhat within categories according to one's place in the occupational hierarchy. The *work persona* involves an extremely important set of conditions, which bear upon the ability to secure and maintain employment. No matter what skills and aptitudes a given individual may possess, he cannot too widely depart from the appearances and behaviors that the *work persona* demands.

The Impersonal Character of Work. The work environment is not only largely public, it is also impersonal. The intimate and highly personal relationships characteristic of love or play are not expected on the job and are usually tacitly, if not explicitly, forbidden. While the formation of friendships is common enough—indeed, many people find their only friendships at work, and the loss of them is often one of the negative consequences of retirement or disemployment—it is expected that resulting contacts are to be carried on away from the work area and outside of assigned working hours (i.e., during lunch, on coffee-breaks, after work). Authority figures at the workplace impose their will through other means than those that prevail in the family or on the playing field. The chief characteristic of the work environment is that it constitutes an assembly of relative *strangers*. The worker must learn how to relate to people who are largely or wholly unknown to him and who have hardly more consideration for his personal feelings and qualities than any other stranger has. This impersonal and distant set of attitudes is often a particularly heavy burden on those who may have particularly strong needs for a more personal relationship: the relatively immature, the handicapped, or even simply the seriously troubled.

Time

One of the most dramatic features of work in modern society is that it is so heavily bound by time. Most workers begin their work at a designated hour and end it at another. Specified times are set aside for eating and for rest-periods or coffee-breaks. If work is required for more than a settled number of hours per day, it is described as "overtime" and may require special compensation. Where the kind of work to be performed permits it, production is rated on a temporal basis, and the worker is expected to turn out a given number of units per hour or per day. Lateness is a misdemeanor, and chronic lateness may be grounds for dismissal. It can be argued that nothing so firmly binds one to the clock as the conditions of work in most kinds of modern industry. Again, the higher one rises in the occupational hierarchy, the greater is the worker's freedom from rigid adherence to specified temporal intervals. This greater freedom from temporal constraints has both its positive and negative features. It is true that people in the higher status occupations are not typically *required* to put in a given number of hours (to "punch a clock"), but the number of hours they work is also not limited at its upper end. While actual data are difficult to obtain, it is believed that the higher executives and professionals put in very long hours as compared to their less-favored employees (De Grazia, 1962).

The degree to which the work environment is enmeshed with time marks it off fairly sharply from the environment of the home or the environments of recreation. To waste time at work is frowned on, but society is indulgent with respect to the use of time in other life spheres. Thus, an inability to discipline oneself to the clock constitutes one of the more severe barriers to an adjustment to work, whatever other favorable abilities or aptitudes an individual may display. On the other hand, how one "spends time" at home or at play is one's own business. For a considerable number of people, adherence to rigid temporal requirements constitutes one of the more onerous demands of the work environment. For a few, an adequate adaptation to work is out of the question, because they cannot or will not meet the demands of time.

INTERPERSONAL FEATURES

Among the various things that characterize the general work environment is that it is manifestly a *social* situation. It is peopled by other human beings, to whom the worker must relate in more or less prescribed, more or less conventionalized ways. In recent years, a great deal of interest has developed among industrial psychologists and sociologists in those aspects of work behavior that are influenced by the social organization of the workplace. Ever since the early Hawthorne studies, an increasingly large literature has described the interpersonal structure of a variety of kinds of work situations. Delbert Miller is not alone in arguing that the "success or failure of the worker depends not alone on his job performance but on how he plays his role in the work group," and he defines a work situation as a triangular set of social relationships involving a worker, a work position, and a work group.[2] While we cannot enter into a detailed examination of the many aspects of industrial social relationships that have been studied, we can specify certain of the major interpersonal demands that work places upon the worker.

Attitudes to Authority

The self-employed constitute an increasingly small portion of the general labor force. Most work is performed under supervision, whether direct or indirect, simple or complex. In small industrial or commercial organizations, the employee may be supervised directly by his employer, while in the large organization there may be very complex networks of increasingly

[2]Major references are the works of Bakke (1953), Miller and Form (1957), Haire (1959), Brown (1954), and Whyte (1961).

remote forms of control. In any case, the individual's reactions to the *demands of supervision*—the manner in which he behaves in response to the work demands made on him by a person or persons in a position of authority—reflect one of the more important demands with which he must cope if he is to adapt to work. The authority of the employer is, of course, far from absolute in modern industry. One of the most pervasive preoccupations of industrial sociology has been to try to elicit the amazingly intricate network of formal and informal constraints that limit the degree to which the work supervisor can effectively influence work behavior (cf. McGregor, 1960; Likert, 1961; Katz, Maccoby, and Morse, 1950). Nevertheless, to a greater or lesser degree and in a variety of ways, the worker must be able to meet certain supervisory demands.

The individual's reactions to supervision have both an "upper" and "lower" bound. On the one hand, once he is past an initial period of habituation to a new job, he must show a desired amount of autonomy. His dependence upon supervision cannot be so great that his work suffers unless he is kept under close and continuous supervision. On the other hand, the degree to which he is expected and permitted to work "on his own" has certain limits, which vary from job to job and situation to situation. The work environment thus demands of the individual worker that he is able to maintain some expected balance between *dependence* and *independence*. The maintenance of an adequate balance, as well as the ability to shift between these behavioral opposites as the situation demands, constitutes a crucial requirement of adaptation to most work situations. It is not too much to say that failures in job performance and subsequent dismissals may more often be due to insufficiencies on this dimension than because of a sheer lack of some required skill or aptitude.

Attitudes to Peers

A second kind of social demand has to do with the *demands of work-peers*. Ever since the studies of Roethlisberger and Dickson (1939), we have been increasingly aware that much work behavior is influenced by the work group. Many individuals experience difficulty in maintaining employment because they cannot or will not conform to the social expectancies of their work-peers. The social demands of co-workers are by no means so obvious as those of the boss, but they are not the less powerful. We are referring here not only to certain expected behavioral standards related to cooperation and competition, but also to more subtle matters of personal interaction. The work behavior of the individual must again meet certain upper and lower bounds, which are set both by the informal consensus of his work-peers and by the demands of his employer or supervisor. He can neither be a "rate-buster" nor so poor a worker that his co-workers must take up the slack for him.

This demand for conformity to the informal standards of the work group is fairly well known and has received intensive study from time to time (Wilensky, 1957). Not so well known, however, is the degree to which an individual's general personal behavior can be grounds for a serious maladaptation to work (cf. Stogdill, 1959). The person who is seen as bizarre or obnoxious by his work-peers, or even simply as a convenient target for "kidding," can be made miserable in a thousand ways. Professionals who deal with the mentally retarded or the emotionally disturbed are familiar with many instances in which such persons could not maintain employment chiefly because they were subjected to so much "kidding" or outright hostility that the work environment became intolerable. Even where these extremes are not encountered, the limited, immature, or disturbed individual may demand from his fellows more than they can reasonably give or may find them to be more indifferent to his personal problems than he can tolerate. Just as the social demands of work require the maintenance of a balance as between cooperative and competitive behavior, they also require a balance between the intimate and the casual. The typical work situation is neither so intimately personal as the environment of the family nor so wholly accidental as the environment of the street. Again, a variable and flexible balance must be maintained between the personal and the impersonal if an adequate adaptation to work is to be made.

CUSTOMS AND MORES

Like any subculture, the work situation derives its customs, behavioral rules, and traditions in part from the general culture of which it comprises a subdivision and in part from its own needs and peculiar history. Earlier we examined the cultural history of work, including both the different meanings assigned to work by different societies in the course of human history and also the kinds of work behavior that different societies have considered appropriate. Here we are concerned with those aspects of the work subculture characteristic of work in the highly industrialized society.

The primary aim of human work is, of course, *production*: the planned alteration of our physical and mental environment so that certain of our biological and social needs can be fulfilled. As we have earlier argued, however, work is not a "natural" or biological activity, like respiration or digestion. Also, except in rare instances, we do not work because of the immediate pleasures attendant upon the activity; such immediate connections between activity and gratification are far more characteristic of the domains of love and play. The gratifications attendant upon work tend to be indirect, roundabout, and heavily enmeshed with complex social arrangements. Essentially, it is the culture that provides the motivations for work and the ultimate rewards for its performance.

The Role of the General Culture

The first major issue in this connection has to do with the *compulsion to work*. Modern society is not able to organize its workers through naked force, as is characteristic of social systems based on various forms of slavery. No one today can be directly compelled to work, either by formal law or by force. Nevertheless, much is implied by the frequently repeated statement that ours is a work-oriented society. A great many formal and informal social arrangements have been developed that have the objective of transforming the nonworking child into the working adult. From comparatively early childhood, the individual is increasingly showered with messages designed to convince him that work is not only a necessary means to certain universally designed ends—maturity, independence, marriage, respect, etc.— but also something good in itself. Not an inconsiderable part of our formal religious teaching is devoted to this conception, although the major established religions approach this issue from somewhat differing standpoints. Similarly, the school is not only designed by society to equip its young with intellectual skills, but is a powerful shaping and modeling institution in its own right. It instills in its captive audiences an entire network of values, habits and attitudes that play a very important function in preparing children for later roles as adult workers. Of course, in addition to such institutionalized forces, of which organized religion and education are merely examples, modern society also has at its command an enormous folklore bearing upon the virtues and rewards of work. To the degree that children incorporate and internalize all these precepts, they become more or less willing workers. Where the massive indoctrination fails and the child grows to physical maturity either with very weak motivation to work or with counter-motivations, he is soon made aware that society has in reserve a powerful array of punishments and deprivations. For most of us, this entire system of cultural norms and sanctions works so well that prolonged periods of involuntary unemployment produce feelings of personal guilt and worthlessness, despite the fact that we may "know" that some massive economic dislocation beyond our control has brought it about.

Although the heaviest cultural guns in modern society are brought to bear upon the motivation to work, there are countervailing forces as well. Many observers of the contemporary social scene (e.g., Bell, 1956; Riesman, Glazer, and Danny, 1950; Whyte, 1956; Goodman, 1960) appear to be convinced that the work-oriented cultural pressures we have been discussing were far more characteristic of the nineteenth century than of the twentieth, and that new pressures antagonistic to the work-culture are arising. These writers express alarm that a rapidly advancing technology is rendering many kinds of work so routinized and mechanical that there is an acute danger that work is becoming meaningless to those who perform it. Further, it is pointed out by some (cf. Harrington, 1962) that increasingly stable "pockets of poverty" are producing a situation in which successive generations of people are excluded from the work-culture and in which children grow to maturity without any of the normal cultural pressures and inducements to acquire the motivation to work. Many other components of contemporary society also serve to balance the overwhelming force of the compulsion to work: the long-run secular trends toward shortening of the working day and working week, the increasing emphasis on recreation and self-development, the moderating influence of the trade unions, and the gradually widening conception that labor is a salable commodity like any other and thus neither a mission nor a duty. On balance, however, the work-orienting forces in our culture appear still to be far stronger than those that press against it, although the latter have the potential of becoming major problems for the industrial society of the future.

The Specific Subculture of Work

Quite apart from the pressures and counterpressures of the general culture, the work situation constitutes a special subarea of culture in itself. Like other subcultures, the subculture of work has its own rather special customs and traditions, assigns roles to people in special ways, develops unique kinds of private languages, and even has its own mystique. One becomes a participating member of the work subculture by a process of enculturation, and this process may be as difficult for some persons as the process of becoming Americanized is difficult for some adult immigrants. Although we cannot here deal with these issues so exhaustively as they merit, we shall single out several features for comment.

Language and Demeanor. A great many occupations demand that their participants acquire special vocabularies and styles of speech, some of which are technical but some of which are also the slang of the trade. In the cases of some of the older crafts (e.g., railroad, construction, the printing trades, many of the learned professions), conversation among habitués becomes almost unintelligible to the outsider, so much so that it becomes almost a secret language, a badge of the occupation. The new entrant is either the object of tacit exclusion or an open butt for derision until he learns the appropriate lingo. Similarly, customs and rituals concerning styles of dress tend to become the special badges of certain occupations. Examples are the high-crowned cap of the railroad engineer, the bright-colored protective headgear of the construction worker, the "gray-flannel suit," the work-shirt versus the button-down shirt, the "neat-but-not-gaudy" clothing required of the female clerical worker, the blazer and flannel trousers that were the trademark of the Oxford don. Quite apart from the special uniforms required of policemen and nurses, these styles of common dress serve to mark off the tyro from the veteran and have the same symbolic meaning as the semisecret occupational language. Both speech and dress, as well as more subtle aspects of demeanor and general behavior, are identifying signs of the members of the subculture of work, in the same sense that these characteristics are used to unite the members of any in-group against "the others."

Gender. One of the more striking features of the work subculture is the extent to which very sharp distinctions are made between men's work and women's work. The division of labor according to sex is probably the oldest kind of differential role assignment in the history of society (cf. Tilgher, 1930) and, although it has changed in detail, is still very powerful. Even in contemporary society, where more than one-third of the labor force is female, there are a great many occupations that are exclusively or almost entirely peopled by one or the other of the sexes, despite the fact that there may be nothing in the required skills that demands such specialization.

The traditional sexual division of labor undoubtedly made biological sense at one time. The ancient male occupations—hunting, the herding of animals, heavy agriculutre—placed premiums on muscular power, physical endurance, fighting ability, and freedom from the requirement to care for children. The occupations of women had to be consistent with their sole responsibility for the nurturing of children. With the rise of modern industry, however, the force of these requirements has greatly diminished. Nevertheless, people still have very firm ideas of what is men's work and what is women's work, and heavy resistance is offered against the crossing of traditional barriers. Although women today work in large numbers, they are largely to be found in light manufacturing (although the foremen and higher executives are usually men), in certain service and consumer industries, in the lower levels of white-collar work, and in such traditional female occupations as nursing, teaching, and social work (where again the administrative and executive positions are often filled by men). For a man to do women's work is seen as demeaning and emasculating, often raising suspicions of latent or manifest homosexuality. Similarly, women who enter occupations traditionally reserved for males frequently have to struggle against the threat of loss of female identification (Roe and Siegelman, 1964).

These distinctions are largely, if not entirely, cultural and social in their origin, at least in highly industrialized societies. There is really nothing in the modern techniques required of the ministry or of medicine that indicates that men should perform them, yet female pastors or physicians are still comparatively rare in the United States. The rapid development of technology has abolished muscle power from most industrial tasks, but most basic industrial production is still carried out by males. While we can expect that the barriers between men's and women's work will continue to erode, since the work environment has so greatly changed, gender will remain a major feature of the work subculture for some time to come.[3]

Status and Role. Another very prominent feature of the work subculture is the degree to which it is permeated by very elaborate provisions bearing

[3]The issues concerned with women at work will be treated in more detail in Chapter 14. Although major changes are taking place in the 1980s, most women are still bound by tradition.

on social status and social roles. Modern industrial, commercial, and professional enterprises are strongly hierarchical in their structure, with clearly
marked pecking orders. The boss is addressed as "Mister," but he in turn
calls his office secretary by her first name. Familiarity tends to travel on a
one-way street. Similarly, the shop foreman is distinguished by his white
shirt and tie, by the pens in his shirt-pocket, and the clip-board in his hand,
while the bench-worker wears less formal clothing. As one moves up the
executive scale in the industrial enterprise, one acquires all sorts of distinguishing features: the rug on the floor, the water carafe on the desk, the
larger and more private office, the private washroom, the executive dining-
room. All these are not merely the privileges of rank; they are also the
jealously guarded marks of status.

Part of the process of becoming a worker, therefore, is the intricate manner of learning how to behave with one's peers, subordinates, and superiors.
That this is not a simple matter for everyone is attested to by the fierce
internecine quarrels that mark many work settings in which people of different ranks are supposed to be performing some cooperative task. Office
frictions are almost a commonplace, and people often leave their jobs or are
dismissed because they cannot relate to their colleagues in accepted and
appropriate ways.

In recent years, industrial psychologists and sociologists have intensively
studied interpersonal relations on the job, with special attention given to
both formal and informal roles and statuses (cf. books by Haire, 1959;
Bakke, 1953; Form and Miller, 1960). The point that is frequently made
turns around the distinction between the "office" and the "person." The
former is defined by a rationally derived set of rules that are developed to fix
authority and responsibility. The behavior of the latter is influenced not only
by the particular characteristics of the individual who happens to "fill" the
office but also by a wide variety of folkways, mores, norms, and values.
These encompass all the animosities and friendships, emotional supports,
and frictions that exist among the people who work in the same shop or
office. The goals and objectives of the informal work group may have nothing to do with or may even oppose the rational goals of production and
efficiency that characterize the formal organization of work. Roethlisberger
and Dickson (1939) were among the first to study the important role of the
informal work group in influencing the process of production, and many
studies have followed since their work.

The Worker Role. The complexities of modern society are such that
most persons must be able to play a fairly large number of differing roles,
some of which demand behaviors that may be quite contradictory.[4] The

---

[4]The concept of *worker-role* and the accompanying problems of role conflict and
role ambiguity have been dealt with most fully by J. R. P. French and R. L. Kahn
(1962) of the Survey Research Center of the University of Michigan. Since these
researches bear directly on the relations of work and mental health, we shall examine them in some detail in Chapter 13 on work stress.

same man may be called upon to be authoritative and decisive within the family, obedient and compliant on the job, cheerful and outgoing with his friends. It is not surprising that some people find these wide shifts in expectations difficult to meet and are unable to play one or another or all of these roles effectively. Since the role of the worker is one of the more important roles people are expected to play, it is useful to summarize the sorts of behaviors that are required.

First, the individual must have some motivation to work, although the precise nature and source of his motivation may vary widely from person to person. Second, he must have some necessary minimum of aptitude and skill. Third, he must be able to conform to certain work-rules. Fourth, he must be able to meet certain minimal standards for productivity and quality. Fifth, he must "look" like a worker, that is, he must meet certain conventional standards for dress, demeanor, and deportment, with the additional proviso that he must have awareness of what is expected from him in different occupations and workplaces. Sixth, he must be able to relate appropriately to various kinds of people on the job, showing the required amount of respect to his superiors and the required amount of camaraderie with his peers. Seventh, he must be able to shift his emotional and cognitive gears well enough so that he can "turn on" all those behaviors appropriate to work and "turn off" all those affects and needs that are mobilized and gratified by other settings.

This is a fairly impressive list of role requirements, and note that only one of the seven components bears upon skill and ability. The process by which the individual learns how to meet the role requirements of working can be described as a process of *work enculturation*. Similarly, people who are unable or unwilling to play the role of a worker, whatever work skills they possess, can be described in terms of *work acculturation*.

THE MODAL WORK PERSONALITY

In describing the general features of the work situation, we have also given a list of specifications for succesful adaptation to work. The individual who can meet these requirements without undue strain or conflict is a participant member—a citizen—of the work subculture, with all rights, duties, obligations, and privileges pertaining thereto. He is able to distinguish the workplace both from home and the playing field and adjust his behavior accordingly. He is able to leave his home to go to work without falling apart in the process. He is capable, within limits, of looking and behaving like the other members of his work group. He can live a public life as well as a private one, and he can reduce his needs for intimacy without undue deprivation. He can regulate his life by the clock, to the degree that the job requires. He can permit himself to be supervised by strangers, without being rendered so angry by supervision that he cannot function, or so servile that he loses all initiative. He can relate to his fellow-workers in ways that they deem acceptable. Finally, he can take on the protective coloration of the local customs and traditions that we have summed up as the "worker role."

It should be perfectly clear that the above-stated list of requirements are those of a *role-model*. Not everyone becomes adept in meeting all of those requirements, and many fall short in meeting one or more of them. By and large, however, they sum up to the kind of *persona* demanded by a work-oriented society. Where accidents of his life-history (severe poverty, physical, mental, or emotional disability, ethnic or religious prejudice, etc.) render a person unable to meet these requirements, he will tend to become classified as vocationally maladapted and will become an object of social concern. It is becoming increasingly likely that the maladapted individual will come to the attention of a corrective or ameliorative agency: a rehabilitation center, a vocational guidance service, an "anti-poverty" program, and so forth. It appears evident that such agencies cannot merely offer the vocationally maladapted a course of vocational training in a given skill area and expect that the person's problem has thereby been solved. The demands that work makes upon people are multidimensional, and the acquisition of a given work-skill is only a part—albeit, an important part—of the adjustment problem. Modern vocational diagnosis requires an estimate also of those areas of the work subculture that the individual has not incorporated or has incorporated very poorly. Corrective action must involve procedures aimed at general work enculturation as well as training for particular aptitudes and skills.

THE TWOFOLD ASPECT OF WORK ENVIRONMENTS

The environmental determinants of work behavior have a twofold aspect. On the one hand, they constitute a set of extraindividual conditions with which the person must somehow cope if he is to work at all. In this sense, they exist outside him, just as the components of a culture exist outside a particular infant who happens to be born into it. In another sense, however, they also exist in his head, since many of the determinants of work behavior play important shaping roles in individual development. Cultural forces are not wholly independent entities; they not only act upon people from without, but they are also *internalized* by their human objects in various ways and to varying extents. Most people are able to meet the demand characteristics of the work environment because they have already been prepared to meet them through a long process of social growth. If we want to know why people work, or—and this is perhaps the more interesting question—why they work in so many different ways, we will have to learn more about the details of this developmental process. Work is not merely a set of responses; it is also a set of adaptations.

Consequently, serious study of work environments is also a twofold task.

One part of the study is cross-sectional and deals with a given moment in time. Its objective is to identify the *present* conditions that influence work behavior. But it is also necessary to determine how past environments have become incorporated in present behavior potentials. In this sense, a comprehensive study of work environments must be longitudinal as well. On the one hand, we need to be capable of specifying a given work pressure (e.g., the demands of supervision). On the other hand, we need to know how the individual was shaped by previous environmental encounters so that he meets this demand in some specified manner. In this chapter, we have attempted to identify the chief pressures and constraints that are characteristic of the "typical" work environment. So far, our analysis has been cross-sectional, in the sense that the demand characteristics of work appear to exist "outside" the person who encounters them. But supervision is effective only to the degree that workers permit themselves to be supervised. We now need to consider the long-range variables, initially functioning as external forces, that play a role in vocational development.

8 | WORK BEHAVIOR AND THE WORK PERSONALITY

So far, we have examined those aspects of human work that comprise a kind of sociocultural environment. We have described some of the more important demands that work environments make upon people, and we have specified that the demand characteristics of work environments constitute one of two sets of variables that together influence the total process of human work. Let us now consider the second set of variables: those that characterize the individual human being who works. In this chapter, we explore the broad categories of psychological baggage that the worker brings with him to the job. The manner and efficiency with which the individual is able to work—including his ability to work at all—is a function of three groups of component factors: (1) the kinds of affects that work arouses or permits, (2) the bearing of work on the individual's conception of his identity as a person; (3) the needs that work fulfills or frustrates.

WORK AND THE AFFECTS

To say that work engages the human emotions, as well as the cognitive and motor aspects of behavior, appears to be stating the obvious. Yet this problem has been little studied. The vast body of literature on man's emotional life—whether literary or scientific—focuses its attention on other life-spheres—love and marriage, friendship and war, play and arts, etc. Until comparatively recently, investigators interested in work behavior were concerned largely with technical and rational matters: the material and organizational variables that influenced productivity, the intellectual and motor skills required for different kinds of work, the manifest rewards attached to work by society at large, and so on. During the past two or three decades, however, students of work behavior have become increasingly aware that the worker does not become an automaton the moment he steps into the place of work.

Since the appearance of the classical summary of the Hawthorne research (Roethlisberger and Dickson, 1939), an entire generation of industrial psychologists has turned its attention to studies of the worker as a feeling and experiencing human being. Unfortunately, the focus of the bulk of these studies has been rather narrow. The general strategy of this body of research has been to attempt to establish relationships between the attitudes of the worker to his work situation (considered as a set of independent variables) and certain aspects of work performance (considered as a set of dependent variables). Various investigators have attempted to develop procedures for measuring or assessing work satisfaction (cf. Hoppock, 1935; Brayfield and Rothe, 1951; Herzberg, Mausner, and Snyderman, 1959), and efforts have been made to relate these indices to such criteria of work performance as productivity, absenteeism, labor turnover, promotion, etc. Excellent summaries of the current state of these research efforts are found in books by Gellerman (1963) and Vroom (1964).

In considering this entire approach to the psychology of work, two observations are in order. First, despite more than two decades of intensive effort, the precise nature of the relationships between work satisfaction and work efficiency remains elusive. Second, *satisfaction* is too abstract a term to tell us very much about the affect sides of work. We will examine each of these issues more closely.

Assuming that reliable measures of job satisfaction can be devised and assuming further that reliable indices of work efficiency are readily obtainable, there is still no reason to expect that any very clear or close relationships should be found to exist between these two sets of measures. Even a minimal analysis of the manner in which work is organized in contemporary society suggests the operation of a great many intervening variables. First, there is the problem of the occupational level of the workers under study. The conditions that influence work behavior and the degree to which job satisfaction can be a significant variable are manifestly very different in the several cases of unskilled laborers, assembly-line workers, foremen, middle-line executives, and self-employed professionals. Among many intervening variables that operate with different force in different occupations are: (1) the degree to which output is under the control of the individual worker; (2) the relative amounts of horizontal and vertical mobility that are realistically possible; (3) the very wide differences in the objectivity and scope of standards of performance; (4) the enormous differences in the nature and kinds of interpersonal relationships that the different occupations entail; (5) the highly differential weights placed on such norms and values as achievement and ambition.

A second set of intervening variables arises in terms of whether the orientation of the study is toward the individual firm or toward an entire sector of the general labor force, that is, whether, for example, we are studying assembly-line workers in general or assembly-line workers in a particular industry (e.g., automotive) or assembly-line workers in a particular unit of General Motors. The conditions that may influence job satisfaction and criteria of efficiency can be expected to vary from department to department, firm to firm, from industry to industry, and even in terms of geographical and ecological considerations. Among probable sources of variation are: (1) the labor policies of the particular industrial unit, including the precise manner in which they are carried out; (2) the presence or absence of a labor union, as well as the manner in which it operates; (3) the variable degree to which more informal forms of worker organization exist (à la Hawthorne); (4) local variations in the demographic and subcultural composition of the labor force; (5) traditional values and norms concerning work, which can vary by industry, by locality, and by firm.

The two sets of intervening variables we have briefly inventoried constitute only some of the more obvious complications in attempting to establish relationships between job satisfaction and work efficiency. It is not surprising, therefore, that inconsistent findings tend to be the rule rather than the exception (cf. Herzberg et al., 1957). Similarly, those studies that report positive findings disclose relationships that are quite weak, accounting, in most instances, for hardly more than 10% of the observed variance in work efficiency.[1] Quite without regard to the amount of error inherent in the various available measures of satisfaction and efficiency, it seems evident that the satisfaction derived from his work by the individual worker is only one of a great many variables affecting his work behavior.

While the research on job satisfaction has called our attention to the fact that work arouses feelings and emotions as well as requiring aptitudes and skills, "satisfaction" is a vague abstraction. It does not reveal the precise kinds of emotions aroused in individuals by the work they do. A person might report himself as "dissatisfied" with his supervisor, but what he actually feels is not made clear. Is the dominant emotion aroused by supervision one of anger? Fear? Feelings of reduced personal worth? Generalized anxiety? Will supervision in general arouse these feelings or does he respond differentially to different kinds of supervisors? Is he the kind of person who simply cannot work well under supervision, or does the kind of supervision offered make a difference? Individuals obviously come into work situations with very different attitudes and dispositions with respect to authority. At one extreme, there are persons who are basically unemployable because any kind of supervision arouses such negative affects that work is intolerable. At another extreme, there are people who cannot work at all unless they are closely and continuously supervised. The supervisor himself may operate in ways that are very authoritative and dictatorial or generally permissive and supportive. The affects aroused by supervision are a highly idiosyncratic affair, varying from person to person both in terms of his ha-

---

[1]We have made this point before in connection with the studies of the Lofquist–Dawis group (see pp. 119ff.).

bitual styles of response to authority and in terms of the kind and quality of supervision to which he is exposed.

What has been largely missing from this field is a "clinical" approach to the problems inherent in the affect sides of work. The research conducted has tended to be exclusively psychometric, with interest focused on statistical relationships between a measure of satisfaction and a measure of work efficiency. The individual as an individual is overlooked, and different persons may get the same "score" on a measure for quite different reasons. While the study of discrete individuals has its technical limits, it is to be hoped that such study will lead to a limited number of characteristic "types" or "styles" of affective responses to work, so that it will eventually be possible to classify people in recognizable subgroups with distinctive properties (e.g., the impulse-ridden, the hostile, the fearful, the anxious) (see Chapter 11). This theory is in accord with the generally accepted proposition that human beings behave, in some respects, like all other human beings; in other respects, like only certain subgroupings of other persons; in still other respects, each person's behavior is recognizably unique.

WORK AND IDENTITY

A great many writers assert that the major psychological problem of contemporary society is the problem of identity (Erikson, 1963; Wheelis, 1953; Fromm, 1948, 1955). Many factors are labeled determinants of the "identity crisis": the population explosion, massive trends toward urbanization, the bewildering pace of technological and social change, erosion of traditional value-systems under the pressures of the scientific world outlook, the breakup of the extended family, and the like. The point stressed is that in less complex and less rapidly changing societies, a great many provisions were in force to help the individual know who he is, but that these supports are being swept away. In former times, it is argued, the individual was clearly aware that he was a full member of a given tribe, a kinship group, a family. He was a noble or a commoner, a warrior or a peasant. He had a place to live and familiar surroundings. He had a prescribed and often very detailed set of religious beliefs, by which he could regulate his behavior. Rituals and initiation ceremonies marked his passage from childhood to maturity to old age. The behavior expected from males was clearly different from that expected from females, and there was no problem of confusion of roles. The issue of who he was could hardly arise. He had a name known to others, a lineage, an extended family, a clearly marked status, and a set of revealed beliefs that guided the important actions of his life.

While this idyllic picture is very overdrawn, emphasizing only certain of the virtues of static societies by ignoring their equally obvious defects, the concept of an *identity crisis* has a certain plausible ring. The huge aggregations of unrelated people in sprawling urban areas, the requirements of modern industry for a highly mobile and ever-changing labor force, the increasing openness of society, the elevation of innovation itself into a major virtue, the immense achievements of the natural sciences—all these have brought many traditional value-systems under sharp attack. Such determinants of identity as name, lineage, religion, race, or nationality are still identifying characteristics to which people cling. However, they are losing their force and have not been replaced by a very adequate set of substitute identifiers.

Although certain traditional marks of identity appear to be eroding, the relationships of work and identity appear to be taking on enhanced significance. People are no longer asked who they are but *what they do*. Children are frequently asked and are frequently quite prepared to answer, "What do you want to be when you grow up?" The expected answer is in terms of some kind of occupation ("I want to be a doctor," "a lawyer," "a professional ball-player," "a teacher," "a nurse," "an engineer"). The expectation may be entirely unrealistic, but the question itself would not be asked in societies where the life-pattern is largely determined by birth and lineage. Where it was once generally expected that a boy will follow in his father's footsteps, it is now safer to expect that he will not. Of course, it is still a great deal easier for the son of a businessman to become a business executive than it is for the son of a common laborer. Our society is still far from completely open, and many millions still suffer constraints imposed by ethnic origin, race, minority group status, social class, etc. But it cannot be doubted that there has been an explosion of expectations, and that the eyes of multitudes are now fixed on what they can become rather than on what they are.

How does this process take place in the life of the individual person? In modern society, the key arena is undoubtedly the school and the critical years from about the age of 5 or 6 on (cf. Erikson, 1963). The goals the child is able to develop vis-à-vis the process of formal education, his ability to achieve, his motivation and opportunity for continued education, are all major determinants of the kind of occupational identity he will attain. Of course, the school does not exist in a vacuum, nor is it the sole determinant of occupational choice. The school is a microcosm of the larger society that it serves and it faithfully mirrors whatever stresses, strains, conflicts, and contradictions characterize the society as a whole. If groups of people tend to be undervalued in society at large, by reason of ethnic status, religion, social class, or other identificatory stigmata, then their children tend to get the least attention in school as well. The child also brings with him into the school certain vital styles of behavior and personality that were imposed by his familial, preschool experience, and these influences persist throughout most of his school life. In addition, he is subject to the influence of non-familial peers and adults, to the subculture of the street, and to the countless communications that come to him via the mass media.

Although his school performance is a complex product of all of these determiners, it is the school performance itself that becomes the crucial determinant of his later occupational role. The school drop-out is mostly confined to unskilled, common labor, since almost any kind of skilled work requires some mastery of the high school subjects. In general, although there is far from a perfect correlation, the more skilled, rewarding, and prestigious an occupation is, the more formal education it requires. The upper limits on the amount of education needed for many higher-level occupations are variable, but these requirements are increasing all the time. Businessmen, who once extolled the virtues of the "school of hard knocks," now want their junior executives to have advanced degrees from graduate schools of business administration. In the United States today, a major portion of one's occupational identity is formulated and fixed by the nature and extent of one's formal schooling.

There are both risks and advantages in the enhanced relation between work and identity. In a society marked by great physical and social mobility, the possession of a recognizable and marketable skill is a great asset. The individual no longer need be bound to a traditional abode or to a kinship group in order to have an identity. He can go anywhere, work anywhere, and still feel that he has a definite role and status. He may end by feeling a stronger sense of identification with his work-colleagues than with his family and childhood friends. But this shift in values entails many dangers and losses as well. Work in modern society is characterized by an elaborate hierarchy of statuses, rewards, and prestige. If the work an individual does is an increasingly important factor in his identity, then people in lower-status positions run the risk of reduced feelings of personal worth. That this is indeed the case is indicated by studies of the mental health of industrial workers (cf. Kornhauser, 1965). Workers in lower-level occupations have many more negative feelings about themselves than those in higher-level occupations, which they attribute to the kind of work they are limited to perform. It may also be questioned whether the gaining of an identity through work is as vital and meaningful to people as the more traditional marks of identity. Compared to the family, the kinship group, the village, or the church, the workplace is relatively cold and impersonal. Also, disemployment and retirement may become a greater threat where work becomes the chief arena for all rewarding interpersonal relations. Studies of the aging worker indicate that cessation of work may involve a major breakdown of important marks of identity (cf. Kutner et al., 1956).

For better or worse, however, in heavily industrialized societies such as ours, one of the important components of work behavior is its function in contributing to one's sense of identity. A great many occupations are characterized not only by distinctive styles of dress, modes of speech, uses of leisure time, but also by differing political, social, and cultural attitudes. An interesting subspecialty of the sociology of work is devoted to systematic study of the life-styles characteristic of various occupations (e.g., the waitress, the physician, the factory worker) (compare the work of Everett Hughes [1959] and his associates). Given that occupations have some influence upon personality style and general behavior, we must avoid the oversimplified inference that the various occupations are characterized by distinctive personality types (e.g., the obsessive accountant, the extroverted salesman, the withdrawn laboratory researcher). On the contrary, it is more likely to be true that there is more variance in personality style *within* occupations than between them. The major occupational categories (law, medicine, factory work) refer to work domains of sufficient internal complexity so that there is room in each for a wide range of occupational roles and a similar wide range of personality styles. Efforts to use personality tests to select for various occupations have met with little success, although there is somewhat more support for the belief that successful practitioners in the various occupations develop differing patterns of interests and attitudes (cf. Strong, 1943, 1955). It seems fairly safe to conclude that the kind of work one does makes some contribution to one's sense of identity and personality style, but work is far from being the exclusive determinant of these personal characteristics. This entire problem needs much more study.

WORK AND HUMAN NEEDS

In declaring that work fulfills or frustrates certain human needs, we are entering the province of motivation. Man is ingenious in inventing needs that his subsequent behavior is designed to gratify. The motivation for work is an extremely complex affair, still not very well understood. At the same time, it is generally agreed that work motivation is one of the most important determinants of work behavior. Phrasing this question in the extreme, why do people work at all? More specifically, why do different people mobilize their energies for work and focus their interests and attention on work in such varying degrees?

Material Needs

At first glance, it may seem silly to ask this question at all, since the answer appears self-evident. People work for money. Although the obvious answer is far from complete, it should not be ignored. Work is, by its nature, an instrumental activity, performed in order to procure the necessities of existence, no matter how broadly the term *necessities* is construed. While modern students of work motivation often appear to be arguing that work behavior is influenced by many motives in addition to monetary reward (Vroom, 1964; Herzberg et al., 1959), it would require some very convincing new evidence and arguments to prove that other motives operate effectively in the total absence of monetary recompense. For economic reasons, the other motives for work may be of greater interest to employers of labor than the strictly monetary motive. An industrialist will be pleased indeed to learn how he can secure increased output without increasing his wage bill. Nevertheless, the monetary rewards consequent upon work constitute one of the primary motives governing the work behavior of the employee. In the modern industrialized society, whether capitalist or communist, money is the essential medium of exchange and the prerequisite for material existence. While the love of money may be the root of all evil, money is also the chief means by which people estimate the quality and quantity of their work.

However, it would be quite mistaken to believe that people work for monetary motives alone. A worker may function ineffectively even when monetary rewards are readily available. Human work is an arena for a great many kinds of human interactions and implicates a great many different motives. One of the signal achievements of 30 years of research into work motivation has been a demonstration of the wide range of needs that are fulfilled or frustrated by different kinds of work. We shall briefly consider some of the more important motivators for work, which operate in interaction with those that are primarily related to economic need.

Self-Esteem

The relationships of work and self-esteem have both absolute and relative aspects. From the absolute point of view, the totally idle tend to be derogated as drones or parasites. Although it is said that our society is becoming less heavily work-oriented, a person still has to have a good reason to be totally idle. He either must be too young to work (still in school), too old to work (officially retired), or too handicapped. There are thus clear associations between work and maturity, work and normality. Being unemployed is never a happy condition and is supportable only to the degree that it is regarded as temporary. Society goes to considerable lengths to ensure that individuals who are not able to work because of some handicapping condition do not enjoy themselves at public expense. Being a worker is a condition for full citizenship in most societies and provides a guarantee for some measure of autonomy and a feeling of personal worth. Being a nonworker is a sign of "second-class citizenship" and is strongly associated with reduced feelings of personal worth. For most workers, the depth of the relations between work and self-esteem are not very evident. Since they are able to work, they are quite free to spend their time thinking about its negative aspects. But those who are unable to work for reasons beyond their control—the victims of technological unemployment, people who are without work by reason of bias or prejudice, the mentally, emotionally, or physically handicapped—tend to perceive unemployment as a calamity and a disgrace.

Self-esteem varies according to the different amounts of prestige associated with different occupations and with different levels within given occupations. It has been repeatedly demonstrated that the various occupations form a very elaborate status hierarchy in such a country as the United States. In a comprehensive study conducted by the National Opinion Research Center (1947), a national sample of respondents were asked to rate 47 occupations for prestige. Some of the occupations that received the top ten ratings were: Supreme Court Justice, physician, high government official, college teacher, scientist, lawyer, minister, engineer, business executive, and banker. Factory owner was twelfth, public school teacher sixteenth, and farm owner eighteenth. The bottom ten occupations included farm hand, miner, service worker, janitor, and share-cropper, with shoe shiner at the bottom. It should be noted that the order of prestige is not identical with relative remuneration, although of course there is considerable correspondence.

Different increments of self-esteem are also implicated in the position a worker has vis-à-vis the promotional ladder within an occupation. Senior executives obviously enjoy more prestige than junior executives, journeyman carpenters more than their apprentices. The negative effects of these promotional hierarchies are somewhat restrained as long as the individual is moving up the rungs. They tend to become severe when he gets stuck at a rung and begins to see younger people pass him by. One of the more frequent causes for serious occupational maladaptation among businessmen is the increasing feeling in a middle-level executive that he has reached a dead-end, that he is being passed over, that he is "over-age and under-grade."

Besides the supports or hazards to self-esteem that may be posed by the vagaries of occupational mobility, the nature of the work environment itself appears to have implications for self-esteem. Wilensky has pointed out (Wilensky, 1961) that the features of work that appear to affect self-esteem may be summarized under three sets of variables: relative freedom from constraint, relative authority and responsibility, and the degree of opportunity for social interaction. Herzberg et al. have offered a complex theory (1959) that distinguishes "job-dissatisfiers" and "job-satisfiers"; the latter generally bear on self-actualization, while the former bear chiefly on the technical conditions of work. Kornhauser's excellent studies (1965) of the mental health of factory workers yield abundant evidence that a person's feeling of personal worth is strongly and negatively influenced by the conviction that he is simply an unimportant cog in a giant industrial machine.

In general, work appears to have important implications for the perception by individuals of their worth as persons, although we must be cautious in assigning weight to this factor. As in the case of material needs, self-esteem is a complex and elusive variable, not easy to measure and quite confounded with other factors (Wylie, 1961). People in the same occupational level may also vary greatly in the degree to which their self-esteem is fulfilled or frustrated by the work they do (Korman, 1967). Work is only one of several major areas of human interaction, and people differ very widely in their commitment to it. It would be a drastic error to believe that all or most members of a given low-status occupation have, as a consequence, reduced feelings of personal worth. Most of the data we have are based on statistical studies of large populations, and there is plenty of room for overlap at the various levels. There is, however, increasing evidence that work is one means by which people assess their personal worth. For some people, it is almost the sole available means. The professional who deals with the problems of the handicapped is frequently impressed by the high evaluation placed on work by people who are prevented from performing it. People who have made a relatively easy adaptation to work may often take it for granted and feel its loss only when, for whatever reason, they become unemployed.

Activity

Another need that work may frustrate or fulfill is the need to be active, to avoid boredom, to fill up the day with things to do. One of the more serious consequences of forced unemployment or retirement, for people who have been habituated workers, is an inability to find enough to do. Similarly, a wealthy individual who has no compelling monetary need to work may seek some kind of employment just to reduce feelings of restlessness that have become intolerable. People in whom this need is strong tend to find vacations a burden and flee back to their work with a feeling of relief. Work also has a function for some in binding their anxieties, draining off inacceptable or inappropriate impulses, "taking their minds off their troubles."

Comparitively little hard information is available on this role of work. Much of what we know is derived from a few studies of the unemployed worker (Bakke, 1934, 1940) during the period of the 1930s and from the reactions of the aged to retirement from work. Much of the rest is based on anecdotal data or on case histories. We also face certain conceptual difficulties in understanding what is meant by such phrases as the "need for activity," or "freedom from boredom." Clearly, what is to be done is at least as important as the mere fact of doing it. Certain kinds of work are, by their nature, so monotonous and repetitive that the mere expenditure of energy is not enough to prevent feelings of the most intense boredom. Also, what is intensely boring for one individual may be relatively stimulating for another. A considerable research literature demonstrates that the nature of the work tasks and the kinds of persons who are performing them are both significant variables in determining the relations of work and boredom.[2]

Although something is known of the differential effects of kinds of work

---

[2]Vroom (1964) presents a useful summary of the extant research on the effects of highly repetitive and simplified work. Two generalizations can be made from these studies. First, the more that work tasks are reduced to one or two highly simplified

on kinds of people, we are on almost entirely speculative ground when we consider the general function of work in meeting the need for activity. Psychoanalysts have theorized that work is a socially approved means for sublimation of the aggressive instincts and that when work is not available the individual suffers from anxiety aroused by the pressure of inacceptable impulses (cf. Menninger, 1942). Ferenczi (1918) described the "Sunday neuroses," a phenomenon in which individuals manage to cope with their personality difficulties during the working week but are faced with an aggravation of symptomatology on their day off (see also Abraham, 1918). I have often observed the same phenomenon in work therapy programs designed to rehabilitate the posthospital mental patient. Such patients frequently appeared more disturbed on Mondays than on the preceding Friday, suggesting that the inactivity of the intervening weekend permitted symptoms to exacerbate. According to the theory, where work can function, for a given person, as an active defense against inacceptable or frightening impulses and fantasies, or where work may serve to drain off energies that might otherwise be put to destructive uses, enforced leisure can simply be a condition for the intensification of anxiety. The resulting higher levels of anxiety, in turn, mobilize all those inappropriate defenses and behaviors we call symptoms.

There is no reason to suppose, however, that work is anxiety-reducing in precisely this way for all or most persons. The role of work in the psychological economy of human beings is extremely varied, and the psychoanalytic theory appears too narrow to account for very much of the variance. For some persons, work itself is felt to be extremely boring and restricting, and some kinds of work are perceived as terribly boring by almost everyone. At the same time, there is some evidence that one of the basic human motives has to do with fulfillment of a general human need for activity. Robert W. White (cf. White, 1959, 1963) has presented us with intriguing arguments that the need for activity is a basic biological need. Although White does not himself draw this inference, human work appears to be one of the chief arenas in which this need may be gratified. This notion receives some support from the fact (cf. Neff, 1968) that one of the chief reasons given for wanting to work by people who are vocationally disabled is that work will alleviate their chronic condition of boredom and inactivity. While this expression may simply be wishful thinking, the same condition is universally reported as one of the disagreeable aspects of forced unemployment. At least in those people who are denied it, therefore, work is seen as a major means for meeting a general human need for activity and stimulation (cf. Berlyne, 1960).

---

operations, the greater the level of dissatisfaction among those that perform it. Second, there is a negative correlation between intelligence and the ability of the individual to tolerate repetitive work.

Respect by Others

The fourth need that work appears to gratify or frustrate to varying degrees has to do with the evaluations placed on "being a worker" by the society in which the worker is a participant. The situation here is quite complex, even in such generally work-oriented societies as our own. On the one hand, being a worker is associated with such positive values as independence, autonomy, "citizenship." The chronically unemployed face a great many varieties of derogation and are grudgingly supported by the state at a minimal level of subsistence. Even quite wealthy individuals derive status from being engaged in some kind of productive work, especially if they derive no monetary income from it. On the other hand, the status of "being a worker" is at best a necessary condition for respect, not a sufficient condition. Two other conditions are influential in determining the amount of respect the worker is "entitled" to receive. First, different kinds of work are associated with different quanta of respect. The second condition has to do with the specific manner in which a given individual performs his work.

The need for respect by others must be disentangled from the need for self-esteem. In practice, they are highly intertwined, but they have a certain measure of autonomy as motives. The two needs reflect quite different questions, viz., "what do I think of myself" versus "what do others think of me." It is certainly possible to encounter persons in whom these two views are quite dissonant. They may have a very low opinion of their worth as persons but believe that others think well of them. Perhaps more frequent are the cases of individuals who place a quite high evaluation on themselves but perceive others as giving them insufficient respect. In its extreme form, the latter kind of case presents the thought process of the paranoid psychotic, in whom delusions of grandeur and persecution are simultaneously present. For the majority of people, however, the opinions of others are a factor in their self-esteem, so that the latter fluctuates within rather wide limits according to whether they receive criticism or praise. Nevertheless, these two sets of opinions are not perfectly correlated across individuals and cannot be treated as identities. Riesman has erected an entire sociology on this distinction, operating with a simple typology of "inner-directed" versus "outer-directed" personality types (Riesman, 1950). People with a very strong need for respect by others would tend to fall in the latter category.

Obviously, the degree to which the need for respect is gratified by work is a function of prevailing value-systems, as well as the degree to which these systems have been incorporated by particular individuals. Historically (see Chapter 2), there have been entire societies in which all kinds of work were perceived as servile—to be performed only by slaves or pariahs—and in which only people who are entirely freed from labor can be respected. In still other societies, only certain kinds of work (pastoralism) are respectable, while others (agriculture) are beneath contempt. In our own society, the respect accorded to "being a worker" is a function of a great many variables and of value-systems that are not free of contradictions. There are sub-cultural pockets—typically those occupied by delinquent and counter-normative populations—in which a worker is a "square"; the highest respect is accorded to those who manage to acquire the perquisites of wealth without working. For quite large numbers of people—particularly those who earn their living through unskilled, heavy, or "dirty" labor—work is simply a burden to be endured; they do not expect to gain the respect of anyone by performing it. At the same time, even in the least skilled and most onerous occupations, it is possible to gain some measure of respect for doing a good job, for being able to "put out." By and large, however, the amount of respect that accrues to work depends on a quite varied set of factors: the amount and kind of training and education that is required; the level of payment; the degree to which the worker is "his own boss"; the amount of economic, social, and political power the position commands; the particular evaluation placed by society on the social importance of the work being done. Generally, people in the higher status occupations expect to receive respect for the kind of work they do and the position they occupy (Centers, 1949), while people in the lower status occupations are reduced to wanting to be respected simply as human beings, but not necessarily as workers (Kornhauser, 1965).

Different attributes are also singled out for respect in the different occupations. The unskilled laborer may be valued for his physical strength and endurance or his ability to tolerate repetitive work. The university professor will be accorded respect for feats within the area of intellectual achievement and will hardly expect it for his muscular prowess. The business executive is admired for his ability to accumulate wealth, even if his success might have been achieved on the basis of the intellectual and manual skills of his employees. The politician and salesman may be given respect for their skills at persuasion, although they may be simultaneously condemned for lack of ethics. It follows also, of course, that a given human attribute that draws considerable respect in one kind of work may be seen as inappropriate or irrelevant in another.

The role of work in meeting the need for respect by others is particularly marked in the attitudes toward work of the vocationally handicapped. In a study I conducted of the attitudes to work of vocationally disadvantaged mental patients (Neff, 1968), a very high weighting was given to statements that have the meaning: "People will respect you if you have a job." In most instances, the kind of work to be done was not a factor, probably because these were people who had never been able to hold *any* type of employment. For some of these patients, however, especially those who had considerable prior education, low-status employment was additional proof that they were not worthy of respect. In general, it is probably true that the association of work and respect is less strong among people who have experienced no difficulty in obtaining work, but the normal worker has been less intensively studied than the more or less severely vocationally maladapted.

Need for Creativity

Whereas the four needs we have so far discussed tend to be universally involved in almost any kind of work, the degree to which work may gratify the need for creativity is rather restricted. Yet the need to do something that reflects one's unique capabilities as a person is strongly implicated in certain kinds of work and equally strongly frustrated by others. While perhaps not so fundamental a motive for work as the others, the need for creativity plays some part in work behavior.

Creativity is an elusive subject, although it has recently aroused the interest of a number of investigators. The research focus has principally been on the nature of the creative process, and the tendency has been to study people who have already been judged to have done something deemed to have been creative. There has been little concern, however, with creativity considered as a need or motive, although it is in the latter sense that we want to examine its relationship to work. For our purposes, "creativity" is not limited to the arts but has a wider area of application. The need for creativity may be thought of as a need for novelty, involving the rearrangement of traditional components into a new and unique pattern. Creativity generally strikes us as a form of human activity that is quite idiosyncratic, expressive of the unique qualities of a particular person. Defined in this manner, the need for creativity would appear to be fulfilled only by certain kinds of work: the labors of the artist, the scholar, the scientific investigator, the industrial innovator, the business entrepreneur, etc.

In another sense, the need for creativity is implicated in work in general. Creativity can also mean the bringing into existence of an additional unit of something with which we are already quite familiar. Creativity here shades off into meanings associated simply with being productive, with achieving something. In this sense, the industrial worker may still feel he is creating something, even though the machine he serves has been originated by someone else. The object or process being produced is tangible evidence that his labor has not been for nought. Only when the process of automation proceeds so far that his connection with production becomes entirely attenuated does the worker feel utterly useless.

The association between creativity and productivity in general, however, should not blind us to the fact that the need for creativity is specifically gratified by only certain kinds of work. People with a strong need to be creative will simply be frustrated by work situations that are countercreative. The widespread rationalization and mechanization of work has presented many people with the requirement to find outlets for their need for creativity in off-work activities. Only a small number of people in modern society are fortunate enough to find in their work an opportunity to create something genuinely expressive of their unique qualities.

IS THERE A WORK PERSONALITY?

As we have examined various theories of work and assessed the available evidence, a general picture has begun to emerge. First, there is considerable agreement that adult work behavior is the outcome of a prolonged developmental process, which passes through a series of distinguishable periods and stages. Second, this process appears to be *adaptive* in nature, that is, the individual is required to cope with a variety of environmental pressures, demands, and constraints. Third, it seems clear that we cannot limit our attention to the particular aptitudes and skills the individual has managed to acquire. All the investigators agree that a great deal more is involved in working than is contributed by whatever cognitive and motor abilities the individual exhibits. To what does all this lead?

Throughout this volume, we have taken the general position that work is a function of two interlocking sets of variables. We have analyzed in some detail one of these sets of conditions (the work environment), but we have not yet systematically considered the other (the work personality). If we question the nature of the psychological baggage that the worker brings to his work, the answers are given in language familiar to personality theory: motives, needs, feelings, coping mechanisms, interpersonal attitudes, defenses, and the like. While correct in principle, this answer seems too general. Do the demands of work draw upon *all* motives and needs of the person, or only certain ones? Is work a function of the entire human personality, or of only a part of it?

To anwer these questions, we first have to come to grips with the general theory of personality and then attempt to see how certain concepts help us understand human work.

THEORIES OF PERSONALITY

It has been waggishly observed that there are as many theories of personality as there are people writing about it. It is true that theories abound, but they share certain common features. First, personality theorists are generally concerned with the emotional sides of human behavior, rather than its cognitive or motor aspects. Second, the primary domain of interest has to do with interpersonal relationships, including whatever the individual feels and believes is true about himself as a function of his relationships with others.

The differences among the theories are largely concerned with how the emotional life is conceptualized. For the classical Freudian, adult emotional responses to others are direct functions of very early interactions between the child and his parents. It is assumed that the primary components of the personality are laid down by the time the child is 5 or 6 years of age, and that these components then function as unconscious determinants of adult interactions. To understand adult personality, or to modify it, it is necessary to "uncover" and reconstruct these early and unconscious determinants. Less orthodox psychoanalysts are concerned not so much with early childhood as with the characteristic ways in which people defend themselves against anxiety in their present interpersonal reactions. Nonpsychoanalytic theories tend, most often, to be "trait" theories. According to this view, people can be placed at points along a series of more or less independent dimensions— "extroversion," "aggression," "dominance," "neuroticism," and the like. In its more sophisticated versions, "trait" theories conceive of the individual personality as a characteristic pattern of points in a multidimensional space or as a unique "profile" of highs and lows across a series of dimensions (cf. Cattell, 1946; Eysenck, 1952).

Although it is obvious that these theories differ drastically in their basic approach, they are all subject to the same failing. Personality theories tend, if anything, to be too general in their application. None of the theorists is wholly wrong, but none is wholly right. Each of the various theories is one-sided, in the sense that one or another aspect of a complex phenomenon has been taken as if it were the entirety. Even more serious is the general belief that whatever is being observed about the behavior of persons in particular situations will serve to account for behavior in any and all situations. Freud accounts for the adult's reactions to authority-figures in terms of the child's responses to the authority of the parent. The "trait" theorist believes that "dominance" is an enduring personal characteristic that will account for one's behavior equally at home, with one's friends, or on a job. However, very few persons—perhaps only the frankest of psychotics—respond to all life situations as if they were identical. One of the most important characteristics of human personality is its flexibility. An individual may have contempt for his father but respect his employer; he may be "dominant" in the home but "submissive" at work.

The central question is whether the personality variables that have been evoked to account for one kind of interpersonal transaction are sufficient to explain *all* transactions. As formulated, the supposition appears implausible. With notable exceptions, human beings display wide response repertories and appear quite capable of discriminating between various types of interpersonal situations. The exceptions turn out to be people whose emotional lives are in severe disarray and whom we label with diagnostic terms as *psychoneurotic* or *psychotic*. These people have been so traumatized by prior interactions that they respond to all situations as if they were identical. Freud may be perfectly right in maintaining that the neurotic is an individual who responds to other persons as if they were replicas of his parents. But, if true, this is precisely why we regard him as "sick." The theory begins to fail when it is simply generalized to account for the behavior of less traumatized people. Normal personality development involves the ability to discriminate between person and person, situation and situation, with a correspondingly differentiated repertory of emotional responses. An angry father evokes one kind of response, an angry friend a different kind, an angry employer still a third.

To say that it is fruitless to search for the unifying elements in a given personality also would be a drastic oversimplification, although at the other extreme. Human personality is neither an entirely monolithic entity nor an aggregate of entirely unrelated fragments. The various aspects of the personality manifest *both* communality and specificity. I may react to all men (in part) in terms of the manner in which I responded to my father. This is appropriate to the degree that all men, including my father, have certain common features. But men differ from each other in a great many ways, and I must respond to the differences as well as the similarities. For normal personalities, the observable differences far outweigh the observable similarities. In the same sense, it may be possible to establish that a given personality trait (e.g., dominance) will account for *some* of the variance of the behavior of the person in certain specified situations. But the same person may behave quite submissively in other situations. The most viable hypothesis concerning human personality is that it is composed of a number of substructures and areas that, although not entirely unrelated, manifest considerable degrees of internal differentiation. The emotional responses that people make to each other appear to be simultaneously motivated by two opposing conceptions: that people are like each other in important ways and different from each other in important ways.

THE SEMIAUTONOMOUS NATURE OF
THE WORK PERSONALITY

The relations of work and personality have a high order of complexity. There are some persons—we suspect they are few—in whom work may generate the same emotions that were evoked in the earliest familial interactions. This kind of person reacts to his employers as if they were his parents, to his co-workers as if they were his siblings. In such cases, we can think of the personality as displaying a high degree of communality, reacting to all situations as if they were the same and displaying certain predominating kinds of emotional responses. For most of us, however, there is only a rather limited, if variable, relationship between the ways in which we respond to intimates and the ways in which we behave on the job. In this sense, work is a function only in part (and to a minor extent) of what is sometimes referred to as the "deeper" layers of the personality. If we are accustomed to think of personality chiefly in terms of the love–hate structures established in early childhood, then there would be little more to say. It is sounder, however, to view the human personality as if it were made up of a number of structures, segments, or areas, all more or less related to each other but exhibiting considerable independence as well. The process of personality development can be looked at as a process of differentiation (cf. Werner, 1948), so that the more developed personality has a more complex infrastructure than was discernible at less mature stages. It is natural for an infant to respond to all women as if they were his mother; but when an adult responds in the same way, we call it pathologically infantile behavior.

It is in this sense that we take the position that the work personality, to the degree that it makes its appearance in adults, arises through a long process of development and differentiation. Its relations to the personality as a whole can best be described by saying that it has a *semiautonomous* character. The term *work personality* refers to the concrete set of interrelated motives, coping styles, defensive maneuvers, and the like with which a given individual confronts the demand to work. These personal attributes constitute a special subarea of the general personality; and its topography is not identical with that of other personality areas. A number of important considerations follow from this notion. First, if personality is made up of a number of semiautonomous areas, a person may manifest severe disturbance in one area of the personality but simultaneously function relatively well in other areas. This possibility helps account for the otherwise mysterious fact that some frank psychotics are able to meet the demands of work with reasonable adequacy. Conversely, some individuals are quite unable to adapt to work but appear to function quite well in other interpersonal areas (e.g., those concerned with sex, marriage, friendship, and the like). A second consideration bears upon the problems of treatment. Psychotherapy may succeed in improving one area of personality functioning, while leaving others quite unaffected.

It is not enough, however, for us simply to maintain that work behavior is mediated by a special subarea of the personality. We need to know the growth of this phenomenon and its unique features.

THE PRODUCTIVE ROLE

Insofar as there is a core to the work personality—a central point to which everything else relates—this core is the manner in which the individual can assume the role of a productive person. It is obvious that work implies output. Something is being produced—an object, a process, a service—which, as a usable unit, did not exist before and which is required to fulfill some human need. It does not matter whether the need in question is "basic" or "acquired," real or illusory. The purpose of work is to bring about some planned alteration of the physical, intellectual, or cultural environment, so that human living can be made more secure, more comfortable, or in other ways more desirable. In the more complex societies, the goals of work can become quite far removed from the concrete aim merely of staying alive. But whatever the kind of work done and whoever carries it out, its basic objectives are instrumental—to produce something.

The productive role has a number of interesting psychological attributes. First, it appears to be the outcome of a prolonged period of personal development. Productivity means nothing to very young children and takes on a variety of different meanings as they grow older. Second, people vary greatly in the ease and efficiency with which they can assume the role of a productive person, and some cannot assume this role at all. We need some idea of the conditions that make for these differences. Third, the requirement to be productive is clearly related to certain prevailing cultural values. Once these values become incorporated, we are in the domain of the motives for work. Fourth, it is not sufficient merely to be motivated for work; one must also be able to cope with a wide array of specialized social conditions. Fifth, the ability to be productive is a function not only of the kind of person one happens to be but also of the kind of work one is required to perform.

In Chapters 2 and 3, we dealt with some of the more important cultural and social factors that can be looked on as the necessary conditions of the work personality. We have not, as yet, confronted the details of the developmental process through which the work personality is shaped, nor the different patterns of work motivations that appear to arise from different features of the developmental experience.

THE DEVELOPMENT OF THE WORK PERSONALITY

Students of child development generally tend to subdivide the entire process into a series of distinctive periods or stages (Piaget, 1955; Erikson, 1959; Werner, 1948). In part these stages are imposed by biological maturation and in part by traditional ways in which societies have institutionalized the care and training of their children. It has become customary to think of these stages as periods in which the child has substantially different developmental tasks to solve. In our own culture, the entire period between birth and adulthood is commonly subdivided into three stages, each of approximately the same length. First, there is the period of *early childhood*, which comes to a close when the child is approximately 5 or 6 years old. The succeeding stage lasts another half-dozen years or so and comes to an end with the onset of puberty; for convenience, it can be called *middle childhood*. After puberty, we think of the child as in the stage of *adolescence*, which gradually merges into adulthood somewhere in the late teens and early twenties. Obviously, this kind of subdivision is very coarse, and the indicated time periods permit considerable variation from individual to individual. But there is a surprising amount of agreement among child development theorists, despite severe doctrinal differences on many other matters, that the three stages are distinctively different. How do these three developmental stages, then, contribute to the formation of those aspects of the personality that bear upon work?

Although there is a very considerable literature on child development, very little is directly concerned with the problem we are here considering. Moreover, the bulk of this literature focuses on the period of early childhood, which, as we shall see, may be less crucial for the formation of the work personality than are later periods of development. Our own ideas concerning the development of the work personality have been influenced by certain suggestions found in the writings of Hendrick (1942, 1943a, 1943b), Lantos (1943, 1952), Erikson (1959, 1963), and White (1959, 1963). We shall separately examine each of these suggestions and then indicate how they may be incorporated in a general theory of the work personality.

Ives Hendrick is one of the few psychoanalysts who has taken the position that the "primary instincts" of sex and aggression are insufficient to account for the full range of human behavior. He became interested in the pleasures that human beings appear to derive, from earliest childhood, in the mere exercise of their cognitive and motor abilities. For the classical Freudian, the pleasure in any action is a derivative or transformation of libidinous pleasure or, alternatively, arises from the satisfaction of native aggression. For such "orthodox" neo-Freudians as Hartmann, adaptive behavior is powered by energies derived from the sexual and aggressive instincts, which become "neutralized" in the process of development (Hartmann, 1958). Hendrick, however, argues that, from earliest infancy, the human being commits an enormous amount of energy to the enterprise of exploring and controlling his environment and derives a great deal of "primary pleasure" from doing so. He believes, therefore, that classical psychoanalytic theory should be amplified postulating a "mastery instinct" (Hendrick, 1943a), an "inborn drive to do and to learn how to do" (Hendrick, 1942).

Lantos, in her early paper (1943), contributes the provocative thought that the transition from pleasure in activity to pleasure in achievement takes place during what Freud called the latency period (roughly from age 5 or 6 to the onset of puberty). She calls attention to a remark of Freud that animals reach adulthood without passing through a latency period and then presents her own view that the importance of this period in man resides in its association with learning and education. Another interesting idea put forward by Lantos (1952) is that the instinctual series is "broken" in man, with the interposition of mental activity between the instinctual need and the gratifying act. Human beings, in effect, engage in "roundabout" activity, in the sense that the objects of adult gratification are usually not *directly* available (as in animals) but must be "worked for." Lantos further suggests that the adult derives pleasure from feelings of independence because this means to him that he is no longer bound by the constraints of childhood. Thus, an adult who is deprived of work feels infantilized, but he is no longer able to turn to the omnipotent parent for security and support.

Erikson's ideas concerning the "life cycle" (1959) are also extremely stimulating. Like Lantos, Erikson suggests that the latency period poses a set of problems that psychoanalytic theory has tended to overlook. As Erikson sees it, early childhood is largely dominated by the mechanics of nutrition and elimination, by play, by early physical mastery (creeping, standing, walking, running), and by the stabilization of relationships to the parents (the Oedipal complex). Only when the child enters the latency period, however, is he ready for new developmental tasks. Erikson identifies the period of middle childhood as the *Industry Stage,* a period of "entrance into life," with the qualification that life must first be school life. In his *Childhood and Society* (1963), Erikson describes this process as follows:

> Before the child, psychologically already a rudimentary parent, can become a biological parent, he must begin to be a worker and potential provider. With the oncoming latency period, the normally advanced child forgets, or rather sublimates, the necessity to "make" people by direct attack or to become papa and mama in a hurry: he now learns to win recognition by producing things. He has mastered the ambulatory field and the organ modes. He has experienced a sense of finality regarding the fact that there is no workable future within the womb of his family, and thus becomes ready to apply himself to given skills and tasks, which go far beyond the mere playful expression of his organ modes or the pleasure in the function of his limbs. He develops a *sense of industry* [italics added] i.e., he adjusts himself to the inorganic laws of the tool world. He can become an eager and absorbed unit of a productive situation. To bring a productive situation to completion is an aim which gradually supersedes the whims and wishes of play. . . . Thus, the *fundamentals of technology* [italics in original] are developed, as the child becomes ready to handle the tools and weapons used by big people. Literate people, with more specialized careers, must prepare the child by teaching him things which first of all make him literate, the widest possible basic education for the greatest number of possible careers. . . . School seems to be a culture all by itself, with its own goals and limits, its achievements and disappointments (p. 259).

We have quoted Erikson at length because he weaves together a number of interesting issues. First, it is clear that, for Erikson, the crises of early childhood are a necessary preparation for later behavior, but do not wholly determine it. Second, he suggests that the conception of being a productive person does not begin to become internalized until the child enters the latency period. Third, he points to the origins of the felt differences between play and work. Finally, he gives us a hint of the importance of nonfamilial persons (teachers), with the school as the arena in which children learn to become productive persons.

Robert W. White, especially in his later monograph (1963) carries the entire argument a step further. He is impressed by Hendrick's observations concerning the pervasiveness of efforts to master the environment, but he sees no need to postulate a new instinct to account for them. Instead, he calls attention to a suggestion by Karl Bühler (1924), that there is an inherent pleasure in the "normal exercise of motor and mental functions" (Bühler called this *Funktionslust*). White has no place in his theoretical system for instincts and instead attributes pleasure to the *arousal* as well as the satiation of any human need. White coins the term *effectance,* which refers to any kind of "exploratory and manipulative behavior, which seems to perform the service of maintaining and expanding an effective interaction with the environment." The feeling of pleasure that accompanies effectance is a *feeling of efficacy*: "a feeling of doing something, of being active or effective, of having an influence on something." White (1963) approvingly quotes Piaget (1937/1954) to the effect that the child's earliest conception of causality arises from feelings associated with his own actions on the environment:

> Ever since the first contacts with the external environment, the child is active . . . ever since the beginnings of his mental life, [the little child] conceives of his own effort as the cause of every phenomenon. . . . Primitive causality may therefore be conceived as a sort of feeling of efficiency or efficacy linked with acts as such. . . .

For White, effectance is an independent ego-energy, which can be observed in infants at birth and to which it is both unnecessary and confusing to relate any other sources of motivation. White also attempts to distinguish effectance from *competence*. Effectance is a generic aspect of human behavior that does not need to be learned. On the other hand, competence is "largely a product of learning . . . a cumulative result of the whole history of transactions with the environment, no matter how they were motivated." Significantly, White (1963:41) at once broadens the concept of competence to include the feeling of *social competence*: "The feeling of being able to have some effect on people, to get them to listen, provide some of the things we need, do some of the things we want, receive some of the love and help we want to give. . . ."

We must also take account of Donald Super's ideas on vocational development. Compared with the others discussed in preceding pages, Super is not a psychoanalyst, or is his primary interest in psychopathology or maladaptation. He is an educational psychologist—possibly the leading psychologist in this field—whose concern is with the vocational guidance and counseling of the millions of children and adolescents in the American public schools. Sited at Teachers College, Columbia University, he has trained a generation of counseling psychologists, who now occupy the bulk of the strategic positions in this growing field of training and research. In an earlier section of this volume, Super's long-term study of vocational development was described (cf. Chapter 6) and his theoretical system examined. Super's interests, of course, are focused on differential career patterns and the mechanisms of career choice—not on the somewhat more elusive issue of the development of the meanings of work-in-general. However, over a period of more than three decades, Super and his team have accumulated a mass of empirical data concerning the vocational ideas of ninth grade boys, including how these ideas shift as the subjects move toward the twelfth grade (cf. Jordaan and Heyde, 1979). We are promised further reports, detailing the vocational behavior of this group of subjects at ages 25 and 36.

Whatever the precise outcome of Super's Career Pattern Study, the data made available so far make it abundantly clear that the work personality is not endowed to us by birth but comes into being through a long process of individual development. Young children have almost no clear notions of the nature of work and also display very little interest in it. Even the 14-year-old boys, who make up the subjects of Super's ninth-grade study, are very obscure about the actual requirements of various kinds of work and have only the vaguest notions of the training needed for various occupations, but there has been considerable movement toward the crystallization of knowledge about work and attitudes to it by the time the subjects are 18 years old. The Career Pattern Study provides considerable justification, therefore, for the belief of the writer that the work personality comes into existence through a long process of development and experience, a process that we shall conceptualize in the following section.

A GENERAL THEORY OF THE WORK PERSONALITY

We stated earlier that the ideas of Hendrick, Lantos, Erikson, and White "point" toward a general theory of work, although none of these writers explicitly states this formulation to be his aim. However, a general theory is precisely what we want to construct.

We start with the proposition that the events of early childhood are less critical for the formation of the work personality than are those of later periods. (Some children are, of course, so traumatized by certain early transactions with the parents that their entire later development is seriously harmed.) The events of early childhood certainly constitute the necessary conditions of further development, but they are not the *sufficient* conditions. The primary developmental tasks that the human being faces in early childhood have to do with nurturance and love. Freud and his followers vividly described the early childhood dramas attending weaning, toilet training, and early jealousies. The manner in which these early crises are resolved may strongly determine how the child relates to his parents and, in some instances, to any other human being. But the emotional habits acquired during these early years principally concern love–hate relationships. The basic emotional problems that the child encounters are how to love and be loved, within the setting of the nuclear family. The young child is, of course, required to master a great many skills, a learning process that may arouse intense affects both in the child and his parents. He must learn how to subsist on solid foods, to void his body wastes in designated ways, to work out complex relationships to members of his immediate family, to dress himself, to speak the rudiments of his native language. But this early period is largely taken up with the vicissitudes of nurturance, love, and play, all of which are almost entirely perceived as ends in themselves. By and large, the young child is not yet being faced with the requirement to do anything that bears directly on the future ability to work.

The critical components of the work personality are apparently formed during the periods of middle childhood and adolescence. To grasp this point, we have to know what takes place when the child must leave his family for hours at a time to go to school. The child is now faced with a novel set of demands and is called upon to make new kinds of adaptations. A great deal more is learned (or *not* learned) in school than a required spectrum of cognitive skills. Many of the requirements of the work-role are first encountered in the school environment. The child gets his first serious conditioning to the clock; he must learn to be at school on time, to stay a fixed number of hours, to divide the day into school-time and play-time. He must learn to accommodate himself to all kinds of strangers (his teachers and schoolmates), with whom he cannot really behave as he may continue to do with his parents and relatives. He must begin the process of adaptation to those aspects of life that are public and impersonal, casual and distant. The child's schooling begins the long process of erosion of the ties that bind him to the parents that ends in the more or less independent existence of the working adult.

Beyond these more subtle conditions of future work behavior, there is one basic demand of the school that is central to all else—the *demand to achieve.*[3] Like other such concepts, the term *achievement* has many meanings. First, it implies some kind of directed activity that is aimed toward meeting some sort of standard. Other connotations of the term have to do with such literal meanings as ''bringing to an end,'' ''reaching a goal,'' ''carrying to a successful conclusion'' (cf. definitions offered in *Webster's*

[3]McClelland (1961) and McClelland *et al.* (1953) have carried on extensive investigations of what he calls the need for achievement (N Ach), a concept originally formulated by Henry Murray (Murray, 1938). McClelland's approach to achievement is to view it as a factor of individual motivation (a ''need'' in Murray's language) and to attempt to demonstrate its association with such behavioral outcomes as success in school, occupational mobility, and even the level of productivity of entire human societies (McClelland, 1961). However, I am concerned with a prior question, which has to do with the origins of N Ach as a human motive. It is being argued here that the pressure to achieve does not really arise until the child is confronted with formal schooling. It becomes internalized as a motive (or rejected and defended against) during middle and later childhood.

International Dictionary, third edition). Intrinsic is the notion of an active performance, indeed even exertion, as if in order to achieve we have to overcome obstacles to "master" something. Achievement also connotes some level of acquired "competence" (White, 1963). An increasingly common usage is found in such phrases as "the underachiever," in which potential to achieve is contrasted with actual accomplishment.

The 5- or 6-year-old child who enters school is confronted with an entirely new set of pressures and constraints, most of which center on the demand to achieve. The preschool years may be stormy indeed, but the child is not required to *produce* anything except a more and more varied set of acceptable behaviors. Once he enters school, however, he is expected to become *task-oriented,* to begin to master a series of skills that are instrumental to some distant end. He is now expected to distinguish work from play, to meet certain externally imposed standards for achievement, to be punctual, to carry out fixed assignments, to live a certain portion of his life under constraints imposed by an extrafamilial social system.

It is our contention that the distinctions between work and play, and between work and love, first begin to take shape in the mind of the child when he is forced to leave his family and playmates for hours at a time to attend school. The preschool child may play at adult work, but everyone is aware that he is playing, and no one demands that he continue. On the other hand, the school child is soon made aware that mastering the alphabet or learning a series of integers is a serious business, and that he is expected to produce something. Certain basic components of the work personality appear to be laid down in the early school years—the ability to concentrate on a task for extended periods of time, the development of emotional response-patterns to supervisory authority, the limits of cooperation and competition with peers, the meanings and values associated with work, the rewards and sanctions for achievement and nonachievement, and the affects (both positive and negative) that become associated with being productive. School is thus a precursor of adult work and provides a set of models for it. It may be gratifying, even beneficial, if the child enjoys his homework, but enjoyment is not the purpose of the process. Basically, he is required to be productive, to be serious, to meet standards, to turn out the required amount of work at a desired level of quality, to meet certain responsibilities.

Of course, school is not the only force that prepares the child to cope with the demands of work. Parents also play a prominent role, but parent–child relationships now begin to differ from those in early childhood. Although parent–child interactions continue to be centered chiefly around nurturance and love, new elements begin to appear in middle childhood. In many ways, the parents begin to convey the impression that it is expected or desired that the child *be* something when he grows up. School achievement may be encouraged or discouraged to variable extents. The parents act to reinforce or to counteract the authority of the teacher. Children begin to become dimly aware that their parents are important to them not only because they are the primary sources of love and nurturance but also because they are models—good, bad, or indifferent—of how grown-ups behave in the outer world. During middle and later childhood, the child begins to develop a set of values concerning work and achievement and probably the initial sources of these developing ideas are his parents. As powerful as parental influence may be, however, it is only one source among many. The larger society also plays its part, through countless and often contradictory messages conveyed by way of the mass communication media and through its public figures. A significant role also is played by the teenage subcultures in which the child increasingly becomes embedded, the values of which are often incongruent with the goals either of the school or the parents. Depending upon the variable strength and congruence among all these influences, the child develops his individual set of attitudes to work.

The available evidence from longitudinal studies (see Chapter 6) indicates that work in the sense of career or vocation has no particular meaning for the child until toward the end of middle childhood. We recall Ginzberg's observation (Ginzberg et al., 1951) that the world of work does not begin to take on real meaning until after the child is 11 or 12 years old. Prior to this age, his vocational aspirations have the character chiefly of fantasy and wish fulfillment. But middle childhood is not necessarily a vocationally empty period. On the contrary, the attitudes and response patterns developed during the early school years may be crucial determinants of the future. The school experience may be relatively gratifying or relatively frustrating. It may be an arena of relative success or relative failure. Parents may play supportive, punitive, or simply indifferent roles. Habitual patterns of response to authority and to achievement are formed fairly early and tend to be self-fulfilling. By the time the child is old enough to think seriously about adult work, some important components of the work personality already exist in embryonic form. Toward the end of middle childhood, children already differ widely in how industrious they are, in the degree to which they can defer immediate impulse-gratification, and in the emotions generated by authorities and peers. Later school experiences serve to consolidate these early tendencies but, in most instances, do not greatly change them.

THE PSYCHODYNAMICS OF WORK

Given that people vary greatly in their ability to assume a productive role, given also that they attribute very different meanings and values to work, it is clear that work behavior must be discussed in psychodynamic terms. The adult worker may be largely unaware of the factors that govern his work behavior. He may tell you cynically or angrily that he works only because he must, but he may feel at loose ends on vacations and feel worthless unless he works. There is ample room in work behavior for all the defensive mechanisms of the ego: rationalization, projection, denial, sublimation, and the like. There is also ample room for conflict and unconscious motivation. Like other broad sociocultural conceptions that are transmitted to the child, those related to work are incorporated and internalized to different extents and different ways. To the degree that they then function as unconscious imperatives, they can then be thought of as components of the superego.[4] Once this takes place, to ignore or violate these precepts can arouse feelings of anxiety, guilt, anger, or personal unworthiness. In turn, the growing child learns to develop all sorts of means of dealing with these feelings, coping methods that have become familiar under the heading of the ego defenses. To the degree that the demand to achieve, to be productive, becomes internalized as an unconscious imperative and to the degree that a network of coping behaviors becomes habitual and automatic—to this degree certain important segments of the work personality become relatively inaccessible to awareness. They then can provide an important dynamic for the continuation of kinds of work behavior that may or may not be appropriate.

SUMMARY

The general source of what we are calling the "work personality" lies in the precepts of society that an individual should play a productive role. In its earliest form, the child is confronted with these demands when he enters some sort of formal educative process. The latency period, which Freud tended to regard as a relatively conflict-free period of child development, is regarded here as the critical period when the child must begin to struggle with the demand to achieve, to be productive. He must learn to give up play for protracted periods of the day; he must endure separation from primary nurturing figures; he must become aware of time, begin to meet schedules, try to complete tasks. He must learn how to deal with what gradually

[4]In classical psychoanalytic usage, the superego comprises the internalization by the child of the precepts of the parents, which then operate as powerful, if largely unconscious, motivators of behavior. Essentially, these precepts constitute a series of prohibitions or constraints. However, the classical usage tends to confine the superego to those precepts and commands of the parents that arise in relation to the vicissitudes of early psychosexual development. It is our belief that the term should be broadened to include the internalization of *other* cultural imperatives as well. In this view, not only the parents but other authority figures are included as agents in the formation of the superego. The internalization of the more broadly social imperatives is also conceived by us to take place over a longer period of child development, particularly during what Freud conceived of as the latency period. The compulsion to work, insofar as it is internally motivated, can be thought of as a superego demand, a demand that may stand opposed to other human needs (to play, to seek affection), concerning which the ego develops appropriate strategies of resolution where it can.

appears to be an almost infinite series of hierarchically organized authority figures, to whom he is not related by ties of blood or intimacy. He must achieve some balance of cooperation and competition with his fellows and find a place within the culture of his peers. At the same time, he is increasingly bombarded with all sorts of messages about the virtues of the productive role, many of which are mutually contradictory.

All children are faced with the demand to achieve, since the process of growth to adulthood involves the mastery of a great many biologically and culturally defined tasks. The compulsion to work, however, is initially entirely external to the organism but becomes internalized to varying degrees and in different forms. Once this demand is internalized in some form or other, it can then become a stimulus for all sorts of feelings of pleasure, gratification, anxiety, guilt, or inadequacy. As a consequence, coping behaviors appear and eventually consolidate into the particular "work-style" of the individual.

The components of the work personality are thus highly complex. People may work poorly or may not be able to work at all for varied reasons. Some might not have internalized the precepts of society to play a productive role; they might not have become enculturated to the work subculture. In other instances, the general demand to be productive might have been internalized, but may be in conflict with other demands of the work situation—the requirement to relate appropriately to peers and authority figures on the job, the requirement to moderate certain needs for intimacy and privacy, the requirement to meet standards imposed by others, and so on. There are a great many people, also, whose styles of work are suitable only for certain kinds of jobs, who can work well, for example, provided the job is routine and unchanging, but who fall apart if the task requires continuous innovation and creativity.

The problems of work behavior are, in large part at least, problems of personality. The work personality should not be identitifed with other personality areas because the demands of work are not identical with the demands of love or play. For this reason, we have described the work personality as a semiautonomous area of the general personality. But work behavior, like love, engages the affects, requires a prolonged period of social learning, is governed by more or less enduring habits of response, is formed by events of which the adult person may be largely unaware. The problems of work cannot be treated or managed with the same techniques that are appropriate for the problems of love. But, in the more severe instances at least, relative inability to work cannot be cured by mere exhortation or even by providing training in some work skill. Work psychopathology implies some area of deficiency or defect in the development of the work personality.

II | CLINICAL ISSUES

THE ASSESSMENT OF WORK POTENTIAL

HISTORY

One of the side effects of industrialization and political democracy has been the development of a massive effort to evaluate and predict work behavior. In the United States, work assessment has become an entrenched institution. To a much lesser extent, British investigators have displayed some interest in the problem, but it has not yet become a matter of much concern in the other major industrialized countries of the world. The reasons lie both in the special history of the United States and in the manner in which its labor force has been recruited.

The early rise of mass education and a powerful tradition of individualism brought about keen interest in measurement of individual difference in ability and aptitude. In a country where—in theory, at least—everyone had equal opportunity and anyone could aspire to any social or economic position, it became an article of faith that the only reason for differential mobility was differential ability. Equality of opportunity was written into the American Constitution, and egalitarianism was a stronger force in the United States than anywhere else. Decisions as to who should get more education or a better job, therefore, could not openly be made simply on the basis of the individual's social class or social status, although tacitly these considerations might have continued to be forceful. However, the Founding Fathers did not legislate equality of ability. Insofar as we can speak of an American ideology, one of its major tenets has been that people can rise through the social system on the basis of their ability, whatever the initial circumstances of their families of origin. We are not here concerned with whether the sought-for abilities were believed to be innate, acquired, or some combination of the two. But the widespread and deeply entrenched conviction that the socioeconomic hierarchy directly reflected a hierarchy of differential individual capabilities made the United States an extremely favorable environment for the identification and measurement of individual differences.[1]

Another set of favorable factors arose from the peculiar conditions faced by American industry. Unlike the situation in Europe, American industry developed under conditions where there was almost no hereditary labor force. Labor had to be recruited almost entirely from the millions of European immigrants who poured into the United States after the Civil War. The bulk of this potential labor force consisted of unskilled peasant labor, which had to be trained, organized, and disciplined for factory work virtually overnight. The result was an enormous proliferation of all kinds of vocational education—in the public schools, in private training institutions, and on-the-job—which was unparalleled in any other country. Like the general educational system and for the same reasons, vocational education also developed its own infrastructure of examinations, tests, and assessment procedures.

Faced as he was with a highly mobile and relatively scarce supply of trained labor, the American industrialist also developed a strong economic stake in work efficiency. Since mass production was an early American invention and often required the aggregation of thousands of employees in a single industrial enterprise, he was more susceptible than his European counterpart to anything that promised to improve the efficiency of employee selection. Personnel psychology—the study and application of techniques of work assessment—thus reached its highest point of development in the United States (cf. Lawshe, 1948; Guion, 1965).

If one attempts an over-all view of the entire field we are considering, it becomes obvious at once that different investigators have approached this problem from very different standpoints and with different objectives. New aims also arose as new problems were encountered. The systematic study of work potential spans a period of approximately some 70 years, from World War I to the present. This period divides itself rather neatly into the two

---

[1]We should emphasize that we are speaking here of the core of an ideology. Practice is something else again, as attested to by the widespread job discrimination still visited upon women and minorities, particularly blacks, and, to a somewhat lesser degree, Hispanics and other immigrants. We shall deal with these matters in some detail in a later section (cf. Chapter 14). This belief, that American democracy is essentially a "meritocracy," has hampered and sometimes defeated efforts to impose "affirmative action" on institutions and occupations that have, in past, discriminated against certain disfavored groups. The opponents of affirmative action overlook the fact that the effects of discrimination are *negative* in the sense that categories other than merit are used to prevent the entry into desired occupations of certain disfavored groups, while the effects of affirmative action are *positive* in the sense that this measure is designed to correct past inequities. Of course, if the desired institutions and occupations do not expand, then the possibility arises of what has been called "reverse discrimination." These issues are still being fought out in the 1980s.

decades between World War I and World War II and the four decades since World War II. Of the four main approaches to work evaluation that we shall describe, two arose and flourished during the period between the two wars and two have come into prominence only since World War II. For identification, we can characterize these four approaches as: (1) the mental testing approach; (2) the job-analysis approach; (3) the work-sample approach; and (4) the situational assessment approach (Neff, 1966). Although the approaches overlap to some extent, they arose to serve different needs, rely on different techniques, and have different areas of application.

THE MENTAL TESTING APPROACH

For practical purposes, the mental testing movement began around the turn of the century, in the efforts of Alfred Binet and his co-workers to develop an intelligence test for use in the public schools of France. What started as an ingenious effort to measure intellectual ability, as distinct from other factors that might influence school performance, soon widened to massive efforts to measure almost every conceivable human ability—including the ability to work. Within a decade, the focus of this movement shifted to the United States, which has become the classical country of mental testing. Terman produced an American version of the Binet in 1916, which became almost indispensable to the American public schools during the next two decades. While the Binet, and its many subsequent versions, was an individual test, the need quickly became apparent for group-testing instruments, which could economically be administered to many persons on a single occasion. The first successful group test of intelligence was the Army Group Examination Alpha (cf. Boros, 1961), which was developed for use in the American armed forces in World War I. During the two decades between World Wars I and II, all kinds of psychometric devices proliferated, with both the schools and industry being the chief consumers. Although the intelligence test is, perhaps, most widely known, thousands of instruments have been designed to measure the most diverse kinds of human abilities, including those required to perform almost every kind of work.

During the early years of the movement, the advocates of mental testing apparently believed that they were in a position to create a panacea for all the problems of selection, recruitment, and promotion in both education and industry. In the 1930s, however, an increasingly intense controversy arose over certain methodological and practical problems involved in psychometric testing, and initial enthusiasms began to dampen. As research data began to accumulate, it became evident that the measurement and prediction of human ability is a much more complex task than it had initially appeared to be, and that many of the assumptions inherent in test construction had holes in them. While we cannot here consider the many problems of psychometric testing in general (cf. Cronbach, 1960), we *are* interested in examining the psychometric test as an instrument to evaluate the potential to work. Tests are still being very widely used for this purpose, although with greater reservations about their utility than some years ago. To the degree that vocational guidance has become institutionalized in the public schools and colleges, part of the data on which the vocational counselor relies is obtained from some sort of program of vocational testing. Most large business or manufacturing enterprises use industrial tests to select and promote employees, and many have developed very elaborate testing programs. To qualify for apprenticeship training, candidates are required to take an extensive battery of tests, and the same is true for entry into a great many civil service occupations. An outstanding example of the massive use of industrial testing is afforded by the development of the General Aptitude Test Battery (GATB) by the Bureau of Employment Security of the U.S. Department of Labor, which, although not released to the public, is in very general use in the various State Employment Services. While there has been a marked tendency toward psychometric sophistication, which has also involved much more caution in the prognostications people are willing to risk, the psychometric test is still the most widely used instrument of industrial selection and appraisal.

What then are the characteristics of the psychometric test as an instrument to assess the potential to work? Its virtues can be stated in a sentence. It is quick, easy, and inexpensive to administer, objective, and reliable. Its limitations will take us somewhat longer to state and arise from its nature as a measuring instrument. To understand what is at stake, we shall have to consider some of the fundamentals of mental test construction.

Given certain assumptions, the process of test development is eminently empirical. First, the investigator collects a large number of brief operations—verbal, numerical, perceptual, or motor—which he has some reason to believe may be necessary components of the kind of work he wishes to evaluate or predict. Second, he collects a sample of persons (the standardization sample) whose work capacities are already known by some other means (foreman's ratings, indices of productivity and quality, etc.). He must take precautions that the people chosen for his standardization sample differ sufficiently widely in work capacity and are reasonably representative of the target population. His third step is to put his standardization sample of persons to work on his sample of tasks. His goal is to include, in the final assessment instrument, those tasks that reliably differentiate his sample of persons according to their known work capacities and to discard those operations that do not do differentiate it. Finally, having produced a provisionally acceptable instrument in this manner, he can then field-test it, by pretesting suitable samples of entrants into the occupation in question and relating their subsequent work performance to their initial test scores. In the course of time, quite powerful statistical techniques have been developed to improve his rigor: correlational analysis, multiple regression procedures, factor analysis, and the like.

This entire procedure seems like a triumph of empirical logic, so that one may be almost astonished to discover that even the most impeccably developed industrial tests have respectably high reliabilities but disappointingly low predictive validity. That is, test scores show an acceptable degree of internal consistency, but relatively little of the actual variation in work performance is being accounted for. Rarely do we find a situation where more than one-tenth to two-tenths of the variation in work performance can be related to the variation in test scores. Of course, even this quite meager result can have some economic utility, especially where the number of potential applicants is very large and something is to be gained by reducing errors of selection by even a relatively small amount. The industrial test, therefore, may be best understood as a mass screening device, characterized by rather large interstices between the fibers of the mesh. Provided the number of applicants is large in relation to the number of available positions, and provided that we pay more attention to the extremes of the distribution of scores than to the intermediate ranges, the tests function to reduce errors of selection by moderate amounts. In the individual case, there is a very high risk of misclassification.

The reasons for this frustrating result are manifold, but some of them lie in the method of test construction itself. There are some very deadly pitfalls in test construction that the test developers have not been able to overcome. The first has to do with the characteristics of the standardization sample. The basic assumption here is that the standardization sample must be representative in certain crucial ways of both the present and future labor force. In a rapidly changing labor force, however, future job applicants may have very different kinds of education and work experience from those that typified the standardization sample, yet the earlier applicants set the norms. We are currently confronted with a hot controversy over the use of standard vocational tests to qualify workers for entry into skilled trades and training programs, where the bulk of these tests were standardized on samples of white workers who had initially higher levels of education and work experience. In such situations, the test acts as an exclusion device rather than as a simple screening intrument (Kirkpatrick, Ewen, Barrett, and Katzell, 1967).

A second major pitfall concerns the apparently innocent requirement that the standardization sample must display wide variance in known work capacity. In many respects, this is the Achilles heel of the entire procedure. Truly objective criteria of work performance are not easy to find. Where reliance is placed on the ratings of foremen and supervisors, a major source of subjective error is introduced at the outset. More objective criteria, such as those based on quantity and quality of output, are not always appropriate to the job in question; where they are available, they are often limited by union regulations or by the more informal understandings that exist among the members of factory work-groups.

A third major pitfall concerns certain crucial differences between the nature and demands of the test situation and the nature and demands of the actual work situation. In the test situation, attention, concentration, and motivation are maximized and under continuous control. In the work situation, however, these factors truly vary and are under very limited control. What must be faced is that the conditions that make for a good test performance—including such variables as "test anxiety" and "test wiseness"—are far from identical with those that make for a good performance in the actual work situation.

The combined operation of these major sources of error has had the effect of considerably reducing our confidence in aptitude testing as a technique of work evaluation. Under proper safeguards, and with firm knowledge that neither the labor force nor the occupation has changed drastically, the tests have some utility as mass screening devices. But we must be aware that the assumptions basic to test construction have a tendency to fail at certain critical points. These weaknesses become crucial when we confront the problem of assessing the vocational potential of people who differ in very important ways from the population sample upon whom the tests were standardized. Even when the population to be tested is not strikingly different from the standardization sample, we are left with a disconcertingly large number of false negatives and false positives. The psychometric tests become almost entirely inappropriate, however, when the problem is to assess the work potential of an ex-mental patient with long-term hospitalization, a borderline mental retardate with no work history, a socially and culturally disadvantaged school drop-out, or the member of a deprived ethnic group. Thus, where the problem is one of individual prediction, or where the population of interest clearly differs from the standardization sample, other techniques of work evaluation are needed.

THE JOB ANALYSIS APPROACH

The second major approach to vocational appraisal—the techniques of job analysis—arose and developed during much the same time period as mental testing, but originated in a different sector of society. While the mental testing movement is largely the product of the university-based psychologist and educator, job analysis originated within industry and has been a major preoccupation of industrial management for some two generations. As its name implies, job analysis focuses primarily on description of the work to be performed and only secondarily on characteristics of the worker. The major investigators in this field have been industrial engineers, efficiency experts, and industrial managers. Indeed, the movement got its start in the work of such men as Taylor and Gilbreth, whose approach was to analyze a given kind of work into a series of time–motion units (see Chapter 3).

While initially focused on providing a rational analysis of repetitive manual labor, the movement rapidly expanded to attempt similar analyses of much more complex kinds of work. The most elaborate and far-reaching set of such job descriptions is found in the *Dictionary of Occupational Titles* (U.S. Department of Labor, U.S. Employment Service, 1949), produced by the U.S. Department of Labor on the basis of a long and fruitful collaboration with industry. Since the initial appearance of the Dictionary, much additional research has been carried out to relate job requirements to specific patterns of abilities and aptitudes among the workers who are required to perform them (U.S. Department of Labor, Bureau of Employment Security, 1956). The General Aptitude Test Battery referred to above (p. 172) was also produced by the Department of Labor because of its interest in work classification and was designed to differentiate kinds of work in terms of the different patterns of aptitudes—verbal, numerical, perceptual, and motor—required to carry them out.

The assumptions and methods inherent in job analysis are, in certain important respects, quite different from those involved in mental testing. In the first place, there is far more emphasis on the actual and direct observation of work performance. The job analyst is not so much interested in potential ability as in *functioning* ability. He wants to know what workers actually do and what they have to know (or can be taught) to function with some required minimum of efficiency. The job analyst tends to be less interested in initial selection than he is in the outcome of a period of on-the-job training.

The mental tester stands at the door, so to speak, accepting or rejecting applicants before their work actually begins. The job analyst, on the other hand, stands in the workplace, observing the new employee at his work, giving whatever training and instruction is deemed suitable, and making a judgment as to the new applicant's potential for future work performance from the work initially done. The chief social instrumentality at the disposal of the job analyst is the probation period, a given period of weeks or months during which the applicant can be dismissed with the least fuss, usually formally fixed by agreement between management and labor and accepted as a condition of employment. The primary assessment instrument is the judgment of the training supervisor or of the job foreman.

The emphasis of the job analysis approach on the nature of the task to be performed, rather than on the human being who is to perform it, is one of its great virtues. In some contrast to the mental testers, the job analysts have both feet planted firmly in the realities. Their base is the factory or workplace. Their clear aim is to adapt the human being to work and to accomplish this by observing and training him while he is actually performing it. Because of the demands of large-scale industry, one of their main aims has been to reduce human variability, to make human work as uniform as possible. To do so, they had to observe work very carefully and write detailed descriptions of every stage and aspect of what were often very complex activities. The result has been the development of a very impressive body of information, which is extremely useful for anyone whose mission it is to evaluate and train people to perform specific kinds of work. Actually, without some acquaintance with this body of fact, the work evaluator is forced to work in the dark.

However, this approach is not without some serious problems. In concentrating on the work-task, the job analyst has often had a tendency to overlook the other term of the equation—the worker himself. While it is possible to reduce human variability considerably, it is not possible to abolish it entirely. As the job analyst became more sophisticated, he found he had to limit his ambitions and pay more attention to human characteristics. Thus, as we have seen, the efficiency engineers began to discover that they had to complement job analysis with attention to human relations in industry. In current policies of industrial management, we see something of a troubled marriage between these two rather discordant elements.

In the over-all sense, however, the work evaluator has a good deal to learn from the job analysis approach. There has been, hisorically, too one-sided an emphasis on the industrial test as the primary instrument for the evaluation of work potential. If work behavior consists of a set of complex transactions between the working individual and his surround, then we need to know what work requirements actually are. The "surround" in this case consists of a detailed set of job requirements, which have been described most exactly by the job analysts. The work evaluator needs to know both terms of the transaction.

THE WORK-SAMPLE APPROACH

The systematic use of the structured work-sample to appraise work potential is largely a post-World War II phenomenon. These procedures were developed to fit the needs of people whose potential for work could not easily be assessed either by the industrial test or by on-the-job observation. This method constitutes an effort to capitalize on the virtues both of psychometric testing and job analysis, while trying to avoid the limitations of both. From the mental testing movement, the work-sample approach took over the procedures of standardization and statistical rigor, thus trying to limit the subjectivity inherent in supervisory judgments. From the job analysis approach, the work-samplers derived the notion that the most realistic way to evaluate work potential is to observe people at work over an extended time-period, thus trying to limit the high order of abstractness inherent in the mental test. Significantly enough, the field of vocational rehabilitation has developed the most elaborate systems of work-sample evaluation, since the psychometric test appears to fail most drastically in assessing the work potential of the physically disabled, the mentally retarded, and the emotionally disturbed. Also, because these specialized populations are difficult to place in industry and because they often require, at least at the start, much more than the usual amount of industrial supervision, some means had to be found to observe their work behavior other than what was available in the typical industrial setting.

Before we examine the advantages and limitations of the work-sample, let us describe it more exactly. Ideally, a work-sample is a "mock-up"—a close simulation—of an actual industrial operation, not different in its essentials from the kind of work a potential worker would be required to perform on an ordinary job. Perhaps the most striking difference between the industrial test and the work-sample is the time-factor. The former typically takes less than an hour to administer and constitutes a cross-section, as it were, of the person's present level of ability. The latter may take several days or weeks and places much more emphasis on the person's ability to learn. More important than time, however, are certain critical differences in the two kinds of situations. The testing situation is most closely analogous to the examination in school; it is designed to measure what has already been learned. The work-sample situation is analogous to the probation-period on the job, without the catastrophic consequence of summary dismissal after a fixed time-period.

The developer of a set of work-samples must start with a detailed job analysis of the kind of work a potential worker would be required to perform on a given job, including how long it will typically take to learn each of the various operations that may be required. He then must take the job into the laboratory, so to speak, and attempt to standardize it, that is, develop uniform methods of instruction, duplicate the materials, tools, and equipment used by industry, work out the amounts of time required to learn each part-operation, and so on. He then must write a manual that will enable the evaluator to make reasonably objective and reliable assessments of the work behavior of future subjects. Having done all this, he has hardly begun. He must now run an appropriate sample of potential clients through his newly constructed work-sample, make predictions as to their future performance, and make follow-up studies to determine the pay-off.

Again, all this sounds eminently reasonable. If we wish to find out whether someone can learn to do something, what could be more practical than to set him to work doing it, under conditions where he can be accurately and reliably observed? There would appear to be nothing wrong with the logic of this approach. The problems, however, lie in its execution. How do we make our choice of the work-samples to construct? Industry is very diverse, and technological change is very rapid. Since the process of developing and standardizing a good work-sample is long and arduous, there is a constant risk of developing an adequate appraisal instrument for jobs that no longer exist. The concreteness and realism of the work-sample are its strongest virtues, but these become vices if the demands of the labor market shift. In principle, the work-sample approach involves its adherents in a continuous race with industrial technology. Obsolescence is always a major danger.

The work-sample approach has also run into some very tangled problems of validation. What are we trying to predict and what criteria are available against which to check our predictions? Are we predicting actual job performance or are we predicting the ability to learn something in a training course? There is evidence that the work-sample procedure does better in predicting the latter than the former (Institute for the Crippled and Disabled, 1968). Typically, the work-sample evaluator has no way of controlling the vagaries of the labor market, while he is in a somewhat better position to see that his recommendations for training are carried out. Since the graduates of training programs are not automatically placed in employment, the work-sampler has no way of knowing if failures of predictions to employment are due to the inadequacies of his appraisal system, to employer biases, or to a host of other uncontrolled factors related to the employment situation itself. While some apparently very well-constructed work-sample procedures are in existence (e.g., the TOWER system developed by the Institute for the Crippled and Disabled of New York City; cf. Institute for the Crippled and Disabled, 1959), there remains considerable uncertainty as to their predictive efficiency.

Granting these very difficult problems, the work-sample approach to work evaluation has much to recommend it. Its virtues are its strong reality orientation, its close simulation of actual work demands, and the unparalleled opportunity it affords to observe actual work behavior in a reasonably controlled situation. Its difficulties are not so much intrinsic as extrinsic. The present situation makes it almost impossible to carry through an adequate test of the efficacy of these systems of evaluation. Typically, a client is evaluated by one kind of social institution (a rehabilitation agency), trained in another kind of institution (a trade school), and employed by a third (a commercial or industrial firm). An adequate research design would require that *all* evaluated clients (both "goods" and "poors") be placed in training and/or in employment, so that it could be determined whether "goods" in fact did well and "poors" in fact did badly. At present, however, only those who are *favorably* evaluated will be recommended for training, and only a portion of them manage to find their way into employment. Given the continued existence of these gaps between evaluation, training, and placement, the utility of the work-sample approach will remain indeterminate.

THE SITUATIONAL APPROACH

The situational approach to work evaluation is the newest method of the four we are examining, originating not much earlier than the mid-1950s. Like the work-sample approach, it is based on an effort to simulate actual working conditions. Whereas the orientation of the work-sample is toward the assessment of specific work skills, the orientation of the situational approach asks a prior set of questions. Can the potential worker work at all?

Can he conform to customary work roles? Can he take supervision? Can he get along with his co-workers? Can he put in an ordinary working day? How does he respond to demands to increase his productivity or improve his quality? Does he work better alone or in the presence of others? Under what kind of supervision does he work most effectively? Does he get so preoccupied with quality that he cannot produce at acceptable rates, or does he try to work so fast that his quality suffers? What are his strengths and weaknesses as a worker?

As we have seen, the work-sample approach has its closest affinities to the techniques of psychometric testing and the procedures of job analysis. The situational approach has a rather different tradition, in part developing from the experiences of the sheltered workshop movement and in part from the situational assessment techniques developed by Henry Murray and his co-workers in World War II (U.S. Office of Strategic Services, 1948). The chief aim of the situational approach is also quite different from the objectives of the work-sample approach. Whereas the work-sample approach focuses on skill-potential, the situational approach focuses on what can be called the "general work personality": the meaning of work to the individual, the manner in which he relates to important other persons on the job, his attitudes to supervisors, peers, and subordinates, the roles he finds it congenial to play. The situational approach tends to be indifferent to particular work skills or specific occupational interests, which gives rise to both its main strength and its chief weakness.

The situational approach to work evaluation is a much looser procedure than the other three methods we have described and varies considerably from agency to agency. One of the early models was the rehabilitation workshop established by the Chicago Jewish Vocational Service (cf. Gellman, Gendel, Glaser, Friedman, and Neff, 1957). The general components of this approach, however, are rather simple. The basic aim is to restructure the ordinary sheltered workshop setting so that certain important features of unprotected employment are more closely simulated. Wages are paid; work is performed on actual commodities destined for sale; foremen are present on the scene who set standards for quantity and quality; regular working hours are maintained and a businesslike atmosphere prevails; the physical setting is designed to resemble ordinary working conditions, and so on. Hopefully, the only (and of course the *vital*) difference between situational assessment in the rehabilitation workshop and ordinary employment is that it *is* an assessment situation, that it is possible to vary all the customary conditions of employment without the overriding concern for efficient production that ordinary employment must require.

Again, all this seems eminently reasonable. If we wish to find out whether a given person can work, it seems sensible to put him in a work situation and find out whether he can peform. If we wish to know what prevents him from working efficiently, it seems reasonable to vary his working conditions and discover what produces his difficulties. In practice, however, there are certain constraints. In the first place, it is obviously impossible to reproduce, within the confines of the rehabilitation workshop, the very wide variety of kinds of employment and levels of skill requirements that exist in industry at large. As a result, the situational assessor tends to make a virtue out of a necessity and takes the position that *any* kind of work will do, so long as it gives him an opportunity to appraise the components of the work personality. He maintains he is looking for the lowest common denominators of work behavior, and that it does not matter to him what kind of work is to be performed. Thus, because it is easiest to establish, we find that the kinds of work that prevail, where situational assessment is being attempted, are usually the simplest types of unskilled assembly, packaging, and elementary clerical operations. So far, this appears to have worked rather well. However, I suspect that this is true largely because these centers have been serving highly marginal populations: the mentally retarded, the severely undereducated and underprivileged, the ex-mental patient with little or no work experience. One cannot be sure that situational assessment, as it is presently organized, would work effectively with fewer marginal clients, particularly with those individuals whose motivation to work clearly depends on the kind of work they are expected to perform.

A second quite serious dilemma facing the situational assessor is that he is rarely in a position where he can determine which aspects of his program cause what effects. The virtue of situational assessment is that it is as close to real life as we can get it, but this also makes it virtually impossible to disentangle the variables that are together producing a total effect. Thus, we remain uncertain as to how much or how little of the total situation we have contrived is essential for our purposes, and it is perfectly possible for a critic to argue that some very different features of work should have been incorporated. Thus, again, the other side of a virtue is a vice.

There is no gainsaying, however, that the situational approach is a highly imaginative and versatile instrument, which has made it possible to produce evaluations of certain types of individuals who hitherto were resistive to any other kind of method. Its limitations should not blind us to its genuine innovative qualities.

VOCATIONAL ASSESSMENT AND VOCATIONAL REHABILITATION

Because of the special problems of the handicapped, rehabilitation professionals have been forced to develop their own assessment devices, which largely fall under the work-sample and/or situational assessment categories. A recent publication of the Arkansas Rehabilitation Research and Training center (Bolton, 1982) suggests that the development of such instruments has become something of a major industry. Compared to the relatively arid

1950s, when hardly anything was available for assessing the vocational potential of the handicapped other than counselor judgement, Bolton describes 10 standardized rating devices that have been developed for research purposes since then. His colleagues in the same volume (Bolton, 1982) describe another 20 or so work-sample and assessment systems, which are now available commercially.

The interesting thing about all of these devices (most of them are simply standardized rating scales) is that they do not limit themselves to cognitive or motor skills, as do most standard psychological tests. Rather, these assessment devices tend to cover a very wide range of attitudinal, personal, and interpersonal behaviors that bear upon all aspects of the typical work situation. They thus further illustrate that adjustment to work is not simply a matter of possessing the requisite motor skills and motivation, but it is, as we have been at considerable pains to point out, a complex adaptation of a whole human being to a very intricate set of material and social demands.

The energy, scientific commitment, and determination of the constructors of these assessment devices can only be applauded. The writer is aware from his own experience that the research required is difficult, very time-consuming, and complex. However, one is permitted to wonder about the ultimate utility of standardized instruments to assess vocational potential. The best of these evaluation systems share the common properties of relatively satisfactory internal consistency and reliability but either unknown or disappointingly low predictive validity. That is to say, the scales are not much help in allowing us to predict who will, or will not, succeed in employment once the rehabilitation process is completed. Then why use them? One answer lies in the fact that they not only serve to focus the attention of the observer on the true complexities of work behavior but that they help the rehabilitation professional to make a determination concerning precisely what it is that is preventing a given person from adapting to work. They are thus important clinical aids, whatever their correlation with ultimate placement and maintenance in unprotected employment.

APPLICATIONS

Instruments and techniques designed to measure work potential are used extensively in two quite different fields: (1) in industry, as a selection device and a condition for employment; (2) in schools, as a basis for vocational guidance and career counseling. In both fields, by far the most widely used instrument is the standardized paper-and-pencil test. In both fields, also, the widespread application of vocational testing has lately come under severe criticism. The sources of discontent with mental and vocational testing differ somewhat in the two fields, related to the differing purposes for which testing has been employed. It will be instructive to examine some of the issues at stake.

In industry (the term is used generically here to refer to almost any kind of paid (employment), the use of mental testing has become so widespread during the past decade or two that the publication and dissemination of standard tests has itself become a substantial industry. If one wishes employment as a typist in an insurance company, a trainee in almost any skilled or even semiskilled occupation, a teacher or a sheetmetal worker, a civil service employee at virtually any level—the first hurdle is to pass a standardized mental and occupational test. Where larger numbers of people apply for one position than can be accommodated at any given time, it has now become customary to develop priority lists based on relative test standing. Obviously more is at issue here than the professed objective of insuring that the person hired can actually carry out the work-tasks to which he will be assigned. In the conditions of the modern labor market, the industrial test now functions as a condition of employment. Recently, serious concern has been expressed that the occupational entry test is not merely a rational selection device, but may function as a discriminatory barrier!

Of course, any selection device has both virtues and vices, but the former appear to have been taken more for granted than the latter. The chief virtue of the standardized occupational test is its presumed objectivity. It has been assumed that the use of objectively scored tests would restrict, if not abolish, the sway of bias and prejudice in hiring and promotion. It is probably fair to say that at least part of the motivation behind the general acceptance of occupational testing arises from the conception of American society as a meritocracy rather than an aristocracy. It is interesting to note, however, that the chief current opposition to the mental test as a condition of occupational entry comes from population groups that have been hitherto denied full access to the opportunity structure: blacks, women, other discriminated-against minorities. It may seem odd that a procedure designed to eliminate prejudice is now being attacked for maintaining biased employment, but there is some merit in the complaint.

In fact, the typical occupational test is not a very good predictor of competence in employment, as we have noted. Predictive validities are low, and there is ample room for error. But there are worse difficulties! As we have seen, the chief operating principle that guides the construction of the typical aptitude test involves the procedure of standarization. The norms that govern task selection and scoring are derived from the performance of "standardization samples," that is, representative groups of persons employed in the occupation in question, whose actual job performance is, at least to some degree, verifiable. An aptitude test, therefore, has a very important historical factor; it reflects the actual job performance of people who worked in the particular occupation at some moment in time. The underlying operative assumption is one of *continuity*: the occupational test is based upon the belief that the best predictor of the future is the past. A major problem now is that the onrush of technological and social change is rapidly making nonsense out of what seemed like a very reasonable set of assumptions. Not only has the social composition of entire occupations changed so radically that the same kinds of people (by ethnic origin, by education, by general social background) are no longer employed or employable in them, but technological innovation has thoroughly changed the kinds of tasks required. It is perhaps not too much to say that, at this juncture, the prime requirement for work adjustment is the individual's ability to adapt to rapid technological changes and to the massive social adaptations that these changes often require. Unfortunately, we have not yet learned how to test for this ability, and the only measures of competence we now have available are not readily reorganized into the rigid format of the standard objective test.

There is thus substantial reason to complain that the standard occupational test may, in fact, be used more often as a rejection device than as a rational instrument to guarantee work competence. The entire apparatus of entry testing is now entering a period of legislative control. Laws are being written into the statute books that require that firms and employing agencies that reject applicants who do not meet certain test norms must demonstrate that the rejected applicants cannot, in fact, meet the work requirements of the jobs for which they applied. The notion is now taking hold that a suitable period of probational employment may be a far more accurate and fairer index of occupational competence than the best-designed occupational test. The agitation (and, of course, legislation) concerning entry tests as exclusion devices has had a chilling effect on their use, and many firms and organizations are either abandoning them or greatly modifying their procedures. Of course, the best test of the validity of any occupational assessment device would be to test everybody and then employ everybody regardless of score, at least for a period of probation. We would then ultimately learn more than we now know about the relationship between test performance and work performance. It goes without saying that there are other things to be gained by this approach. People who are not test-wise, who are traumatized by testing situations, or who do not achieve high test scores for reasons other than work competence, will have a chance to show what they can do on the job, under quite different pressures for achievement and over a longer period. Short of this millenium, we would hope that current exposures of the relative invalidity of industrial testing, combined with the wide protests against their use as exclusion devices, will produce greater caution and wisdom in their general use.

Criticism of vocational testing in school situations has taken a different turn from what we have seen in industry. The issue here is the manner in which occupational aptitude and interest tests typically have been used in vocational guidance. Dale Prediger, who is himself a leading member of the test-production establishment (he is currently Director of the Development Research Department of the American College Testing Program), has written a useful survey of the present situation in vocational testing (Prediger, 1974). Prediger observes that the traditional trait-factor approach to vocational guidance is increasingly being subjected to severe criticism. His language in describing the traditional methodology is worth citing:

> These applications at their worst involve a one-shot "test 'em, tell 'em," square-peg, square-hole process whereby an individual's characteristics are analyzed in conjunction with the characteristics of occupations in order to find a match indicating the occupation to be entered (Prediger, 1974, pp. 325–326).

Prediger is quite ready to concede that this use of vocational assessment devices (vocational tests in particular) is "static, sterile, limiting, directive, generally unworthy of professional attention."

Complaints about the use of vocational tests in vocational guidance are not limited to their relative invalidity, although this issue has also received a good deal of recent attention. A number of important studies have appeared that seriously question the degree to which occupational success can be predicted from scores on occupational aptitude and interest tests (cf. Ghiselli, 1966; Goldman, 1972; Thorndike, 1963; Pucel, Nelson, and Mohamed, 1972). But this problem, as serious as it is, is not the only one inherent in the use of vocational tests in career guidance. A much more damaging criticism comes from such vocational development theorists, such as Super and Crites, who believe that final occupational choice is preceded by a prolonged and uneven period of exploration, during which occupational interests (and aptitudes) are very far from any sufficient degree of crystallization that can be measured or which, if measurable, can be quite deceptive. Super's studies of the vocational development of 14-year-old boys have convinced him that the high school years, for most, are a period of questioning and fumbling. It would thus be a disservice to attempt to freeze a person's ultimate vocational choices by administering vocational interest and aptitude tests during these formative years. But, in current practice, it is during the later high school years that occupational tests are most heavily employed.

Of course, Prediger is eager to convey to his readers that the baby should not be thrown out with the bath water, and there is some reason to listen to him. Whatever their misuse, the better occupational tests are distillations of vast amounts of useful information about the kinds of work-tasks found in a wide variety of different occupations and about the kinds of people who appear to succeed in them. The taking of an occupational interest test can itself be a useful means of gathering information about what one might be expected to do in a particular occupation and even about the beliefs and stereotypes that prevail among some of the people who work in it. The problem is to avoid the lure of prediction. If the vocational test could simply be regarded as an expert and encapsulated description of typical tasks and people, which can be utilized judiciously in arriving at tentative decisions regarding educational programs, then some of the present dangers might be avoided. The trouble is that in a success-oriented society such as ours, the prediction of occupational success has a strong, if illusory, appeal.

SUMMARY

From this brief overview of the chief approaches to vocational evaluation, it should be apparent that the choice of method will, to a considerable degree, depend on our objectives. If what is needed is a mass screening device, which will enable us to select for certain kinds of employment those persons who possess a necessary minimum of certain abilities, then certain psychometric tests may serve reasonably well. If we want to know what a worker actually must do on a given job, then some form of job analysis seems to be required. If we want to assess an individual's ability to master a particular skill, then it is likely that the structured work-sample is appropriate. And if we wish to know whether a given person can work at all, or what causes him to work very poorly, then it seems that the simulated work-situation will give us the best information. No one of these four methods can do everything; each deals with a restricted facet of a many-faceted problem.

One of the major stumbling blocks lying in the way of improving our systems of vocational evaluation is that very meager resources exist with which to field-test the newer procedures in actual industrial settings. Once the client leaves the confines of the evaluation center, we are no longer in a position to observe his future work behavior on an actual job, so that we can ascertain the reasons for his success or failure. Our outcome criteria tend, therefore, to be very crude, essentially boiling down to the all-or-nothing criterion of employment versus unemployment. We have been able to develop no means of observing our evaluated client in actual employment as intensively as we observed him during the evaluative phase. It would be highly desirable to provide a system of work-trials in unprotected industrial settings, which would provide opportunities for professional observation. At present, however, and for many obvious reasons, once a client is lucky enough to be absorbed by private industry, he disappears from sight. Until the professional evaluator gains some opportunity to observe his clients on an actual job, genuine validation of the work-sample and situational procedures will remain inadequate. In this respect, the British, with their widespread system of publicly owned Remploy enterprises, are better off. Whatever way it is managed, however, greater access to industry is a fundamental requirement, if the developing systems of work evaluation are to be adequately validated.

10 | THE TECHNIQUES OF WORK ADJUSTMENT

VOCATIONAL GUIDANCE

In all ages, some people could not or would not adapt to the demands of work. Until comparatively recently, however, this was not regarded as a *social* problem that required any kind of ameliorative effort by organized society. Every reasonably able-bodied person was considered to be quite capable of working. The chronically unemployed were simply looked upon as drones or parasites and generally felt to lack some essential moral quality. Of course, certain categories of the population—the very wealthy, the very young, the very old, the severely physically disabled, married women— were exempt from this kind of general disapprobation. But otherwise, especially for males of working ages, the nonworker was generally assumed to be a person with marked defects in will and moral character. To the degree that remedies were available, they consisted either of exhortation or some kind of punitive action. Vagrancy has long been classified as a statutory crime, and the adult male without visible means of support is still regarded as a legitimate object of police surveillance. Not too many years ago, public workhouses were in existence in both England and the United States, to which the chronically unemployed could be sentenced for indefinite terms of forced labor.

Toward the end of the nineteenth and the beginning of the twentieth centuries, these public attitudes began to shift. It is perhaps more accurate to say that new ideas began to appear, since the older attitudes are still very powerful. Many people still look upon the chronically unemployed with a mixture of derision, contempt, and suspicion. We have a large vocabulary of derogatory terms to describe the adult nonworker: "bum," "idler," "parasite," "ne'er-do-well," and the like. The difference is that it has now become more legitimate to think about this problem in psychological, rather than merely in moral, terms. Closely linked to these newer ideas is the conviction that the chronically unemployed ought to be given "treatment" rather than subjected to derogation or punishment. There has thus arisen, during the past few decades, a new kind of professional specialty, the essential objective of which is to provide some kind of psychological assistance to the vocationally disadvantaged. The most common name for this new kind of specialist is the *vocational counselor,* often also described as a counseling psychologist.

Modern vocational counseling is now an established professional specialty, with all the customary marks of professional identification: advanced university degrees, professional associations, and scholarly journals. It is, however, one of the younger specialties, which has passed through a number of shifts of emphasis and is still in the process of attempting to define its objectives. During much of its early period, during the first two or three decades of the twentieth century, the few people interested in vocational problems were essentially working for broad social reforms. The pioneers were social workers or educators, who became convinced that vocational guidance ought to be one of the basic functions of public education. From the beginning, therefore, there was a strong orientation toward the school as the primary arena for counseling, which remained its chief focus for many years. In the decades since World War II, however, there has been a hyperdevelopment of interest in the vocational problems of people who are no longer in school. Some 60 universities now maintain graduate training programs, at the Master's or Doctoral levels, which are designed to produce a new kind of professional: the *rehabilitation counselor.* The focus here is on the vocational problems of the disabled or handicapped adult. Also, since World War II, the vocational psychologist (more often referred to as the *counseling psychologist*) has acquired specific occupational status, both in the universities and in various types of public and private agencies.

For most of its 60-odd years of existence, vocational counseling as a professional specialty was dominated by a single conception—to fit people to the kinds of jobs for which they were best suited. Given this definition of the counselor's role, his professional task was seen as having three interrelated aspects. First, he had the responsibility of obtaining accurate information about job characteristics and opportunities. Second, he needed to be able to assess the individual's capabilities and interests. Third, he needed to fit these two sets of data together so that the individual could enter that occupation for which he was best suited. The model assumes, of course, that people are quite capable of making rational choices, if they are provided with sufficient information about the world and about themselves. Following from the requirements of the model, the bulk of the available research for many years was focused on occupational information and the techniques of vocational assessment. Acquisition of know-how in these two fields of investigation still makes up a large part of the university training of the typical vocational counselor.

This conception of the counselor's role has come under criticism in recent years as being both too mechanical and too "rational." The matching of individuals and jobs has turned out to be far from simple. Available tests of vocational aptitudes and interests have relatively low correlations with occupational choice, leaving much of the variance in vocational behavior entirely unexplained. This is not only because the tests are not accurate enough but because the tested individuals do not behave like automatons. Even where adequate job information has been provided and the testing battery appears to point in a well-defined direction, it does not follow that the individual will passively accept whatever recommendations are deemed appropriate. It has slowly become obvious that human decision making is not solely dependent upon the ability to reason from fact to fact but is also heavily influenced by emotions, feelings, attitudes, aspirations, and similar "irrational" factors. To the degree that this problem has become recognized, vocational counselors have become aware that more is needed than the acquisition of occupational information and the administration of tests.

In addition to being confronted with the relative failure of basic assumptions, other kinds of questions have arisen. Is the vocational counselor merely a technician or does he have other professional responsibilities as well? Does his task end with the imparting of vocational information or must he also play some kind of therapeutic role? If inadequate vocational behavior is not simply a direct result of lack of information, does he not have to get involved with whatever else is causing the difficulty?

During the past decade or two, these questions have become increasingly insistent. As a result, vocational counseling is in the process of establishing itself as one of the "helping" professions, like social work, psychiatry, and clinical psychology. As is the case in these professions, the counselor now tends to see himself as an active therapeutic agent, whose primary task is to bring about *changes* in maladapted individuals. To do so, he has been compelled to familiarize himself with many of the problems and techniques with which his fellow professionals have been struggling for many years. At the same time, the counseling psychologist is not simply a clinical psychologist under another label. His concerns are chiefly with those personal adaptations that facilitate an adjustment to work.

In Chapters 7 and 8, we have described in some detail the differences between the coping behaviors demanded by the world of work and those that are required by other life-spheres. Although these differences have not always been easy to see, they account for the fact that counseling psychology has become something of a distinctive specialty and has both selected and developed a rather distinctive array of therapeutic techniques. Vocational counseling still includes the proper utilization of occupational information and may involve the client in taking an array of vocational tests, but these procedures are no longer considered to be the core of the process. Super (1957) has defined counseling, as the process of helping a person to develop and accept an integrated and adequate picture of himself and his role in the world of work. One then tests this concept against reality and converts it into reality, with satisfaction to himself and benefit to society." This is a fairly elaborate and ambitious set of objectives and obviously goes far beyond the mere transmittal of vocationally relevant information.

Like all movements of social reform, vocational counseling has its share of extreme positions. Some influential leaders in the field (e.g., C. H. Patterson of the University of Illinois) have become so annoyed with the inadequacies of routine psychological testing that they seem ready to outlaw the use of tests. One of the more extreme adherents of this point of view (Arbuckle, 1961) states flatly that it is the duty of the counselor "to remove himself from any phase of testing if at all possible."

What is being argued here is that the real problems of work behavior are not at all (or, at least, not primarily) in the realm of cognitive and motor abilities but have to do with the "nonrational" aspects of behavior: feelings, emotions, perceptions and misperceptions of the self, and similar psychological qualities. The giving of occupational information may be simply gratuitous, and the administration of the standard psychological tests may simply distract attention from the basic problems at issue. What is needed by the vocationally maladapted individual, according to this view, is a kind of *psychotherapy*. Anything else is of doubtful utility at best and a positive hindrance at worst. The group for which Patterson is an articulate spokesman (cf. Patterson, 1964) feels strongly that a kind of reality-oriented psychotherapy is the core of the counseling process. To the degree that information-giving and test-administration can play any useful part, these operations can be relegated to a technical aide and may be most useful *after* therapeutic counseling has come to a successful conclusion.

As a specialty, vocational guidance thus has tended to divide into three distinct phases of activity, each of which was dominant at a particular historical period, although all have tended to persist to some degree. In the early 1900s, about all that the new vocational experts could provide for their clients was information about jobs. Job analysis has continued as an important subspecialty, but it is now carried on mostly by economists and engineers. Starting in World War I, a new dimension was added—psychometric testing. The development of more reliable and sensitive testing batteries is still a major activity but is less prominent than it was 30 years ago. After World War II, vocational counseling began to be conceived of as a form of therapy or treatment. Because of the nature of the problem, all three forms of approach have persisted, although it is fair to say that the first two enjoy less current prestige than the third. Now under discussion is whether therapeutic counseling differs in any particular ways from the kinds of treatment traditionally offered to emotionally disturbed individuals by psychiatrists and clinical psychologists.

THERAPEUTIC COUNSELING

The idea that vocationally maladapted individuals may need some kind of psychotherapy is not new. As we have seen, however, very few psychiatrists and clinical psychologists have directed their attention to the problems of adjustment to work. To the degree that they have thought about it at all, most of these specialists take the position that inadequacy at work is simply one of the consequences of an underlying neurosis or psychosis. From this point of view, the therapeutic strategy follows as a matter of course. Assuming that the underlying emotional illness can be successfully treated, an adjustment to work should then be one of the incidental treatment outcomes. Unfortunately, it is not quite so simple. It has been repeatedly observed that many frank neurotics and psychotics are quite capable of working, and that there are also people who are unable to adjust to work but who do not appear to be emotionally ill. This kind of uncomfortable finding has led the counseling psychologist to the conception that he needs a specialized treatment strategy of his own.

It is no accident that the patron saint of therapeutic counseling is Carl Rogers, rather than Sigmund Freud. Rogers wrote his highly influential first book (Rogers, 1942) after some years of experience in a university counseling center. His patients had been bright and articulate college students, who were referred to his clinic because they could not measure up to a relatively high standard of intellectual achievement. Clearly these young people had emotional problems, but they were not necessarily of the same quality and intensity that the psychiatrist encounters in his ordinary office or hospital practice. Many of them appeared able to function fairly well in other life-spheres, but they had severe scholastic problems despite more than adequate intelligence. In these cases, a full-scale "uncovering" psychoanalysis appeared both too drastic and too time-consuming to meet the immediate problem. What to do?

It was Rogers' hunch that the core difficulties these students faced were in the areas of self-understanding and self-acceptance. They generally tended to be people who had either unrealistically high conceptions of what they should be or unrealistically low conceptions of their personal qualities and capabilities, or both. What was needed, then, was a procedure whereby they could be helped to improve their understanding of their own feelings, attitudes, and abilities. The result was what Rogers came to call "client-centered counseling." In the Rogerian version of psychotherapy, no assumptions are made about causative factors. The client is encouraged to talk about anything that he thinks is relevant to his problems, and the therapist plays the role simply of helping the client become aware of his real feelings. In this situation, the therapist does not interpret, offer advice, or make judgments. He simply operates as a catalyst or "reflector," stressing and making manifest whatever actual feelings the client is conveying. In effect, the client does all the therapeutic work; the therapist's role is to structure the session so that the client gradually understands the true nature of his feelings. In Rogers' view, the therapist should be neither an interpreter, an analyst, nor a guide, because all these roles divert the attention of the patient from the task of self-analysis. Self-analysis is conceived of as the primary aim and virtually sole object of the therapeutic process.

It is easy to see why Rogers' views of psychotherapy have proved to be quite congenial to the needs of counseling psychology. First, Rogers was himself a university-trained psychologist, rather than a medically trained psychiatrist as most American psychoanalysts are. His sphere of operations was the university, rather than the hospital or doctor's office; his patients were students in trouble rather than "sick people." Second, his language is notably free of medical or psychobiological terminology. Everything could be thought of in terms generally familiar to the academic psychologist. Third, one could be trained as a Rogerian therapist within the university setting, without having to win the acceptance of another profession (psychiatry), which has not been notable for its readiness to give equal status to its psychologist colleagues. A fourth reason is somewhat less obvious but may even be more compelling. Most counselors carry out their professional lives either in educational institutions or in agencies whose specific function is described as vocational rehabilitation. The nature of their professional tasks thus stimulates a strong concern in how people cope with environmental demands. In the eyes of many of these men, the subtleties of psychoanalytical theory have a semimystical and unreal flavor. On the other hand, Rogers' views, and especially the case-studies he presents to exemplify them, are closely akin to the kinds of problems they encounter daily in their own professional work.

Despite the existence of considerable doctrinal controversy, I believe that current differences of opinion concerning therapeutic strategy have a good deal to do with style and emphasis rather than with substance. All the current varieties of psychotherapy are "talking" therapies; the basic procedure is to bring about a prolonged verbal dialogue between the patient and the therapist. All require the establishment of a special "therapeutic relationship"; the therapist strives to be seen by the patient as an understanding, nonjudging, and accepting figure, to whom anything can be told without fear of rejection. Both the Rogerian and the Freudian agree that emotional problems reflect unconscious conflicts and inappropriate defenses, although they may disagree widely on what they believe to be the sources of these difficulties. The vaunted "passivity" of the Rogerian therapist may be more apparent than real, since he intervenes at least to the extent of helping the client to understand his real feelings. The psychoanalytically oriented therapist is also trained to avoid active intervention, except perhaps toward the end of the entire therapeutic process; his role is not to advise or instruct but merely to "interpret."

To the degree that there are substantial differences between therapeutic counseling (whether Rogerian or not) and traditional clinical psychotherapy, these differences have more to do with the area of the personality that is of primary interest. The counseling psychologist tends to be more concerned with those emotional dispositions that influence career, work, and achievement. On the other hand, clinical psychiatrists and clinical psychologists are more concerned with the ability of the patient to cope with the demands of personal intimacy. Interestingly enough, both the counselor and the clinician assume that effective treatment of one area of the personality will have a beneficial effect on all others. The clinician has always believed that vocational problems are simply a function of emotional maladjustments in other life-areas. Similarly, from his own vantage point, we find Super (1957;301) arguing that "emotionally maladjusted persons who have genuine problems of vocational adjustment, which can be worked on directly, will find that improvement in the latter will bring about improvement in the former." Unfortunately, both the counselor and clinician appear to be subject to the common failing of professional optimism. It is possible to improve a person's vocational adaptation without making any noticeable dent on other life-problems (Gellman et al., 1957) and the reverse, as we have previously noted, is also true. A person who manifests psychological disturbance in several life-areas may require a number of different kinds of professional service. Whether the various services can be conveniently provided by a single professional or by several is largely a matter of the professional division of labor. What needs recognition, however, is that help with one problem does not necessarily result in the solution of all of them.

The theories of personality that lie behind clinical psychotherapy and therapeutic counseling are all developmental and dynamic. Present dilemmas of personality are understood to be the consequences of earlier traumatic experiences, which the person has largely "forgotten" at the level of awareness but against which he is still defending himself by currently inappropriate maneuvers. For the clinician, the relevant past experiences are those involved in the earliest interaction between the child and the parents, while the counselor is largely concerned with later facets of development.

The most common term in the language of the counselor is the self-concept (derived from Rogers), and it is generally assumed that the most important aspects of this psychological property are formed in middle and later childhood. These differences in theory appear not so much contradictory as complementary. Our attitudes to intimates may well be strongly influenced by very early parent–child interactions, although it has not been easy to establish this link by hard empirical evidence. Similarly, our attitudes to work and achievement may largely be a function of later events, when the sway of parents is less decisive and certain extrafamilial demands have become more insistent. It is also quite possible that child development is an "epigenetic" process (as Erikson puts it), in the sense that earlier experiences have a powerful influence on the ways in which later experiences are incorporated. But, as we have noted above (pp. 91–92), one of Erikson's most stimulating ideas is that personality develops through a series of critical stages, with each stage being determined only in part by the events of prior stages. In effect, the clinician is interested in what has taken place at the earliest stage of child development, while the therapeutic counselor tends to be more concerned with the events of later stages. Clinical psychotherapy and therapeutic counseling differ not so much in their basic techniques as in the kinds of life-problems that are of primary interest. Helping an individual to adapt to work requires examination of one of the semiautonomous areas of the personality (see Chapter 8), which largely takes shape after the years of early childhood have come to an end and is subject to both familial and other-than-familial influences.

These differences between clinical psychotherapy and therapeutic counseling have considerable theoretical and practical importance, since they reflect our current understanding of the relations of work and personality. However, the chief significance of the rise of therapeutic counseling is that it involves the recognition that work adjustment is not simply a logical–rational process that might be managed more efficiently by the large-scale use of electronic computers. The closer we examine work behavior, the more we become aware of its emotional components. Attitudes to work are not only a function of what a person *knows* about the world of work but also what he thinks and feels about himself as a person. The therapeutic counselor works in the domain of "feelings" just as the clinician does, but he is concerned with feelings about work and achievement rather than feelings about love and intimacy.

GROUP METHODS

By far the most usual kind of therapeutic situation, whether we are dealing with therapeutic counseling or clinical psychotherapy, can be described as dyadic: one patient, one therapist. During the most recent period, however, chiefly during the 1960s, considerable interest has developed in treating people in groups. In part, this interest may be accounted for by the obvious economies of effort. The very limited number of trained therapists can thereby serve a larger number of people. But it would be a mistake to believe that economy of scale is the sole purpose currently attributed to the group methods. The adherents of treating people in groups have developed a fairly elaborate rationale to justify this technique and even something of a private mystique.

The group methods have a complex parentage. Their theoretical background derives more from modern social psychology and industrial psychology than it does from the traditions of individual clinical practice. For some decades, the dynamics of small-group interaction has been a fertile field of research for a large number of experimental social psychologists (cf. Cartwright and Zander, 1960). Similarly, industrial psychology has long had a strong interest in the roles of the foreman and administrator and has carried out a great many studies of the intricacies of group leadership (e.g., Argyris, 1962; Haire, 1959; Bavelas, 1950). The latter group has even gone so far as to develop a special kind of group therapy situation (called the "T-group"; see Bradford, Gibb, and Benne, 1964) designed to train the business executive in more effective behavior in interpersonal situations arising on the job. Central to many of these studies is the hypothesis that the behavior of people in groups takes on new dimensions because of the physical presence of others, thus that the full range of human behavior cannot be known if people are studied only as individuals. Following from the principle that the whole is more than the mere sum of its parts, the social group is thought of as having a psychological life of its own, with distinctive properties that cannot be wholly derived from the individual attributes of its members. As might be expected, the precise nature of these alleged distinctive properties has been the subject of considerable controversy.

The counseling psychologist has been more strongly inclined toward the utilization of group therapy than his colleagues in clinical psychiatry and psychology. Again, it is my belief that this is related to the somewhat different kinds of problems on which the various helping specialties are focused. A great many of the demands of work and achievement are heavily social in character. As we have maintained earlier (see Chapter 7), the world of work is predominantly "public" rather than private. One of the major requirements of the adjustment to work is the ability to interact in certain appropriate ways with other people present on the scene. The group therapy procedure has proved to be a useful technique for the detection and amelioration of this sort of maladaptive behavior in work situations. However, this is not to say that group therapy has become the preferred technique for the counselor, nor is it correct to say that clinical psychotherapists are wholly uninterested in it. It is simply that the method may have more genuine utility in therapeutic counseling than in psychotherapy generally. Some exposure to the methods of group therapy has become a fairly common feature of the training of counseling psychologists, while it is still a comparatively rare feature of the professional preparation of clinicians. Most of the authoritative spokesmen in counseling psychology (Bennett, 1963; Lifton, 1961) advocate a judicious combination of individual and group therapy, regarding the latter as capable of adding desirable dimensions to the former. Nevertheless, it is fair to say that the group methods have a more obvious function in adapting people to the world of work than they may have where the focus of attention is on other kinds of intrapsychic difficulties.

NONVERBAL TECHNIQUES: THE REHABILITATIVE WORKSHOP

The common feature of the various forms of treatment we have so far discussed is their heavy reliance on verbal communication. Psychotherapy, whether group or individual, can be distinguished from other kinds of treatment by the fact that it is a *talking* therapy. What the therapist is intent on establishing is a prolonged and intense dialogue between the patient and himself. In the case of group therapy, an objective is the promotion of verbal communication *among* patients as well. None of this is particularly inappropriate. After all, language is the chief means that people have of understanding each other. At the same time, many mental health professionals have always been committed to a determined search for nonverbal methods of treatment.

Ever since the advent of psychoanalysis, the profession of psychiatry has been sharply split between people who believed that mental illness was essentially a neurological problem and those more psychoanalytically oriented psychiatrists who tended to conceive of mental illness as some kind of massive interpersonal maladjustment. The preferred methods of the former are physical and biochemical treatment of what is seen as simply another variety of organic disease. The latter regard the "talking" therapies as the prime treatment method and look upon medication as little more than a palliative. Most clinical psychologists are in the second camp, partly because they have been heavily influenced by psychoanalytic theories and partly because they have, of course, no legal right to prescribe medical treatments. One of the consequences of this division of labor is that the more biologically oriented psychiatrist tends to be concerned with treatment of the psychoses, which are often particularly resistant to the establishment of viable verbal communication, whereas the preferred patient of the psychoanalyst or clinical psychologist is the psychoneurotic. One must be able to talk in a relatively coherent and systematic fashion in order to participate in psychotherapy, and the neurotic is not so disturbed that verbal communication is virtually out of the question. This peculiar division of labor perpetuated itself the more easily because the nature and causes of the emotional disorders are still largely scientific mysteries. In the absence of any very clear evidence of what they are dealing with, the helping professional is at liberty to choose whatever approach is most congenial to his temperament, interests, and particular background.

In the field of vocational behavior, there is also a difference of opinion about the appropriateness of various treatment modalities, but it is caused by somewhat different circumstances. There are probably no vocational counselors who believe that vocational problems can be solved through the techniques of medicine. On the other hand, there are a fairly large number who feel the need for some alternatives to the verbal psychotherapies. One of the pressing reasons is that many of their clients are poorly educated people who are markedly deficient in verbal skills. Another reason is that the adjustment to work seems to require a good deal of genuine reality-testing, during which the individual experiences what it means to play the worker's role. Many of these experiences cannot be put into words in formal psychotherapy. Others can only be encountered in the work situation itself. The result has been a search for nonverbal methods of treatment for the vocationally maladapted. These other methods are no more "biological" than is ordinary psychotherapy, but they tend to be manipulations of objective situations rather than words.

The chief nonverbal instrumentality that has developed within vocational counseling is the so-called rehabilitative workshop. The rationale of this type of treatment modality is essentially akin to the notion of "learning by doing." In this case, both the counselor and his client are in a position to learn something that is difficult to ascertain by other means. A large number of vocationally maladapted people are in a very poor position to discover why they cannot find or maintain employment. Modern competitive industry has neither the time nor the will to convey to the worker the reasons for his poor performance or to give him much assistance in improving his competence. Most often he is simply told he cannot meet the average level of performance and is laid off as quickly as possible. The very impersonality and remoteness of most work situations is a guarantee that the counselor will normally have only a very dim idea of what he is supposed to treat. Obviously, this sort of situation is very different from other kinds of personal dilemmas, in which the patient is usually full of circumstantial detail about his problems, even though he may initially totally misunderstand their import. On the other hand, the vocationally maladapted person knows he cannot work, but there is very little he can tell the counselor about it. Also, the clinical psychotherapist may sometimes be able to interview the people who are most important in the patient's emotional life and even involve some of them directly in the treatment process. The vocational counselor, however, can rarely learn anything very useful from interviewing the client's employer—who is both too unconcerned and too unobservant to tell him anything very material—and he certainly cannot draw both the client and his supervisor into a conjoint therapeutic situation.

The rehabilitative workshop is, as it were, a contrived version or simulation of actual work. We have already become familiar with this device as one of the vehicles for vocational assessment. It is, however, also a treatment modality in its own right. To function as a means of therapy, certain conditions must be carefully provided. First, the facility must provide a reasonable simulation of the important demand characteristics of working environments. In other words, it must be as much like an ordinary job as is possible. Wages and working conditions should be quite comparable to those in ordinary industry. The work performed should be "realistic" in the sense that it is not make-work. The client is made aware, ultimately at least, that he is expected to perform according to customary standards of quality and quantity. Both co-workers and supervisors are present on the scene, and the opportunity must exist of confronting the client with the full range of interpersonal relations that he will encounter on the job. To be effective, this type of treatment program should be quite realistic in terms of physical layout, kinds of work to be done, levels of compensation, quality of supervision, hours of work, and the like.

Of course, if it is to be therapeutic, it cannot be identical with ordinary employment. Since the objective is to bring about changes in the work personality, the ineffective worker cannot be summarily discharged after a few days of poor performance. The rehabilitative workshop, therefore, must include features that are not present in unprotected employment. The most important difference is the role of the shop foreman. In the ordinary work situation, the prime responsibility of the foreman is to see that the work is done. Productivity is his overriding concern. If he is particularly understanding, or has been instructed in "human relations," he may be aware that production can be negatively influenced by personal problems; but he has very limited time and scope to concern himself with the work-problems of the individual. In the rehabilitative workshop, however, the foreman plays a far more complex role. He must be in a position to observe the client for a sufficiently protracted period so that he can detect what is preventing an adjustment to work. He then must be able to manipulate those conditions of work that will help the client move toward a more adequate set of work behaviors. He must do all this while still "acting" like an ordinary work supervisor in an ordinary work situation. It can be seen that this is a fairly demanding set of role requirements, requiring specialized training and considerable flexibility.[1] It also necessitates a much larger number of foremen for a given number of workers than is the case in industry. Experience has suggested that the ratio of client–workers to foremen cannot be more than approximately 5 to 1, otherwise the foreman has great difficulty in meeting the demands of his therapeutic role.

[1] In the original facility that served as the prototype for the rehabilitative workshop (Gellman et al., 1957), it was felt that only trained professionals could meet these complex role requirements. The innovators of this facility felt it would be easier to train psychologists to act like foremen than to train industrial foremen to act like psychologists. It is not at all certain, however, that the rehabilitative workshop must be *entirely* staffed by professionals, since this matter has not yet been put to any decisive experimental test. It is possible, although perhaps unlikely, that industrial people can function as foremen in the rehabilitative workshop, provided they are carefully selected and adequately trained. The most difficult technical problem of the

In addition to the complexities of the foreman's role, there are other important differences between the rehabilitative workshop and ordinary work. The rehabilitative workshop cannot function effectively unless it is understood by everyone to be temporary and transitional. It is in no sense to be regarded as a place of permanent sheltered employment for the ineffective worker. The client is to stay in it only as long as he can benefit from it, and benefit means being able to leave it for regular employment. The period of stay in the facility must thus have a defined temporal limit, although the length of this period is a matter of some dispute. Some rehabilitative workshops operate on the basis of a fixed duration of service for everyone. The client who cannot make sufficient progress during this fixed period is simply dropped or referred to some other kind of facility. Other workshops permit clients to remain for variable amounts of time, depending upon the particular client's needs and difficulties. Advocates of a fixed period of service rest their case on the argument that an indefinite time period encourages dependency on the part of the client and indecisiveness on the part of staff. On the other hand, the more flexible procedure seems better attuned to client variability. In any case, the service must end at some point, whether it lasts 10 weeks, 6 months, or 1 year; otherwise the objective of bringing about behavioral change simply shifts to the provision of sheltered work.

As a therapeutic medium, the predominating characteristic of this type of facility is that the influence that is brought to bear upon the client is situational rather than verbal. This does not mean, of course, that there is *no* verbal communication. Foremen talk to workers and workers talk to each other. It is assumed, however, that the primary agents of therapeutic change are the nonverbal features of the total work situation. The client is induced to test the reality of what it means to work by a wide variety of available procedures. Monetary compensation may be systematically varied. He may be placed to work by himself or with others. The foremen can adopt different kinds of supervisory demeanors, ranging from a high degree of supportive permissiveness to a high degree of authoritative control. Violations of ordinary work-rules can be tolerated or given various degrees of negative sanction. Standards of quality and quantity of production can be enforced or ignored. The chief objective of all these maneuvers is to confront the client with all the customary conditions of work in a planned and systematic manner, so that the individual's particular work problems can be assessed

therapeutic workshop is maintenance of the necessary balance between the businesslike atmosphere of ordinary work and its basic professional aims. Some professionals can play both roles fairly well; others cannot. The professional tends to find it congenial to be too "soft," the industrially trained foreman too "hard." Additionally, the ambiguities of the role requirements may cause both types to overcompensate in undesired directions. This is one of the aspects of the rehabilitative workshop that needs much further investigation.

and the necessary corrective measures systematically applied. These steps can be carried out with very little verbal interchange between staff and client.

None of this implies that the workshop cannot also provide the more conventional verbal therapies. In fact, the client's workshop experiences and the therapist's knowledge of the client's work behavior can be marked assets for the therapeutic hour. Many clients can develop enhanced understanding of what is happening to them in the workshop if they can talk it through with a knowledgeable professional. Even in these cases, however, the workshop is providing the core therapeutic experiences, and largely on a nonverbal basis. Where therapeutic counseling is deemed advisable (it need not be for all cases and may be inappropriate for some), it should take place outside of ordinary workshop hours, as would be the case if the client were attempting to hold an ordinary job. Some workshops achieve this objective by engaging their clients in group therapy sessions at the close of the working day in order to provide them with the possibility of talking over their problems and difficulties. The provision of some form of therapeutic counseling or psychotherapy, however, should not act to diminish the reality aspects of the workshop.

The prime purpose of the rehabilitative workshop is not merely to provide sheltered employment. Of course, it must do so for a limited time, since we can take for granted that its clients will be people who would be fired within their first few days of ordinary employment. But, sooner or later, the client must be faced with work as it really is, with the condition that everything is being done to help him tolerate it. The workshop must operate on the basis of a systematic procedure, whereby work pressures are increased until they approximate those prevailing in unprotected employment. However permissive the staff must be at first, it cannot remain so indefinitely. The client who can work well only under unusual conditions will continue to fail in ordinary industry.

In its essential respects, the rehabilitative workshop is an effort to create an artificial "small society." To the degree that it recreates the customary demands of work, the client encounters whatever have been his chief problems. He does so, however, under conditions in which he can be adequately observed and also under circumstances where the relevant variables can be placed under some measure of social control. The actors in the drama are the "employer" (the workshop director), the "foreman' (the professional trained to play this role), the "personnel worker" (the therapeutic counselor), and his "co-workers" (the other clients). Since these are all available on the scene, it is possible not only to observe his reactions to other human beings on the job but also to vary the roles of these figures in ways designed to strengthen the client's tolerance for stressful situations. The foreman can be—as the plan or situation demands—supportive, matter-of-fact, or controlling. The "employer" can be benign or demanding. The counselor can be helpful and sympathetic or stern and critical. The client's relations to his co-workers can be altered in a variety of ways. He can be placed in a group of workers who are more productive than he is or less productive; it can be seen how he handles the problem of a co-worker who is provocative or disturbed; the client can be helped to achieve the necessary balance of competition and cooperation. Without having at once to cope with all the relatively demanding features of the labor market, the client is able gradually to familiarize himself with the routines of work. The rehabilitative workshop can thus be looked on as a kind of enculturative medium, in which the requirements for entry into the world of work can be more readily incorporated. If, as many therapists say, traditional psychotherapy is some kind of process of resocialization, then the rehabilitative workshop has similar features. The essential difference concerns the means through which therapeutic messages are transmitted. In psychotherapy, the necessary vehicle is the spoken word. In the rehabilitative workshop, it is the entire work environment that "speaks" to the client and with which the client is encouraged to interact.

THE DEVELOPMENT OF ADJUSTIVE TECHNIQUES

From the standpoint of the 1980s, it can be perceived that nonverbal treatment techniques of the type described in the preceding section have been fairly widely adopted within the field of rehabilitation of the handicapped. The rehabilitation workshop pioneered by the Chicago Jewish Vocational Service was adopted as a model by the Division of Vocational Rehabilitation of the U.S. Department of Health, Education and Welfare, which financed its establishment in a number of other vocational agencies throughout the country. In certain respects however, the Chicago model (the Vocational Adjustment Center, or VAC) has proved both too expensive and too cumbersome for really general adoption. The workshop setting has become very widespread in rehabilitation agencies, but, more often than not, important aspects of the model are found difficult to execute and are dropped (e.g., the requirement that trainees are paid according to a graduated wage-scale, or that foremen be trained professionals, or that there must be rigid adherence to a fixed time-schedule). While the original developers of VAC believed that such features were crucial, many rehabilitation agencies throughout the country have found them difficult or impossible to implement.

The techniques of adjusting people to work have developed in two directions since the early 1950s, when they first started taking shape. The first of these calls itself *behavioral analysis* and is modelled on the theories of operant conditioning identified with B. F. Skinner (1953, 1974). These techniques were first applied to treatment of severely withdrawn psychotics by Ayllon and Azrin (1968) in the form of the so-called "token economy" and

have been widely applied to problems of vocational rehabilitation by Fordyce (1971, 1976). A very good summary of this approach is provided by
Marr (1982). The methodology of behavioral analysis seems about as far as
one can get from the techniques familiar to us in verbal psychotherapy. This
approach to treatment boils down to two procedures: (1) the identification
and *objective* measurement of improper or unwanted behaviors *and* of
desired behaviors; (2) an essentially nonverbal conditioning procedure designed to stamp out the unwanted behavior and enhance the desired behavior; the outcome of the treatment is, again, measured objectively. These
behavioral methods have some enthusiastic adherents in the field of vocational rehabilitation and have helped to focus our attention on the pressures
emanating from the work environment. They have been, however, too often
presented as a panacea when, in fact, behavioral techniques appear to work
best with certain specific kinds of persons (e.g., severely withdrawn psychotics, people with fairly massive mental retardation, very young children).
This approach also seems to work best in highly structured situations such as
mental hospitals, where all crucial aspects of a patient's life are under
observation and therefore capable of being manipulated. In freer situations,
the presumed object of the behavioral analysis may simply take himself out
of the treatment situation.

The second direction that work-adjustive techniques have taken may
simply be described as *psychosocial*. The basic assumptions are: (1)
maladaptation to work is a function of complex social interactions between
the person and the work setting; (2) therapeutic intervention involves a
process of reeducation, which takes place both in verbal and nonverbal
terms. Hershenson has provided a theoretical model for this kind of adjustive training (cf. Hershenson, 1981). The psychosocial approach involves
assessment of a great many aspects of work other than specific work skills
(the meaning of work, self-concept, relations to co-workers and supervisors,
etc.); once the major problems have been identified, the task then is to apply
whatever educative process appears most suitable. In its employment of
adjustive techniques, the psychosocial approach is quite eclectic, using a
range of methods from conventional teaching and lecturing, through group
counseling and workshop methods, to behavioral techniques where suitable.

SUMMARY

The field of vocational service has a history of some 60 odd years, if we
include the pioneers. During this period, it has undergone some marked
shifts in outlook and objectives. Most of its energies were devoted at first to
the procurement and transmittal of occupational information and to the
development and administration of standard vocational tests. This type of
service is still, by far, the most frequently encountered. Despite the acknowl-

edged limitations of these procedures, it is fair to say that they have had some value in meeting the minimal vocational needs of the majority of the population. During the past two or three decades, the vocational expert has begun to turn his attention to people who have severe problems in adapting to work, with a resulting rise of vocational counseling as a distinctive professional specialty. The shift from "guidance" to "counseling" implies an increasing belief that the problems of adjustment to work are, in some sense or other, problems of personality. Where these problems are severe, they cannot be solved by the giving of occupational information or the administration of tests. Some type of reconstruction of relevant areas of the personality appears to be required. The result has been an increasingly intensive search for appropriate methods of treatment.

The common characteristic of the therapeutic methods we have been discussing is that they are concerned with the emotional and affective sides of work behavior. They are quite analogous, therefore, to the traditional clinical methods that have been developed to deal with the disturbed personality. Where we have found differences in technique, they can be attributed to the fact that the ability to work has, in part at least, its own unique set of determinants.

III | WORK AND MENTAL HEALTH

11 | PSYCHOPATHOLOGY AND WORK: SOME CONCEPTUAL ISSUES

It may seem obvious that many of the issues so far discussed have direct bearing on the problems of mental illness and mental health, but until very recently, this connection has been far from clear to most mental health practitioners. Clinical psychiatry and clinical psychology have, historically, concerned themselves with a quite different set of issues. These helping professions have largely focused their attention on what, for want of a better term, we may call *psychiatric symptomatology:* obsessions, delusions, hallucinations, thought disorders, inappropriate affects, problems of impulse control, and the like. Generally, the medical model, at least in this country, has governed the activities of most mental health practitioners. The basic tasks are *diagnosis* (identification of the particular disease entity presumed to be responsible for the particular mental aberrations and misbehaviors observed) and *treatment* (amelioration of symptom severity at the minimum, and eradication of the disease entity, at the maximum). During over 100 years of devoted research and practice, psychiatry and psychology have achieved many technological advances: the development of elaborate and complex systems of psychiatric nosology, sophisticated assessment devices, many kinds of psychotherapy; and a wide armamentarium of psychotherapeutic drugs. In cases where treatment fails—and this is often the case in dealing with the more severe mental disorders such as the schizophrenias—psychiatry has also heavily concerned itself with what could be called the *management* of mental disorder (how to arrange the lives of people who seem unable to exist, without unbearable friction, in ordinary human society).

The appropriateness of the medical model in clinical psychiatry and psychology has, of course, been challenged both within and without the field. Some psychiatrists and psychologists and an array of social scientists have argued that what we are dealing with here are essentially "problems in living," not "diseases." While this may seem like a distinction without a difference, it reflects important differences in points of view. The dissenters from the medical model—and these are frequently identified as social psychiatrists and social scientists—tend to view the mental and personality disorders as the result of failures in the socialization process that all human beings must undergo; correspondingly, there is a tendency to use the term *assessment* rather than *diagnosis* and to speak of *reeducation* rather than *treatment*. The goal of the socially oriented practitioner is not to achieve a "cure" of a "disease" but to bring about a more adequate adaptation to the demands and requirements of the larger society. The emphasis is on "coping" rather than on "health." It seems fair to add that dissenters from the medical model are still rather rare on the ground, and that the overwhelming majority of clinical psychiatrists and clinical psychologists see their task as the identification and treatment of mental illness.

MENTAL ILLNESS

Given that this appraisal is valid, we at once confront a set of rather murky problems. What is *mental illness*? The very existence of this term implies that there must be some important differences between *mental* illness and *physical* illness, but what are these differences? The meaning of "illness" is fairly straightforward. Dictionaries are very terse on "illness" and simply give its synonyms: disease, malady, ailment. Under "disease," the *Random House Dictionary of the English Language* says the following:

> 1. *Pathol.* a condition of an organ, part, structure, or system of the body in which there is incorrect function resulting from the effects of heredity, infection, diet, or environment; illness; sickness; ailment. 2. any abnormal condition in a plant that interferes with its normal, vital physiological processes, caused by pathogenic microorganisms, parasites, unfavorable environmental, genetic, or nutritional factors, etc. 3. any deranged or depraved condition, as of the mind, society, etc.: *Excessive melancholy is a disease.* 4. decomposition of a material under special conditions: *tin disease.*

The first of these definitions causes us no difficulties; it simply describes the domain of the medical and biological sciences. Diseases are seen as malfunctions of the organs, organ systems, or biochemical structures of living organisms. The tasks of medical science are: to identify the organic system that is malfunctioning and to discover the causes of the malfunction (*diagnosis*); to intervene with physical procedures (medication, surgery, diet-control, etc.) in order to restore the malfunctioning structure to what is described as normal functioning (*treatment*). Definition 2 above extends to plants, whereas definition 1 is limited to animals. When we reach definition 3, however, the language and focus changes. We now encounter qualifiers such as "deranged" and "depraved," applied to "mind" and "society." We have left the rigorous domain of biology to enter upon the somewhat more rarified areas of philosophy, psychology, sociology, even morality. It may be appropriate to ask whether or not the meaning of a commonly used word is being stretched too far when the term *disease* is used to refer to: (1) the breakdown of biochemical material such as lung tissue or heart muscle; (2) the appearance in a person of what looks like irrationally assaultive or seclusive behavior: (3) the manifestation in a human society of unstable functioning, such as severe economic depressions, wars, or revolutions. The term *sick society* has even been applied to human groups who are presumed to have undergone a critical decline of previously strongly held moral and ethical codes (e.g., Nazi Germany).[1]

We have grappled with the concept of *disease* because the so-called diseases of the mind appear, in a number of important respects, to be quite unlike the diseases of the body. These differences seem so fundamental to some psychiatrists and social scientists that serious questions have been raised concerning whether the mental disorders are diseases at all, at least in the stricter biological sense of the term *disease*.

While it is generally agreed that if there is an impaired organ in question, that organ must be the central nervous system (loosely, the brain), a century of research has so far been unable to determine the causes of impaired brain functioning or even the precise nature of its impairments. A number of investigators are firmly convinced that hereditary and constitutional factors play a role in the genesis of certain of the more severe mental disorders (e.g., schizophrenia), but the evidence adduced remains ambiguous for a number of technological and methodological reasons. Similarly, although it has been amply demonstrated that certain biochemical substances (the psychotherapeutic drugs, such as thorazine and lithium) can ameliorate some manifest psychotic behaviors, it remains uncertain as to whether these substances are directly *curative* (curative in the sense that specific drugs can be shown to attack and destroy that bacilli responsible for certain specific bodily diseases) or merely control certain of the *sequaelae* of a mental disorder, such as the anxiety and confusion generated in a person who is seriously misperceiving the world and the people around him or her. Again, although there is controversy about their effectiveness, a major treatment modality for the mental disorders is composed of the so-called talking therapies (psychoanalysis, psychotherapy), but no one maintains that a prolonged dialogue with the patient can cure a brain tumor, an impaired kidney, or the unwillingness of a person's bone marrow to produce adequate quantities of red blood cells.

Above all, the mental disorders appear to have very powerful con-

[1]One may denounce the operations of the Nazi regime as evil and destructive without necessarily thinking of them as the behaviors of a "sick" society. In fact, to describe murderous and inhuman actions as "sick" seems merely to water down our traditional conceptions of good and evil and gain nothing in the process. The planned and systematic extermination of entire ethnic groups (Jews, Gypsies, etc.) were outcomes of a coldly rational political policy, not the consequences of some irresistible impulse.

sequences for the general *social adjustment* of the affected individual. In fact, it is a central feature of the more severe mental disorders (the psychoses) that they massively disrupt the social arrangements and basic social attitudes that enable people to live and function within ordinary human society. The afflicted individual appears unable to tolerate the most minimal obligations of family life. He or she seems unable to form or maintain normal friendships or finds such relationships disrupted or destroyed. In most cases, a fairly severe mental disorder renders the person unable to work in any kind of gainful employment. The heavily "social" flavor of the mental disorders[2] is attested to by the fact that the best studies of treatment outcome (cf. Strauss and Carpenter, 1974; Strauss, 1983) use as criteria of recovery not only evidence of the eradication of the more florid psychotic symptoms (delusions, hallucinations, thought disorders, etc.) but also such criteria as whether the "recovered" patient can remain outside the walls of a mental hospital, whether he or she can maintain a marriage or relate without disruption to other people, whether the person can find or maintain some kind of gainful employment. All this has led some current writers to argue that the mental and personality disorders are not diseases at all (not, at least, in terms of the primary medical definition of disease) but must be thought of as "social breakdown syndromes," failures or impairments in the complex networks of socialization processes through which the child is taught to take his or her place in society.

Having discussed the term *mental disease* and its ambiguities, we should hasten to declare that we need not take a position in this controversy. Whether or not the mental disorders are "true" diseases in the biological sense of the term, it remains a fact that these disorders have massive social consequences for the afflicted individual. It is with certain of these social consequences that we deal here.

The appearance in a person of a serious disorder of thought and behavior—whatever its origin or nature—typically renders it difficult or impossible for the individual to cope with ordinary familial demands, hold unprotected employment, or pursue a career. Medical psychiatry has never been indifferent to these social aspects or consequences of these disorders and, in fact, has included them in its lists of "symptoms." Amelioration of these social disruptions is regarded as the ultimate goal of treatment. Traditionally, however, and with few exceptions, psychiatrists regard themselves

---

[2]The reader will note that, in the past few paragraphs, we have begun to use the phrase "mental disorder" rather than "mental illness." This is because the term *disorder* implies nothing about the sources, locus, or nature of the process that is seen to be somehow disarranged. While not free from its own conceptual difficulties, the phrase "mental disorder" has the advantage that we may use it without necessarily implying that some system of the body has broken down. The sources of "mental disorder" may be physical, environmental, personal, or whatever combination of all these that science eventually determines fits the case.

as *medical* specialists, trained to deal with what is most frequently defined as "primary" or "first-rank" psychiatric symptoms (delusions, hallucinations, thought disorders, inappropriate affects, etc.), leaving to others the task of correction or amelioration of what is seen as the social consequences of these "primary" symptoms. These other professionals tend to be nonmedical specialists: psychologists, social workers, rehabilitation specialists, "change agents." Many of these professionals may subscribe to the belief that basic to the mental disorders are certain imperfectly understood hereditary, constitutional, or biochemical factors that it is the task of the medical sciences to disentangle and treat, but this belief does not govern their practice. Trained, as they are, largely in the social rather than biological sciences, they see their task as directed at correction of the "secondary" symptoms of social disruption.

The writer numbers himself among those whose task it has been to deal with the social disruptions consequent upon mental disorder. He is a psychologist, not a physician. His training and biases, therefore, incline him toward social and interpersonal explanations of mental disorder rather than a search for a biological substratum. But the particular theoretical biases of the writer are not terribly relevant, in this instance, to what is to be written here, except where the writer explicitly engages in the game of theory-building. The relations between work and mental illness, between mental illness and social behavior generally, are sufficiently close and complex so that an exhaustive treatment is desirable. One may subscribe to the aforementioned distinction between primary and secondary symptoms of mental disorder (as it happens, the writer does not), but it need not follow that eradication of the so-called primary set will, by itself, cause the "secondary" set automatically to disappear. We have, unfortunately, too many instances of people whose more florid signs of mental disorder have long vanished but who seem quite unable to function adequately outside the walls of a mental hospital. Much of the content of this chapter and of the two to follow, is devoted to demonstrating that *both* the "first-rank" symptoms *and* the social disruptions need treatment, perhaps simultaneously.

MENTAL HEALTH

In considering the conceptual problems of the term *mental illness,* we have noted a number of ambiguities. But what of *mental health?* Both in medical and common usage, the term *health* is defined as a state characterized as "freedom from illness or pain." Mental health, then, would be seen as the absence of mental illness or mental anguish. But this essentially negative definition has seemed inadequate to many writers, and there have been strenuous efforts to attach more positive meanings to the term *mental health.*

Some years ago, a leading social psychologist (Jahoda, 1958) was commissioned by the Joint Commission on Mental Illness and Health[3] to conduct a survey of "positive" conceptions of mental health. The objective of the survey was to clarify a variety of efforts to give meaning to what is described as a "vague" term: *mental health.*

Jahoda began her task by disposing of three conceptualizations of mental health that she found unsuitable or generally inadequate. The first of these is the familiar notion that mental health is to be defined as the absence of mental disease. This she summarily discards on three counts: first, because the criteria themselves of mental disease are ill-defined, confusing, and, often, contradictory; second, because, except in extreme cases, the borderline between what is regarded as normal and abnormal is dim and difficult to fix; third, because cultural relativism suggests that what is seen as normal in one society may be regarded as abnormal in another and therefore that the "evaluation of actions as sick, or normal, or extraordinary in a positive sense often depends largely on accepted social conventions" (Jahoda, 1958, p. 13).

The second notion that is summarily discarded by Jahoda is the use of "normality" as a criterion for mental health. Here she cites the contributions of cultural anthropology, whose work can be regarded "as a series of variations on the theme of the plasticity of human nature and, accordingly, on the vast range of what can be regarded as normal" (Jahoda, 1958, p. 15). There is an additional difficulty. The term *normality* conceals two quite different concepts: normality as *statistical* frequency and normality as a set of ideas of how people *ought* to function. The mathematical model for statistical normality is the so-called normal (or Gaussian) curve, marked by very low frequencies at the two extremes, with the bulk of the cases concentrated at or near the average. This mathematical model works very well in describing the distribution of such population characteristics as height or weight but rather poorly in connection with such demographic features as family income or years of education. It may also lead to the mistaken judgment that whatever exists in the majority of cases *is* the desired social norm. Intelligence tests administered to large, unselected populations of school children tend to yield distributions approximating the normal curve, but this does not cause us to declare that scores close to the average are most

---

[3]The Joint Commission was set up by an Act of the U.S. Congress in 1955 to "analyse and evaluate the needs and resources of the mentally ill in the United States and make recommendations for a national mental health program." During the following two decades, the Joint Commission produced a series of very important studies of all aspects of psychiatric theory and practice in this country, of which the Jahoda volume was the first published. The Commission's final report, *Action for Mental Health* (Joint Commission on Mental Illness and Health, 1961), has been profoundly influential in altering prevailing methods of care of the severely mentally ill in the United States. The report provided documentation for passage of the Kennedy Mental Health Act of 1963, which shifted the locus of care of the mentally ill from the traditional mental hospital to the "community."

desirable. Similarly, it is easy for us to think of mental retardation as a variety of abnormality, but the equally infrequent "genius-level" performance is not seen as abnormal. Statistical frequency, on the one hand, and the standards in a given society of how people *ought*, on the other, to behave are far from identical, although frequently confused. The idea of normality as the criterion of positive mental health does not meet the test.

The third criterion of mental health that Jahoda questions at the outset is that there must exist some sort of state of "well-being." As Jahoda points out, however, well-being or "happiness" flows from a kind of conjunction between what a person wants out of life and what life has to offer. A person who is sublimely happy in the face of highly adverse circumstances is usually seen as either a saint or an idiot, neither appellation falling within the framework of the normal. A state of well-being may, under certain circumstances, be *one* of the criteria of mental health, but it is insufficent to serve as the chief criterion.

Having disposed of three popular meanings of mental health that she found more or less deficient, Jahoda next examines the rather extensive psychiatric and psychological literature. She organizes the various approaches encountered under six major categories, as follows.

1. *Attitudes toward the self.* The healthy person is one who is aware of his own assets and limitations and who is accepting of them (Mayman 1955; Allport, 1937). He is realistic about his own capabilities and liabilities (Fromm, 1955). He can accept himself without complacency (Maslow, 1950). He has developed an adequate sense of *ego-identity* (Erikson, 1950).

2. *Self-actualization.* The key issue here is the realization of one's potentialities (Goldstein, 1940; Lindner, 1956).

3. *Integration.* This idea has become prominent among psychoanalysts identified with ego psychology (Hartmann (1939, 1947). Hartmann argues that a truly rich personality requires achievement of a balance among the various psychic forces implied by the terms *id, ego,* and *superego* without exclusive domination of one of three sets. Kris (1936) has supplied the useful phrase "regression in the service of the ego" in describing the essense of the creative personality.

4. *Autonomy.* Here we are concerned with the independence—dependence continuum, with the former seen as the positive pole. Foote and Cottrell (1955) talk of the degree to which an individual's actions are governed by a stable set of internal standards. Riesman (1950) has coined his well-known set of characterological types: tradition-directed, other-directed, self-directed; in his view, the latter are the most healthy.

5. *Perception of reality.* The operative issues here are (a) freedom from need-distortion (Jahoda, 1950; Barron, 1955); (b) being sensitive to the needs of others (Foote and Cottrell, 1955).

6. *Environmental mastery.* This last category is the most inclusive. It turns on the basic themes of *success* and *adaptation*. The issues covered include:

(a) the ability to love (Hacker, 1945; Erikson, 1950); (b) adequacy in love, work, and play (Ginsberg, 1955); (c) adequacy in interpersonal relations (Washington State Department of Health, 1951; Fromm, 1955); (d) being able to deal with situational demands (Sanford, 1956; Wishner, 1955); (e) ability to adapt (Hartmann, 1939; Chein, 1944); (f) problem-solving (Jahoda, 1953).

We have reported Jahoda's survey at some length because it drives home the point that the definition of mental health is far from a simple affair. Although many of these criteria appear to overlap and the boundaries between others are quite vague, it seems clear that we are dealing here with a multidimensional conception. It is also clear that the listed criteria make up a set of social and cultural values, and that we cannot talk of mental health without being enmeshed in ideological consideration. In passing, we note that the ability to work is only listed once. We regard this as something of a deficiency in our current conceptions of mental health, and we shall compensate for this deficiency in the remainder of this chapter.

WORK AND DISORDER

Given the complexities and ambiguities involved in "mental illness" and "mental health," and also given that the primary approach to the disorders has been, in our opinion, rather narrowly medical, it should not be surprising that we still know relatively little about the place of work in these two great domains of human behavior. This is not to say that it has been totally overlooked. Examination of the literature discloses two quite different lines of enquiry and practice. The first of these bears on the quite varied roles of work in the severe mental disorders: the psychoses. As it has developed, we will refer to this line of research and service as the field of *psychiatric rehabilitation*. The second line of enquiry has developed with industry as an aspect of personnel work and has to do with *work stress*. We shall deal with these two problems in subsequent sections, but, before we do so, we need some general remarks to set the stage.

In Chapters 7 and 8, we have argued that work is a form of social behavior: the ability to work and the manner in which one works are functions of very complex processes of socialization. We also have placed considerable emphasis on a further argument that our basic attitudes to work are formed not so much within the family setting but in extrafamilial situations (e.g., the school and the street). It was indicated that this process of socialization was long and complex, involving the internalization of many messages from the larger society, some of these messages being quite explicit while some are implicit. We acknowledged that there were many ways in which such a process could go wrong, and we delineated some of the forms of work pathology. We did not, however, describe the relations between the domain of work behavior and the psychiatrically defined forms of personality disorder that we know as the psychoses and psychoneuroses. This is because we were anxious to establish that the domains of work adaptation and personality adaptation were not identical. In effect, we were separating the domain of work from the domain of love. We were led to draw this distinction because of our experience that successful treatment of a personality disorder did not necessarily bring about an adaptation to work. We also observed the converse, that is, people who seemed to be able to adapt to work despite the continued existence of a fairly severe mental disorder.

While it is worthwhile to distinguish the spheres of work maladaptation and personality disorder, if we can show that their internal phenomenal structure and etiology are not identical, it is also possible to leave the impression that there is no connection whatever between these two behavioral domains. Such an impression would be manifestly wrong. There is massive clinical evidence that development in a person of a massive thought disorder or affective imbalance also disturbs those coping mechanisms by which the individual adapts to work, although this outcome does not occur in all instances. Similarly, even a relatively milder neurotic disorder may interfere with the person's ability to meet certain vital work demands. The correlation between the severity of an emotional or mental disorder and the ability to work is not perfect, but it is also not zero. One of the aims of the field of psychiatric rehabilitation is to restore or facilitate the ability to work even where the underlying mental disorder persists uncured. It should be noted, however, that the field of psychiatric rehabilitation would not exist at all if it had not been observed that one of the life domains often disrupted by a mental illness is the domain of adjustment to work.

TOWARD A CLINICAL PSYCHOLOGY OF WORK

It is regrettable that we have very little hard information on the relations of work and mental disorder. We pointed out earlier that the enormous body of literature on psychopathology is almost wholly silent on maladaptive work behavior, partly because of the manner in which psychological services are organized and delivered. As a consequence, we lack an adequate taxonomy of maladaptive work behaviors, in vivid contrast to the almost overabundant body of fact on the general symptoms of mental disorder. The problem is that the available information tends to focus on intrapsychic processes, rather than adaptive behaviors. Thus, we know a good deal about the kinds of thinking defects, delusions, hallucinations, and other cognitive impairments that, taken together, lead to a diagnosis of schizophrenia. Similarly, we can recognize disturbances of affect and mood, the manifestations of extreme anxiety, the presence or absence of irrational fears, and the like. We are certainly aware that many of these "mental" impairments must have effects on the ability of the person to cope with any of the major demands that living makes on him—including the demand to work. What has so far eluded us, however, is the precise nature of these effects. In part, our ignorance arises from the fact that the mental health professional rarely has the opportunity to observe the disturbed patient *in situ* (i.e., while he is actually at work). In part, it may be because the right questions have not been asked.

If we are right in our hypothesis that work behavior is dependent, at least to some degree, on a semiautonomous area of the personality, then we need to begin to accumulate information on the various ways this sector of the personality can go wrong. The importance of this consideration becomes obvious if we grasp the essence of the manner in which the clinician actually operates. On the one hand, the clinical practitioner must constantly keep in mind that each new case is a unique individual, whose experiences and reactions cannot be assumed to be identical with those of anyone else. On the other hand, he could not begin to deal effectively with the patient unless he was able to perceive that the particular problem that plagues the patient is an example of a more general *class* of problems, which his entire experience has trained him to identify. He is able to say to himself that what the patient tells him suggests that there may be a neurotic or psychotic process at issue, and he will deal with the patient accordingly. In practice, the skilled clinician is constantly moving back and forth from the "uniqueness" of the patient to the manner in which the patient exemplifies a general class of patients. The training of the clinician not only involves enhanced sensitivity to "uniqueness"; he also is required to digest vast quantities of information on the general characteristics of the mental disorders. He must know the extremely varied ways in which intrapsychic processes can go wrong, so that he can see the general in the particular case. The ability to classify, to subsume the particular under some larger and meaningful category, is one of the major components of any science. While an exact taxonomy of the mental disorders is still elusive, we know a good deal about many broad classes of symptomatic behaviors, and the clinician could not operate without them, despite the many complaints concerning the inadequacy and incompleteness of standard classifications of mental disorder.

The trouble is that the many rich and detailed descriptions of the mental disorders include very little about disorders of work. Very recently, however, a still very limited body of knowledge has begun to accumulate, largely from observation of the behavior of mental patients in simulated work settings. Almost no knowledge, as yet, has come to us from ordinary, competitive industry, partly because very few mental health professionals are sited in industrial firms and partly because of complex issues related to confidentiality and labor–management relations. The meager information that is currently available is limited in two ways. First, it chiefly concerns the work behavior of a very specialized subgroup of human beings: people who have been committed to a mental hospital with a diagnosis of a psychotic disturbance. Second, the setting in which their work behavior has been observed (typically a simulated work situation of some type—whether sheltered or rehabilitative) is not necessarily identical with the conditions of ordinary, unprotected work. Within the limits of these *caveats,* we are not so wholly ignorant about maladaptive work behavior as we were a few years ago.

The following presents a highly tentative and preliminary nosology of types of maladaptive work behavior. Before this preliminary classification is undertaken, however, a few words should be said about the theory of human types.

TYPE THEORY

One of the oldest and most strongly held ideas about personality is that people can be classified into distinctive types. These conceptions have persisted for thousands of years and appear to reflect a powerful human need to impose some kind of order on the phenomena of nature. There is nothing, of course, intrinsically wrong in the desire to place things into ordered categories. In fact, the entire scientific enterprise arises from the need to classify. Many sciences (e.g., botany) involve very little else. In a more basic sense, it would be impossible for the human being to function at all unless he could classify the myriad kinds of stimulation that constantly play upon him. Since the requirement to respond appropriately to others is a major life demand, it obviously would be very convenient if the complexities of human relationships could be reduced to a few simple varieties or types. Various schemes for the classification of personality are almost as old as the history of written languages, and many works of genius in art and literature have endured because they seem to exemplify recognizable human types.

Despite the persistence of these ideas, it has been very difficult to establish them on a scientific basis. Human personalities are obviously extremely complex and tend to resist being easily and conveniently pigeonholed. It is also necessary to point out that there has always been a seamy and obscurantist side to typing people. Too often, entire human groups are given some kind of label only for the purpose of disposing of them in some negative manner ("all Greeks are liars," "Jews are untrustworthy," "salesmen are extroverts," "professors are impractical and absent-minded"). In American psychology, type theory has generally tended to be regarded as a discreditable enterprise, and there has been a good deal of research devoted to demonstrating that popular classifications of personality are without foundation. Studies of prejudice have provided ample evidence of what is called "stereotyping," in which imagined properties are assigned to entire human populations in order to classify them as inferior. Efforts to type human beings have come under particularly sharp attack when the unifying category is some national, racial, ethnic, religious, or socioeconomic characteristic. These obvious and regrettable instances of human bias have tended to place the entire typing enterprise under a cloud. The counterargument, which seems more scientifically respectable and more humane, is that people are basically all alike. A more exact way of stating this opposing proposition is that if personality differences exist, they are found among *individuals,* rather than between groups.

When given even the most superficial examination, most type theories are easily shown either to be entirely fictional or gross oversimplifications. Contrary to Galen, people are not sanguine because they have too much blood or irascible because they have too much bile. Similarly, it has been comparatively simple to demonstrate that typing according to race, nation, or social group is predominantly based on bias and ignorance. The fallacy of the traditional typologies is that a single part or trait is elevated to the position of the whole. This may be a kind of convenient mental shorthand, but it is scarcely a serious theory of human personality. Despite all these difficulties, the nagging thought persists that there *are* personality types, if we only knew how to define and measure them. In its more sophisticated form, the modern search for types is taking the form of a search for characteristic *patterns* of personality traits, with the implicit assumption that there must be a limited number of ways in which human traits arrange themselves, from person to person.

Resort to some sort of theory of types appears most frequent when the objects of interest are the phenomena of psychopathology. The familiar psychiatric nosologies are essentially efforts to provide classification of sharply different personalities. People are spoken of as *obsessive–compulsives, anxiety neurotics, sociopaths, schizophrenics,* and the like. Although there is a great deal of continuing controversy about the precise referents of these terms, the explicit assumption is that an individual who receives a given diagnostic label shares significant behaviors with other members of his class. At the same time, it may be recognized that the diagnostic label does not exhaust the content of the described personality. Persons whom we have good reason to call schizophrenic are found to differ very widely in other aspects of personality. For some authorities, this simply implies that there are "types" of schizophrenia (Beck, 1954). Other experts take the more cautious position that the psychiatric classifications describe "symptoms" rather than people; it is thus possible for almost any kind of personality to display a given set of symptoms.

Perhaps the most palatable view of type theory, with which the majority of personality theorists would probably agree, consists of a series of interrelated propositions. The first states that people *are* all alike, in the sense that the same basic traits are detectable in everyone. However, these common qualities can be arranged differently in different people. This leads to the second proposition, which states that personality is made up of a number of attributes, but it is their *organization* that constitutes the essence of human uniqueness. We begin to approach a theory of types when it is further maintained that there are only a small number of *patterns* of trait organization, and that large numbers of people can be defined as being more like one pattern than another. The core notion here is that groups of people can be marked off from each other in terms of what is predominant or subordinate in their personalities, granting that these adjectives are attached to a common fund of personal qualities. In this sense, everyone is, at times and under certain conditions, aggressive, passive, withdrawn, fearful, anxious, and the like. But people may be said to differ from each other in the sense that one or another (or a *set* of these qualities) may *predominate* in their personalities. It is currently more fashionable to use the phrase "personality style" rather than "type" to describe these more subtle views, but we are obviously still dealing with an effort to classify personalities.

MALADAPTATION TO WORK

Certain broad patterns of work behavior can be observed, suggesting the possibility that there are types or kinds of work psychopathology. Most people who cannot play a productive role have problems in any or all of the various segments of the work personality. They may have various amounts of difficulty in relating to authority figures; their interactions with work peers may arouse uncomfortable or inappropriate affects; they may find all sorts of negative meanings associated with work. However, the common elements of the work personality give the appearance of being arranged differently in different persons. In evaluating the observations to follow, it should be kept in mind that they are all highly tentative. They consist of a set of clinical impressions derived from studying clients in a rehabilitative workshop setting of the kind described in Chapter 10 (Neff, 1959). Like all such impressions, they require empirical confirmation. They will be useful only to the extent that different kinds of dilemmas ought to elicit different strategies of treatment.

We have been able to observe five individual types or patterns of qualities that appear to lead to failure in work. By no means can every client be made to fit one of these categories, and we know little concerning the frequency of their appearance. They may be thought of, perhaps, as modal points around which sufficient clustering takes place so that they are brought to the attention of the observer. The characteristics that describe a type are found, to some degree, in almost everyone. A given individual can be "typed," therefore, only when certain selected characteristics appear to predominate. The following five types were reconstructed from the case-reports of the foreman–professional in the rehabilitative workshop. In effect, they are clinical pictures of different varieties of work psychopathology.

Type I

The first general category includes people who appear to have major lacks in work motivation: They have a negative conception of the role. We can hypothesize that in these individuals the precepts of society in relation to work have not been internalized or incorporated; in a sense, the superego is defective or undeveloped, at least in this area. The ego perceives the precepts of society as alien not only to itself but to the entire personality and maneuvers to resist or evade them. In some cases, depending on other social variables, the resulting feelings and motivations may verge on the sociopathic ("work is for squares"; "stealing is better than working"). In less extreme cases, there seems to be a general indifference to the productive role; work serves no vital needs of the personality. Impulse gratification appears to be the rule, simply because there are no important internal constraints acting to prohibit it.

Such persons may be compelled to work under powerful social coercion but will meet only the most minimal standards of productivity and then only under close and continuous supervision. In its pure form, this characterological type is rather infrequent in our society. As a subordinate element in the work personality, it must be fairly common, since society has gone to a good deal of trouble to arrange a complex series of rewards for productivity and an equally complex series of punishments for being unproductive. In rehabilitation settings, problems of work motivation are apparently frequent enough so that there is considerable talk of "remotivation" projects. In the rehabilitative work situation we have described, this characterological type tends to be rare in its most pronounced form because such persons usually do not follow through on referral. Where they do appear, they frequently quit early in the program or are administratively terminated as unfeasible.

Type II

The second general category includes individuals whose predominating response to the demand to be productive is manifest fear and anxiety. These cases are quite common and probably constitute the most frequent characterological type. For persons in this category, the precepts of society in relation to work are internalized and strong, perhaps too strong. Unfortunately, the individual has also learned to believe that he cannot meet the standards of being a productive person, that he is inept, incapable, or impotent. The result is an endemic and generalized anxiety that lies very near the surface and is mobilized by almost any aspect of the work situation. The quite ordinary behavior of supervisors and co-workers may be interpreted as major threats to an already precarious self-esteem. In some instances, the anxiety may be so general and so immobilizing that the individual has little choice except to withdraw from work altogether. More often, the individual's work behavior is characterized by large swings in productivity in response to events that others may see merely as annoying irritants. Criticism, whether real or fancied, has a destructive effect, and the more that this sort of person is ordered to improve his performance, the worse it gets. These persons are typically acutely uncomfortable when forced into a competitive role, since competition with one's fellows involves too many risks of failure. Even the cooperative role is difficult because cooperation may involve a demand for equality of performance, and the individual's self-esteem is too damaged for him to take this lightly.

Although the anxious client often appears more acutely disturbed than others, he is frequently more responsive to a skillfully executed rehabilitative regimen. What he appears to need above all else is the experience of success, an experience that appears to have been markedly rare in his life development. Common to the life histories of those clients is that they have been failures at everything—at pleasing their parents, at achieving in school, at winning acceptance among their peers, at achieving anything in life. At the same time, they have incorporated the demand to achieve and were thus continuously faced with the discrepancy between wish and performance. Under these circumstances, it is advisable to provide supervision that is relatively benign and supportive for a somewhat more extended period than is usual and to shelter the client from aspects of work that may be too immediately threatening. Frequently, however, the anxious client shows marked gains in the rehabilitative workshop setting without any special treatment. Perhaps this is the first time in his life that he has encountered people in authority who take even the slightest interest in his personal feelings and welfare, and he finds that he can perform in a setting in which his efforts are not being constantly depreciated. On the other hand, it must be conceded that such progress may be transitory and become dissipated as soon as the anxious client is forced to face the harsher conditions of the actual labor market. It was very often noted that the anxious client was able to make good progress during the middle period of his stay in the rehabilitative workshop, only to reinstate much of his negative symptomatology during the last week or so as he is faced with the prospect of termination. It was also noted that the anxious client, more than others, could not be abandoned to his own devices, even after an initial job placement was successfully made. Such clients generally required an extended period of follow-up counseling, including several job placements, in order to minimize their expectation of continual failure and maintain whatever gains were made in the initial rehabilitative process.

Type III

The third typal category is composed of people who are predominantly characterized by open hostility and aggression. In these persons, the precepts of society in relation to work are internalized imperfectly and are perceived as restrictive and hostile demands. Anger lies very near the surface and is very easily aroused. The ego is alert to protect itself from attack by others and uses angry aggression as the chief strategy. Attack is the best defense. These people often work well enough if they are left entirely alone, a condition that the more ususal work situation does not permit. They are, of course, hypersensitive to any threat, whether real or fancied, and can develop severe grievances even in relatively neutral interpersonal environments. Supervisory criticism of any kind is perceived as an attack and is actively resisted. Work peers are regarded as potentially dangerous, and the slightest disagreement may be magnified into an open quarrel. In its most extreme forms, these kinds of behavior manifest themselves in the paranoid psychoses. In less severe manifestations, Type III people are so immobilized by anger that their productivity suffers and they either quit or are discharged.

It is interesting to note that this type of work psychopathology is not usually a barrier to initial employment. Such persons are often quite readily placeable, unless the disorder is so far advanced that they cannot contain their anger even in the employment interview. As workers, they are often quite able, since they have considerable energy and drive. They are not marked by the simple unwillingness to participate in the work culture that characterizes Type I, nor by the extreme fear and anxiety of Type II. Their problems do not lie in the abilty to *find* employment but in the ability to *maintain* it. While Types I and II typically present themselves to the rehabilitation agency with a history of no previous employment, Type III people have frequently held many jobs, each for a brief period of time. The most common reason given for dismissal is an inability to get along with others.

Type III clients appeared to benefit least from the ameliorative procedures available in the rehabilitative workshop. They often seemed to adapt very well to the early stages of the program, probably because the kind of supervision initially offered is highly benign and accepting. But as soon as the conditions of supervision shifted toward those more typical of unprotected work, their habitual reactions of anger and aggression became manifest. It was very difficult to keep these clients in the program, and they made up the bulk of the early drop-outs and administrative terminations. To the degree that their anger was acted-out, an additional problem arose related to the maintenance of treatment regimens for other clients. By and large, it would appear that the typical rehabilitation agency is least well-equipped to deal with the hostile client, and this type undoubtedly comprises the largest sector of treatment failures.

Type IV

This category includes people who are characterized by marked dependency. Here we can speculate that the precepts of society are perceived in the same way in which the young child perceives the commands of parents or teachers. The child becomes aware very early in his life that his welfare depends on the all-powerful adult, but this relationship is initially highly concrete and global. The important thing is to please mother (father); the reasons for doing this or that are still imperfectly understood. In instances where the nurturing figures are highly dominant and consistently demand total compliance, the child may begin to perceive any kind of independent behavior as intolerably threatening. The kind of authority figure that is internalized is an omnipotent figure who must be *pleased* at all costs; the chief defensive strategy is a kind of childlike compliance. In adulthood, when these trends are pronounced, the chief impression made on others is of childlike expectations and maneuvers. Type IV people do not discriminate very well between the demand characteristics of work environments and those appropriate to the home or the school. A familiar instance is the person who works well in order to please the foreman but who lacks any other substantial motivation. Such individuals are able to produce effectively only under very close and continuous supervision, a condition that is impossible to sustain in ordinary unprotected employment.

The Type IV client presents both a challenge and a possibility in the rehabilitation workshop setting. On the one hand, this kind of client makes heavy demands on the patience of supervisory personnel by the essential irresponsibility of his work behavior and by his continuous hunger for emotional sustenance. On the other hand, these are people who had never really experienced any reward for independent activity, which can be provided by the rehabilitative workshop. The tactic of choice is to praise the client for any sign of being able to work on his own and to withdraw approval for continued dependence. Money wages often mean a great deal to these people, since in typical cases they have never earned and disposed of their "own" money. It is frequently necessary to ensure that the client does not simply turn over to his parents whatever he makes and then have it "given" to him as an "allowance." The chief objective in Type IV cases is to give training in coping with some moderate degree of independence.

The highly dependent person cannot easily tolerate placement in a work setting marked by considerable impersonality. It is typically necessary to make a quite selective placement, even in cases that have shown some benefit from independence training in the rehabilitative setting. Such clients will work best in a small enterprise in which supervision is close and paternalistic. In a work atmosphere that can go some distance toward meeting their strong need for personal contact and approval, they make surprisingly effective and loyal workers, although initiative and responsibility are not the strong points of their work behavior. The chief difficulty is that most work environments cannot provide the kind of continuous and warmly supportive supervision that the Type IV individual requires.

Type V

The fifth and final category of work maladaptation consists of people who display a marked degree of social naiveté. In these people, the precepts of society relating to work were not incorporated because they were never really perceived in the first place. The ego possesses no strategy to deal with this aspect of reality because it never had to face the problem. There is no understanding of work, no conception of oneself as a worker, no knowledge of the demands and realities of work environments. It should be emphasized that the problems manifested are those of simple ignorance, rather than those of rejection or resistance. Many disabled young people, who have been unusually highly protected both in the family and the school, are found in this category. They have never been required to perform any chores or household duties; they have been accustomed to be relieved of meeting ordinary standards for performance and are often blindly convinced that such standards do not apply to *them.* Typically, they have lived their entire lives in highly sheltered settings and are simply unable to grasp what is being demanded of them when they are confronted with any ordinary work environment.

The naive client is encountered with considerable frequency by rehabilitation agencies. Children who have congenital impairments or who have suffered a severe disability very early in life often become "special" persons within the family setting. Where the parents are both guilty and benign, a certain degree of overprotection is almost inevitable. Such children spend most of their time at home and are thus isolated even from the competitive hurly-burly of street play. Less is demanded of them both at home and in school, and the rudiments of what we have described as the work personality simply remain undeveloped. Such people often display rather bland, pleasant, essentially empty personalities, because they have never had to struggle with frustration or disapproval. On the negative side, they may be almost totally unprepared to cope with the routine demands of unprotected environments.

For the socially naive, a transitional and tutorial work experience is an essential requirement of becoming a worker. The rehabilitative workshop serves as an arena in which the client can learn to play the role of a worker. The great asset of the Type V client is the very blandness and emptiness of his general personality development. He is neither resistive, hostile, nor fearful; and the quality of his dependency is not such that independence is perceived as a danger. He is simply ignorant of what is expected of him! He is not accustomed to travel on his own; he is not bound by the clock; he has never been expected to be productive. On the other hand, he has not been punished or rejected, since he has been sealed off from situations in which these consequences might arise.

Under proper circumstances, the rehabilitation program becomes an opportunity for social learning, which he accepts as blandly as he has been taught to accept everything else. Interestingly enough, the parents of the Type V individual may present more of a problem for the rehabilitation agency than does the client himself. The parents remain eager to "protect" the client and foresee all sorts of dangers in unprotected employment. Even where the agency is convinced that the client has made sufficient progress to tolerate ordinary employment, the family may resist or sabotage a job placement because of their fears that "something may happen." Nevertheless, the vocationally disadvantaged individual who best fits the Type V paradigm is typically the most successful client of the rehabilitation program, since it is, for him, a relatively uncomplicated educational experience.

AN EMPIRICAL STUDY

These five "types" of maladaptive behavior must be regarded as hypothetical. They appeared to have considerable utility in work with disturbed clients, but their method of derivation was entirely subjective and impressionistic. I had an opportunity to provide some evidence that they are more than convenient fictions. In a large-scale study of factors involved in the rehabilitation of the former mental patient (Neff and Koltuv, 1967), systematic data were collected to find out if this sort of notion could be confirmed. Two aspects of the problem were studied: (1) the reliability or consistency of the typing process and (2) the relationships, if any, between these global personality types and various rehabilitation outcomes.

The procedure involved the development of a rating scale, which would permit a number of professionals to supply independent ratings of what appeared to predominate in the behavior of the client. This instrument was called a *Coping Scale* and included categories drawn from the five maladaptive types. In addition to the five basic personality types described above (*fearful, dependent, impulsive, naive, hostile*), two others were added that were thought to reflect the special problems of the discharged mental patient: *withdrawn* and *self-deprecatory*. Each typal category was defined by a brief descriptive paragraph, and pilot work was carried out to ensure that the judges had a common understanding of what was implied. The full scale is presented below.

Categories and Supporting Definitions of the Coping Scale

Fearful (F). Among other things, this sort of individual may be tense, fidgety, jumpy, uneasy, may be frequently troubled or worried, may be afraid and timid in his relationship with others, may be afraid to establish contact with others, may seem mousy, may shy away from things and people.

Dependent (D). This kind of individual might give the appearance of being impotent in dealing with the world by himself. Among other things, he may frequently ask help from others, may rely on others for support, may be unable to initiate action on his own, may place himself in the position of making others direct him, may be highly compliant, may seek others' approval.

Impulsive (I). Among other things, this sort of individual may rarely see a task through, may be unable to stick to a plan of action, may flit from one thing to another, may be unable to delay the gratification of his impulses, may immediately seek to satisfy his desires, may easily become enthusiastic about something and then rapidly lose his enthusiasm.

Socially naive (SN). This kind of individual may be unperceptive when it comes to the needs or feelings of others, may not realize that his behavior elicits reactions from others or has an effect on them, may be socially inept, may not seem to know what is appropriate in ordinary social situations.

Withdrawn, apathetic (W). Among other things, this kind of individual may be bland, lethargic, may lack vitality, may give the impression of being indifferent to things going on around him, may lack emotional responsivity, may seem very easygoing and uninvolved.

Self-deprecatory (SD). Among other things, this sort of individual may point up and willingly talk about his deficiencies, may be highly self-critical, may talk about his ineptitude, may derogate his qualities and abilities, may generally run himself down, may express self-doubts.

Hostile (H). Among other things, this sort of individual may be angry with others most of the time, may be subtly negativistic, may contradict and argue with others, may do things to irritate and annoy others, may be sarcastic, may belittle or insult others, may criticize others.

Scoring and Results of Study

Each of 100 successive clients was independently rated by an average of six different professionals, who were in a position to observe his behavior during the first 2 weeks of a year-long program of vocational rehabilitation. The judges were asked to rank these broad kinds of behavior in terms of their predominance in the client's make-up and then also to rate each category on a 4-point scale. If a category was thought to be "very predominant," it was given a score of 1; "somewhat predominant" was assigned a score of 2; "slightly predominant" a score of 3; "not predominant" was scored 4. The scores were then treated as quantities and submitted to statistical analysis.

The results of this study were fairly gratifying. In the first place, the scale displayed an acceptably high amount of reliability. The professional people who had contact with the clients were able to differentiate between them on the basis of the scale categories and showed a considerable measure of agreement concerning what was dominant and what was subordinate in the client's make-up. The manner in which an individual was typed also had some bearing upon his service career. Clients who were initially described as predominatingly impulsive or socially naive were more prone to leave the rehabilitative program before completion than were the others. Another interesting finding was that clients who managed to finish their assigned work programs were not only less impulsive and naive but also *more* self-deprecatory. In relation to the ultimate outcome criteria of this entire research project, the clients with the poorer postservice work records turned out to be those who were initially characterized as dependent, naive, or fearful (cf. Neff and Koltuv, 1967).

The significance of these findings is enhanced by the fact that the investigators were unable to find any systematic relationships between severity of disability and the various outcome criteria of the study. What appears to be at issue is not so much the presence or absence of blatant psychotic symptoms but the over-all manner in which people tend to cope with a major life demand. However, people with a history of psychosis do not find it easy to adapt to work. There is ample evidence that the ex-mental patient finds it very difficult to find or maintain employment (Gurel, 1963; Freeman and Simmons, 1963). What is at issue here is that blatant symptomatology may simply be the outcome of a lifetime history of inadequate interpersonal relations. Whether or not an individual is frankly psychotic, at the moment he is being confronted with the demand to work, may be less crucial than his general style of relating to any demanding social situation. At the same time, it is clear that not *all* psychotics are unable to adapt to work. Those who apparently have the greatest difficulty are marked by certain specific personality styles—poor impulse-control, excessive fearfulness and timidity, dependence and immaturity.

RESEARCH NEEDS AND POSSIBILITIES

It is unnecessary to reiterate that we have very meager knowledge, as yet, of inappropriate or ineffective work behavior. The clinical observations reported here are little more than subjective impressions. Moreover, these impressions were derived through observing a highly restricted and specialized sample of persons in a quite atypical kind of work environment. All that we have so far must be thought of as no more than a few tantalizing glimpses. We have been able to define a few kinds of "response-styles" that appear to constitute barriers to an adjustment to work. On the other hand, we cannot pretend to have exhausted the varieties of maladaptive behavior, nor do we have any idea of their frequency of occurrence. It would appear that we have little more than a set of plausible hypotheses, which undoubtedly need both supplementation and confirmation through wide and controlled observation of ordinary people in ordinary work situations.

To summarize our beliefs concerning work psychopathology, the familiar, psychiatrically defined mental disorders—the psychoneuroses, the psychoses, the character disorders—are not, by themselves, the *sufficient* conditions of maladaptation to work. In addition to whatever personal problems they have, people who are unable to work are unable to tolerate or accept the demands of work as a social situation. They may be unable to accept work-discipline or may need more supervision than the ordinary work situation is in a position to supply. They may be so hypersensitive and fearful of others that the sheer presence of other people is an intolerable burden, or they may be so dependent and childish that they make unacceptable demands upon the people with whom they have to work. They may have never internalized those social norms that bear upon the demand to achieve and thus the basic elements of the role of the worker remain alien.

Unfortunately, these assertions are in the realm of belief, not fact. What is needed to confirm them (or disconfirm them) is a prolonged series of research investigations of people at work, so that we can know more than that a person was discharged or quit because "he couldn't get along." Such research is easier to propose than to accomplish. To carry out the kinds of studies that are needed, the mental health professional would have to be much more closely integrated with industry than has hitherto been the case. In effect, the clinic would have to be sited within the factory, so that inappropriate work behavior could be observed and assessed while it is actually taking place. To achieve such a major rearrangement of the delivery of mental health services, the disinterest and resistance of both management and labor would have to be overcome. It must be admitted also that few members of the mental health professions see the need for such a development. At the same time, there are the beginnings of some concern about the mental health of working people and some initial recognition that the proper site to do something about it is the workplace itself (cf. McLean, 1967). A few very large firms have employed clinical psychiatrists and psychologists, and a few labor unions have experimented with the provision of mental health services under their union health plans. The entire problem, however, is being approached with extreme caution and reserve because of the many fears and mutual suspicions that at once become aroused. While we are still very far from being able to study and treat the working person on the work site, the door may be opening to such a possibility.[4]

---

[4]Helping to open the door is a recently organized agency called the Center for Occupational Mental Health, headed by Dr. Alan McLean of Cornell University Medical College. The Center is attempting to bring together industrialists, labor leaders, and behavioral scientists to focus on the mental health problems of the worker. The Center systematically provides information on occupational mental health to the National Clearinghouse for Mental Health Information of the National Institute of Mental Health.

12 | WORK AND THE PSYCHOSES

It cannot be our purpose here to enter upon the manifold and enormous complexities of the severe mental disorders (e.g., the schizophrenias, manic-depressive disorders). What is noteworthy about the psychoses, however, is that they are not only marked by a familiar, if still poorly understood spectrum of psychiatric symptoms—hallucinations, delusions, confusion, agitation, depression, thought disorders, etc.—but that the psychoses are also accompanied by massive disruptions of the individual's most basic interpersonal and social adjustments. Such hard-won social coping processes as those involved in the ability to work, the maintenance of even minimally adequate family relationships, the capability of managing the most essential living arrangements, are often materially disorganized or wholly destroyed. It is this peculiar combination of the *symptomatic* and the *social* that has made the psychoses a major management problem for organized society as well as a set of intolerable problems for the afflicted individual. Complicating this picture is that these disorders and disruptions tend to be of relatively long duration, leading to what appears to be chronic or permanent disability.

There are two aspects of the relations of the psychoses and work that are of interest to us here. The first of these has to do with some of the consequences of the *deinstitutionalization* movement, a major shift in treatment philosophy that is currently confronting the psychiatric establishment with some crucial problems. The second concerns the development within medical rehabilitation of a new subspecialty: *psychiatric rehabilitation*. We shall deal with these two issues in the present chapter.

DEINSTITUTIONALIZATION

The best definition of this weighty term has been given by a sociologist connected with the National Institute of Mental Health (Bachrach, 1976) and repeated by her in a more recent volume on this issue (Bachrach, 1983): "deinstitutionalization . . . a process involving two elements: (1) the eschewal of traditional institutional settings—primarily state hospitals—for care of the (chronically) mentally ill, and (2) the current expansion of community-based services for the treatment of these individuals."

Human societies have never quite known what to do with their mentally deranged members, and their disposition seems to have been more a reflection of whatever social and political ideology happened to prevail at a given time than of a well-defined body of factual knowledge (Foucault, 1965; Jones, 1972; Grob, 1973). For thousands of years, the "insane" were thought to be victims of divine or demonic possession; typically, they were turned over to the religious establishment, incarcerated in almshouses or prisons, or simply driven out of their communities and left to starve. With the rise of the scientific world outlook—toward the end of the eighteenth and beginning of the nineteenth centuries—deranged behavior gradually came to be regarded as a disease of the brain and became the responsibility of the medical establishment for treatment and care.

It can hardly be doubted that this shift in conceptualization—often spoken of as the first great revolution in mental health care—represented a great step forward in common humanity. However, the special aspects of the severe mental disorders—their long-term character, their consequences of massive social disruption, their apparent intractability to successful treatment—have made them a problem of great complexity for medical management. These unique features of mental disorder also made for the rise of an equally unique medical institution: the mental hospital.

In the United States, the mental hospital or asylum dates back to the mid-1800s, when Dorothea Dix initiated a notable reform movement to take the mentally ill out of the prisons and almshouses in which they were currently incarcerated and to place them to live in benign medical institutions under the care of physicians rather than jailers.[1] The 100-year history of the mental hospital, however, is almost the classical example of the aphorism that the road to hell is paved with good intentions. Originally established as refuges (Bockoven, 1963), indifference and overcrowding led to their becoming more like prisons (Goffman, 1961), isolated and self-contained small societies (Stanton and Schwartz, 1954; Caudill, 1958) and, incidentally, public medical facilities operated by the various states. The population of patient residents, in what had become essentially merely

---

[1]Thomas Szasz (1961, 1963, 1973) has repeatedly argued that this is a distinction without a difference, that the psychiatric establishment simply acts as an arm of the state in getting rid of the unwanted and dangerous by labeling unwanted deviance as mental illness. Szasz's views are, perhaps justifiably, regarded as extreme, but, as has recently been pointed out (Gorenstein, 1984), the controversy over whether mental disorder is best thought of as a disease remains unresolved. Whatever the case, Szasz's much publicized books have served a useful function in calling attention to the more unpleasant aspects of institutional psychiatry and have provided some of the steam that is driving the movement to deinstitutionalization.

custodial facilities, reached a census of some 560,000 persons in 1955 (Kramer, Pollack, and Redick, 1972). This was the high point! Since then, the deinstitutionalization movement has brought about very large and comparatively rapid declines in the state hospital census of patients. In 1976, the figure stood at 193,000—a 65% deline in a period of 20 years.[2] Although most of the 300-odd state mental hospitals now stand more than one-half empty, social and political factors have, so far, prevented their total abolition.

It is perhaps too easy to derogate the public mental hospitals for their peculiar social isolation, their deprived social and psychological environments, and even their character as "snake pits" (Deutsch, 1948), but it should not be forgotten that these institutions were established originally in the spirit of a great movement of social reform, and that the problems that instigated this reform movement have by no means vanished. It is true, however, that the state hospitals became terribly overcrowded, and that living conditions in them deteriorated as a result of budgetary pressures and social neglect. Initial therapeutic optimism shifted toward pessimism and even what is often called "therapeutic nihilism" as causes and cures remained elusive. But it is also a fact that the state hospitals provided a kind of refuge for people who, for a variety of reasons, were extruded from ordinary society, and the problem of meeting this need remains with us. Second, for a hundred years, the mental hospitals were virtually the only sites for serious research into the psychoses. It was in the laboratories of certain of these institutions, for example, that many of the psychoactive drugs in current use were first developed, and virtually all controlled experimentation takes place within their walls. Also, the first major techniques of social intervention and social treatment were begun in the mental hospitals themselves (Jones, 1953).

Whatever the mental hospital's past or present virtues, however, it has become a casualty of what can best be described as a major shift in mental health ideology, a kind of paradigm shift (cf. Kuhn, 1970). The current efforts to find alternatives to the custodial mental hospital are only the latest phase of a general trend toward enhanced humanitarianism, which was one of the major outcomes of World War II. Early in the 1940s, a movement began to "unlock the doors," designed to involve the patient in self-care and self-government (cf. Jones, 1972). This important movement led to drastic changes in the structure and functioning of public mental hospitals. It was fostered not only by the new humanism but by simultaneous observation and reports of the dilapidation and deterioration observed in many "backward" chronic psychotics, a dilapidation now thought to be a function not of the disease process per se, but a result of prolonged living in an environ-

---

[2]Given the general population increase over the period, this two-thirds decline is an underestimate of the true decline in the mental hospital residence rate.

ment drastically deprived of social and intellectual stimulation (Wing and Brown, 1970).

However meager the evidence (cf. Wing and Brown, 1970; Honingfeld and Gillis, 1966; Goldman, 1965), the notion that the mental hospital itself could produce deleterious psychotic symptoms has become something of an article of faith in administrative psychiatry and has been a major element in the generation of structural changes in the management of mental illness. Experimentation began in the late 1940s and early 1950s with patient self-government, with efforts to stimulate the hitherto passive patient to play a role in his own care and maintenance, with nonprofessional and lower professional staffs of the hospitals in enhanced treatment roles, with various schemes of resocialization including sheltered and rehabilitative workshops (Paul and Lentz, 1977) and, ultimately, with drastic changes in admission and discharge policies. The result has been the deinstitutionalization movement and its accompaniment—the current active search for alternatives to hospitalization.

Deinstitutionalization under Review

By the mid-1970s, the movement to liquidate the mental hospital began to run out of steam. A few of the most dilapidated institutions actually closed, but new (smaller) ones were established; the total number of public state hospitals has remained about the same (ca 330). The census of resident mental patients has tended to stabliize at about 180,000. However, the bulk of these hospital residents are no longer long term. The average patient is now "released" within a few weeks or months, although we have become increasingly aware of an alarming new statistic: the readmission rate. Of any given 100 dischargees, 30–40 are back within the following 12 months and, if the period of review is extended to 4 or 5 years, the return rate rises to 50–60. A matter of somewhat greater concern, however, is that early discharge does not seem to have the positive effects that were anticipated when the deinstitutionalization movement began.

Adequate follow-up studies are expensive and difficult to carry out. Our knowledge of the posthospital careers of discharged patients remains piecemeal and fragmentary. A few things are known but none are very reassuring.[3] According to the Group for the Advancement of Psychiatry (GAP), over one-half of dischargees are now living in unlicensed, in-adequately supervised boarding homes or welfare hotels, supported by public welfare, and without any professional assistance whatever. The GAP

---

[3]A number of reports have appeared that focus on the problems of early discharge. Among the more definitive are: (1) Bachrach (1976); (see also Bachrach, 1983); (2) Comptroller General of the United States (1977); (3) the Group for the Advancement of Psychiatry (undated).

report further states, as an example, that in Manhattan alone in 1973, some 25,000 ex-mental patients were living in single-room occupancy (SRO) welfare hotels, under extremely impoverished conditions. This situation is not limited to the United States, although in countries with more elaborate social welfare systems, such as England, the picture is somewhat softened. Wing in England and Cole in the United States estimate that only from 5 to 20% of ex-mental patients make any kind of acceptable social adjustment in the community. Similarly, in reviewing data from a number of studies, Anthony, Buell, Sharrett, and Althoff (1972) have shown that very few ex-mental patients manage to secure stable, paid employment (estimates range from 10 to 30%), with the bulk subsisting on public welfare. There is increasing evidence that the discharge of ex-psychotics to their families of origin place heavy burdens on the already strained family relationships, and that the families of patients become less eager to accept them the more frequently the patient is readmitted and subsequently discharged.

Perhaps the most comprehensive examination of the deinstitutionalization movement and its consequences is the report by Bachrach (1976). Approaching the problem from the point of view of a sociologist, she argues that the current problems of the deinstitutionalization movement arise from the fact that its proponents have never fully understood or acknowledged the basic social functions of the public mental hospital. Her basic position is summarized in a citation from a paper published in 1964 by Robert M. Edwalds, the arguments of which, she feels, have been largely ignored or discounted. According to Edwalds (1964, quoted by Bachrach)

> Primary functions demanded of the state mental hospital have included (A) public safety and the removal from society of individuals exhibiting certain kinds of socially disruptive behavior; (B) custodial care of persons who, by reason of mental disorder, cannot care for themselves or be cared for elsewhere. . . . Treatment and rehabilitation of the mentally ill has always been, at best, a secondary function of the state mental hospital. For many years, it was not considered part of the function of the state hospital at all. Today treatment and rehabilitation are usually officially regarded as the primary functions of the state mental hospital, leading to a remarkable amount of self-deception and confusion on the part of society and the personnel working in these hospitals.

Bachrach adds that Edwalds is of the opinion that the very use of the term *hospital* to refer to these institutions is misleading, and that the term conceals understanding of their basic social functions.

Although she never quite says so, it appears clear that Bachrach feels that the secret agenda of the deinstitutionalization movement involves the ultimate abolition of the public mental hospital. Her fear is that as a consequence two of the main functions of the mental hospital will have been lost (i.e., protection and custody). The conclusion of her monograph is worth stating in full:

The deinstitutionalization movement—a movement intended to counteract the effects of dehumanization in mental health care—can best fulfill its promise if certain conditions are met. Individual mental hospitals are most effectively superseded in accordance with the aims of the deinstitutionalization movement when (a) there is a thorough understanding of the functions they serve in American life; (b) consensus is reached as to which of these functions is to be continued or discontinued, or which functions should be added; (c) effective alternatives are established in community settings for the accepted functions; and (d) sufficient time is allowed for the systematic and orderly implementation of new programs and transfer of functions (Bachrach, 1976, p. 64).

Her specific recommendations involve: (1) more attention to effective screening of patients, both for institutionalization and deinstitutionalization; (2) an end to territorial arguments as to what constitutes the "best" site for treatment; (3) close supervision of community residence facilities; (4) a decisive expansion of community-based services available to (and *delivered* to) the discharged patient; (5) genuine continuity of care.

On paper, it appears that Bachrach's recommendations are unexceptionable, and that the community mental health movement should regard them with extreme seriousness. There is no doubt that a great many disturbed persons have been discharged "to the community" in the absence of an established network of community support services. It is true also that many disturbed patients have been poorly prepared for discharge, and that many now live "in the community" under conditions not very dissimilar from those they suffered in the back wards of the traditional mental hospital. It is also worth asking whether the rush to early discharge has not only ignored certain of the basic reasons why the mental hospitals came into existence in the first place (protection, isolation, custody) but also has not enquired whether the society at large still wants these functions to continue. Above all, it appears that the provision of an adequate community support structure should be our first priority.

But some nagging questions remain: Do we really know *how* to screen? Are we in a position to specify exactly what *kinds* of community-based services are required to meet the needs of the very wide variety of discharged patients? Is society ready (will it ever be ready?) to receive the former psychotic back into its collective bosom, in contrast to keeping them safely hidden away in the mental hospital? Given the fear and distaste aroused in most people by psychotic disorders, can we expect families and public authorities to deal humanely and correctly with people who have suffered a psychotic episode, particularly when some measure of desocialization has been a sequel to or an accompaniment of the mental disorder?

Our current inability to find available answers to these questions, combined with the incapacity of available community facilities to absorb large masses of dischargees, has produced something of a counterreformation within the mental health field. A number of authoritative spokesmen are now saying that the effects of prolonged hospitalization on the development of incapacity have been greatly overestimated, and that discharge does not appear to lead to termination of incapacity. There is also increasing concern that early intervention and efforts at prevention do not appear to have affected the course of the more severe disorders. Chronicity remains chronicity, whether it is manifested by prolonged residence in a mental hospital or by equally prolonged subsistence on public welfare in a community boarding home. There is even greater concern being expressed that former or potential residents of the mental hospital are now being abandoned to the tender mercies of rapacious or indifferent managers of the nursing-home industry, who are neither able or willing to provide them with even the minimal treatment and maintenance services available in the better-run public hospitals.

The ideas involved in what I am calling a counterreformation need our close attention, whether or not we are prepared to agree with them. It is being reasserted, for example, that the psychoses are organic diseases, with prominent genetic components, which are thus relatively impervious to social intervention. Recent research has lent some support to the belief that genetic determiners play a role in the predisposition to psychosis, although we are still without knowledge of what these defective genes might be, and even further from knowing how they interact with postnatal events and experiences. Better controlled studies of the genetics of schizophrenia, while still inconclusive because of persistent problems of diagnosis and sampling, have lent some support to the belief that the psychoses may have hereditary components and are likely to yield more to biological than to social manipulation. Current excitement over advances in molecular biology has provided a supportive climate for the reformulation of this quite traditional belief.

The counterreformation also represents a kind of inevitable reaction to some of the unsupported claims made by enthusiasts within the community mental-health movement. In this connection, we will examine two issues: chronicity and the problems of psychiatric rehabilitation.

CHRONICITY

Observations of the dilapidation of long-term patients in the traditional mental hospital comprised one of the most powerful stimuli of the movement toward deinstitutionalization and community-based treatment. These observations, within the framework of the deteriorated and impoverished environments within many public mental hospitals, encouraged the belief that the mental hospital itself was the *agent* of chronicity. It was logical to infer, therefore, that transformation of the custodial hospital into a short-term intensive treatment center could make a major contribution to the abolition of chronic mental illness. This inference led easily to the belief that severe mental disorder was best treated on an out-patient basis, thus permitting retention and development of whatever social ties the patient still possessed. Prevention of hospitalization was stated as a primary aim. Admission and readmission were read as treatment failures. The view was advanced that the mental hospital was to be no more than one link in a network of social and medical services to be utilized (if it was necessary at all!) for the speedy amelioration of the more florid and unmanageable psychiatric symptoms. The pattern here is akin to the acute disease model of general medical practice, where hospitalization is the last resort and where the bulk of treatment takes place in the out-patient clinic or the doctor's office.

Unfortunately, we cannot yet assert that the acute disease model is any more appropriate for the severe mental disorders than was the traditional custodial model. Chronicity is still with us, although we have had to redefine it. A few years ago, the chronic psychotic was a long-term resident of a back ward of a custodial mental hospital. Today, he or she is likely to be living on relief or SSI in a boarding home or welfare hotel, almost certainly unemployed, and making a very poor social adjustment by any standard. Chronicity is now defined by multiple readmissions and severe dependency rather than simply by long-term hospital stay. In attempting to free the patient from the deleterious effects of an impoverished environment within the walls of the hospital, we have simply shifted these disordered people to an equally impoverished environment located "in the community." We have gone from the frying pan, into the fire!

PSYCHIATRIC REHABILITATION

This developing subspecialty is the child of a marriage (perhaps marriage is too strong a word) between institutional psychiatry and vocational rehabilitation. It came into existence as a result of the shift in mental hospital policy toward early and rapid discharge, which began to gather steam in the late 1950s. The psychiatrists in charge of the public mental hospitals believed—correctly as it turned out—that many of their charges were too traumatized or desocialized to be able to adjust outside the protecting walls of the mental hospital without some expert assistance. Moreover, the medically trained psychiatrists within the mental hospitals—and their nonmedical allies such as psychiatric nurses and psychiatric social workers—saw their expertise as lying in the area of eradication of psychiatric symptoms, not in what was seen as a process of social adjustment. Another type of professional had to be recruited to deal with the posthospital careers of discharged mental patients. The new professional turned out largely to be the vocational rehabilitation specialist who, up to the 1950s, had been concerned exclusively with physical disability. At the federal level, this meant the beginnings of collaboration between two hitherto unrelated divisions of the U.S. Department of Health, Education and Welfare: the National Institute of Mental Health and the Division of Vocational Rehabilitation. For the vocational specialist to be able to help the discharged mental patient, some major changes had to take place in both his training and orientation. It will be instructive to see how this has taken place.

The Field of Vocational Rehabilitation

Until scarcely three decades ago, the problems of the disabled person in our society were dealt with as if they were almost exclusively of a medical character. The prevailing image was that of the "cripple," a person who had suffered some sort of chronic and irreversible impairment of his sensory capacities or skeletomuscular structure. The attention of the health professions was directed primarily toward the techniques of physical restoration, on the basis of very considerable progress in the techniques of surgery and repair of tissues, advances in medical engineering, and in development of the procedures of physical therapy. It was generally assumed that, if the medical procedures were successful, the patient would automatically pick up the broken strands of his life and function as well (or almost as well) as he had before. The various medical specialties concerned with disability were not unaware that disabled people might have problems that could not be solved by direct treatment of the physical symptom. But the entire tradition of medical training and practice made it inevitable that the rapidly developing specialties of physical medicine (psychiatry, orthopedic surgery, prosthetic technology, industrial medicine, etc.) would concentrate on the eradication and amelioration of biological symptoms and defects, leaving to others the possible psychological and social problems of the person who "has" the symptom. Unfortunately, the "others" were not yet on the scene. An uncomfortable impression began to arise that there were too many cases that were medical successes but social failures.

In recent years, however, an increasingly diverse body of professionals have begun to devote themselves to the problems of the disabled person. Undoubtedly, the most prominent impetus was World War II. The gravity and destructive character of the conflict required the mobilization and training of huge technical and human resources to deal with the problems of wounded and traumatized soldiers and civilians. In addition, one of the aftermaths of World War II—in the United States and in most of the developed countries of the world—was a marked concern for new issues of human welfare. In England and in some other European countries, this concern took the form of what has come to be called the Welfare State—an evolving complex of new governmental arrangements designed to underwrite the health and welfare of the entire citizenry. In the United States, with its different history and social structure, these trends have not been, as yet, so thoroughgoing, but the past 30 years have seen an enormous increase in the availability of public funds for the solution of a number of human problems. The official responsibility of the federal government for these matters was made manifest by the establishment in 1953 of the Department of Health, Education and Welfare (HEW), with a Secretary of cabinet rank. The great broadening of the scope of services to the disabled is largely attributable to the work of one of the sections of the Department, the then Office of Vocational Rehabilitation (OVR).

The history of this Office is itself an illustration of the broadening of interest in the total welfare of disabled persons. Until World War II, OVR had been a relatively small agency, whose mission had been to stimulate appropriate services to the physically disabled. Created initially in 1917 to aid the wounded veterans of World War I, enabling legislation was passed by Congress in 1943 to widen the scope of the agency's efforts to include service to the mentally retarded and the mentally disordered. During the following decade, the funds made available to the agency were greatly expanded and diversified. It was authorized, in 1955, to launch an extensive program of grants-in-aid for research and demonstration projects and to fund training programs designed to produce badly needed professional manpower. In 1963, OVR was further expanded, raised to the level of a major department of HEW, and retitled as the Vocational Rehabilitation Administration (VRA). In 1967, a major reorganization of HEW grouped VRA with certain other service agencies of the Department to form a new division titled the Social and Rehabilitation Service (SRS).

Throughout this entire period of very rapid expansion and reorganization, this federal agency has been firmly oriented toward *restoration of the disabled person to the world of work.* The very considerable influence of this federal agency has expressed itself in a reorientation of the entire field of services to the disabled. By the 1960s, medical service to the disabled had become only one component—albeit a very important one—in a network of services aimed at *adaptation to work.* The result has been the rapid development of a multidisciplinary attack upon the problems of the handicapped person, under the slogan of commitment to what is coming to be known as "comprehensive" rehabilitation. This approach includes at least three components: medical services, social services, and vocational services. The great weight now given to the vocational component is attested to by the fact that VRA reports its annual statistics in terms of the numbers of individuals who have been "rehabilitated into employment." Adjustment to work has thus become, as it were, the chief criterion of the relative effectiveness of whatever other forms of service the client has received. We shall return to this issue.

The commitment of our federal government to full employment during this period, was one of the major elements in the broadening of services to the disabled beyond its prior focus on medical problems. Another element arose as a tangential consequence of World War II—the greatly increased public and professional interest in psychological and psychiatric matters. The surprisingly large number of draftees rejected for psychiatric reasons, the relatively high frequency of psychiatric casualties in the armed forces, the massive efforts during the war and afterward to train needed mental health personnel—all of these were major factors in drawing both lay and professional attention to the apparent pervasiveness of problems of emotional disorder.

One of the side effects of the greatly expanded interest in psychological and psychiatric issues was the invasion of traditional fields of medicine by notions that were, hitherto, quite alien. Thus, we had the appearance of what came to be called psychosomatic medicine (cf. Wittkower and Cleghorn, 1954; Dunbar, 1954). With some excesses at times, claims began to be put forward that many traditional somatic diseases—tuberculosis, cardiac conditions, stomach ulcer, colitis, asthma, etc.—especially diseases of a chronic or long-term nature, had powerful psychological conditions not only in their *sequelae* but also in their etiology. Similarly, there has been a hyperdevelopment, in the postwar years, of psychiatry as a major specialty. This development has not only included an increased number of medically trained psychiatrists but has also been marked by the appearance of new, nonmedical specialties (e.g., the clinical psychologist, the psychiatric social worker, the vocational specialist, and even sociologists and anthropologists). While not all of these specialties are "new," the novelty lies in their increasing involvement (not without frictions!) in the problems of direct patient care. This greatly broadened and deepened public and professional concern with what is being increasingly called "mental health" has become manifest within the framework of a radical transformation of the theory and, to some extent, the practices of patient care.

The combined influence of these shifts in ideology and outlook—our greatly increased concern for the health and welfare of our entire citizenry, our national commitment to full employment, a coincident great expansion of interest in psychiatric and psychological issues—has led to a basic reconceptualization of the problems of the handicapped person. It is now taken for granted that the disabled individual may face a very wide range of problems, the solution of which requires a broad spectrum of professional experts. Whether the disability in question is a physical injury or impairment, whether it is defined as mental deficiency or mental disorder, it has become evident that medical treatment can be only one facet of what is often a many-sided problem.

Consider the classical case of an adult male laborer who has lost his right arm, above the elbow, in an industrial accident. Obviously, his most urgent initial need is for competent surgical and hospital care. His next need is for the fitting of an appropriate prosthetic device to restore some semblance of two-arm and bimanual functioning. This requires the intimate cooperation of a whole crew of experts—orthopedic surgeons, physiatrists, orthotic and prosthetic technicians, physical and occupational therapists. But even when he makes a good physical recovery and acquires (and learns to use) a suitable prosthesis, his problems may be far from over. The loss of a limb is not only a physical trauma but a deep psychological and social wound as well.

Depending upon the severity of his reactions to the loss, depending also upon his prior state of emotional stability and interpersonal development, he may require psychiatric, psychological, or casework assistance to accept his disability and to use his artificial arm without intolerable discomfort, guilt, or shame. He may require a good deal of help in working out new relationships with his family and friends. He may, and very often will, need vocational retraining and specialized vocational services to find employment. If his former occupation involved heavy and unskilled labor, and if he cannot now return to this kind of work, he may have to be given special educational services, including basic literacy training. Thus, returning the patient to some modicum of his former level of functioning frequently requires the services of an almost bewildering variety of experts—ranging from the orthopedic surgeon at one extreme to the vocational counselor and social worker at the other. As Fishman sums up this complex process in a report of research on amputation (1962:39):

> As the ability to use the prosthesis more automatically and subconsciously increases, as the client's awareness of being physically limited and different becomes less threatening, and as the amputation becomes a minimal source of interference in his familial, vocational and social activities, the elements of successful rehabilitation have been approached.

Clearly, a great many of the problems of the disabled person are not medical at all, although the latter are obviously a precondition for all else. A drastic impairment of the body may involve encountering and solving an entirely new set of psychosocial barriers to a life adjustment.

What we have implied of the adult patient with a traumatic physical injury applies with still greater force to people with congenital disabilities or to those unfortunate persons who suffered major impairments in early childhood. In the cases of traumatic accidents to adults, a stable set of social arrangements and adaptations can be badly disrupted—not the least of which concern the ability to work. But where the impairment exists from birth, or occurs during early childhood, critical components of cognitive and personal development may be blocked or seriously distorted. Whether we are dealing with such congenital physical disabilities as cerebral palsy, or whether the problem manifests itself in the form of inadequate mental development (e.g., mental retardation), or whether we are encountering the consequences of long-term mental disorder, something new has been added. We cannot now assume that the patient has encountered those experiences that normally lay the basis for an adequate work personality. It may be necessary to provide training in the elementary requirements of the work-role, even before any effort is made to provide the individual with some specific work-skill. In these instances, effective rehabilitation tends to become a very complex, protracted, and difficult affair.

For all these reasons, the scope of modern services to the handicapped has become very wide indeed. In certain respects, the most striking single feature of the rehabilitation movement has been the degree to which it has become preoccupied with the psychodynamics of the adaptation to work.

Some Definitions

Before proceeding further with the relations of work and disability, certain necessary terms should be defined.

Rehabilitation. There is no precise way of defining the term that has become associated with the entire field we are considering. The definitions supplied by standard dictionaries denote such concepts as *restoration* and *reinstatement.* As the term is used in relation to modern practice, however, there are a number of important connotations. The first of these has to do with the fact that there are many kinds of physical, mental, or emotional disorders that, in the present state of medical science, leave behind them some kind of chronic or permanent residual impairment. In this sense, the most frequently stated objective of rehabilitative procedures is not so much "curative," in the sense of complete elimination of the impairment in question, but "ameliorative," in the sense of bringing the person to a maximal level of functioning, *within the limits of a continuing deficiency of some kind.* In one of the pioneering texts on rehabilitation medicine (Rusk and Taylor, 1953), the goal is stated as follows: "Lacking specific measures in the cure of many of the chronic diseases, medicine must look to rehabilitation to teach those afflicted by disability to live and work as effectively as possible."

A second connotation of the term has to do with facilitation of the ability to work, to find gainful employment. The overwhelming, perhaps one-sided, emphasis on vocational objectives that has permeated the field of rehabilitation presents one of its clearest distinctions from the therapeutic goals of the other helping professions. We earlier pointed to the influence of federal agencies (particularly the Vocational Rehabilitation Administration of the Department of Health, Education and Welfare) in insisting that entry into gainful employment be the over-all success criterion of any funded rehabilitation program. The research and service professionals involved with the handicapped have thus been obliged to learn a great deal more about human work than they otherwise might have done. Much of what we now know about work has been derived from studies of the handicapped worker. At the same time, the overriding preoccupation with gainful employment has been both a blessing and a curse. On the one hand, this sort of success criterion has the virtue of being both objective and readily measurable. On the other hand, it has also functioned as something of a straitjacket and might have promoted some tendency to select those clients for intensive rehabilitation service who appear to show greater promise of eventually entering gainful employment.

A third important connotation of the term arises from the professional recognition that the disabled person in our society appears to encounter some of the same problems faced by disfavored minority groups. It is increasingly believed that the rehabilitative process must concern itself with the overcoming of powerful psychosocial barriers, related both to the attitudes of others to the disabled person and to the attitudes of the disabled person to himself. In this sense, the problems of the disabled person are seen to have a strong social–psychological component.

In terms of all these connotations, the term *rehabilitation* has come to imply a many-sided and multidisciplinary process, which follows after the acute phases of an illness or disorder. Its objectives are essentially ameliorative or adjustive. The goal is an "optimal life adjustment" within the limits of a continued physical, mental, or emotional impairment.

Disability versus Handicap. In common usage, these terms tend to be treated as synonyms. In the field of rehabilitation, however, it has become customary to attempt to distinguish clearly between them. By and large, the term *disability* is reserved for some sort of medically diagnosable condition, whether the disability in question is physical, mental, or emotional. On the other hand, the term *handicap* implies that the disabled person finds himself (or is found) to be disadvantaged in relation to some desired life objective. It follows that not all disabilities, or all levels of intensity of a given disability, are handicapping. Similarly, individuals may be handicapped in relation to some vital life objective without being disabled, in the technical sense of the term.

This matter is not merely of semantic interest. Hamilton (1950) makes the point that a disability is a condition of impairment that has an objective aspect, while a handicap is "the cumulative result of the obstacles which disability interposes between the individual and his maximum functional level." Wright (1960) argues that a handicap can only be meaningfully appraised in terms of the cultural setting within which a person lives, including knowledge of the social goals toward which the individual wishes to strive. Whether a disability is, in fact, handicapping, tends to be a complex question, related in part to the manner in which the person perceives himself and, in part, to the manner in which society deals with him. When we use "disability," we are referring to a "condition of the organism"; when we use "handicap," we are in the realm of interpersonal relationships and social consequences.

In rehabilitation practice, the serving agency will typically see people who are *both* disabled and handicapped, simply because people with nonhandicapping disabilities will not accept referral. But even when both sets of problems are presented, it cannot be assumed that there is any very clear or simple relation between a given disability and any particular set of personal or social consequences. Everything depends, as it were, on the person who "has" the disability. It has proved to be impossible to establish any monotonic kind of relationship, for example, between the intensity or extent of a disabling condition and the severity of related handicaps. In discussing the behavior of patients with cardiovascular disability, White-house (1962) points out that "the person's accustomed pattern of response to threat is perhaps the most significant clue to the nature of his reactions to heart disease." At another extreme, there is evidence that such relatively "mild" impairments as a disfiguring skin condition of the face are almost certain to bring about relatively severe personal and social maladjustments. We are dealing, therefore, not only with issues related to the premorbid "personality" of the disabled person but also with powerful sociocultural norms and expectancies.

In summary, then, a disability is a permanent, residual limitation or impairment that may or may not interfere with an optimal life adjustment. The objective of the rehabilitative process is to overcome or minimize the possible handicapping effects of a disabling condition. For our purposes, we are interested in those aspects of disabling conditions that, again depending upon the case, have negative effects on the adaptation to work.

THE COMMUNITY MENTAL HEALTH CENTERS AND PSYCHIATRIC REHABILITATION

By 1955, the overcrowded and deteriorated conditions in our public mental hospitals had become sufficiently a public scandal so that the U.S. Congress was moved to set up a study commission called the Joint Commission on Mental Illness and Mental Health. The Commission was very wide-based, including leading representatives of psychiatry, psychology, social work, and a number of social science disciplines. The task put before the Commission was to make recommendations for what Alfred Deutsch (1948) had aptly called "the shame of the states." During the subsequent 5 years, the Joint Commission issued a number of important studies, culminating in a final report titled *Action for Mental Health* (Joint Commission, 1961). It was the recommendations of the Joint Commission, or at least certain of these recommendations, that provided the basis of what has come to be known as the Kennedy Mental Health Act of 1963. This historic bit of legislation, with its subsequent amendments, has provided the legal structure for the massive changes in mental health management of the past decade or two. It will be instructive to review these recommendations.

The Joint Commission summarized its final proposals under five headings: Research, Manpower, Services, Public Education, and Costs. The central theme of these recommendations can be summarized by the term *diversification.* Mental illness was seen as a disorder with many ramifications, some of which went far beyond the borders of the biomedical specialties. Thus, under the heading of *Manpower,* it was urged that there was need not only for more and better-trained psychiatrists, neurologists, and biochemical specialists, but that special emphasis should be placed on the recruitment and training of many kinds of *nonmedical* personnel: psychologists, social workers, rehabilitation specialists, employment counselors, as well as a wide variety of less formally trained paraprofessional "mental health workers."

Under the heading of *Services,* the recommendations of the Joint Commission were quite far-reaching. In effect, they called for a major structural shift from state hospital care (then the primary means of management of severe mental disorder) to "community care," thereby providing a rationale for what is now called community mental health, or community psychiatry. First, the Commission called for the establishment, nationwide, of a network of community mental health clinics (now called community mental health centers), based on catchment areas limited to populations of 50,000 persons. Second, it called for the development in every community general hospital of a psychiatric unit organized for short-term intensive treatment. Third, the Joint Commission insisted that all state hospitals should be limited in size to 1000 beds, and that larger units should be phased out or converted to other uses as quickly as possible. Fourth (a recommendation of extreme importance in the light of current problems), the Commission emphasized that the "objective of modern treatment of persons with major mental illness is to enable the patients to maintain themselves in the community" and therefore that "after-care and rehabilitation are essential parts of all service to mental patients" (Joint Commission, 1961, p. xvii). To achieve the latter goal, the Commission recommended support and development of the following kinds of services: day hospitals, night hospitals, aftercare clinics, public health nursing services, foster-family care, convalescent nursing homes, rehabilitation centers, work-services, and ex-patient groups.

With current controversies in mind, it is of considerable importance to note that the Joint Commission was fully aware that this panoply of services would be certain to cost a great deal more money than was currently being spent for service to the mentally ill. Since it was already clear that the various states and municipalities could not dispose of the required sums, the Commission took the radical step of recommending that the federal government establish a mental health budget to assist the states in carrying out services to the mentally ill.

In light of these recommendations made over 20 years ago, what is the current status of care for the mentally ill? To use a cliché, it may be said that we have made two steps forward and one step back; pessimists among us may declare that we have made only *one* step forward and *two* steps back. In effect, one-half of the job has been done, but the relative absence of the other half might have placed the average person with a severe mental disorder in a worse position than he was in a generation or so ago. These are rather strong statements requiring documentation.

There is no doubt that the worst excesses associated with the custodial mental hospital have been largely eliminated, that average length of mental hospital stay has been greatly reduced, and that intensive treatment and rapid discharge are now the rule rather than the exception. Very large numbers of elderly patients, who once comprised the majority of the denizens of the so-called "back wards," have been transferred to nursing homes where, some critics argue, they receive less care and protection then they formerly received in the hospital. The price of early discharge and easier admission has been enormous increases in readmission rates. Chronicity, which once was defined in terms of long-term residence in a mental hospital, has been redefined to describe a situation of multiple readmissions. Whether this is a gain or a loss remains to be appraised.

The chief outcome of the Mental Health Act of 1963 has been the establishment throughout the nation of over 600 community mental health centers. It cannot be doubted that these centers provide psychiatric services to large populations who, hitherto, had no access to any kind of professional mental health care. The 1963 Act has also supported the addition to many municipal general hospitals of planned psychiatric units. Recent studies of these new centers, however, have disclosed a major problem. *By and large, these community-based centers have served the milder rather than the severe disorders.* For example, in 1974, only 8% of all net releases from public mental hospitals found their way into community mental health centers. Similarly, of all persons who received a diagnosis of schizophrenia, 283,000 were reported as being treated in mental hospitals and only 29,000 as being treated in community mental health centers. While I am far from saying that the community mental health centers have not lived up to expectations, it is clear that they are not providing much service to the severely disturbed. In retrospect, it could not have been otherwise. By statute, the community mental health centers have been organized for early intervention, rapid turnover, and brief in-bed treatment when required (the typical limit for in-bed treatment is 21 days, and the average stay is less than that figure). They are, therefore, hopelessly ill-equipped to provide the long-term, supportive services that a great many former state hospital patients appear to require. More serious, the community mental health centers have not been obligated to provide the rehabilitative, work-oriented, and community-support services that were mandated by the original recommendations of the Joint Commission. The Department of Health, Education and Welfare, which is responsible for administration of the federal mental health legislation, has recently enjoined that they do so, but no funds have yet been appropriated that would make this very costly effort possible.

It also must be conceded that the ideology of psychiatric rehabilitation suffers from some of the same limitations that characterizes that of the community mental health centers. There is a kind of inflated therapeutic optimism, which may be a response as much to the exigencies of funding practices as to genuine conviction. The outcome criteria by which the success or failure of rehabilitation projects are most commonly judged have been: (1) reduction of the frequency of rehospitalization and, (2) the ability to find and maintain paid employment. All of these projects are time-limited, and it is rare that a given patient receives more than 6–12 months of planned services. Additional follow-up activity typically takes place for another 12–18 months, but this is usually limited to information-gathering. The ex-patient who manages to find his way into a rehabilitation program must make substantial progress toward the goals of the program during, at most, 1 or 2 years of posthospital service. If such progress cannot be achieved, the patient is recorded as a failure and dropped from the rolls. Thus, like the community mental health centers, the extant psychiatric rehabilitation projects are not equipped to provide long-term care.

It is difficult to assess the efficacy of current psychiatric rehabilitation practice, since the programs are small in number, limited in capacity, highly selective in whom they admit, and have still largely a "demonstration project" nature. So far as I can estimate, not more than 3–5% of discharged patients find their way into such projects, and from one-quarter to one-half of this small proportion are reported as having dropped out or been terminated before the planned services are completed. An appraisal of a number of these projects (Anthony, 1972) reports that there is some moderate effect on the employability of ex-hospital patients but little influence on the frequency of re-admission of the samples studied. Worse, if follow-up is extended to as long as 5 years, it is reported that even those patients reported as successes during the initial year of follow-up tend to lapse back into their initial states of desocialization, rehospitalization, and dependency. My own judgement of current psychiatric rehabilitation practices indicates that they do not have, up to now, any noticeable impact on the posthospital careers of the more severely mentally disordered. Of course, there is something of a logical circle here. People who are labeled as chronic psychotics are precisely the ones who do not respond either to treatment or to current rehabilitation service.

WORK AND SEVERE MENTAL DISORDER:
THE PRESENT SITUATION

At present the relations of work and the psychoses remain largely ambiguous.[4] The deinstitutionalization movement has brought about fun-

---

[4]There is some indication that a fresh look is being taken at the relation of work and mental disorder. In March 1982, the first national conference on Work and Mental Health took place, under the aegis of Dr. John Strauss, Professor of Psychiatry

damental shifts both in the manner in which severe mental disorder is managed and in the ways the psychoses are conceptualized.

A few things seem undebatable. First, the massive changes that have taken place within our public mental hospitals are basically positive and almost certainly irreversible. It is extremely unlikely that we will ever return to the hugh custodial establishments of a generation ago, when long-term commitment was the only means available for the management of severe mental disorder. Brief and essentially voluntary commitment, active treatment, and early discharge are now the rule and show every liklihood of remaining so. On the other hand, the mental hospital does not appear to be in process of being entirely "phased out," as was once the hope. In 1950, there were 322 such institutions; in 1974, there were 323. It is true that their annual censuses have been more than halved, but there are peculiarities. Admissions to mental hospitals were 152,000 in 1950; they were 374,000 in 1974. Of course, net releases were a negligible figure in 1950; releases totaled 389,000 in 1974, and this figure is larger than the admissions counted in that year. The contemporary public mental hospital is a swinging door rather than a prolonged place of custody and is highly likely to remain so.

The second thing about which we can have reasonable confidence is the irreversibility of the shift from hospital-based to community-based service. Although they remain precarious in funding and organization, the community mental health center and general hospital psychiatric units have increased in number year by year since the early 1960s. Patients reported as under care in community mental health centers have increased from 271,000 in 1968 to 1,327,000 in 1974, despite reduced budgets and federal hostility during the federal administration of the period.

A Rubicon appears to have been crossed, but the road to Rome remains beset with difficulties. In my opinion, some of our most serious problems arise from the fact that we have not yet confronted certain of the features of severe mental disorder. The massive social disruption that accompanies certain of the psychoses (or, possibly, constitutes their essential nature) is not easily influenced by a few weeks of in-hospital treatment, even if this is

---

at the Yale School of Medicine, and Dr. Sheila Akabas, Director of the Industrial Social Welfare Center of the Columbia School of Social Work. Some 35 people attended this conference, including psychiatrists, psychologists, social workers, rehabilitation specialists, and representatives of the U.S. Department of Health and Human Services. One of the major issues of this initial working conference was the role of work in the treatment of the severe mental disorders. A second conference, involving some of the same people, took place in September 1983 at the behest of a newly organized Work and Mental Health Section of the Center for Prevention Research of the National Institute of Mental Health. Again, the emphasis was on the role of work in psychiatric treatment. The writer was a participant in both of these conferences.

followed by a year or so of efforts at social restoration. The more uncritical proponents of community treatment may be overlooking at least two real possibilities. First, it is possible that a psychotic episode is, for many people, merely a more florid expression of a lifetime of poor and precarious personal and social adaptation. For such people, restoration of the premorbid state (an objective implied by the prefix *re* in rehabilitation) may simply mean return to a situation of general inadequacy. It has been determined that the best predictor of posthospital employment is premorbid employment stability, and this is precisely what many victims of psychosis appear to lack. Second, there is the possibility that, for still other people, a severe psychotic episode (combined with the reactions of others to it) is so damaging to the individual's social fabric that the most heroic measures currently available will not restore the set of social competencies that we ordinarily take for granted: those competencies required to cope with families, with work, with civil authorities, and with friends.

There is, of course, a third possibility, although the state of present evidence does not compel us to accept it. Unfortunately, it is also true that we are in no position to deny it. It remains possible that the psychoses are genuine medical diseases, with prominent genetic components, that are triggered by social circumstances that the more fortunate among us would experience as simply more or less stressful. If the latter possibility is true, then it would be unlikely that we could hit upon *any* plan for social intervention that totally would prevent the occurrence of psychotic behavior in afflicted persons. The stress–diathesis model of the etiology of mental illness permits a theory much like this one.

Whatever the facts as to etiology, it seems clear that people who undergo a psychotic episode are extremely heterogeneous in their life-long adaptation patterns, both before and after the initial outbreak. At one extreme, there are some for whom a psychotic break is merely a temporary, if serious, disruption. These are people who had achieved a reasonably competent life-style and are able to return to it with little or no assistance. This subgroup contains the most obvious beneficiaries of the deinstitutionalization movement. At the other extreme, there are people for whom a psychotic episode is an exacerbation of a life characterized by desocialization, disorganization, and dependency. Between the extremes, there are all sorts of variations around the basic themes of capacity and incapacity. Neither the traditional mental hospital nor the present network of community-based treatment programs has been able to face up to the facts of heterogeneity or been flexible enough to encompass them.

The chief dilemma of current pressures for short-term treatment and time-limited rehabilitation is that these measures, however desirable for many mentally disordered persons, are simply not appropriate for that substantial subgroup whom we call *chronic*. The term *chronic* here is something of a misnomer and carries the flavor of therapeutic failure. We use the term to refer to those patients who remain impervious to treatment, whose psychotic episodes recur with frustrating frequency, and who are observed to be making very poor social adjustments. It is these people who swell the readmission rolls, who live highly marginal lives in boarding homes and welfare hotels, and whose odd, bizarre, and disheveled public appearance has often become the subject of community outcry. Chronicity has also played a role in differential diagnosis: The more chronic the disorder, the more likely it is to receive the label of *schizophrenia*. More transitory disorders, in people with a history of adequate social competence, are more likely to be thought of as affective disorders or schizoid tendencies.

Although it runs against the grain of the helping professions to admit it, we must declare that there is a substantial portion of ex-psychotics—we do not know how large—that remains impervious to current treatment methods and is largely unresponsive to the most devoted efforts of active rehabilitation. What, then, are we to do? Must we throw up our hands and call for the reestablishment of the traditional mental hospital? Or are there alternative means of providing the life-long care, protection, and stimulation that some of our ex-psychotics appear to need? I think that there are alternatives, although to meet these alternatives will require modification of some strongly held ideological positions.

The helping professions have a strong commitment to change and progress. The physician records a therapeutic success when a diseased condition changes into a healthy condition. The rehabilitation specialist counts a success when a person who was formerly unable to cope with some major social demand (i.e., life outside the hospital or maintenance of paid employment) is now able to do so. Perpetuation of disease tends to be regarded as a medical failure, just as perpetuation of severe dependency is seen as a rehabilitation failure. Nobody likes failures, and they may be liked less in our own country than in some others. Funds, support, and prestige accrue to those who can report successes. There is not much glamor, and less current reward, for the provision of more or less permanent service and care to a sector of our population that remains uncured, unrehabilitated, and unchanged. Yet, more or less permanent care, at a range of levels, may be precisely what is needed by an indeterminately large sector of our de-institutionalized patients.

We can specify what is needed! There is a need for benign residential units in which manageably small groups of ex-patients can live together under the supervision of people trained to play the roles of surrogate parent and surrogate friend. Living as we do in a work-oriented society, in which employment plays a major role in contributing to feelings of personal worth and well-being there is need for a widespread network of sheltered work programs on the assumption that some ex-psychotics will never be able to meet the personal and performance demands of ordinary unprotected employment. These work programs should encompass a wide range of types of service, from total sheltering, at one extreme to transitional work experiences, at the other. ideally, we need to continue into the community certain of the more positive features of the traditional mental hospital, while avoiding the impersonality, bureaucratization, and neglect that were almost inevitable accompaniments of the rise of very large and isolated establishments.

We are saying, in effect, that the deinstitutionalization and community mental health movements must face up to some very unpalatable facts. More accurately, we are saying that the society at large must confront these unpalatable facts. Given the present state of knowledge and practice, we can neither "cure" some of the more severe mental disorders nor even make substantial progress toward the resocialization of some of the people afflicted by them. This is a bitter pill indeed, and we have reason to believe that neither the helping professions nor society at large are ready to swallow it. Yet, swallow it they must, or there is considerable danger that many psychotics will be abandoned or attacked, as they were abandoned or attacked before the advent of the traditional mental hospital.

13 | WORK STRESS

THE STRESS SYNDROME

So far in Part III we have considered the relation of work and mental disorder largely in connection with the very severe disorders (i.e., the psychoses) which involve almost total disruption of the individual's hard-won social adaptations. However, it must be conceded that the severe disorders affect, at most, not more than 1–2% of the working population and can be safely ignored by most of us. On the other hand, it can be stated with some confidence that all of us at times, and a good many of us more frequently, encounter and must deal with something called "work stress." We are here in the realm of rather large-scale phenomena, so much so that a considerable research and speculative literature has accumulated around the concept of *work stress*. It has also attracted the attention of two large and powerful federal agencies: the Occupational Safety and Health Administration (OSHA) of the U.S. Department of Labor and the National Institute of Occupational Safety and Health (NIOSH) of the Department of Health and Health Services. Private industry has also responded by providing both financial support and access to relevant working populations.

The magnitude of interest and scholarly attention has not resulted, unfortunately, in a situation where the concept of *work stress* is free from ambiguities and contradictions. As expressed by Stanislav Kasl and Sidney Cobb (1983, p. 445) two prominent authorities in this field:

> The day is yet to come when a reviewer of stress research is challenged because he overestimated the extent of conceptual and methodological disagreement in the stress field. The term "stress" continues to be used in fundamentally different ways: (1) as an environmental condition, (2) as the (subjective) appraisal of an environmental condition, (3) as the response to that condition, and (4) as the relationship between environmental demands and the person's ability to meet these demands. Passionate pleas for uniformity of usage or for the adoption of one particular definition go unheeded.

This entire field of study and research is comparatively new, dating back less than 30 years, although industrial psychologists and engineers have studied the relations of certain working conditions, worker productivity, and worker "morale" for a much longer period (see Chapter 3). The specific notion of "stress" was formulated by a biomedical researcher, Hans Selye, in an influential book (Selye, 1956). Selye saw certain modern "conditions of life" as inherently life-threatening, directly causing increased frequencies of such diseases as essential hypertension, peptic ulcer, and coronary heart disease, which he called the "general adaptation syndrome." He also carefully distinguished between the external physical conditions ("stressors") and the resultant physiological reactions ("strains"). Much of the ensuing research has, however, tended to abandon this neat distinction, leading to confusion as to whether stress is best understood as a noxious physical factor external to the organism (a given level of noise, a particular frequency of movement of an assembly line, a given quantity of supervision), a subjective *perception* (the external factor must be *seen* to be distressing by the affected individual), or a physiological condition whether conscious or not (increased blood pressure, reduced thresholds of irritability, etc.). Psychologists working in the field have tended to treat stress as if it were an essentially subjective experience; for example, a fairly widely used definition (McGrath, 1970) sees stress as "a (perceived) substantial imbalance between demand and response capability under conditions where failure to meet demand has important (perceived) consequences" (p. 20). Much of the confusion arises from the fact that studies of stress have encountered many complexities and difficulties, not the least of which have been that people embedded in an allegedly stressful situation display a very wide variety of reactions to it, ranging from no discernible effect at all to very severe breakdowns, including even death. The literature on work stress provides us with classical examples of the interaction between objective and subjective variables, or what we have in earlier chapters called a "transaction." One of the interesting things about the literature on work stress is that it amply reinforces the notion that the psychological and/or physiological baggage that the worker brings to the job requires equal billing with the particular job conditions that happen to exist.

However, it is possible to be too preoccupied with conceptual unclarities. As Holt (1983, p. 421) puts it in an excellent review of the literature on occupational stress:

> Put in commonsense terms, the basic proposition of the whole field of OS [occupational stress] might be expressed thus: some aspects of many kinds of work have bad effects on most people under certain circumstances. . . . The prevalent research paradigm is *stress* (independent variable)—*undesirable consequences* (dependent variable) under certain parametric conditions (moderator variables), which are not always included.

In the remainder of this chapter, we shall examine some of the variables intrinsic to stress and see how they further our understanding of the nature of human work.

KINDS OF STRESS

Comprehensive surveys of the research literature (Holt, 1983; Cooper and Payne, 1978) indicate that a great many aspects of paid employment in the United States have been investigated as a possible source of stress. The results of these studies suggest that almost any aspect of working—at certain levels and under certain conditions—can produce in working individuals an extremely wide range of undesirable consequences. All this might well lead us to the conclusion that work itself is stressful, until one also encounters studies (Cobb and Kasl, 1977; Jahoda, 1979) showing that its absence (unemployment) is also a considerable source of stress. Of course, in a heavily work-oriented society—in which both one's economic welfare and psychological well-being are dependent upon being able to find and hold reasonably well-paying employment—such a result is far from contradictory.

In his listing of stress variables studied, Holt (1983, Table 25–1, pp. 422–423) distinguishes between objective and subjective stressors, but it does not seem to me that this is a useful distinction. Under the former, Holt lists such studied variables as: physical properties of the work setting (e.g., noise, extremes of heat and cold), time pressures (e.g., nonstandard shifts, deadlines), job changes (e.g., unemployment, promotion, and demotion). Under subjective factors we find: role-related variables (e.g., role ambiguity, level of responsibility, degree of control, and a host of variables related to person-environment fit). That the objective–subjective distinction is somewhat strained is shown by the fact that included among the former are such obviously interactional variables as "responsibility overload" and "participation" and that included under the latter heading are such ambiguous variables as "job complexity," "inequality of pay," and "supervisory pressures and behavior."

It seems more useful to draw the general conclusion that, under certain conditions and for some persons, work can be stressful. We are again reminded, as we have emphasized in earlier chapters, that work is not a "natural" human activity but is something that we must "learn" to do. Moreover, as we showed in Chapter 7, work is carried out under conditions imposed by the particular society or culture in which one happens to be embedded and, indeed, can be thought of as a particular subculture of its own. As we examine the variables listed in Holt's Table 25-1 (1983), one discerns the general properties of work settings that were examined earlier in Chapter 7: the properties of the work site, the degree to which work is bound by time, the special interpersonal features of the work situation (relations to supervisors, peers, and subordinates), the needs fulfilled or frustrated by working (material needs, avoidance of boredom, need for self-respect and the respect of others, need for creativity and autonomy), and the incidental features of the general work environment (blue-collar versus white-collar, manual versus mental, public versus private, etc.). In the earlier chapters, we were simply describing what we thought to be the intrinsic features of work in modern society. The difference simply is that in the present chapter we are considering the darker sides of what most people take for granted.

We are thus again made aware that work can be a curse as well as a necessity, at least at certain times, for particular people, and at certain specified levels of intensity and degree. In examining the effects of the various conditions placed under study as possible sources of stress, we should also note that these effects of stress are never uniform across individuals exposed to a given source of stress but vary widely across individuals and occasions. Thus, the title of the Kasl and Cobb study of the effects of unemployment (Kasl and Cobb, 1983) is "Variability of Stress Effects among Men Experiencing Job Loss." The Kasl–Cobb study was a well-organized and well-controlled study of the effects of an anticipated plant closing on a group of employees. Both a physical examination (uric acid level, serum cholesterol, etc.) and attitudinal measures were the data of the study as the subjects went through anticipation of plant closing, actual job termination, a period of unemployment, probationary reemployment, and stable reemployment. Interviews were conducted on five occasions (a few weeks before the plant closing, a few weeks after, 4–5 months later, 1 year later, 2 years later). Suitable control groups of employees who were not involved in job loss were followed for the same length of time and received the same assessment techniques. In discussing their results, Kasl and Cobb state that, although group averages differed statistically in the expected direction, many individual subjects showed no effects at all. Moreover, an *adaptation* effect seemed to make its appearance, such that subjects who might have initially shown both physical and mental signs of anxiety and depression at job termination would return to previous levels fairly quickly. There was also some evidence suggesting that subjects with higher scores on a test of their psychological defenses showed less anxiety effects and appeared to adapt more quickly. Like work behavior generally, work stress is also subject to individual variation.

It seems fair to conclude that the field of stress research and practice, while potentially important and socially valuable, is still at an early stage of development. Although a fairly large number of stressor variables have been subjected to study, only a small number have received more than a single investigation. There has been time, so far, for little of the patient replication and verification that is needed for the establishment of what could be said to be a body of scientific knowledge. Rather, the net has been set very wide, but the holes in the mesh are equally large. This becomes evident when we examine effects of stress.

THE EFFECTS OF WORK STRESS

In his review of stress research, Holt describes over 50 studies of the consequences of stressful situations, all carried out during the 1970s. The unfavorable consequences studied range from specific biological indicators of strain (increased pulse rate or blood pressure, changes in serum cholesterol or uric acid concentration, catecholamine excretion, and the like) through such complex psychological dimensions as job dissatisfaction, fatigue, or alienation, to the possibility of increased frequency of defined disease entities (heart disease, hypertension, peptic ulcer, etc.). Quite global behavioral syndromes have also been studied, such as "mental health," depression, alcoholism, drug abuse, suicide, and "antisocial behavior." Again, the net has spread very widely.

A close examination of these studies shows that the relationships between stressors in the workplace and unfavorable reactions on the part of people exposed to them must so far be characterized as (1) modest in strength if present at all; (2) quite indirect in the sense that stressors are effective only if certain intervening states are brought into being, such as lowered self-esteem; (3) thoroughly interactional, in the sense that they appear to be maximally effective only with certain kinds of work personalities under certain conditions.

The difficulties in the way of drawing precise relationships between stressful situations and biological signs of unfavorable reactions to stress are perhaps best shown by two authoritative studies on the reactions of professionals and executives—two groups that can be best relied on to be able to articulate their problems. Caplan carried out an extremely meticulous study of such indicators of coronary heart disease as blood pressure, serum cholesterol, and serum uric acid among 390 executives and professionals in industry from whom he elicited self-reports of degrees of stress experienced on the job (Caplan, 1971, Caplan et al., 1975). In this study, zero correlations were reported between the indicated signs of potential heart disease and the reported measures of job pressure. In another study of 400 middle managers in an aerospace company (Chadwick, 1980), the investigator found that the physiological signs typically studied as indicators of a potential for heart disease (uric acid, blood glucose, dopamine, and cholesterol) correlated with pulse rate and blood pressure but not with heart attacks or with the only good predictor of heart attacks, the so-called personality Type A (see below). Of course, these problems may simply reflect some of the difficulties involved in medical research, where investigators are often trying to relate the immeasurable with the imponderable!

That the relationships between job stressors and mental states is indirect was shown in Kornhauser's famous study (1965) of auto workers (see discussion in Chapter 3). Kornhauser's study has been replicated for other occupations (Gechman and Winer, 1975; Ronan, Cobb, Garrett, Lazzeri, Mosser, and Racine, 1974). The point here is that the necessary intervening variable between work stress and mental health is a complex set of attitudes summed up in the phrase "job satisfaction." A good review of this literature is found in Katzell, Yankelovich, Fein, Oornatti, and Nash (1975).

The literature examined here is destructive of certain widely held beliefs about the relationships between kinds of work and such disease entities as coronary heart disease and peptic ulcer. People who have fallen victim to these diseases are often told that they must diminish their work loads or seek occupations believed to be minimally stressful. By far the largest number of studies are of the relations between coronary heart disease (CHD) and various working conditions (e.g., work overload, time pressures, excessive production demands). The results of these studies can best be described as ambiguous, with both negative and positive finds reported (House, McMichael, Wells, Kaplan; and Landerman, 1979; Falger, 1979; Haynes and Kannel, 1978). Again, as above, there appears to be a necessary intervening variable, the so-called Type A behavior pattern (cf. Jenkins, Rosenman, and Freedman, 1968).

There is an even more disappointing finding on the ambiguity in the association between peptic ulcer and work stress. A widespread popular belief is that people react to certain work demands by developing stomach ulcer. The specific studies of this presumed relationship (Susser, 1967; Weiner, 1977) find both positive and negative results. One might expect that people in very pressured occupations (e.g., air traffic controllers) would display higher rates of peptic ulcer. One study (Cobb and Rose, 1973) found that they did, but another (Caplan et al., 1975) was not able to replicate this finding. It would again seem that a complex net of intervening variables may need to be studied to tease out the reason for these contradictory findings.

The absence of clear and unequivocal causal relations between work conditions deemed to be stressful and unfavorable or pathogenic reactions on the part of people exposed to them suggests that the problems in this sort of research are more complex than the investigators initially assumed. We are forced to the conclusion that the relationships between stressors and effects of stress are not one-to-one but more complicated in nature. If intervening or moderating variables must be invoked, what are they and how do they come into being? A theory of work behavior that attempts to account for these ambiguities is the theory of person–environment (P–E) fit, evolved by an important research group at the University of Michigan. We shall examine this theory in the following section.

PERSON–ENVIRONMENT FIT AND JOB STRESS

For the most part, the study of work stress has tended to be rather atheoretical. The bulk of the investigations reviewed by Holt and others have been looking for direct causal links between some aspect of the work situation and a variety of undesirable consequences on the side of the worker. All too frequently, a direct causal link has either been very difficult to establish or the effect size is so small that very little justification is provided for any efforts at reforming them. In trying to account for the meagerness of positive findings, the researchers have pointed to the complexity of work settings, to the presence typically of a great many moderating and intervening variables, and to the fact that the working populations, whose behavior is being studied, run the gamut of variability of response. This hardly tells us much, since the investigators might well have been aware that work behavior is very complex to begin with.

There is, however, one group of researchers who have attacked the issues of work stress with a reasonably well-worked-out behavioral theory already in hand. Their work merits special examination. Since the early 1960s, a research group headed by John R. P. French and Robert L. Kahn at the University of Michigan (specifically, the Social Environment and Mental Health program of the Institute of Social Research) have carried out an exemplary series of studies of the relations of work and health (cf. French and Kahn, 1962). French and Kahn are social and industrial psychologists, whose theoretical views derive from those formulated by the late Kurt Lewin, a gestalt psychologist often described as the father of experimental social psychology. Lewin believed that the social behavior of people can best be described in terms of the interaction between the needs of the individual and the ways in which social environments fulfilled or frustrated these needs. Extrapolating from this point of view, French and Kahn have worked out a theory that finds that mental and physical health are a function of the "goodness of fit" between the person and the environment. In the case of work stress, the relationships to be studied are between what the worker brings to the job and what the work setting both demands and provides for the worker. We need to examine this theory in some detail and analyze the evidence presented for it.

The French–Kahn theory of work stress is essentially interactional and is similar in many ways to the work behavior theory of Lofquist and Dawis (see Chapter 6) and the writer's own ideas about the nature of human work (Chapters 7 and 8). The theory is fairly straightforward on the surface but complex in its generation of variables for study. As Kahn puts it in a recent paper (Kahn, 1983, p. 5).

> The basic idea of the P–E fit model is that individual adjustment consists of goodness of fit between the characteristics of a person and the properties of that person's environment. . . . A further distinction is made between objective facts—things as they really are or might be assessed by an objective, expert observer—and subjective facts—things as they are perceived by the person whose adjustment or well-being we wish to understand.

Thus, according to this view, two basic measures of fit are required: (1) the fit between the objective environment and the actual characteristics of the person (the objective person) and (2) the fit between the environment as perceived by the person (the subjective environment) and the beliefs and attitudes the person has about himself (the subjective person). A very large part of the activities of the Michigan group has been devoted to developing reliable measures of measuring the four conceptual domains (objective environment, subjective environment, objective person, subjective person).

The Michigan group tends to view P–E fit in terms of the relationships of supply and demand. The job presents the worker with certain demands (a range of work skills, amounts of required output, levels of supervisory pressures, kinds of social behaviors demanded, etc.); the supply consists of person's ability to meet these demands; stress and strain arise when there is some discrepancy between supply and demand. Here, demand is on the job side and supply on the worker side. But the theory also provides for the reverse. Workers have certain demands (needs, goals, preferences, aspirations) and look for jobs that will provide a supply of resources for meeting these demands. Stress and strain can arise when there is a discrepancy of some size between the demands on the side of the person and the ability of the work setting to fulfill these demands.

An interesting inference from the theory is that, under certain conditions, the amount of stress experienced by workers in certain settings might be U-shaped, rather than being a simple monotonic function of intensity. This is related to the problem of too much and too little. It is easy to see that strain may arise if the job demands more than the worker can supply or if the worker demands more than the job can supply. But it is also true that job-demands may be too little (the worker is overqualified). As a given factor proceeds from low to high, the reactions to that factor may proceed from high to low to high.

A study by Caplan et al. (1975) is cited by Kahn to illustrate the complex nature of the relationship between given job properties and the intensity of worker reactions. Caplan, a member of the Michigan research group, questioned over 2000 workers in over 20 occupations about the relation between job complexity and feelings of depression, anxiety, and dissatisfaction. Physiological measures of strain (blood pressure, heart rate, etc.) were also measured in a smaller subgroup. The results show the relative importance of P–E fit. When the relation between job complexity and depression is studied for the entire group, *disregarding individuals,* a direct but weak relationship of a positive nature is found. In general, there is a direct, but moderate, tendency for workers doing jobs of lower complexity to evince more feelings of depression than workers in jobs of higher complexity. However, a much stronger, or U-shaped relationship, is found if workers are asked how much job complexity they prefer. The data show that for the subgroup who state that job complexity is preferred, tasks of low complexity and very high complexity induce fairly strong feelings of depression, but these feelings drop off sharply in the middle ranges of job complexity. A pattern of variables on the side of the person thus functions as a set of moderating variables, affecting the strength of the relationship between a purported stressor and a feeling of strain.

Another kind of intervening or moderating variable is demonstrated in a study of the relation between job dissatisfaction and workload. According to common wisdom, as workload increases, so should job dissatisfaction. Harrison, another member of the French–Kahn group, (1978) has shown that this relationship holds good for such occupations as assembly-line worker and police officer, but a very sharply marked U-shaped relationship is reported for administrators. The latter appear dissatisfied with too little work as well as with too much. Again, there appears to be a formidable interaction between the characteristics of the worker and the properties of the work situation.

From these studies the Michigan group has drawn the conclusion that industrial reforms designed to decrease worker dissatisfaction and improve morale may not have the same or similar effects on all workers. The conception of P–E fit clearly implies that the relationships between given working conditions and specific signs of stress or strain are inclined to vary with certain attitudinal patterns on the side of the person. This is not to say that working conditions believed to be deleterious should not be eradicated or that the positive features of work should not be enhanced. Their results serve as a warning, however, that the beneficial results of a given reform may be masked by the fact that a given substantive change may increase morale among one subgroup of affected workers and either have no effect or actually reduce morale in another subgroup of employees in the same work situation.

From the point of view of this writer, the researches on P–E fit of the French–Kahn group provide us with evidence of the genuine complexity of work behavior, a degree of complexity about which the writer has speculated in earlier chapters. It is worth noting, however, that the researches so far carried through may yet fall short of the true level of behavioral complexity that is aroused by work settings in modern industry. Harrison's review of P–E research (1978) suggests that off-the-job factors, such as the amount of support given to the worker by his family or personal intimates, may also reduce expected amounts of job strain. One may add that the amount of experienced job stress may be influenced by the degree to which the individual worker feels that *all* work is more or less unpleasant, and that changes in particular work aspects are not expected to bring about notable improvements (i.e., a certain level of resigned fatality may be a moderating variable). One might also invoke the degree to which the given individual is capable of adapting to unpleasant or noxious work settings for a wide variety of situational and/or personal reasons.

Of course, the utility of the P–E fit theory can be appraised only in terms of the degree to which it adds to our understanding of the relationships between alleged stressors and presumed unfavorable consequences on the side of people who are embedded in the situations deemed stressful. As Kasl (1978) has pointed out, the results so far are "only mildly encouraging. The question is whether use of P–E fit measures can strengthen the observed effects between given stressors and a number of measures of worker reactions (job dissatisfaction, somatic complaints, depression, anxiety, irritation). In reanalyzing the data reported by Caplan et al. (1975) and Harrison (1976), Kasl shows that P–E measures do not show their superiority except for depression and then only for certain occupational groups (administrators but not assembly-line workers) and for certain specific sources of stress (job complexity but not role ambiguity). As Kasl himself concludes, however, P–E fit indicates the complicated nature of the things being studied here and suggests possibilities for research methodology that should not be ignored. It convinces us for the nth time that the study of human organisms in natural environments cannot be reduced to the "pure" models of single-variable research.

THE WORKER AND THE WORK SETTING

It is worth noting that some of the best examples of the interactional character of much of the research on human behavior is to be found in the literature on work stress. It would appear that the strongest evidence of the effects of particular stressful situations is obtainable only when moderating variables are taken into consideration. We shall here consider two sets of these moderating variables. The first set constitutes variables on the side of the person, which can perhaps best be described in terms of the mediating effects of types of work personalities. The second involves the moderating effects of social factors.

Perhaps the best case for the differentiating effects of personal factors in work stress is the now well-known distinction between Types A and B behaviors as contributors to the risk of coronary heart disease (CHD). CHD refers to those breakdowns of heart function that produce the intense pain associated with angina pectoris and can lead to the extremely dangerous disease known as myocardial infarction, which involves destruction of heart muscle tissue. Associated consequences of heart function failure are what is known as "strokes," where the vital blood supply to the brain is interrupted, resulting in the rapid destruction of crucial quantities of brain tissue. Loss of speech, paralysis, and, frequently, death are some of the consequences of strokes. CHDs and strokes are associated, both in the popular mind and in medical lore, with "stress." Since CHD is the leading cause of death, the past two or three decades have seen an enormous mass of research designed to pinpoint the factors causing it and to design measures to ameliorate its effects. Although many factors have been implicated (obesity, high blood pressure, cigarette smoking, etc.), considerable attention has been paid more recently to a set of factors that only can be described as a type of work personality.

The researchers who have identified the Type A syndrome (Jenkins, 1971, 1976; Rosenman, Friedman, Strauss, Wurm, Kositchek, Hahn, and Werthessen, 1964, 1970;) speak of four interrelated personality traits: (1) strong orientation toward achievement; (2) perfectionism, (3) strong commitment to job or profession; (4) high expenditure of energy and relative inability to relax. Type A is not a kind of stress reaction but has been identified as an enduring behavioral pattern that interacts with stressful factors in the work situation to enhance the risk of serious diseases, such as CHD. Correspondingly, Type B people (people who are low on this combination of traits) are relatively immune to the same stress-inducing variables that produce disease in their opposites. Data supporting this conclusion have been produced in a range of researches, ably summarized by Jenkins (1976).

This Type A syndrome perhaps has been most thoroughly studied by Rosenman and his co-workers, who carried out the Western Collaborative Group Study over an 8-year period. An elaborate structured interview on life and behavioral style was administered to a group of male workers, who were then followed-up 4.5, 6.5, and 8.5 years later. The evaluation technique was, in effect, a "double-blind" procedure. The behavioral patterns of the subjects were appraised without knowledge of the existence of possible disease entities, and, subsequently, diagnoses of disease were made without knowledge of behavioral type. The results showed a strong relation between the Type A personality pattern and risk of CHD. In a recent survey of these findings, McMichael (1978) points out quite correctly that this sort of finding was anticipated a generation or two ago by the founders of psychosomatic medicine.

In its broadest sense, the research on Type A as related to stress and CHD provides another illustration of the role of personality factors in work behavior (see Chapters 7 and 8). We should keep in mind, however, as we have stressed earlier, that the psychological baggage the worker brings with him to the job is far from being the only set of factors we need to examine. We must also consider what we have called the "demand characteristics" inherent in the work situation (see Chapter 7). Among these factors that we must accept as "conditions" of work behavior are the *social* aspects of the work situation, which we referred to in the opening paragraph of this section as the second set of moderating factors.

Among others, Cassel (1976) has stressed the importance of psychosocial factors in, depending upon the case and the setting, either increasing the experiences of anxiety and tension or diminishing them by serving as protective buffers. Work in modern society is a heavily socialized kind of behavior, as perhaps it always was (cf. Chapter 2), albeit to lesser or different degrees. The typical work setting requires that the worker interact with a wide variety of different persons who are playing a wide variety of different roles (work peers, supervisors, subordinates, the "public," etc.), and considerable flexibility is required in order to respond appropriately to these different work personnae. Also, kinds of work vary in the degree to which they contribute to such need patterns as self-respect, respect by others, levels of social status, and similar personal characteristics.

However, much of the research in this field has focused on what could be called non-job factors, such as "social support." Cassel and Tyroler (1961) report an interesting, if somewhat inconclusive, study of the relation between sociocultural status and physical health. The site of this health survey was a factory sited in Eastern Appalachia which, for some decades, had drawn its work force from the relatively isolated mountain peoples of western Kentucky and eastern Tennessee. The investigators compared two groups of workers: those who were the first of their families to leave the traditional mountain communities for work in the factory town and those whose fathers had worked in the same factory before them and who were already a generation removed from what has been pejoratively described as "hill-billy" life. The research hypothesis was that the former would show a higher proportion of stress-induced diseases than the latter. The results supported the hypothesis, and the investigators concluded that the second generation workers had made a successful subcultural adaptation, which the first generation workers had not yet had time to do. Of course, it must be noted that subcultural adaptation, the factor that the investigators believe to be the main factor at work here, is far from being the only variable involved. The differences between the two groups might well relate to the fact that the two sets of workers were raised in quite different *physical* environments: the isolated mountain valley and the industrial town; certainly, different disease-producing conditions prevail in these two quite different physical settings, and culture may have less to do with the research results than appears on the surface. However, it must be conceded that this is an interesting and novel direction for stress research and deserves further study.

A more job-related kind of social factor in work stress was reported by Caplan (1971). Caplan studied the effects of stress among a group of NASA administrators, scientists, and engineers. Among a great many other findings, he reported that such presumed stressors as role ambiguity and work overload produced greater signs of strain (both psychological and physiological measures were used) among workers whose relationships with supervisors, peers, and subordinates were described as poor than among workers who enjoyed good work relations. Of course, we cannot yet be certain that the strain levels reported are a function of inadequate social relations, a set of unrelated job stressors, or both together in some indeterminate combination.

An interesting study by Wells (1977) pinpoints the source of social support. Studying a sample of some 1800 blue-collar workers in the rubber industry, Wells separates the moderating effects of four sources of social support: supervisor, co-workers, wife, friends, and other relatives. The measures of strain included such psychological aspects as job satisfaction and self-esteem; job-related items such as productivity, concern for quality, etc.; health outcomes such as symptoms of angina, ulcer, frequency of colds, and neurotic symptoms. The reported results show that the support of wives and of supervisors were much more effective mitigators of the effects of stress than were the other two support variables: co-workers and friends. All this seems very plausible, but the data also suggest that the moderating effect of social support factors on signs of stress and strain may be quite small and even inconsistent. It seems clear that much more study is needed.

WORK STRESS AND MENTAL HEALTH

The best and largest-scale studies of work stress have been in the medical domain. Following the notions of Selye, investigators have examined various aspects of work settings and have tried to establish links between certain of these features and specific physiological indicators (blood pressure, serum cholesterol, uric acid concentration, etc.) on the supposition that excessive changes in the latter determinants will also increase the frequency of specific diseases: CHD, peptic ulcer, stroke, etc. As we have seen, it has not been easy to establish direct causal links between presumed stressful features of work situations and resulting disease processes, and a variety of intervening and moderating variables have been invoked to account for what may be justly described as weak or inconclusive findings. The Type A syndrome in CHD is perhaps the best known, but many others have been studied. Nevertheless, despite these ambiguities, it is possible to draw the conclusion that, under certain conditions and for certain persons, there are features of modern work settings that appear to be responsible for unwanted and undesired organic consequences.

Unfortunately, the relations of work and mental health are even vaguer and more uncertain than those disclosed in the studies of work stress and physical illness. In part, this is because the mental disorders, especially those toward the mild end of the mental disorder continuum, are themselves difficult to measure and establish. A more serious problem is the virtual impossibility of separating work and nonwork sources of stress. We can anticipate here many instances of circularity, where cause and effect relations become hopelessly entangled. A given feature in the work setting (work overload, supervisory pressure, etc.) may bring about a set of reactions characterized by enhanced irritability or depression. To the degree that the worker brings these feelings home with him, there may be resultant strains on his marital or personal life. To the degree that the latter become severe, they may in turn affect performance on the job. This presumed sequence of events may of course start in the other direction, originating in the personal domains of the worker's life and subsequently affecting job performance. The source of causation may ultimately be a matter of where one chooses to start one's investigation!

This degree of causal indeterminacy, however, has not prevented some writers from making very wide claims about mental effects of job stress. Ivancevich (1980) has estimated the costs to industry of stress-related consequences in a rather hortatory book addressed to industrial managers. He begins by declaring that alcoholism costs industry some $20 billion dollars a year, to which he adds an $18 to 25 billion loss due to absenteeism. Citing a recent estimate of a $17 billion dollar loss due to stress-induced mental dysfunctions and adding other presumed costs of stress, he arrives at a cost of stress of some $75–90 billion annually, or some 10% of the gross national product. Ivancevich believes this estimate is conservative, if we include the dollar costs of hospital and medical expenses, costs rising from familial disruptions, and the costs of premature death and/or forced retirement. Whether such estimates can be directly related to work stress or are a function of much more general pathogenic conditions in the society at large is quite moot.

Even if the losses in production are not so large as has been estimated, it is quite likely that they are considerable. It has recently been reported that in Britain, during the 15 years prior to 1980, absenteeism attributed to physical illness rose 15%; during the same period, however, days lost attributed to mental health problems rose by 152% in men and 302% in women. Whether this finding can be directly related to work stress or is a function of a range of nonwork factors remains uncertain. Again, alcoholism is reported as a major problem, but the causes of alcoholism are many and varied.

STRESS AND WORK: GENERAL CONSIDERATIONS

Although conclusive and unequivocal research findings appear to be in somewhat short supply, research and service programs flowing from the basic ideas of stress are widespread and developing. The presumed relations of work stress to such serious industrial problems as absenteeism, reduced productivity, poor worker morale, the increased costs and disruptive nature of physical and mental illness—all these have drawn the attention of industrial managers, who have opened their factories and records to concerned investigators and often made considerable financial contributions to the research effort. All this is in rather sharp contrast to the virtual total unconcern of private industry in the rehabilitation or sheltered employment of the severely disturbed. Clearly, management has great hopes for the former kinds of research efforts and very little for the latter.

However this may be, the research on work stress has provided the writer with considerable support for his own theories about human work behavior. The investigators in this difficult field, who have struggled with the effort to establish the effects on workers of presumed work stressors, have become abundantly aware of the enormous complexity of work behavior and its manifestly interactional character. What they have had to invoke as intervening or moderating variables, in order to account for unexpectedly weak causal effects, is what we have called the "psychological baggage" that the worker brings with him to the job (i.e., the *work personality*). In examining specific work demands, these researchers have been compelled also to study specific needs on the side of the worker, thus providing further evidence of the interactional or transactional nature of work behavior (see Chapters 7 and 8 and the Dawis–Lofquist Minnesota studies, Chapter 6). Although it is clearly banal to invoke the notion that "one man's meat is another man's poison," it appears to be true that a given work stressor may have undesirable effects on workers whose pattern of attitudes and needs make them particularly sensitive to the stressor in question, whereas other workers in the same situation may show little or no effect. Perhaps we do not have to be told again that work behavior is a highly complex affair, but the literature on work stress leaves us with no other conclusion.

IV | SOME CONTEMPORARY PROBLEMS

14 SOCIAL BARRIERS

We have repeatedly observed here that work is a social activity, and that the manner in which people work is a function of the social situations in which they find themselves. The ability to work is, of course, a characteristic of the human being as a member of a particular biological species, but it also depends on sociocultural conditions. In this sense, work is not a "natural" activity but is a product of a long period of historical and individual development. All societies exhibit more or less elaborated and institutionalized means designed to transform their playing children into working adults, although it is obvious that the procedures utilized and the kinds of workers desired vary greatly from society to society. There are also massive variations *within* societies, particularly within modern, highly industrialized societies. It is a fact of contemporary life, in complex societies such as ours, that not all people are presented with inducements to become workers. Some are presented with *barriers*! It is also true that certain of the barriers to employment faced by certain sectors of the population are now under severe attack, although it remains to be seen how soon they will be overcome. In the present chapter, we shall deal with some of the problems vis-à-vis work faced by certain massive social groupings: women, minorities, and the handicapped.

WOMEN AND WORK

Before the 1960s, there was some general awareness that women were far from being treated as full and equal members of the labor force, but this was not yet seen as a major social problem. A striking phenomenon of the 1960s, however, was the rise of a powerful movement among women (particularly in the United States) for egalitarianism in all aspects of social living, including those aspects that bear upon work. In order to grasp what is at issue here, it will be helpful to review the differing work roles that have historically been assigned to men and to women and also to document how these roles have been changing.

269

Until quite recently, very little of the literature on work has been concerned with working women. In fact, the term *worker,* in its literary connotations, appears implicitly to refer to a *man* and is specifically qualified to read "woman worker" when the context requires it. Yet, from the point of view of human history, no human society could be a viable economic enterprise without the labors of their women. In some societies, the women perform the major kind of useful work. Why the comparative silence about the woman worker? There are women who will argue that this is simply because almost all of the literature on work has been produced by males, and we are merely seeing another example of the pervasive manner in which sex roles have been historically stereotyped. While ordinary bias is undoubtedly a factor, it is not the whole story.

Current relations of women to work are in a state of flux. Attitudes to work that have prevailed for centuries are now being sharply challenged by some striving and articulate women, and certain of the challenges have divided women as much as they have confused and angered men. Although we need more perspective to be sure about it, we seem to be passing through a kind of social revolution that may have the long-run effect of shaking up a great many traditional social arrangements. As in any social revolution, particularly in its earlier stages, we are bombarded by a great many differing doctrinal positions. There are extremists who argue that women cannot be really freed for work and career unless all the traditional arrangements for sex and marriage are radically altered. There are moderates who refrain from attacking such basic institutional arrangements and who simply want to improve the possibilities for work and career for any woman who wants to engage in them. There are women who wish to retain the traditional roles of housewife and mother and resent being called slackers and slaves by their more militant sisters. There are also a great many varied attitudes among men, ranging from affirmation of the most crass stereotypes to total acceptance of the justice of women's rights. The present writer cannot here engage in a full discussion of the politics of the women's movement. We are, however, interested in developing a theory of work behavior, and, since women work as well as men, we cannot be indifferent to the woman worker.

A number of highly intricate and involved issues are at stake here. First, as we have insisted throughout this volume, work is a highly socialized enterprise. The attitudes to work we display as adults are the outcome of a long process of social learning, during which a wide variety of social norms are internalized. One issue we will have to face is whether, and to what degree, the social norms vis-à-vis work are different for boys and girls. But cultures change, and social change is virtually the hallmark of our present society. We will have to estimate the impact of massive technological change on traditional social norms.

A second complicating issue has to do with conceptions about the nature of work, which largely came into existence during the Industrial Revolution and have persisted since. As we have seen, the spread of the factory system introduced the idea that work is not really work unless it is paid for. This close association between work and wages appears to have resulted in a situation where the expenditure of energy in household tasks or in the care of children is not generally thought of as work but as some sort of "natural" activity. In addition, modern work is not only paid for, it is also generally performed away from the household. We need to examine the force of these distinctions and understand their effects on other social arrangements.

A third issue we will have to study involves the effects of massive advances in the technology of work. With regard to women, technological change has been a two-edged sword. On the one hand, it tended to *divide* the activities of women between unpaid household labor and paid work. On the other hand, technological advances have also stripped most kinds of work of what were once thought of as "masculine" requirements (i.e., superior physical strength or mobility). Technological advance has thus placed women in a kind of *double bind.* Much of what they do in the home—no matter how necessary to the economic welfare of the family unit—is no longer thought of as work and is not recognized as such by direct payment. At the same time, women are now capable of entering virtually any occupation and meeting its requirements as well as men do. All this has become aggravated by the gradual trend of modern society toward greater egalitarianism and toward a situation in which the kind of work one does is not only a mark of identity but the chief source of social respect. It is in this sense that many women today are experiencing a kind of crisis of identity. Traditional female pursuits (household maintenance and the care of children) no longer appear so attractive as the kinds of independence, identity, and prestige that may derive from paid work.

There has probably always been a division of labor between males and females. Initially a function of the biology of reproduction, this division has been enforced by varied cultural arrangements. The idea that work is a *primary* obligation for males and, at best, a secondary obligation for females is, however, a recent development. During the hundreds of thousands of years that the human animal was chiefly a hunter–gatherer, the women worked at least as hard and certainly as much as the men did. It is true that hunting was mainly a male activity, particularly the hunting of large, swift, or dangerous animals. It is true also that men typically fabricated everything needed for the hunt—tools, weapons, snares, angling equipment, boats, and the like. But virtually everything that was eaten, worn as clothing, or lived in as a habitation was prepared or fabricated by the women.

Similarly, in societies organized around relatively undeveloped subsistence agriculture, the women do virtually all of the field work, while the breeding and care of cattle and draft animals is the work of men. Even in the more developed peasant societies, in which a considerable and varied agricultural technology has already made its appearance, women spend a large portion of their time working in the fields, with the entire family functioning as a productive unit. Where either hunting or subsistence farming is the principal economic activity, the division of labor is not between work and "no-work" but simply between different kinds of work tasks. In part, these distinctions may derive from differences in physical strength, but their most obvious source has to do with responsibility for the care and nurturing of children. So far as we have any knowledge of human history, the latter has always been primarily a female responsibility. Freed of this responsibility, men can be more mobile, can perhaps do heavier work, risk greater dangers, and undertake all the requirements for attack and defense. But the labors of women, bound by the responsibility of care for children, were as demanding, frequently more time-consuming, and certainly as vital to the continued existence of the community. Whether the nurturing of children was ever conceived of as "work" in the same sense as food-gathering or field labor is a moot point still being hotly debated, but it can hardly be doubted that the latter activities *were* work, and that young girls were trained from early childhood to undertake them. While we have very meager information on the attitudes to work prevailing in older societies, there is anecdotal evidence that skill in preparing hides and making productive gardens were assets for marriage and matters of prestige in tribal and subsistence societies.

The notion that work was principally a male responsibility was probably a consequence of urban growth and the development of industrial technology. In the cities, a distinction was drawn between paid and unpaid labor, and it gradually became customary to think of only the former as genuine work. This distinction became sharper, of course, with the rise of the factory system and the firm establishment of a money economy. *Work then increasingly became something performed away from the home and for which one was paid a wage.* In the early years of the Industrial Revolution, many women (and small children as well) became paid factory workers, particularly in textiles and weaving. But reforms of the worst horrors of the new factory system, plus the availability of vast supplies of male labor due to rural overpopulation and displacement, soon eliminated most working women as the factory system spread. By the end of the nineteenth century in the technically developed countries, the labor force became predominantly male, with women confined chiefly to the domestic services.

In industrialized societies, there is so close an association between work and monetary compensation that we have become accustomed to think of the "working woman" only when she is doing something for which she is paid a wage or salary. Between bearing children and endless household labor, the wife of a male factory worker might wear herself out at an early age, but this was not considered work because it was not *paid for* directly. An employed female domestic is considered to be a worker because money changes hands, but the identical labors of the housewife are simply considered the "natural" accompaniments of marriage and childbirth. While a

woman is unmarried or is not directly responsible for the care of her children, she may be expected, or even required, to work for wages. But it is still
widely believed that the nurturing of children is the prime responsibility of
women. Given the definition of work as paid labor, there is obviously a
conflict between the requirement to care for one's children and the requirement to work. Although by this time over one-third of the United States labor
force is female, it has been shown that women work in paid employment in
much larger numbers *before* they become mothers and *after* their children
are old enough not to require continuous care (Smuts, 1959). Of course, no
such association with the presence or absence of children is found in the
case of the male worker.

Given the enormous changes brought about by urbanization and industrialization, given also the current close association between work and
money, girls and boys have increasingly faced very different cultural demands and pressures with regard to work. In technically advanced societies,
such as ours, boys are made aware in a great many ways that they are
expected to "make a living" when they grow up. While girls are not wholly
exempt from these pressures, the overriding cultural imperative for the
young girl is to "get married." There consequently has developed a widespread and deeply held belief that the work of women is only incidental and
temporary. Although this belief is illusory, at least in part, it is held not only
by most men but by very large numbers of women. Far fewer women than
men are able to regard their work as their *principal* life-vocation, or at least
to be as single-minded about it as men usually are. It has become customary
to think of the married, male worker as the "breadwinner"; income brought
in by the married, female worker tends to be looked on as contributory,
rather than essential.

In the face of these powerful traditions, one of the most remarkable
phenomena of the past two decades has been the rapid rise and power of
movements among women aimed at egalitarianism in all aspects of life,
especially in the sphere of work. This drive toward full equality has not been
without complications and setbacks, as exemplified by the 10-year long,
ultimately unsuccessful struggle to ratify an Equal Rights Amendment (ERA).
The wording of the ERA was almost absurdly simple ("equality of rights
under the law shall not be denied or abridged by the United States or by any
state on account of sex"). Although work was not mentioned, it was seen as
guaranteeing equal pay for equal work, regardless of gender. Moreover, it
was seen by its proponents as providing the legal basis for the entry by
women into any occupation and also preventing, by statute, the continued
existence of any kind of job discrimination based on sex. The ERA was
passed in both houses of Congress by the necessary two-thirds majority in
March 1972 (an historic date!) and, as the required second step in the
amendment process, was then turned over to the states for the necessary
ratification by three-quarters of the states within a 5-year period after pas-

sage by Congress. By 1978, 35 of the states had done so but three states had not (38 states were required for passage of a constitutional amendment). After a bitter fight, Congress extended the time of ratification from March 1979 to June 1982. Unfortunately, by the time the extended date was imminent, the ERA had still not secured ratification by the three additional states, and, in June 1982, the amendment was declared dead. What had happened?

Many alternative explanations have been offered to account for the ERA debacle, although none is completely satisfying. The protracted battle over the ERA undoubtedly raised the hackles not only of some male workers and legislators but also of certain women associated with the more conservative sectors of the population. The ERA opposition put forward arguments that its passage would open the door to the conscription of women into the armed forces and their use as combat troops. Charges were raised that the proponents of ERA were interested in the destruction of the traditional family, and that their secret agenda was directed not to female equality but female superiority and separation. The national women's movement was probably also hurt by its unwillingness to separate itself from the small minority of extremist antimale and lesbian elements among its membership, who received media attention far out of proportion to their actual numbers and influence. It is, more than likely, however, that the ERA was a victim of the trend toward conservatism in the national elections of 1980. The fundamentalist and neoconservative groupings that were active in the election of the new Administration were united in their opposition to the ERA and virtually guaranteed its failure.

Although this initial effort to pass an equal rights amendment to the U.S. Constitution did not succeed, I do not believe we have heard the last of it. We should also note that the thrust of the proposed amendment contrasts sharply with previous labor legislation concerned with the woman worker. In the past, the main concern of reformers was for *protection* of the woman worker rather than equality. During the nineteenth and early twentieth centuries, feminists and women trade unionists fought for legislation that would protect women from particularly heavy or dangerous working conditions. Banned as particularly injurious to women were any working conditions or types of work that might have a negative influence on childbirth or on effective motherhood. For example, it was prohibited to employ women in excessively hot or wet kinds of work or as night workers, all under the aegis of protection, not equality. The enactment of such protective statutes was long considered a major achievement of the earlier women's movement and was particularly prized by many women in positions of trade union leadership. Passage of the ERA therefore, was, opposed initially by some women labor leaders, but pressures for equality, in the long run, turned out to be overwhelming, and the older women leaders ultimately gave the ERA their support. Nevertheless, it is clear that ratification of the ERA, in its 1972 language, might have rendered moot a vast network of protective ordinances, and perhaps this also made for lukewarm support in certain quarters.

There are some complex problems involved here. It can hardly be doubted that the majority of working women today are in a relatively small number of "female" occupations: office work, light factory work, certain service occupations, teaching, social work, nursing (Bancroft, 1958; Women's Bureau, 1969). It is hardly an accident that a good many of the jobs reserved for women, and to which women are frequently restricted, bear some resemblance to the duties of family care and household maintenance. Even in those occupations in which they predominate in numbers, women are generally denied the higher executive and administrative positions. For example, the overwhelming majority of public school teachers are women, but school principals and superintendents are generally men. This situation is exaggerated the higher one goes in the educational network. A recent study of higher education (Oltman, 1970) showed that women were underrepresented at every position level. Even where women manage to achieve academic positions, they are paid lower salaries, are negatively affected by antinepotism rules, and have greater difficulty achieving tenure (Harris, 1970). A recent study of hospital administration (Dolson, 1967), where women constitute the majority of the labor force, showed that women occupy only 21% of the administrative positions, were paid less at the same job levels, and took longer to achieve executive status.

One would be hard put to account for these dramatic differences by citing the technical qualifications for most kinds of work and attempting to relate these to alleged differential capabilities of men and women. Research designed to find sex differences in intellectual and motor performance has yielded meager results, and it is generally taken for granted that the sexes do not differ in ability to learn. At the same time, the tremendous advances of industrial technology have rendered largely unnecessary the one asset that males have historically displayed: superior physical strength and endurance. It seems obvious that what is at stake here is the force of powerful and ancient cultural traditions.

Even if we are ready to concede that occupational discrimination is a function of culture rather than a judgment on capability, we are still some distance from equitable solutions. While culture is eminently subject to change, not all aspects of culture change at the same rate, and some appear to have remained stable for thousands of years. One such component of human social relations, which appears to have successfully resisted cultural change, involves the responsibility for the nurturing and care of children. So far as we have any knowledge of human history, women always have had the primary responsibility for child care, with men playing, at most, supportive and auxiliary roles. In the face of the most thoroughgoing cultural changes, in the face also of the virtual disappearance of the *extended* ("three-generation") family in modern, industrialized societies, this relation-ship has persisted without much change. Even in societies that have at-tempted to institutionalize child care in order to free mothers for work (in the Israeli *kibbutzim,* for example), the professional caretakers are women. This division of responsibility has persisted so intractably that one would be tempted to regard it as simply biological in origin. But man is so plastic an animal that there is no form of human behavior that is not, somehow, influenced by culture. Even the care of children has been influenced by technological change. In principle, at least, it is possible to imagine arrange-ments where males can be at least as much involved in child care as women now are. Of course, we have no way of anticipating the effects on children of such a massive alteration of ancient child-care procedures. It may well be that children will develop "normally" only if they are reared principally by women in their early years, but we have no way of proving the case. Obviously, children need "mothering," if mothering means the delivery of tender and solicitous care, but whether such care can also be delivered by men remains to be seen. Certainly, there may be unwanted consequences, but we do not know what they may be.

We have entered into this digression on the care of children because it appears to be one of the more impermeable barriers to full equality of men and women with respect to work. By and large, boys are raised to become workers first, husbands and fathers second. Girls are still raised to be wives and mothers first, workers second. Assuming that girls continue to be brought up with the entrenched idea that marriage and children are primary objectives, assuming further that society continues to arrange things so that the care of children and maintenance of the household are largely female responsibilities, women's attitudes to work will show more ambivalence than those of men.

Of course, reforms are both possible and necessary. Society can invest adequate sums in the provision of nurseries and day-care centers, thus free-ing many women for occupational careers. We can certainly legislate equal pay for equal work (an Equal Pay Act was passed by Congress in 1963 but has been ineffectively administered). We can legislate equal opportunity for training and promotion, and such a provision was written into law in 1972. Ratification of an Equal Rights Amendment might also extend the base for equality in the labor market. But full equality will require some fundamental shifts both in cultural attitudes and in prevailing social arrangements.

In the United States in the second half of the twentieth century, men and women are becoming increasingly equal before the law, and many of the more glaring social inequalities are being minimized. It is still largely true, however, that the two sexes are far from being interchangeable units in the labor force. This is true even when training and aptitude are apparently equivalent. In an extensive study of men and woman lawyers, for example, it has been shown that men earned about $1500 more on their first job than did women, and, after 10 years of legal practice, only 1% of women were earning $20,000 or more as compared to 9% of the men (White, 1967). This may reflect not only the ordinary operation of bias and prejudice but also the frequently observed fact (cf. Kaley, 1971) that professional women have a *dual* responsibility, while their professional husbands can be more single-minded. In families where both members of the marital pair are working professionals, the woman is still chiefly responsible for home maintenance and child care.

The relations of women to work in modern society are more difficult than appears on the surface. To use the language of a federal study (President's Task Force on Women's Rights and Responsibilities, 1970), it is "a matter of simple justice to abolish all legal barriers to full equality." But the achievement of such legislative equality is still only a partial solution, as desirable as it may be. The brutal facts are that the overall life-tasks faced by men and women in our society are still sharply different, and these differences undoubtedly have a powerful effect on attitudes to work. Sex-role stereotyping starts very early in life, possibly from infancy. Little girls are expected to be pretty, docile, and winsome; they are expected to play with dolls and to simulate domestic activity. Little boys are expected to be strong and venturesome; their play is marked by rivalry and is seen as a preparation for competitive games and sports. Boldness, aggression, and rivalry are seen as unfeminine. Passivity, docility, and attachment to the home are looked on as desirable feminine traits, and little girls may quickly learn that such behaviors are rewarded. These sex differences, in the kinds of social norms presented for internalization, have powerful effects. It has been shown that, as early as the third grade, girls and boys display sharply different occupational fantasies, with girls dreaming of such occupations as nurse and teacher and boys opting for what they think of as more adventurous and dangerous occupations. In her studies of vocational development in children, Tyler has observed that these differences are already present in the first grade and are sharply crystallized in 10-year-old children (cf. Tyler, 1951, 1955, 1964).

This sort of sex-role stereotyping does not taper off as children get older but, if anything, becomes more demanding. Teen-age girls are confronted with the strongest possible pressures to prepare themselves for marriage and for entry into "feminine" occupations. Although obviously interested in sex, marriage is still far from the minds of most teen-age boys. In a widely cited study done 30 years ago, Singer and Stefflre (1954) found that male high school seniors expressed desires for jobs that offered power, prestige, and independence, while senior girls aspired to occupations that were oriented toward welfare and social service. Although more recent studies have found some shifts in the statistical proportions, these sex-linked occupational differences are still very powerful.

It is not easy to draw clear conclusions in rapidly changing situations, and it can hardly be doubted that the relations of women and work are currently undergoing massive change. Women in increasing numbers are entering professions and occupations that were hitherto the exclusive prerogative of males; achievement of a legal framework for labor force equality seems well on the way; institutions and industries that are under any kind of public regulation are under very strong pressures to implement sexual equality at all levels. At the same time, perhaps the most accurate word we can use to describe the present relations of women and work is *ambivalence*. The relative weight of marriage and work is still sharply different in the two sexes. For boys, work is an indispensable instrumental activity that lays the basis for everything connected with adulthood: independence from the natal family, identity, the means of supporting one's own family, etc. For girls, work and marriage involve conflicts and tensions and may easily come to be alternatives rather than complements. The primary objective required of boys is instrumental achievement; girls are still required to be "feminine." Much of this distinction is attributable to massive social stereotyping, but it is none the less powerful. The basic source, however, may be found in the traditional division of social responsibility within the family, particularly as it relates to responsibility for the care of children.

While social prediction is, at best, a chancy business, it seems safe to say that women will play larger roles in the labor forces of the technically advanced countries. This will both require and produce a great many other massive social changes, some of which are already in process. The traditional distinctions between masculine and feminine occupations are rapidly eroding as technology undermines the requirements for physical strength and endurance. The traditions of responsibility for child care are also subject to change, although these cultural norms are more ancient and more resistive to change. We will undoubtedly see a wider provision of creches and day-care centers than now exist, thus freeing more women for work. We can also venture the prediction that in families in which both members of the marital pair are oriented toward work, there will be increased sharing of many household duties. There is some anecdotal evidence that this is already taking place, but it is probably uneven and unbalanced. Working men have been increasingly reported as "helping" their working wives, but it is obvious that "helping out" is not the same thing as basic responsibility. But we need not expect the total abolition of the natal family, as some extremists in the women's movements now advocate. As a unit, the natal family has changed radically throughout human cultural evolution, and we can confidently expect further changes in the future. Exactly what form they will take cannot now be foreseen, but we can assume that the pressures for egalitarianism will, in the long run, change certain of the relations *within* the family, as they have outside of it.

The relations of women to work are a neat example of the high degree to which work is a sociocultural enterprise. As we have repeatedly pointed out, work is not a "natural" activity of human beings, although of course it is the biology of the human species that makes work both possible and necessary. Human children become adult workers through a long process of social learning, and we must admit that the social norms presented to little girls— even in industrialized societies—are markedly different in important respects from those presented to little boys. The attitudes to work of most women, therefore, are marked by a kind of ambivalence and a degree of conflict with which men need not contend. The work personality does not develop in a vacuum but is itself a product of social norms and social arrangements. As the latter change, so does the former. The time may not be far distant when work and marriage, for women, are no longer contradictory goals. Given the changes in ideas and social arrangement that now appear to be taking place, they can become complementary aims, as they now are for most men.[1]

ETHNIC MINORITIES AND WORK

It is unnecessary to provide documentation here for the fact that there are large categories of the population in the contemporary United States that are blocked from full access to the work opportunity structure. Somewhat euphemistically referred to as ethnic minorities, they include blacks, Puerto Ricans (plus other groups of Latin American origin), other Mexican-Americans (Chicanos), native Americans, and certain smaller groups of recent immigrants from undeveloped countries. We are not dealing here with insignificant numbers, since together these groups amount to approximately one-fifth of the total United States population. It is not at all easy, however, to provide an appraisal of their relations to work. In part, this is true because there are extreme risks to thinking in terms of stereotypes. The various ethnic minorities differ markedly from each other in social history, cultural characteristics, and in the social barriers they face. There are even wider within-group differences, with a selection of individuals running the gamut from severe social deficit at one extreme to full social achievement at the other.

---

[1]There appears to have been slower progress toward equality for women in the labor market than might have been anticipated. According to a recent article in the *New York Times* (January 16, 1984), a senior official of the Census Bureau has reported that in 1980, white women entering the labor force were paid only 83% of the average wage of white men joining the labor force. It was noted that during the 1970s, the gap between entry pay for white women and white men widened rather than narrowed; in 1970, white women entering the labor market were paid an average of 86% of the hourly wage of white males in entry occupations. Black women lagged still further behind in absolute terms, although they had made a slight relative gain during the decade (black women in entry occupations in 1980 earned 79% of the white male entry average hourly wage; 77% in 1970). Excellent treatments of the issues involved are found in two recent books: Matthaei (1982) and Kessler-Harris (1982).

Ethnic minorities are far from being monolithic groupings, and it is both nonsensical and dangerous to speak of *the* black or *the* Puerto Rican. There are, however, certain common problems faced by these minorities: high rates of unemployment, restriction for most to the lower and more poorly paid occupations, inadequate and interrupted schooling, and inordinately large numbers of people at poverty and near-poverty levels.

As in the case of women, a major phenomenon of the present decades is the strength and power of the struggle by ethnic minorities to achieve full access to the work opportunity structure. Like the women's movements, the minority movements have won some measure of public recognition and governmental support, but there is a long way to go. Both movements face entrenched social barriers that reflect strongly held biases and stereotypes. Both groups contend with widespread popular beliefs that they are physically or mentally inferior to their more successful competitors.

There are, of course, important differences between the lot of women and the lot of male members of disfavored minorities. We have argued that the problems of women vis-à-vis work are still heavily influenced by traditional conceptions of male and female social roles. In general, because women are still assigned the major responsibility for household care, they cannot be so single-minded about work and career as can men. As we have indicated earlier, women tend to be confined to a limited number of "feminine occupations," and they are expected to be fully committed to work only *before* they have children and perhaps *after* their children are grown. The problems faced by the male members of disfavored minorities are very different. For example, black or Puerto Rican boys are fully expected to become workers when they grow up, just as are the boys in more dominant social groups. We are dealing here not with differing social role conceptions but with the existence of social arrangements and prejudices that confine the members of these ethnic minorities to the lowest rungs of the occupational ladder. Women and minorities thus face quite different social binds. The message heard by many girls is that they are expected to be mothers first and workers second. No such ambivalence about work is conveyed to the children of disfavored minorities. They *know* that they are expected to become workers. Unfortunately, they also know that they are expected to provide the prime source of relatively unskilled, common labor—unrewarding in pay and unstable in tenure.

There is a kind of self-fulfilling prophecy inherent in this situation. If most members of disfavored minorities are to wind up in laboring occupations, then a great deal of schooling, or the achievement of scholastic proficiency, can be looked on as irrelevant luxuries. This can not only affect the quality and quantity of schooling that is provided to minority children but can also influence the manner in which they receive whatever schooling they get. There is abundant evidence by now that a great many minority group children lag behind others in acquisition of basic scholastic skills and show significantly higher dropout rates as they approach school-leaving age. Although there are devoted exceptions, their teachers too often acquire the belief that these children are dull, unteachable, and even "brain-damaged." Early school failure is, of course, a major catastrophe in a society that relies on the school to prepare its children for adult work. One factor plays upon the other. Children become disinterested and unmotivated in school because they become aware that schooling is not, for them, a ready passport to rewarding employment. As a result they are also taught badly. Since the school is not only a place in which cognitive skills are to be transmitted but also an arena in which important components of the work personality are to be acquired, it can be seen that the minority child is doubly disadvantaged.

Similarly, high rates of unemployment and an expectation that the jobs to be found will be dull, routine, unrewarding, and without the prospect of advancement can have insidious personal effects. We have seen earlier that the motivation for work is highly complex. Work is not merely the primary means for meeting material necessities. It also fulfills or frustrates a number of important individual needs: the avoidance of boredom, the acquisition of self-esteem, the respect of other persons, and, in fortunate cases, the need for some measure of creativity. In heavily work-oriented societies such as ours, the kind of work one does is a mark of identity and a source of prestige. If members of disfavored minorities tend to be confined to kinds of work that are low in the status hierarchy, then they can readily come to believe that they are not worth any more, and many positive aspects of work can lose their meaning.

While it is generally recognized that the children of these ethnic minorities do more poorly in formal schooling than their more favored counterparts and, once working age is reached, tend to be confined to routine, low-paying, and unstable jobs, there are sharp differences of opinion about the reasons. Correspondingly, there are widely differing proposals for remedies. It is hard to imagine an issue that is more controversial than the rights of ethnic minorities nor one that is so easily capable of dividing and polarizing modern society.

There are a number of obvious reasons. First, the American economic system is not currently expanding at the same rate as it did in former decades. The new entrant to the labor force now finds himself faced by the entrenched opposition of people who have already struggled up from the lowest rungs of the occupational ladder and have no desire to see themselves displaced. Second, advances in industrial technology have greatly reduced the demand for unskilled common labor. In the past history of the United States, the European immigrant was generally able to penetrate the economic system only at its lowest levels, but he needed no great amount of schooling and literacy to do so. While most first generation immigrants had to spend their entire lives as largely unskilled workers, many were able to become skilled workers and craftsmen. In time, their children and grandchildren were able to use the public schools to such effect that many moved into white-collar and technical occupations, and even into the professions. The work available to the first generation immigrant might have been as dull and unrewarding as that currently offered to the new minorities, but there was at least a great demand for workers and some prospect of stability in employment. The immigrant youth of past periods could leave school at an early age and be reasonably confident of finding a job. If motivated enough, he could undergo on-the-job training or enter the apprenticeship system to prepare himself for skilled work and higher rates of payment. These guarantees and opportunities appear to be far less available than they were a generation or two ago. The lowered rate of industrial expansion and the sharply reduced demand for common labor make the path to upward mobility more tortuous than it was in the past.

At least three strongly differing viewpoints have been advanced to account for the work problems of disadvantaged minorities. The oldest and probably most pervasive argument is that the economically disadvantaged are simply *racially inferior*. This belief is subscribed to more widely in the less-educated sectors of the American public, but it is by no means confined to them. Unfortunately, a belief in racial differences is most vehemently expressed by workers in the lower white-collar and skilled jobs, positions which are the immediate targets of upwardly mobile blacks and the members of other disfavored minorities. A second viewpoint shifts the argument away from biology to questions of culture. This type of explanation is far more frequent among the more educated and is expressed fairly widely by many social and behavioral scientists. In this second viewpoint—most simply defined as a theory of *cultural deficit*—the educational and work problems of the disadvantaged are explained in terms of inappropriate life styles and preindustrial social structures. Sharply different from either of these explanatory viewpoints is a position that holds that the problems of these ethnic minorities are simply a function of *denial of opportunity*. It should be no surprise that this stance is favored by many spokesmen for particular ethnic minorities, but it is also subscribed to by a large proportion of social reformers and by an impressive array of social scientists.

Convictions about the innate inferiority or superiority of different races and ethnic groupings are by no means limited to the contemporary United States. Unfortunately, racism has an extremely ancient human history. It is probably at least as pervasive among tribal and less advanced peoples as it is in the industrially advanced nations. Convictions of constitutional inferiority have been advanced as a justification for slavery and as a rationalization for military conquest. It has apparently been extremely convenient to believe that people who are "different" from us (whoever "us" happens to be) are also, in most respects, worse. These convictions have been undermined by the spread of democracy and egalitarianism since the Industrial Revolution, but they have by no means vanished.

From the scientific point of view, of course, genuine race differences have proved to be very difficult to establish. There is even some question whether an adequate methodology for doing so is currently available. As we have had occasion to remark, *Homo sapiens* is so heavily socialized and enculturated that innate characteristics become highly elusive. Perhaps the best case in point is afforded by the current controversy over the heritability of the IQ. During the past 18–20 years, a hot debate has been generated among some behavioral scientists concerning the degree to which performance on intelligence tests is a function of genetic variation. This is an old issue in intelligence testing, which has passed through a number of ups and downs during the half century since psychometric testing became widespread in the United States. Earlier, it was simply taken for granted that IQ differences were largely attributable to variations in native endowment. This understanding was sharply challenged by a number of studies in the 1930s and 1940s, in which evidence was presented that *group* differences in intelligence test performance (differences in average IQ between socioeconomic classes or ethnic groups) could be accounted for by differences in environment (Klineberg, 1935; Neff, 1938; Skodak and Skeels, 1949). The result was that most of the present generation of psychologists became very cautious about the genetic origins of IQ differences between social or ethnic groups. Probably in response to renewed pressures for racial equality, there recently has been a flare-up of controversy about the heritability of the IQ and its significance for ethnic and social differences. In the late 1960s, Jensen (1967, 1969, 1970) began publication of a highly publicized set of studies that attempted to demonstrate that four-fifths of IQ variation is attributable to hereditary factors, and Herrnstein (1971) added fuel to the controversy by insisting that variation in occupation and income is largely attributable to variation in innate endowment. These views provoked systematic rebuttals by many other behavioral scientists, but the Jensen–Herrnstein position has had a serious public effect.

Whatever the ultimate outcome of this controversy, there is some question whether IQ differences have any bearing upon the problems of socioeconomic classes or ethnic groupings. As an assessment instrument, the intelligence test was devised to provide educators with a means of distinguishing between children who were failing in school because of cognitive limitations and those who were failing because of lack of motivation, emotional instability, or lack of interest, In terms of both its structure and content, the standard intelligence test is best thought of as a device to measure scholastic potential. Its highest correlations are with measures of actual scholastic achievement in the primary grades. In part because of progressive restriction in range, in part also because other variables begin to play larger roles, correlations between IQ and school grades are larger in the primary grades than in high school, larger in high school than in higher education. Correlations between intelligence test performance and occupational levels are small and can best be described as "modest" (Jencks, 1972, p. 187).

There is a more serious conceptual difficulty. The IQ, as a score, is a ratio of an individual's mental age (his performance on tasks that can be solved by an average child of a given age) to his chronological age. In practice, an individual's score may range from below 20 for a severe mental defective to close to 200 for some unusually gifted performers. But inferences concerning socioeconomic or ethnic status are based on *group averages*. The range of individual differences in IQ *within* any social group is far larger than *between* group differences. The latter are on the order of 15 or 20 points. For example, the children of common laborers in the United States yield an IQ average of about 96; the children of professionals, about 116. Similarly, a random selection of black children will yield an IQ average of about 85; a random sample of white children will average about 100. Even if we were to accept as proved that a significant portion of individual variation in IQ is attributable to genetic factors, we are still at a loss to account for the relatively small average differences between large social groups. This is because we cannot make the assumption of environmental equivalence between social and ethnic groups and because a mean IQ difference of the order of 20 points is well within the limits of variation attributable to environmental effects. The most cautious conclusion we can draw, concerning a presumed relationship between innate endowment and occupational competence, is that the decisive evidence is lacking. Given the limitations of the standard intelligence test, the entire issue of the source of ethnic differences must still be regarded as an open question. Thus, at best, the racial hypothesis remains unproved. This does not prevent it, however, from being rather widely believed.

To the degree that it is believed that differences in occupational status are a function of differences in innate endowment, remedies are hard to come by. At the extreme, we hear arguments for selective breeding, proposals that bear uncomfortably on genocide. More modest proposals involve the idea that we ought to provide only a limited vocational education for "inferior breeds," equipping them to carry on the common labor that is still required in many sectors of the economy. For the convinced adherent of the innate inferiority of disadvantaged minorities, the provision of advanced education is simply a waste of society's resources and an invitation to disaster.

Despite the probability that some version of the racial inferiority viewpoint is fairly widely held, it is *not* the officially professed view of makers of public policy. Much more prominent is a second viewpoint, which states in effect that the educational and work problems of certain ethnic minorities are a function of *cultural* deprivation. In many respects, this second viewpoint is far more palatable in a democratic country than the notion that large sectors of the population are genetically inferior. The theory of cultural deficit also carries with it a number of proposals for remedy. The only problem with the theory is whether it is in fact an accurate description of the occupational problems of ethnic minorities.

The cultural deficit theory is presented in differing versions, depending upon the particular ethnic minority under discussion. With reference to blacks, it is argued that their adaptation problems have four sources: certain residuals from the African cultural past, the effects of the long history of slavery in the United States, the consequences of living in semiserfdom after emancipation in the American South, and the influences of the so-called subculture of poverty in the modern industrial city. Puerto Ricans and other Latin Americans are said to be handicapped by language problems and by their background in impoverished peasant societies under semifeudal regimes. Native Americans who leave the reservations for jobs in the cities are described as preindustrial and nonurban, caught between sharply differing societies and unable to identify fully with either. The large Mexican–American population of the Southwest and West also have language problems and are thought of as bearing the cultural characteristics of relatively backward peasant societies. Taken together, these alleged cultural differences are invoked to account for relatively poor performance in the American school system and for attitudes to work that are more characteristic of preindustrial, rural societies than of the highly urbanized, technically advanced United States.

The cultural deficit viewpoint has been criticized as simply a more refined form of racism. It has been claimed, with some merit, that there is not much practical difference in being discriminated against because of biological inferiority or because of cultural inferiority. In both cases, the operative practice is discrimination, and the reason given is inferiority. However, it would be hard to find a spokesman for an ethnic minority who would agree with the notion that he and his people are inferior by constitution, whereas the conception that certain cultural differences may be disadvantageous in the economic struggle is certainly more reasonable. More significantly, the cultural deficit view has stimulated some massive efforts at remedial reform: the Head Start programs, compensatory educational practices, the introduction into school programs of material on the cultural history and achievements of certain minority groups, efforts to install bilingual education, and the like. All of these programs are too recent in origin to have yielded many positive results, and some have been poorly conceived or inefficient in administration. Still, there is a close association between the cultural deficit theory and social reform. The reformers in this field are not infrequently charged with being paternalistic (cf. Gordon, 1974). It is also claimed that they are assimilationist, that is, they see no particular virtue in maintenance of the ancient and valued cultural identifications of these ethnic minorities. Cultural differences tend to be seen as cultural deficits. But, of course, if the narrow objective is to penetrate the peculiarly American opportunity structure, and this *is* the objective of most of the reforming

programs, then a great many differing cultural norms may simply be abandoned as a matter of practical necessity. The trouble is that we do not really
know which cultural traits allow adequate adaptation to the requirements of
American society and which are really irrelevant. Unfortunately, there is a
tendency to throw the baby out with the bath water.

There is the third view concerning the problems of disfavored minorities.
It starts with a flat denial of the deficit hypotheses—whether the alleged
deficit is attributed to biology or culture. This viewpoint simply and straightforwardly argues that the problems of disfavored minorities arise from social
deprivation, from the denial of opportunity. The changes demanded are
basically socioeconomic in nature. It is pointed out that the common property of most children of disfavored minorities is their *poverty*. The consequences are a litany of difficulties: inadequate and congested housing,
insufficient nutrition, lowered physical health and meager medical care,
lack of cognitive stimulation in families where the parents are themselves
illiterate or semiliterate, lack of the experience of success, and lack of successful adult models. All these difficulties are further compounded by poorly
financed and overcrowded schools and by discrimination and prejudice in
hiring practices. Poverty thus has many of the characteristics of a vicious
circle, from which it is difficult to escape. The remedies proposed are as
direct and as straightforward as the theory: improved housing, improved
medical care, better schooling, better jobs. That these political and economic aims may be difficult to achieve is beside the point. The central
difference between the deficit theories and the opportunity–denial viewpoint is that the former tend to blame the victim for his difficulties, whereas
the latter puts the onus on society and sees the remedies in social change.

It is perhaps not necessary to affirm that the views of the present writer are
closer to the third view than to the other two. The case for genetic differences
in endowment is not only extremely difficult to make but also highly im-
probable in terms of what we know about the biology of the human species
and about human history. There are too many historical instances of initially
backward people making astounding material advances under the impact of
favorable conditions. The millions of European immigrants who came to the
United States in the nineteenth century were originally spoken of in much
the same derogatory terms, displayed some of the same social characteristics, and faced many of the same kinds of discrimination in employment as
do current ethnic minorities. Within two or three generations, the bulk of
their descendants have overcome most of the social barriers with which they
were faced and are now to be found at virtually all levels of the work
opportunity structure. Of course, the European immigrant had the advantage
of entering a rapidly expanding industrial system that could utilize vast
amounts of unskilled labor. It must be admitted that more is required of the
current entrant to the labor force than a strong back and a willingness to
labor. It must also be conceded that many kinds of work today require more

schooling than was the case a generation or two ago. But this may simply mean that society must invest larger resources in the education of its poor than it has hitherto found convenient. This process may involve needed provisions for on-the-job training as well.

The difficulty with the cultural deficit viewpoint is that it is compounded with socioeconomic deprivation. So long as the bulk of the families of these ethnic minorities are poor, we cannot have confidence in the independent effects of cultural differences. These cultural differences may in fact exist, but they may not at all be the direct causes of inadequate school and work performance. The Coleman report (Coleman, 1966) has made the point that the largest single source of variance in scholastic performance is attributable to a single variable: the socioeconomic status of the child's family of origin. This does not, of course, tell us exactly what is at fault or where to seek the remedy. But the socioeconomic variable cuts across a great many and varied families, including large numbers that are not associated with any of the disfavored ethnic minorities. Since it is impossible to disentangle the effects of cultural differences and of economic deprivation, the cultural deficit viewpoint must be looked on as equivocal at best.

During the period since 1960, some extraordinary measures have been proposed (some actually implemented) to improve the economic status of the black sector of the population in the United States. Among the most extraordinary were a set of policies that were somewhat euphemistically tied together under the term *affirmative action*. This term referred to a series of federal policies, starting in the early 1960s, to require universities and professional schools to recruit larger numbers of black students, to reach at least the proportion of blacks in the general population on pain of losing their federal subsidies if they did not comply. Gradually, this policy became extended to the employment practices of federal and state agencies and eventually to any kind of employment or educative process in which public money was involved. The result has been some increases in the number of black students in elite university and professional schools and, again, the entry of black workers into a number of hitherto white-only occupations (e.g., skilled construction work). This process was brought to something of a screaming halt by the successful suits of whites claiming "reverse discrimination" (e.g., the famous Bakke case, decided in his favor by the Supreme Court in 1978) and, during the 1980s, largely halted by a new and more conservative federal administration. But, during the period, some notable progress appeared to have been achieved by blacks, at least in certain areas. If we use such a crude but objective measure as years spent in school, for example, it would appear that the white–black gap has largely been overcome. According to Census Bureau data, in 1960, approximately 7–8 years of schooling were achieved by blacks and 11–12 achieved by whites; in 1980, approximately 12 years of schooling were achieved by blacks and about 12.5 by whites.

It comes as something of a shock, therefore, to come across a report (Center for the Study of Social Policy, 1983) that shows that the income gap between blacks and white is as large in the 1980s as it was in the 1960s. According to a study comparing Census data for 1960, 1970, and 1980, median family income for blacks was only 56% of that for whites in 1980 and was 57% in 1960 (the difference is not significant). There were absolute increases in median family income in both groups, but, despite the marked gains in education, blacks remained as far behind whites in income as at the start of the 20-year period. The report found two principal reasons for the continuation of this large discrepancy: first, a sharp drop from 1960 to 1980 in the percentage of black men over 16 who are employed (from 74% in 1960 to 56% in 1980) and, second, a parallel sharp increase in the number of families with dependent children headed by a woman (from 20% in 1960 to 47% in 1980. It would take an intensive socioeconomic analysis to tease out all the factors involved in these trends, but it seems obvious that, whatever the reasons, blacks face severe barriers in obtaining and maintaining paid employment.

In general, it seems more productive to tinker with the opportunity structure than to tinker with culture. It is true that work requires the internalization of a complex set of social norms, but these norms are not restricted to particular countries or races. It is also easier to legislate equality of opportunity than to implement it. But until we can disentangle the effects of poverty from the effects of culture, it is simply wrong (and unjust) to attribute to the latter what may be a direct function of the former. We could determine the effects of culture on modern work only if we were able to eliminate or hold constant the effects of poverty. But it is unlikely that we would ever make the effort to do so, since the problems that originally aroused our attention would already have been solved.

DISABILITY AS A STATUS CONDITION

As we have stressed in earlier chapters, the sheer ability to work, that is, the motor and cognitive skills required to carry through a given work task, is far from being the sole determinant of an adequate adjustment to work. Work takes place in a kind of sociocultural environment, which has its own unique set of social norms, customs, rituals, and demands. Adaptation to work requires the internalization by the worker of certain culturally determined values and goals. Successful work adaptation is, therefore, a complex result of many interrelated factors—of which some of the most important are social and interpersonal in character. While the sheer ability to perform a task is certainly a necessary condition of adjustment to work, it is clearly to a sufficient condition. There is abundant evidence that a great many people lose jobs or are unable to obtain them because of factors quite remote from their actual or potential capabilities.

A good deal of what we now know about adjustment to work has come from study of the handicapped worker. It must be emphasized that many of the problems of the disabled individual are *psychosocial* in character. They have to do with the conceptions he develops of himself as a person and as a worker, the attitudes and behaviors of others *to* him (including his own beliefs concerning these attitudes), and the meanings he ascribes to his disability and to work. We can learn much about the demands of work by examining some of the problems peculiar to disability.

One of the chief problems faced by the disabled person is the existence of a vast body of folklore and traditional notions about disability that have accumulated over thousands of years. The crippled, the blind, the mentally deficient, and the insane have always been regarded as "different" by the rest of the human race. In most instances, these conceptions of "difference" carry a strongly derogatory flavor, although some societies tend to attribute supernormal powers and superior status to particular disabling conditions e.g., epilepsy and schizophrenia. Of this massive set of stereotypes, some arise from simple ignorance concerning the nature of disability, others involve misconceptions and misinterpretations, and still others are the products of superstition and magical thinking. Only very recently have we begun to disentangle some of these ancient and strongly held ideas, although we are still far from overcoming their persistent influence.

In the first place, it makes more sense (cf. Wright, 1960) to speak of a "person with a disability" than to use the shorter and less awkward phrase: "a disabled person." Contrary to popular belief, it is extremely rare to encounter a patient whose disability influences all, or even many, aspects of his total psychological functioning. An obvious example is the individual with severe problems of gait, who yet remains perfectly adequate manually. In the same sense, a person may be in only a partial state of remission from a prolonged schizophrenic episode, but his ability to work may be entirely unaffected. The point here is that disaster tends to strike the body in a fairly selective manner. A given disability may impair a single bodily function, but it is highly unusual that its effects are so pervasive that the person is rendered totally incapable. Thus, one of the initial strategies in rehabilitation practice is to look for other assets upon which to build an ameliorative program.

Second, a series of intensive studies of special disability groupings has begun to cast doubt upon ancient notions that there is a kind of one-to-one relation between given disabilities and particular kinds of associated personality structures. When physicians first began to think about the possible psychological implications of certain physical diseases, it was appealing to think that certain kinds of persons might be prone to certain types of disease (e.g., "the cardiac personality," "the ulcer personality," "the epileptic personality") (cf. Alexander, 1955; Engel, 1954, 1955; Grinker, 1955; Dunbar, 1954). Unfortunately, evidence for these claims continues to be elusive. Garrett and Levine (1962), in summarizing the evidence in a collection of monographs on a wide range of types of disability, conclude that the similarities in the psychological problems and reactions common to the disabled are far more striking than typological differences. The range of cognitive, affective, and behavioral response-patterns in the repertoire of the disabled appears to be as diverse as that displayed by nondisabled persons. Disability is no respecter of persons and may afflict the intelligent as well as the dull, the emotionally stable as well as the emotionally unstable, the outgoing as well as the withdrawn. What seems to cut across all forms of affliction is the "style" of coping behavior that the individual has developed and with which he confronts any of life's tragedies and problems.

A third general view of the nature of disability associates it with the conception of some sort of *loss*—of a part of the body, of a sensory capacity, of an ability or competency, or even of an expected or established place in society. It is assumed that the disabled individual looks upon himself as deprived and feels bitter and angry. In this connection, Dembo, Leviton, and Wright (1956) have carried out an extremely interesting and provocative study of the reactions of adults to severe traumatic injury. They point out that the initial reactions of the amputee or paraplegic are very similar to the feelings of *mourning* and *bereavement* that follow the death of a cherished person, but they also make it clear that patients varied widely in the intensity and duration of these feelings. At one extreme, some patients' feelings of loss and bereavement were so intense that they felt that their lives were over, while at another extreme some individuals succeeded in wholly denying to themselves that they were handicapped at all.

Obviously, this is the realm of the psychological defenses. We can expect that disabled people—depending upon their predominating character-styles—will mobilize any of the effective and ineffective defenses familiar to students of psychodynamics: denial, projection, reaction-formation, repression, and the like. One of Dembo et al.'s more interesting observations is that a period of mourning, providing it is worked through, appears to be something of a necessary condition for an eventual adequate adjustment. She notes that patients who wholly denied any feelings of misfortune appeared to make less adequate recoveries than those who passed through a period of intense mourning. For our purposes, it would seem that feelings of bitterness, loss, and mourning are perfectly normal consequences of severe bodily injury, but they are not necessarily enduring states. The common attribution of such feelings to all disabled persons, regardless of the time elapsed since the disability was incurred, is simply another of the many stereotypes about disability.

The most serious aspect of the social status of being a disabled person is that it involves a fairly impressive array of essentially negative attitudes (see Yuker, Block, and Campbell, 1960; Siller, 1967). A number of writers on the social psychology of prejudice (Barker, 1948; Gellman, 1959; Wright, 1960) have drawn an analogy between the entire social position of the

disabled and that of disfavored minority groups. Like the members of derogated religious or ethnic groupings, the person with a manifest disability
faces the task of overcoming many social barriers in order to live the kind of
life enjoyed by a favored majority. He suffers, for example, from severe
restrictions of employment opportunities, not only because of employer
prejudices but also because of negative attitudes on the part of potential
co-workers. He often encounters considerable difficulty in carrying on a
"normal" social or recreational life, including rejection by desired love or
marital partners. Similarly, he may find that certain qualities are attributed to
him because "this is what crippled people are like," so that he is being
treated and perceived not as a unique individual but as a member of a
derogated class.

Like many analogies, however, the parallel drawn between disability and
minority group status glosses over some important differences. First, there
are clear differences in the reality factors at work in the two cases. By this
time, expert opinion is fairly unanimous that racial and religious groupings
do not actually differ in basic human capacities and potentialities. On the
other hand, it cannot be denied that there are disabling conditions that result
in genuine impairments of functional capacity. While the extent and significance of such functional losses are readily exaggerated, some disabled persons may not be able to function so well in certain areas as the nondisabled.
One of the important areas of difficulty has to do with work and employment. The overcoming of very real bias and prejudice is only one of the
many problems faced by the disabled in adapting to work. Certain kinds of
physical disability may require physical alterations in the work setting (e.g.,
ramps instead of staircases, certain modifications of machines). Other types
of disability may place certain limits on the number of hours of continuous
labor or may require more rest periods than is customary. While such
arrangements may not be very costly, they constitute departures from ordinary work routines. The more that industry becomes mechanized and routinized, the more that workers tend to be treated as interchangeable units,
the more difficult it is to fit disabled people into the work situation.

Another important difference between the lot of the disabled and that of
minority ethnic or religious groups arises from the very special kind of social
isolation from which many disabled persons suffer. Identification with other
disabled persons does not carry with it the kind of group sanction and inner
compensation that may accompany minority group status. There are no
cultural traditions that will give a disabled individual the feeling that he is at
least a member of something, of a persecuted minority if nothing else. It is
infrequent that a disabled child is a member of a family whose parents and
siblings share the same disability. As Wright (1960) and others have indicated, the social isolation of many disabled people may be extreme. Unlike members of minority groups, they may not be able to avail themselves
even of the dubious joys attendant on identification with a "subculture" but

must bear the burdens of being "different" with none of the rational or irrational compensations of counteridentification. In this connection, the self-help organizations for the crippled and disabled have the possibility of playing important social roles, but they remain quite limited in scope and visibility compared to the massive counterorganizations of most ethnic and religious minorities.

It should be noted also that not all of the social dilemmas of the disabled person are responses to derogation. He may also be faced with social problems when he is *not* derogated, either because other people may simply be unaware of certain handicapping features of the disability or even because others may attribute some supernormal connotations to certain disabling conditions. When the disabled individual himself does not recognize the limits imposed by his conditions, we speak of "denial of illness" (cf. Weinstein and Kahn, 1955). When others do not perceive that a disability may restrict certain expected behaviors (e.g., getting out of a car, carrying a food tray, shaking hands), the situation may involve sudden frustrations of normal expectations that provoke embarrassment at the minimum and outright rejection at the extreme.

Because of the weight of certain legends, some people may gratuitously endow the disabled with mystical qualities that transcend actual human capacities. Wright (1960) calls this process *anormalization* and defines it as the attribution of "certain unusual characteristics, even supernatural ones, so that ordinary expectations do not apply." An example is the belief that the blind have supernormal hearing or that they possess some "sixth sense" of spatial localization, like the radar-like senses of bats and porpoises.[2] Despite our inability to demonstrate that these special powers actually exist, these half-legendary misconceptions can be very tenacious.

In general, disability may handicap a person vis-à-vis work in three fundamental ways. First, a disability may impair or limit certain functional abilities and aptitudes that are required by specific kinds of work. Second, the disabled person may have to cope with the many kinds of negative and aversive feelings that some disabilities arouse in other persons—both employers and co-workers. Third, a disability may, under certain conditions, arrest, distort, or block the development of what we have earlier described as the work personality. So far, in this chapter, we have largely concerned

---

[2]After surveying the available evidence on this issue, Axelrod (1959) concludes that it has not been possible to demonstrate that blind persons have any special auditory or tactile abilities. Raskin (1962) reports that some of the early blind display what he calls "obstacle perception"; they appear able to detect a large obstacle (e.g., a wall) before blundering into it. However, a number of investigators cited by Raskin have demonstrated that the skill rests on the use of aural cues related to pitch changes in sound reflected from the obstacle. Not all blind persons show this ability, but, presumably, most can learn it, as can sighted individuals as well.

ourselves with issues related to the first two of these problems. Our discussion will not be complete unless we examine the third.

What we are concerned with here are some of the vicissitudes and vagaries of individual personal development. The major thesis of this book is that work behavior is *learned* behavior, and that the process of learning takes place over an extended period, from early childhood through late adolescence and early adulthood. It should not be surprising, therefore, that an early disability may have the effect of denying the person those experiences, interactions, and environmental pressures that gradually transform most of us from nonworking children to working adults. Among the many kinds of clients encountered in rehabilitation practice, there are always some who can best be described as cases of *work-acculturation*. They have either never learned to play the role of a worker or have been desocialized for so long a period that the work-role has become alien. Whether because of massive overprotection or rejection, they simply cannot cope adequately with the range of social and interpersonal demands that characterize ordinary work situations. In effect, they have to learn to play the role of a worker before they can be taught any particular work-skill.

Interestingly enough, this kind of difficulty is only now being recognized as a problem. Rehabilitation practice is still largely focused on specific impairment of function, with considerable attention also on measures designed to overcome employer resistance to employment of the disabled. Prevailing rehabilitation ideology has been based on the tacit assumption that, given willingness to work, all that is required is restoration of impaired functioning, some retraining in a new work-skill, and a willing employer. It was always admitted that some disabled persons were "unmotivated" for work, but this problem was simply regarded as a defect of will. To the degree that the field has begun to take responsibility for the ex-mental patient, the mental retardate, the congenitally brain-damaged, and similiar instances of prolonged and early disablement, it has become more obvious that more may be involved than the correction of an impairment, the provision of a work-skill, or proclamation of a campaign to hire the handicapped. This accounts for recent interest in the *rehabilitation workshop,* a facility in which the disabled person is not taught any particular work skill but is confronted with a simulated work-environment in which he can learn what work is all about.

It is also being slowly and reluctantly perceived that some disabled people may not be able to make a full adjustment to the demands of work in competitive industry, whether because their residual impairments are insufficiently compensated, or because industry is not sufficiently flexible to permit the necessary adjustments, or because major defects in the work personality are not easily correctible. Within the framework of our best current services to the handicapped, there remains a residue of disabled persons who appear too handicapped to be able to cope with the work demands of unprotected employment. Although some agencies provide sheltered and semisheltered forms of gainful work, they are markedly limited in scope and resources. Solution of the multitudinous problems of the handicapped worker requires advances on three fronts. We need to continue to improve our professional services to the disabled persons, and we need to continue to break down the barriers to employment of the handicapped in ordinary industry. All else failing, we need considerable expansion of various transitional and semisheltered facilities to provide some kind of useful and gainful work for those who cannot compete for unprotected employment.

WORK AND SOCIAL CHANGE

THE ENVIRONMENT AND THE WORKER

Human work is an exceedingly complex and many-faceted phenomenon that has been studied and commented upon from many vantage points—as an economic factor, a social institution, a focus of politics, a set of events in history, and as a moral value. The various studies of work that we have examined—whether economic, sociological, historical, or technological—have been useful to the extent that they have contributed to our understanding of work as a *psychological* phenomenon. We are in no sense suggesting that the psychology of work is primary to all else, or that it has any greater importance. We have emphasized this feature of work simply because we believe that it has received insufficient attention and remains rather poorly understood.

Our primary concern has been with those features of work that make problems for people, that elicit inappropriate or maladaptive behavior. Our standpoint, therefore, has been akin to that of the *clinical* psychologist, whose concern is with people in trouble. In order to deal with disturbances of personality, the clinician must know a great deal about *normal* behavior. The task of helping people with their vocational problems, however, has been made particularly difficult by the relative inadequacies of our general theories of work. Accordingly, we have devoted the bulk of our energies in this volume to an effort to formulate such a general theory. In effect, we have taken the position that it is quite impossible to understand why some people *cannot* work unless we have a fairly good grasp of why most people *can*. If a well-developed theory of work behavior already existed, we would have spent all our time, rather than a minor portion of it, in discussing various ways in which the work personality can be maladapted and in suggesting possible remedies.

Our contention has been that work is a severe problem for some people because it is a function of two quite distinct sets of variables, which need not be in congruence and may, at times, be flatly in contradiction. One of the sets of factors is an array of work-demands, which arise in terms of the technical and social characteristics of work environments. Interacting with these "external" conditions are all those personal characteristics that the individual worker brings with him into the work situation—his motives, feelings, attitudes, emotions, preconceptions, and values. We have designated the former as *work demands* and the latter as the *work personality*. Both sets of variables have important temporal, as well as structural, characteristics. The demands of work are a function of the kind of society we are examining and of long cultural traditions. The work personality is a function of the individual life-experience. The latter is, of course, heavily influenced by society and culture, but there is ample room for variation in terms of idiosyncrasies of personal development.

Maladaptive work behavior can be elicited by any facet of the work environment and by any component of the work personality. One individual's chief problem may be his inability to tolerate ordinary supervision without experiencing so much anxiety, fear, anger, or hostility that his production suffers. Another person may be unable to distinguish work from play or may confuse both with the demands for intimacy that prevail at home. Still another may be unable to endure the many challenges and frictions that inhere in relations to co-workers. While we have described some frequently occurring maladaptive patterns, we have by no means exhausted the problem. More important than an individual's degree of resemblance to a "type" is an exact description of his unique individual difficulties, whatever they may be. Diagnostic evaluation involves a search for those features of the work personality that in the individual case permit or encourage unacceptable responses to the demands of work.

Most people manage to make some sort of acceptable adaptation to the demands of work. But this obvious assertion is no more meaningful than a similar statement that most people are able to marry and raise families. Statements like these tell us something about the structure of society but very little about the complexities of the adaptive process. This process can go wrong in a great many ways, and resulting disruptions of behavior can be comparatively slight or very severe. When there is only a very moderate degree of incongruence between certain requirements of work and particular personal attributes of the individual, we think of him merely as being "dissatisfied" with his work. He may continue to perform it because he has to, but he perceives it either as less rewarding than he feels it ought to be or as the source of unwelcome irritations and discomforts. In some cases, a particular employment situation, not work itself, is the problem. The remedy at hand, assuming opportunities are available, is to change jobs. More often, the job-change simply brings more of the same or produces fresh difficulties.

Where this pattern is repeated, we can begin to *suspect* that some kind of personality problem is at issue. We cannot, however, blandly assume that there is a personality problem at the core of all, or even most, instances of dissatisfaction with work. Many kinds of work in modern society are intrinsically unrewarding, either because of traditional levels of compensation and work requirements or because of cultural notions concerning occupational prestige. Satisfaction and dissatisfaction are highly relative terms; they depend very heavily on the concrete situations in which people find themselves. The trained professional needs to be alert to those instances in which the individual appears to be *more* dissatisfied with his work than the objective conditions appear to warrant. This is not an easy judgment to make! It requires a considerable degree of technical skill and an intimate knowledge of prevailing work environments.

Like all human dilemmas, the problems of work may yield to manipulation of the environment relatively readily in some cases, especially where it is possible to bring about massive changes in the conditions of work. In other cases, the solution may require some kind of thoroughgoing alteration of certain components of the personality. Ideally, it should be possible to alter both sets of variables in whatever manner the individual case seems to require. To the typical helping professional, however, the demands of work may seem beyond his power to control, while the amelioration of personality problems is, after all, his special field of expertise. This limitation of his powers should not provoke him to misleading diagnoses, although it is easy to see the sources of his bias toward the personal.

In order to maintain the required balance, we cannot here overlook those major problems of work maladaptation where the characteristics of environments are particularly insistent. What we are concerned with here is the extent to which individuals may become maladapted to work because of major social changes in the conditions under which they are required to perform it. The effects of social change on work are both obvious and subtle. In heavily industrialized societies such as ours, even rather minor technological changes may render entire occupations superfluous, presenting their practitioners with sudden problems of major work adjustment. In a less obvious sense, our values and norms concerning work are under continuous pressure. Formerly highly valued kinds of work may lose prestige, whereas others become more strongly valued. In the United States during only a very few decades, we have witnessed the virtual disappearance from the scene of the independent working farmer and of the highly skilled craftsman. Another instance is the shift in the proportions of blue-collar and white-collar workers, the latter now comprising the majority of the labor force.

Therefore, we cannot ignore the effects of massive social change, even more because really massive social changes have important effects on attitudes, including, of course, what people think about work. Of the many current relations between social change and work, three problems appear to be crucial: (1) the effects of automation on work, (2) the relations between poverty and work, and (3) work and productivity.

AUTOMATION AND THE WORKER

It is not at all easy to make an objective appraisal of the effects of technological change on the conditions of work. The introduction of a new industrial process has always benefited some and harmed others. Major technological breakthroughs are two-edged swords, which can have very different effects on the lives of different people. As a result, it is very difficult to discuss them dispassionately. Whether a given innovation is seen as a great benefit or an unmitigated evil depends on who is looking at it and from what vantage point. The burgeoning literature on automation is a case in point.

The term *automation* has become current only in the past decade. It refers to the development of the *fully* automatic machine, which is not served and controlled by a human worker but by an electronic computing system. In the offing is the conception of the fully automated factory, in which the entire process of production is carried out by machines alone, making the human machine-operator almost entirely redundant. The marriage of electronic control devices to productive machinery is still very new but is spreading very rapidly. According to a report (by Seligman 1966), there were only 35 process-control computers in operation in 1960; in 1965 there were 600 such installations. The implications of this development appear so vast and incalculable that there is already talk of a "second Industrial Revolution" (Wiener, 1961; Friedmann, 1955). Automation has been heralded as a tremendous blessing and condemned as a terrible threat. From either viewpoint, its advent will undoubtedly greatly alter the meaning of work for huge numbers of people.

Major technological advances have always had very considerable effects on the relationship of the worker to his work. For thousands of years, work was performed with the use of hand-tools under circumstances where the available sources of energy were the forces of nature—human muscle-power, draft animals, wind, and water. Although no direct evidence has been gathered, it has been theorized that there was a very close and intimate relation between the worker and his product. Work could be thought of as an essentially private and personal activity, which permitted the worker to express in his product—whether it was produced for his own use or for exchange—his own personality, skill, ingenuity, and creativity. To the degree that we can speak of industrial technology during this long period of human history, it consisted chiefly of an elaboration of hand-tools and the acquisition of personal work skills. The best example was the work of the artisan or handicraft worker, who was able and willing to incorporate in his product some of the qualities of a work of art. Our archeological museums today are crowded with objects and implements that were once fabricated for utilitarian purposes but are often characterized by considerable beauty and individuality. Ever since the rise of the factory system, some writers have looked back upon the preindustrial era as a Golden Age, when work was a dignity and a joy.

Whatever was, in fact, the meaning of his work for the artisan—and it is quite possible for us today to exaggerate its positive qualities—the consequence of the Industrial Revolution was the virtual disappearance of the handicraft worker. This, of course, did not take place at once, even in the rapidly industrializing countries, and there are many areas of the world today where work is still largely carried out by hand. But the application to work of nonhuman and nonnatural sources of power—first steam and later electricity—had the ultimate effect of transforming work from an essentially private and personal activity into something that was both public and impersonal. Whereas the artisan was capable of putting his own impress on the product, the factory worker is engaged in serving machinery that turns out an anonymous product. The critics of industrialization have always argued that this process ends by reducing the worker to a mere appendage to a machine, thereby splitting the intellectual and creative aspects of work from its merely manual aspects and stripping it of all personal dignity and interest. The only reason left for working is monetary necessity.

While this picture may be overdrawn, it seems plausible that the factory system might have confronted the worker with a double kind of alienation. Not only was he alienated from the means of production, as Marx pointed out, but he also was alienated from the product. It was no longer *his* product, in any sense. If anyone could claim to have produced it, it was the entrepreneur, since he controlled, organized, and planned all the processes by which it came into existence. In his book on modern industry, Seligman (1966 p. 368) describes these dismal consequences in vivid language:

> In the historic process of transferring his energy into a commodity the control of which rested in other hands, however, man really lost control of himself. Objects created by work passed into another realm, distinct from and basically hostile to work. It was the world of marketable goods, where man was opposed to himself in the most profound meaning of the term, for marketability was the antithesis of the free activity engendered by work. What was virtually a component of human nature became a mere instrumentality. Work was freed from tools, craft, and community and was metamorphosed into a commodity with a price tag attached to it. The significance of work was twisted: man became a laborer, without a sense of being or engagement in the meaningful. As a laborer he engaged in uniform activity, mere expenditure of energy. Yet work was once a diverse phenomenon, gathering esteem by its very particularity and providing joy in the articles produced. There was human delight too in its structure and organization and in the comradeship gained from other workers. There was a sense of dignity in work. Unfortunately, the elements of craft—spontaneity, exuberance, and the freedom to perform—which made work, play and culture virtually identical have been irretrievably lost.

It is not easy to ascertain whether Seligman is right. In the absence of any evidence as to the meanings that the artisan attributed to his work and with very meager information on how the modern factory worker perceives *his* work, this sort of thoroughgoing assault on the consequences of technology is only an educated guess. It is possible also that the critics of the factory system tend to idealize the work of the artisan and to overemphasize the dehumanizing features of the factory system. Man is an extremely adaptable animal and usually manages to find something good in almost anything he does. It is very likely that the spread of the factory system, with all of its implications, brought about thoroughgoing changes in the meaning of work for a great many people.

But not all of these changes were necessarily so negative as the critics appear to think. The factory system also made work a *social* activity, which had the long-run consequences of making it subject to public scrutiny and legislative control. In order to operate the factory, masses of workers had to be brought together in a joint work-site. Inevitably, this led to the development of social interactions, if only to share their mutual misfortune. The result was the organization of formal and informal work groupings and the eventual rise of the trade unions. While this sort of development was hardly intended by the entrepeneur, who typically resisted it with determination and ferocity, the widespread recognition of unions has undoubtedly restored to the worker some elements of dignity. The socialization of labor has had more subtle consequences as well. The factory became a site in which friendships could be formed and through which common interests could express themselves. Many workers found their friends, their acquaintances, and even their spouses within the walls of the factory. This has become so much the rule that one of the negative consequences of retirement is that many stable social contacts are thereby disrupted; the retired worker tends to become a socially isolated person. One of the common reasons workers may give for staying on a particular job is because they like the people there. Similarly, a frequent reason for quitting is an inability to form satisfactory personal relations at work.

But what of automation? Despite the vast dislocations that accompanied and followed the Industrial Revolution, despite the harnessing of the worker to the machine, the prior effects of technology did not threaten to make work an entirely superfluous activity. If anything, in the countries in which industrialization has become most widespread, work came to be regarded as a highly respectable and desirable way of life, to which all sorts of social and moral values were imputed. Assuming, however, that fully automated production spreads at exponential rates, as some economists appear to believe, will work no longer be a primary human activity? In a heavily work-oriented society such as ours, where enforced idleness is not only an economic disaster but is also psychologically unbearable for many, such a development would indeed be revolutionary. Norbert Wiener, perhaps the leading theorist of computer technology, is convinced that full automation is imminent and argued that we are not really preparing ourselves to cope with its consequences. His observations are worth quoting at length (Wiener, 1961, pp. 27–28):

> The automatic factory and assembly line without human agents are only so far ahead of us as is limited by our willingness to put such a degree of effort into their engineering as was spent, for example, in the development of the technique of radar in the Second World War. . . . There is no rate of pay [now] at which a pick-and-shovel laborer can live which is low enough to compete with the work of a steam-shovel as an excavator. The modern industrial revolution is similarly bound to devalue the human brain, at least in its simpler and more routine decisions. . . . [In] the second revolution . . . the average human being of mediocre attainments or less has nothing to sell that is worth anyone's money to buy.

Wiener is talking about the ultimate abolition of any need for the slightly skilled and semiskilled workers, who now make up a considerable sector of the modern labor force. It has also been argued, by others, that the marriage of the electronic computer with sophisticated machinery will make many kinds of *skilled* occupations just as superfluous. Electronically controlled machine-tools already exist that do not require the labor of highly skilled machinists. Many of the skilled clerical occupations are imperiled by the incorporation of bookkeeping and auditing machines into computer systems. Even the printing trades—once "aristocrats" among skilled workers—have fought a losing battle against wholly automatic methods of setting and composing type. Thus, the spread of the fully automatic machine threatens the position of the highly skilled worker as much as it makes the relatively unskilled worker almost entirely redundant.

Assuming that the introduction of fully automatic machinery continues at an unchecked pace, and assuming further that the sole operative force in society is the desire of industrial management to reduce unit-costs, automation might well prove to be an unmitigated disaster. But we have learned, through hard experience, that economic prophecy is very risky. The aims of industrial management are by no means the sole determinant of economic affairs. Although they have a high order of priority, they operate within a very complex network of countervailing forces.

Even if we could predict the rate at which industry will introduce fully automated processes, a great many questions remain unanswered. What resistances, for example, currently exist or will appear in the system? How will society react to greatly increased rates of man-hour productivity? By increased institutional unemployment? By shortened hours of work? By permitting entry into the labor forces at later ages than is now customary? By earlier retirement? By shifts in the mix of producers' and consumers' industry? By vast expansion in the resources allocated to education, recreation, and culture?

Technology does not exist in a social vacuum, particularly today. While some groupings in American society are certainly still "more equal" than others, the days when the captain of industry was the sole arbiter of the worker's fate are long gone. Although we may face a period of intense conflict and widespread dislocation, the situation is not entirely without remedies. Just as one of the long-run consequences of the first Industrial Revolution was a shortening of the working-day and working-week, the second Industrial Revolution may bring about even more drastic reductions of work-time. Just as another consequence was mass education and a continuing shift in the direction of more years of education for more people, this process can be radically extended. Just as social and economic planning has lately become respectable, it can be greatly expanded. All these measures, of course, may have their limits, but we are currently very far from reaching them.

We can get a clearer grasp of the issues as stake if we compare the viewpoints of Ben Seligman, an American labor economist, and Georges Friedmann, a French industrial sociologist. Both men have written very informative and provocative books on automation (1966 and 1955, respectively). Both were keenly aware that the breakneck development of machine technology is stripping work of many of its positive meanings, reducing "joy in work," and threatening the status of work as a major sphere of life activity. Seligman, however, is deeply pessimistic about the future, whereas Friedmann ends his analysis on a note of cautious optimism.

The differences arise from two quite different perceptions of the relations between men and machines. In a number of ways, Seligman's analysis is more simplistic than Friedmann's. He tends to look upon the machine as an unalloyed evil, which gradually has stripped man of all control over his own labor and now threatens to abolish work as a meaningful human activity. The "notorious victory" in the title of his book (Seligman, 1966) is the victory of the machine over man. Thus, in his final chapter, he associates himself with those writers (Mumford, 1944; Goodman, 1965; Marcuse, 1964) who oppose science and technology because they believe that material progress has led to a separation of men from nature and from each other. Like De Tocqueville, whom they frequently quote, these men appear to be nostalgic for the Golden Age of the independent craftsman and "village democracy."

In contrast, Friedmann treats the development of machine technology as a two-edged sword (1955):

> Mechanization leads to a simultaneous and contradictory dual evolution: on the one hand, subdivided tasks increase in number, bereft of initiative and responsibility, and of overall views. This is the "despiritualization" of work. On the other hand, there appear . . . preparatory tasks, tool-making, supervisory work, work in the construction of complex machines, which require

training. Much more than this, work . . . in which, as a result of mechanization, the operation on material has become separated from the worker's hand,
no longer requires speed or strength of execution, but precision and attention;
that is, not quantitative but qualitative characteristics. The quality of work in
this case shows the worker's ability. Thus, the process of despiritualization and
respiritualization of labor accompany one another.

Friedmann is quick to point out that much more despiritualization has so
far taken place than respiritualization. But he also insists that there is "no
rigorous determinism in either of those evolutions. . . . [t]he choice itself
depends on the socio-economic milieu in which the evolution takes place."

We see that Seligman and Friedmann have basically different conceptions about the social order as a whole. Seligman appears to view society
statically. Because the primary motive for technological change has been
private profit, with very little concern for general human welfare, he
assumes that this tendency will always prevail. Friedmann, on the other
hand, is not ready to assume that the social relations within which industry
operates are settled for all time. He believes that the unalloyed sway of
"private profit" has been tempered in the past and can be further modified
in the future. Human history is marked not only by technological change but
also by social change. Automation, Friedmann believes, will certainly in-
tensify current social conflicts, but the ultimate outcome of these conflicts is
not foreclosed.

Of one thing, though, we can be fairly certain. If technological progress
ultimately has the effect of greatly reducing the present large portion of our
lives that we commit to work, then the meaning of work itself will undergo a
qualitative change. Instead of devoting such a large portion of formal education to preparation for work and career, the entire educational process may
have to be restructured to permit other objectives. Current patterns of child
development, which give high priority to the development of the work
personality, will need to be modified. Some very strong cultural values will
have to change. Unfortunately, it is all too likely that we will not do very
much about these drastic problems until the crisis is upon us. The meaning
of work may then be very different from what it is today, but its contemporary meanings are quite different *now* from what they were a few centuries
ago.

POVERTY AND THE WORKER

Matthew Huxley, in an address to the American Orthopsychiatric
Association in 1964, observed that the "war on poverty" in the United States
was a highly novel social enterprise. He thought it represented a break with
past traditions in several respects. In the first place, he knew of no other
instance in which the U.S. government had taken the position that a large
sector of its population was in danger of being *permanently* impoverished. It

had always been tacitly assumed that poverty was a local and temporary condition, which might require crisis assistance but was in no sense a structural feature of our system. In the past, the remedy for unemployment was the creation of more jobs through general increases in production. Because this remedy no longer seemed to work for increasing segments of the populations a new attack seemed necessary.

Huxley also stated that we were for the first time undertaking to solve the problems of people who hitherto had been almost entirely ignored by social reform. According to Huxley, we have always tacitly distinguished between two kinds of poor people—the "deserving" and the "undeserving." The former were thought to be people who were motivated to work, anxious to support themselves and their families, but simply denied the opportunity because of adverse circumstances. They were, in effect, full citizens of the world of work, who were in temporary difficulty for reasons beyond their control. The social legislation of the 1930s—unemployment compensation, social security, wages and hours laws, guarantees for collective bargaining—was chiefly aimed to assist the "deserving" poor. But there had been very little provision for the "undeserving" poor—the "shiftless" and the "unmotivated"—except the dole. Huxley's major point was that the "war on poverty" was something new, because it was now being publicly recognized that poverty, under certain circumstances and for certain people, can be a self-perpetuating condition.

We cannot here discuss the complex economic and political problems that have restricted the "war on poverty" to a series of skirmishes rather than a major offensive. We can agree with Huxley, however, that some quite revolutionary ideas are involved, whether or not they are as yet being fully implemented. The core conception of the "war on poverty" is that there are certain environmental conditions that, unless altered, will permanently prevent some people from ever establishing themselves as stable workers.

It is somewhat disconcerting to discover that we know very little about what it means to be a member of the subculture of poverty in the United States. Economic and sociological data indicate that a considerable sector of our population is sealed off from the mainstream of American society by a series of more or less impermeable barriers. Harrington (1962) and others have called our attention to the self-perpetuating nature of modern poverty, so that it is already possible to speak of pockets of hereditary unemployment. We have been made aware of the degree to which ethnic and social factors are intrinsic to the problem, and this not only has weighed heavily on our collective conscience but also has contributed to many social and political fears and upheavals. But as soon as we begin to ask ourselves serious questions concerning the *psychology* of poverty—what it is that the poor person thinks, feels, believes, desires—we are forced to fall back on the doubtful resources of speculation, guesswork, and remote inference.

We are not entirely lacking in information. Most of what we know has been obtained through study of the blatant casualties of the economic battlefield—the hospitalized mentally ill, the institutionalized criminal or delinquent, the narcotic addict, etc. We cannot assume, however, that the extremely disordered are necessarily typical of the mass of any given population, even if it can be shown (cf. Hollingshead and Redlich, 1958; Srole, Langner, Michael, Opler, and Rennie, 1962) that higher frequencies of every kind of major human problem are associated with the condition of being poor. Not only are the poor sealed off from participation in the affluent society, they also tend to be sealed off from observation.

Our knowledge concerning attitudes to work has largely been obtained through study of individuals for whom the sheer ability to work is not the major problem—the student who has available a range of occupational choices or the employed worker. An exception to this rule is the growing literature on vocational rehabilitation, dealing with the meaning of work to the handicapped person. While there is a certain analogy between being physically disabled and economically disadvantaged, the analogy is far from perfect. There may well be, however, some common features to the two kinds of problems, particularly those bearing on the conditions of development of an adequate work personality.

A good case can be made that the male child of the very poor faces considerable difficulty in acquiring the components of the positive work personality. To the degree that early play-at-work requires both adequate role models and minimum equipment, he will very likely have neither at his command. If he is a child in a fatherless family, being brought up by his mother and an array of female relatives, then he will have difficulty imagining the role of the male breadwinner. Even if the father is present in the home, there are no great inducements to use the father as a model of what adults do when they work. The father is likely to be unemployed or, at best, a poorly paid, exploited, and unskilled laborer. Not only are educational toys at a minimum or nonexistent, but there is evidence that the children of the poor are discouraged from playing with ordinary household objects for fear of breakage (cf. Stone and Church, 1968). Thus, even the preschool life of the child of the poor may be lacking in those very early stimuli and experiences that are the initial shapers of the work personality.

Whatever is lacking in the early experiences of the slum child immediately becomes exacerbated when he enters school. Enough has been written about the slum school to make us all aware of its deficiencies merely as an educational institution. But the slum schools are also very inadequate arenas for the formation of an appropriate work personality. Overcrowded and rundown, staffed frequently by teachers who are more eager to transfer than to teach, oriented more toward the maintenance of discipline than the provision of a stimulating educational experience—the slum school becomes something merely to be endured and to be escaped from. Not only is the child in the slum school frequently unable to become task-oriented in any meaningful way, but he may also be entirely unable to secure any gratification through achievement. He is soon enough made aware that he lags behind the grade norms of more favored children, and this gap tends to widen the longer he is in school. He gets very little training in concentration, and he becomes aware that achievement is not really expected. Supervision is most often authoritarian, rather than encouraging or supportive. Thus, the demand to achieve may hardly be internalized at all. Correspondingly, the peer culture that surrounds him is hardly conducive to the formation of positive attitudes toward work. Because rewards for achievement are generally lacking, the peer society is more than ordinarily committed to impulse gratification and to systematic resistance to authority. Under these circumstances, it should hardly be surprising that the child of the slums may become "unmotivated" to remain in school and then drops out as soon as possible. Unfortunately, he has been as ill-prepared to become a worker as to secure an advanced education.

One might suppose that an incidental function of the slum school is to produce people who are motivated to work, even if only to escape from school. But the slum school is capable of producing only one general *kind* of worker (we are aware of many exceptions to this rule): the "outer directed" and unskilled laborer, who works only under close and continuous supervision and for whom the only alternative is starvation. But this kind of worker is not only becoming redundant in the face of rapid technological progress, he is also becoming an anachronism in relation to our current ideas of social progress. We no longer have "poor laws" on the books to compel people to work. Our welfare legislation makes it possible for the nonworker to live "on relief," although we take considerable pains to make this mode of existence quite unattractive. The net effect of the slum school, however, is to turn out increasingly large numbers of people who become more or less permanent citizens of the world of poverty, for whom work has little positive meaning, who have been unable to acquire those habits, attitudes, and behaviors that make up the core of the positive work personality, and who simply augment the army of the relatively unemployable.

Of course, influences other than those related to the family and school also shape the work personality, but these also must be counted as generally negative in the case of the child of the slums. He is made aware through many media that ours is a work-oriented society and that there are many rewards contingent on achievement, but he is also made aware that the people who hold the good jobs are not like him or his relatives and friends. They speak differently, they dress differently, they have different interests, they may even belong to different ethnic and racial groupings. They appear to belong to a different world, from which he is at worst entirely excluded or at best merely tolerated as a marginal member. Given this entire set of life experiences, it seems likely that such children will develop to adulthood with only negative or indifferent attitudes to work and with very meager resources to function as productive workers.

In stressing that the consequences of extreme poverty can be psychologically damaging, we are by no means arguing that the remedy is to provide psychotherapy for everyone. For many reasons, this method would be both wildly impractical and generally ineffective. But it is almost equally unrealistic to believe that all these manifold problems can be solved merely by attempting to provide the victims of poverty with a specific work-skill of some kind. Not only are the very poor generally lacking in employable skills, but they also have been ill-prepared to acquire them. The problem is that the severely underprivileged need a great many different things, and they need them virtually all at once. To attempt to make up only one of a number of interrelated deficiencies is to risk renewed failure. The task is not hopeless, but it needs a many-sided and comprehensive attack. A successful assault on the employment problems of the very poor should include measures that can create positive attitudes to work. For at least some of the extremely deprived, we will need to develop elaborate simulations of actual work, in which positive work behavior can be systematically and immediately rewarded. It has not been sufficiently recognized that one of the consequences of extreme poverty may be inability to fulfill the basic requirements of the work role.

It is in these respects that current antipoverty programs, with all their virtues, appear to lack one very important component. Various job corps and youth-opportunity projects now in effect report alarmingly high dropout rates, for which there are undoubtedly many reasons. But, to the degree that some of these young people are cases of severe work acculturation, a high dropout rate can be expected. It is possible that we will need to devise a kind of total, ameliorative environment in which the deprived person can learn to assign a wide range of positive meanings to work. An available model is the rehabilitative workshop, in which work is done on real commodities, in which real wages can be paid on a scale related to productivity, and in which a trained staff can manipulate the variables crucial to work adjustment in a systematic manner. In this kind of setting, the deprived individual can learn to get some gratification out of working and begin to feel that it is possible, through work, to gain some measure of respect and self-esteem. Such procedures have not as yet been seriously applied to the socially disadvantaged, as they have been to the handicapped worker, but it is a step that the antipoverty movement may have to undertake.

Of course, a great more is at stake in the "war on poverty" than the provision of adequate employment. The problems of poverty in the United States are enormously complicated by ethnic and racial issues, which we have not touched at all. It is still far from certain that our society is willing and able to provide decent jobs for the very poor, even if they are trained and motivated to fill them. Our intention has merely been to emphasize that growing up in the world of poverty can be psychologically crippling as well as economically disastrous. The Head Start programs are designed to prevent the *onset* of some of these crippling conditions. But we do not have to abandon the adult. If our intention is to eradicate unemployment among the severely disadvantaged members of the adult labor force, simply providing training in employable skills is not enough. We will also have to take steps to endow the very poor with full citizenship in the work-oriented society, from which they have been systematically excluded.

WORK AND PRODUCTIVITY

It seems appropriate to end this chapter with some comments on the current war of words over what has been presented as a catastrophic decline in the productivity of the American labor force. I use the word comments advisedly since it is too early to make a definitive assessment of the evidence and also not easy to extract kernels of truth from the outpourings of special pleading currently coming from both management and labor. Nevertheless, it seems possible that we are facing some major shifts in the social conditions under which work is performed in modern America, and we should be cognizant of these changes, assuming we can specify them.

Much of the excitement and controversy has been generated by the successful penetration by the Japanese automotive industry of the domestic and foreign markets for American cars and the effects of the less well-publicized but very substantial imports of foreign steel products, which have raised havoc in our own very basic steel industry. Complicated by a world-wide economic recession, the result has been an epidemic of plant closings all over the country, the disemployment of hundreds of thousands of workers in steel, automotive, and allied industries, and a consequent outcry in the communications media. Representatives of industrial management at once charged that the whole problem was due to excessive labor costs, claiming that organized labor was pricing American products out of the market, while at the same time protecting the workers from the imposition by management of improved industrial discipline. Spokesmen for organized labor responded by accusing management of short-sided profit-taking and reckless reduction of the allocation of funds needed for research and development. Observers who sought positions of neutrality tended to conclude that there were elements of truth in both sets of charges.

Actually, the issues of work and productivity are many and complex. For our purposes here, we need to know to what degree changes in productivity are a result of possible changes in work behavior. To put this more bluntly, can we relate these problems of the market place to actual changes in the work motivation and work behavior of the American worker in certain key industries, or are we seeing the operation of certain very large social forces that are operating beyond the grasp of the individual employee? Of course, this may not be an either—or proposition at all but a phenomenon accountable for in terms of a long and interrelated set of factors, of which labor and management activities are only two among many. We reveal no secret when we say that the latter is likely to be closer to the real state of affairs.

Of course, we need to know what it is we are talking about. What is productivity? Given that we agree on what it is, how is it best measured? Given accurate measurements, what are the factors leading to increase or decrease? To what degree are these changes, once detected, temporary or permanent trends?

According to a recent publication of the Committee for Economic Development (CED) (1983) the "productivity problem involves a complex set of issues, some more serious and more intractable than others" (p. 8). The writers of this valuable report indicate that there are major disagreements about the definition of productivity and its measurement, about the factors that produce change in productivity, and about the policies designed to make a difference in whatever changes have been noted. They make a contribution, however, in bringing together the conclusions about which there is at least a minimum of disagreement.

To define productivity, the CED reports to a familiar input—output model: Productivity, they say, measures the relationship between outputs (the amounts of goods and services produced) and inputs (the quantities of labor, capital, and material resources used up in producing the outputs). This seems fairly straightforward until one sets about to consider how to measure both output and input. Measuring output, the CED points out, is far from a simple matter. This is particularly true when the issue is the measurements of services rather than the simple enumeration of the quantities of given commodities, such as cars or cameras. How does one measure productivity in the health service industry or in education? This becomes a serious question when one reflects that for some years it has been true that a larger proportion of the American labor force is employed in service industries than in manufacturing.

If output is hard to measure, total input presents even greater difficulties. The CED report cited notes that productivity ratios are often publicly discussed as if there was only a single input (i.e., labor). On the other hand, the CED points out that a great many interrelated variables are involved on the input side: production techniques, capital equipment, the skill of the labor force, managerial performance and decisions, the rate of capital utilization, the scale of operations, materials flow, product mix, the state of labor—management relations, and the quality of the work environment. They could have added such large and even more unmeasurable factors as the cultural history and nature of the country involved, the distribution of its labor force over the broad domains of agriculture, manufacturing, and service, the relative standard of living, and other possible background determiners.

The most common measures of productivity among input–output economists are *labor productivity* and total-factor or *multifactorial productivity*. The former measures productivity as a simple function of man-hours worked or man-hours paid for. The latter measures not only labor productivity but also the utilization of plant and equipment, energy, and materials used up. It is very instructive to compare the two kinds of measurement. For example, it has been reported that in Japanese industry, in an 8-year period from 1965 to 1973, labor productivity increased at the very impressive rate of 11%. However, when one examines, for the same period, the growth in the contributions of capital, energy, and materials, one sees that the bulk of this apparent change in rate is made up by increases in the rate of capital formation and materials flow. Labor productivity in Japan for this period increased at only 0.8% (CED, 1983, p. 11). Before Americans begin to rejoice at this apparent down-grading of Japanese productivity, they should note that total-factor productivity in America has increased at a progressively lower rate during the same period and actually turned negative during the period 1979–1981.

It begins to be rather clear that before one can attribute changes in labor productivity to shifts in work motivation or other aspects of work behavior, a host of other economic factors must be examined: changes in the rate of capital formation, proportions of gross product devoted to research and development, the composition of output (the distribution of the gross national product between goods and services), changes in composition of the labor force (sex, age, race, education, work experience, etc.), shifts in cost and utilization of natural resources (especially energy), and developments in the world market. In addition, there are a number of more intangible factor that can have major effects on managerial decision making: preoccupation of management with short-term rather than long-term consequences, inflation, federal monetary policies, tariff policies, and defense outlays.

Faced with this comparatively enormous set of economic factors, some of which have been under study and others merely the subject of speculation, it seems sensible to defer any further comments on the relations of work behavior and productivity. Certainly, the entire situation vis-à-vis productivity seems too complex and too unresolved for us to draw any conclusions bearing upon the motivation to work or the overall factors governing work behavior.

16 WORK IN PERSPECTIVE

The basic aim of this book has been to construct a coherent theory of human work. Our interest in this problem was, at first, rather parochial. We simply wanted to know why some people appeared unable to adapt to work, although they were physically and mentally equipped to do so. It seemed insufficient to say that they were simply "unmotivated," since some of them seemed very anxious to achieve a stable work adjustment. What stood in the way? The effort to answer this question has taken us very far afield. An individual's ideas about work, his manner of working, and the values that work has for him appear to be determined by an extremely complex network of factors. Some of these factors relate to events and circumstances within the life-history of the individual, while others appear to reflect the history of the entire human species. Similarly, some of the determinants of work behavior appear to be clearly personal—individual styles of feeling, emotion, thought, and action. Other determinants appear to be clearly external—the physical, social, and cultural conditions of work. Inevitably, our search has led us into very diverse fields of knowledge: archeology, anthropology, and history; economics and politics; biology and engineering; philosophy, sociology, and psychology.

This prolonged search has shown that work is, above all, a *social* enterprise, which takes on different forms, depending upon the particular variant of human culture in which it is embedded. Man is not only a heavily socialized animal, he is also an *enculturated* animal. One of our most significant findings is that work has different meanings in different human cultures and, in the more complex societies, may have specialized meanings peculiar to a particular subcultural enclave. It is also obvious that, within a society, cultural norms are not internalized by different persons in precisely the same way or to the same extent. While we are prepared to believe that culture is a prime source of the motivation to work, cultures are not monolithic or wholly distinctive entities. They are distillations of old and new ideas, ancient and modern practices. Certain ideas may tend to dominate, giving the culture whatever distinctive properties it possesses, but other ideas are still pervasive. Thus, in a strongly work-oriented society such as our own, it is quite possible for people to believe that certain kinds of work, if not all work, are inherently demeaning and degrading. On balance, however, it seems fair to say that the motivation to work is largely a function of culture, and that it varies according to the socialization process through which cultural norms are internalized.

Another highly significant conclusion arises from our efforts to write a definition of work. Work is a distinctively *human* activity, although other animals carry through a great number of work-like activities. The direct links between instinct and action appear, as it were, to be "broken" in man. While animals other than man are generally limited to living in the world as they find it, man is capable of *altering* the features of his environment so that life will be (as he sees it) more secure, more satisfying, or more pleasurable. So far as we can discover, the essentials of what is meant by work are to be found in this "planful alteration of certain features of man's environment." Human beings have learned to preserve and maintain their lives through extremely roundabout procedures involving an amazingly complex network of social relations, culturally determined ways of doing things, and an immense weight of technology. We have succeeded in so altering the "natural" environment that there is already some danger that we are rendering it unfit for continued habitation. That some of us now live in an almost entirely artificial environment (the modern city) has become fairly obvious. But it is important to recognize that even the most "primitive" of men were capable of controlling and altering their environment. The fabrication of tools and weapons, the control of fire, the development of protective clothing—all these involve the planful and directed use of energy to alter something in the environment. This instrumental and alterative aspect of work also largely serves to differentiate it from love and from play.

One reason work is so difficult to define is that man is extremely clever in imputing meanings to the things he does. Thus, the more obvious dictionary definition, that work is "undertaken for gain," is only one of many meanings attributed to it. People work also to "pass the time" and may face intolerable amounts of boredom and restlessness if they are idle for protracted periods. For complex social reasons, work has been interlocked with self-esteem and has become one of the major ways in which people evaluate their worth as persons. Similarly, from a slightly different vantage point, people are accustomed to give respect to others according to the kind of work they do, a posture that reflects a very elaborate status hierarchy based on occupations and roles. It would also appear that a number of more subtle feelings may be aroused or frustrated by work, *viz.*, the desire to achieve something, to be creative, to leave some mark on an otherwise indifferent world. The motivation for work thus can be complex, with quite different motives predominating in different individuals, or even in the same person on different occasions. The complexities of work motivation have considerable practical significance, since they undoubtedly influence the manner in which one works as well as the felt consequences of disemployment. This is, so far, a brand-new field of research, which will repay intensive examination.

In its broadest possible outline, we have evolved what is essentially a "two-factor" theory of work, with the proviso that each of the "factors" is made up of a complex network of many variables. One set of variables describes the human beings who are confronted with the demand to work; the other set describes the critical features of the work environment. Work behavior is seen as a kind of *transaction* between the working individual and his "surround." Of the many aspects of this complex transaction, we have singled out three for special emphasis. These are: (1) the semiautonomous operation of the work personality; (2) the existence of a distinctive work subculture; (3) the conception of a taxonomy of distinctive forms of maladaptation to work. These matters merit some final comments.

THE WORK PERSONALITY

The notion that work behavior is a function, in part, of a semiautonomous area of the personality is fundamental. There are, of course, important implications for therapeutic strategy. We have insisted that the experiences of early childhood are the *necessary* but not the *sufficient* conditions of adult work behavior. We have called attention, as others have done less systematically, to the critical importance of the period of middle childhood (the school years) in laying the foundations of the work personality. The early experience is not irrelevant, however, and in some instances, it must be admitted, the early childhood experience is so traumatic that later experiences cannot really be incorporated at all. The severely autistic child cannot profit from schooling because he is wholly preoccupied with much earlier developmental problems. Similarly, the adult psychotic may "regress" to stages characteristic of infancy. In some of these cases, however, it has been found possible to develop those areas of the personality that bear directly on work, without basically altering any of the "deeper" layers of the personality.

The significance of this result for the practical worker is that inability to work may be ameliorated without the prior requirement of intensive and prolonged reconstruction of the entire personality. An additional implication is that people may be helped to adjust to work who are considered difficult to treat by conventional psychotherapeutic means. The long-term chronic schizophrenic, for example, may be helped to adapt to work by means of a specifically work-oriented treatment process. To the degree that the ability to work is relatively autonomous of competencies in other life areas, the possibility exists of solving certain problems while leaving others largely unaffected. This possibility provides an asset for the developing "new look" in the mental health professions, which is called *community mental health.* It should be emphasized that we are not arguing here for a substitution of work-oriented treatment for other treatment modalities. We are also not arguing that work is a "cure-all" for mental disorder. We are merely saying that adaptation to work can be achieved even where other areas of the personality remain badly disorganized. This is simply one of the consequences of the fact that human personality does not appear to function as a monolithic entity but as a set of more or less related functional areas.

THE WORK ENVIRONMENT

The second conception that is intrinsic to the theory is that the process of adaptation to work is essentially a process of enculturation. If this is true, then there must be a set of cultural norms and practices that, taken together, we can define as the *work subculture.* We have described its distinctive properties, which we have conceptualized as a set of environmental demands. The attention given to these matters may be justified on several counts. First, we have suggested that important segments of the work personality are established *developmentally* through internalization of components of the work subculture. In this sense, any bit of work behavior can best be understood in terms of present or prior transactions between a behaving individual and a set of work pressures or demands. Second, it becomes possible to regard the maladapted individual as an *acculturated* person; he may simply not perceive important segments of the work subculture, he may misperceive them, or he may perceive them as alien.

One of our major conclusions is that knowledge of the work subculture is an indispensable requirement for the rehabilitation practitioner. He not only needs to know the general demands of various work situations but also must often know the particular features of work that the individual client finds predominantly oppressive. The simulated work environment of the rehabilitative workshop is an effort to reproduce some of the more important demands of work. In a less well-defined way, the same is true of the work-sample approach to vocational evaluation. In such settings, it is possible to determine what the client finds particularly difficult to manage. Therapeutic strategy can then take the form of helping the client to cope more effectively with whatever feature of the work subculture he finds most troublesome. Depending upon the case, this can involve an emphasis on therapeutic counseling, on environmental manipulation, or on whatever combination of the two techniques seems most appropriate. All this is based upon the explicit assumption that man is essentially a socialized and enculturated animal, and that behavioral deviance is largely a consequence of failures in socialization.

MALADAPTATION TO WORK

Even a cursory reading of this book will convince the reader that we know very little as yet concerning the psychopathology of work. Until very recently, this was not really recognized as a serious scientific problem. We have been forced to resort to a good deal of speculation, much of which may turn out to be quite unfounded. Our aim has been to call attention to the evident need for a clinical psychology of work behavior. Inappropriate or ineffective work behavior cannot solely be attributed to the lack of specific work-skills. If work makes demands on feeling and emotion, as well as requiring certain cognitive and motor skills, then the problems of adaptation can become very complex. There are many people whose biographical pasts have ill-prepared them to meet the demands of work. This is markedly true when the work situation appears to mobilize negative affects—fear or anger in some persons, feelings of inferiority and self-depreciation in others. Although we have generally conceptualized work as a social problem, the specific experience of each working person is individual and idiosyncratic. To give him effective assistance, we need to know him as a person, not merely as a representative of a class. What is *his* unique understanding of the meaning of work? What features of the work environment are significantly traumatic for *him*? Which of the many variants of treatment will be most effective in *his* particular case? Such questions are the special province of the clinician, who must always be sensitive to the uniqueness of the in-dividual case.

Then, it might be asked, why our evident interest in typology? In Chapter 11, we made a strenuous attempt to evolve a taxonomy of types of mal-adaptive work behavior, although we knew full well that empirical data were largely insufficient and that much of the interpretation was im-pressionistic and speculative. Why then make the effort at all?

The problems of interest to the behavioral sciences can be arranged in a three-dimensional space. Along one axis are all those activities that are common to the entire human *species;* along another are those things that are common to particular human *groups;* along the third are the unique be-haviors of particular *individuals.* The classification of people into behavioral subgroups has importance in itself, since the classification of phenomena is one of the major goals of the scientific enterprise. But it is also vital for the therapeutic enterprise. If one or another behavioral component pre-dominates in different people, the amelioration of their problems may re-quire somewhat differing techniques. The conception that all people are basically alike was one of the great liberating ideas of the modern period. Thus, the components of work behavior that we have described are prob-ably present in all of us. This is one axis of the problem. At the same time, there may be a finite number of different patterns in which these com-ponents are arranged, making it possible to designate "typical" subgroupings. This is the second dimension of the problem. Finally, every human being has had a unique set of biographical experiences and has developed his own unique style of coping with problems. This is the third axis. The therapist must know all of them, although he may find that his daily practice draws more heavily on the second and third.

THE FUTURE OF WORK

Prediction is, at best, a risk in a rapidly changing world. In the technologically advanced countries, innovation is the prime fact of life; it is taking place now at such a breakneck pace that adaptation to it is being perceived as a major human problem. The forces of change are currently penetrating many sectors of the world that, hitherto, had been frozen into a given set of social and economic relations for many centuries. Masses of people are migrating from country to town, cities are taking on the features of the megalopolis, all sorts of powerful traditions are being undermined. Nothing seems more certain than that we can expect very massive social, economic, and political change. What, then, is the future for work?

It may seem a perfect illustration of Parkinson's Law that there is a sudden explosion of interest in work as a major sphere of human behavior, at the very moment when we seem to be in a position to abolish it. In reality, the situation is not so simple. Work is still a major life-sphere and will remain so indefinitely. The onrush of science and technology is bringing about massive changes in the conditions of work, but it is still very far from diminishing the need for it. We are witnessing fairly drastic shifts in the composition of the labor force, based on reduced need for common labor at one extreme and for the highly skilled manual artisan at the other. Peasant labor is clearly becoming redundant, with a consequent influx into the cities of millions of people from the countryside. Primary producers of manufactured goods are already a minority of the American labor force, with continuing expansion of the numbers of workers employed in distributive, merchandizing, commercial, and white-collar occupations. In the advanced countries, the workday and the work-week are shorter, retirement is earlier, entry into the labor force later than was the case a generation or two ago. These are all trends that bear watching, but work is still very far from being eliminated as a major human enterprise.

However, we are becoming increasingly aware that the *will* to work is not a God-given natural resource, like air or water. One result of the conquests of science is that we are now beginning to question everything. When aspects of life that everyone took for granted are put under the microscope of controlled observation, they begin to look different. All sorts of sturdy beliefs and unconscious preconceptions begin to be challenged. We are becoming sensitive to the fact that workers are not born but *made*. In itself, this idea does not sound very revolutionary. But once the idea is grasped, we begin to have all sorts of second thoughts about the aims and techniques of the process through which a nonworking child becomes an adult worker.

Of course, the scientific outlook is not the only devil in the machinery. During the past few decades, all sorts of social arrangements that doomed most of humanity to unremitting labor have been undermined. A man's color, his lineage, his social class, or his nation of origin need no longer determine whether he spends his life as a worker or as a drone. Modern egalitarianism insists that both the rich and the poor, the powerful and the weak, shall perform some kind of useful work. They may not be equally compensated, but there is little disposition to support idlers at either end of the economic continuum. The *right* to work has been made a matter of basic law in many countries. With rights come duties! We can no longer *compel* people to work—whether by the force of feudal and semifeudal arrangements or by condemning them to starvation if they do not. On the other hand, we are now willing to spend billions of dollars annually to help people become workers if their only alternative is living as an idler on the public purse.

All these social, technical, and ideological shifts are undoubtedly changing the meanings imputed to work. Probably few people still see work as the path to Godliness, for revealed religion is no longer a powerful social force. Work may also be losing some of its intrinsic virtues with the development of mass production and the increasing pervasiveness of machinery. We may even be approaching a situation where the clear nexus between work and money may become somewhat diluted, so that our incomes and life-styles may no longer so unequivocally reflect the particular kinds of work we do. It is also quite possible that formal education may have to give more concern to the constructive use of leisure. But none of this implies any immediate risk that work will become a negligible part of human existence. What the very remote future holds in prospect, none of us can now say.

Work is neither a blessing nor a curse but simply one of the major conditions of man's existence. Through work, a naked half-ape, equipped with neither fang nor claw, has been able to establish his sway over stronger and better-armed animals, virtually extinguishing the latter in the process. Through work, we have domesticated useful animals, tamed the land, learned to control many of the indifferent and inimical forces of nature. Through work also, we have developed the most efficient means of subjugating and killing our fellow men, which, of course, is the darker side of the process. The entire aggregate of human culture, for better and for worse, is a product of work; without work, it is difficult to say how we would have become human at all.

Like many other human characteristics, the ability to work has dual aspects. We can use it to destroy ourselves as a life species, or we can use it to improve our lot on earth. Since knowledge is power, further study of work may instruct us in better ways of harnessing and controlling this awesome human energy. It has been said that we are halfway up the tree! If our ancestors were arboreal, it might be more accurate to say that we are half-way down to earth. The long record of man on earth has been a history of the blind conquest of nature through work. But the more we know *why* we work, what we are working *for,* what are the *consequences* of our labor, the more we will be in a position to control our destinies.

BIBLIOGRAPHY

All of the titles below have been cited in the text. For the reader who wishes to further pursue some of these issues, titles indicated with an asterisk (*) are recommended.

Abraham, K. "Observations on Ferenczi's Paper on 'Sunday Neuroses'" (1918). In *The Psycho-analytic Reader*, edited by R. Fliess. New York: International Universities Press, 1948.

Alexander, F. "The Logic of Emotion and its Dynamic Background." *International Journal of Psycho-analysis* 16 (1955).

Allee, D. "American Agriculture—Its Resource Issues for the Coming Years." *Daedalus* 96 (Fall 1967), 1071-1081.

Allport, G. W. *Personality*. New York: Holt, 1937.

American Psychiatric Association. *Troubled People on the Job*. Washington D.C.: The Association, 1959.

American Psychiatric Association. *The Mentally Ill Employee: His Treatment and Rehabilitation*. Washington, D.C.: The Association, 1965.

Anderson, E. *Plants, Men, and Life*. Boston: Little, Brown, 1952.

Anderson, N. *The Hobo*. Chicago: University of Chicago Press, 1923.

Anthony, W. A.; Buell, G. C.; Sharrett, S.; and Althoff, M. E. "Efficacy of Psychiatric Rehabilitation." *Psychological Bulletin* 78 (1972):447–456.

Arbuckle, D. S. *Counseling: An Introduction*. Boston: Allyn and Bacon, 1961.

*Arendt, Hannah, *The Human Condition*. Chicago: University of Chicago Press, 1958.

Argyle, M. "The Relay Assembly Test Room in Retrospect." *Occupational Psychology* 27 (1953):98–103.

Argyris, C. *Interpersonal Competence and Organizational Effectiveness*. Homewood, Ill.: Irwin, 1962.

Aristotle. *The Politics*. Translated by T. A. Sinclair. Baltimore, MD.: Penguin Books, 1962.

Astin, A. W., and Holland, J. L. "The Environmental Assessment Technique: A Way to Measure College Environments." *Journal of Educational Psychology*, 52 (1961):308–316.

Axelrod, S. *Effects of Early Blindness: Performance of Blind and Sighted Children in Tactile and Auditory Tasks*. New York: American Foundation for the Blind, 1959.

Ayllon, T., and Azrin, N. H. *The Token Economy: A Motivational System for Therapy and Education*. New York: Appleton, 1968.

Bachrach, L. J. *Deinstitutionalization: An Analitical Review and Sociological Perspective*. Mental Health Statistics, Series D, No. 4, *DHEW* (ADM 79-351). Washington, D.C.: U.S. Government Printing Office, 1976.

Bachrach, L. J., ed. *Deinstitutionalization*. San Francisco: Jossey-Bass, 1983.

Bagdikian, B. H. *In the Midst of Plenty.* New York: The New American Library, 1964.

Bakke, E. W. *The Unemployed Man.* New York: Dutton, 1934.

Bakke, E. W. *Citizens without Work.* New Haven: Yale University Press, 1940.

Bakke, E. W. *The Fusion Process.* New Haven: Labor and Management Center, Yale University, 1953.

Bancroft, Gertrude. *The American Labor Force: Its Growth and Changing Composition.* New York: Wiley, 1958.

Barker, R. G. "The Social Psychology of Physical Disability," *Journal of Social Issues* 4 (1948):28–38.

Barron, F. "Toward a Positive Definition of Psychological Health." Paper presented to Convention of American Psychological Association, 1955.

Bavelas, A. "Communication Patterns in Task-Oriented Groups." *Journal of the Acoustical Society of America* 22 (1950):725–730.

Beck, S. *The Six Schizophrenias.* New York: American Orthopsychiatric Association, 1954.

*Bell, D. *Work and Its Discontents.* Boston: Beacon Press, 1956.

Benedict, Ruth. "Anthropology and the Abnormal." *Journal of General Psychology* 10 (1934):59–82.

Bennett, Margaret E. *Guidance and Counseling in Groups.* 2d ed. New York: McGraw-Hill, 1963.

Berlyne, D. E. *Conflict Arousal and Curiosity.* New York: McGraw-Hill, 1960.

Berrien, F. K. "The Effects of Noise." *Psychological Bulletin* 43 (1946):141–161.

Bettenson, H. S., ed. *Documents of the Christian Church.* New York: Oxford University Press, 1947.

Blauner, R. *Alienation and Freedom: The Factory Worker and His Industry.* Chicago: University of Chicago Press, 1964.

Boas, F. *The Mind of Primitive Man.* New York: Macmillan, 1911.

Bockoven, J. S. *Moral Treatment in American Society.* New York: Springer, 1963.

Bolton, Brian, ed. *Vocational Adjustment of Disabled Persons.* Baltimore, Md.: University Park Press, 1982.

Bordin, E. S. "A Theory of Vocational Interests as Dynamic Phenomena." *Educational and Psychological Measurements* 3 (1943):49–65.

Boros, O. K., *Tests in Print.* Highland Park, N.J.: Gryphon, 1961.

Borow, H. ed. *Man in a World of Work.* Boston: Houghton Mifflin, 1964.

Borow, H. "Apathy, Unrest, and Change: The Psychology of the 1960s." In *Vocational Guidance and Human Development,* edited by E. L. Herr. Boston: Houghton Mifflin, 1974.

Bottomore, T. B. and Rubel, M. (eds.). *Marx, Karl, Selected Writings in Sociology and Social Philosophy.* New York: McGraw Hill, 1956, pp. 169–170. [Translated from *Marx-Engels Gesamtausgabe,* Section I, Vol. 3, pp. 85–86, by T. B. Bottomore.]

Bradford, L. P.; Gibb, J. R.; and Benne, K. D. *T-group Theory and Laboratory Method.* New York: Wiley, 1964.

Bramel. D., and Friend, R. "Hawthorne, the Myth of the Docile Worker, and Class Bias in Psychology. *American Psychologist* 36 (1981):867–878.

Brayfield, A. H., and Corckett, W. H. "Employee Attitudes and Employee Performance." *Psychological Bulletin* 52 (1955):396–424.

Brayfield, A. H., and Rothe, H. F. "An Index of Job Satisfaction." *Journal of Applied Psychology* 35 (1951):307–311.

Brown, G. H. "United States Population." In *World Almanac and Book of Facts.* New York: Newspaper Enterprise Association, 1972.

Brown, J. A. C. *The Social Psychology of Industry.* London: Penguin Books, 1954.

Buehler, C. *Der menschliche Lebenslauf als psychologisches Problem.* Leipzig: Hir-zel, 1933.

Bühler, K. *Die geistige Entwicklung des Kindes.* 4th ed. Jena: Fischer, 1924.

Burch, W. R., Jr. "Resources and Social Structures: Some Conditions of Stability and Change." *Annals of the American Academy of Political and Social Science* 389 (1970):27–34.

*Buxton, L. H. D. *Primitive Labour.* London: Methuen & Co., Ltd., 1924.

Cantril, H. "Perception and Interpersonal Relations." *American Journal of Psychiatry* 114 (1957):119–126.

Cantril, H.; Ames, A.; Hastorf, A., and Ittelson, W. "Psychology and Scientific Research." In *Explorations in Transactional Psychology,* edited by F. P. Kilpatrick. New York: New York University Press, 1961.

Caplan, R. D. Organizational Stress and Individual Strain: A Social Psychological Study of the Factors in Coronary Heart Disease among Administrators, Engineers and Scientists. Ph.D. dissertation, University of Michigan, 1971.

Caplan, R. D., Cobb, S., French, J. R. P., Harrison, R. V., and Pinneau, S. R., Jr. *Job Demands and Worker Health: Main Effects and Occupational Differences.* DWEW (NIOSH) Publication #75–160. Washington, D.C.: U.S. Government Printing Office, 1975.

*Caplow, T. *The Sociology of Work.* Minneapolis: University of Minnesota Press, 1954.

Carey, A. "The Hawthorne Studies: A Radical Criticism." *American Sociological Review* 32 (1967):403–416.

Cartwright, D., and A. Zander, eds. *Group Dynamics: Research and Theory.* 2d ed. Evanston, Ill.: Row, Peterson, & Co., 1960.

Cassel, J. C. "The Contribution of the Social Environment to Host Resistance." *American Journal of Epidemiology* 104 (1976):102–123.

Cassel, J. C., and Tyroler, H. A. "Epidemiological Studies of Culture Change: I. Health Status and Recency of Industrialization." *Archives of Environmental Health* 3 (1961):25–33.

Cattell, R. B. *Description and Measurement of Personality.* New York: World Book Co., 1946.

Caudill, W. *The Psychiatric Hospital as a Small Society.* Cambridge, Mass.: Harvard University Press, 1958.

Center for the Study of Social Policy. *A Dream Deferred: The Economic Status of Black Americans.* Washington, D.C.: Center for Study of Social Policy 1983.

Centers, R. *The Psychology of Social Classes.* Princeton, N.J.: Princeton University Press, 1949.

Chadwick, J. F. "Psychological Job Stress and Coronary Heart Disease." In *New Developments in Occupational Stress,* edited by R. M. Schwartz. Cincinnati: NIOSH, 1980.

Chapanis, A. *Research Techniques in Human Engineering.* Baltimore: Johns Hopkins Press, 1959.

Chein, I. "The Awareness of Self and the Structure of the Ego." *Psychological review,* 51 (1944):69–80, 304–314.

*Childe, V. Gordon. *Man Makes Himself.* London: Watts & Co., 1936.

Childe, V. Gordon. *What Happened in History.* New York: Penguin Books, 1946.

Clarke, G. *From Savagery to Civilization.* London: Cobbett Press, 1946.

Cobb, S., and Kasl, S. V. *Termination: The Consequences of Job Loss.* Cincinnati: National Institute for Occupational Safety and Health, 1977.

Cobb, S., and Rose, R. M. "Psychosomatic Disease in Air-Traffic Controllers: Hypertension, Diabetes and Peptic Ulcer." *Journal of the American Medical Association* 224 (1973):489–492.

Coleman, J. S. *Equality of Educational Opportunity.* Washington, D.C.: U.S. Office of Education, Department of Health, Education and Welfare, 1966.

Committee for Economic Development. *Productivity Policy: Key to the Nation's Economic Future.* New York: Committee for Economic Development, 1983.

Comptroller General of the U.S. *Returning Mental Patients to the Community: Government Needs to Do More.* Report to Congress. Washington, D.C.: U.S. Accounting Office, HRD-76-152, 1977.

Cooper, C. L., ed. *Stress Research: Issues for the 80s.* New York: Wiley, 1982.

Cooper, C. L., and Marshall, J. "Sources of Managerial and White Collar Stress. In *Stress and Work,* edited by C. L. Cooper and R. Payne. New York: Wiley, 1978.

Cooper, C. L., and Payne, R., eds. *Stress at Work.* New York: Wiley, 1978.

Cottrell, W. F. *Energy and Society: The Relation between Energy, Social Change and Economic Development.* New York: McGraw-Hill, 1955.

Cressey, P. G. *The Taxi-Dance Hall.* Chicago: University of Chicago Press, 1932.

Crites, J. O. *Vocational Psychology.* New York: McGraw-Hill, 1969.

Cronbach, L. *Essentials of Psychological Testing.* 2d ed. New York: Harper & Row, 1960.

Curwen, E. C., and Hatt, G. *Plough and Pasture: The Early History of Farming.* New York: Schuman, 1953.

Dahl, R. *After the Revolution?* New Haven: Yale University Press, 1970.

Dalton, M. *Men Who Manage.* New York: Wiley, 1959.

Dawis, R. V., and Lofquist, L. H. *A World of Work Adjustment.*

*De Grazia, S. *Of Time, Work and Leisure.* New York: Twentieth Century Fund, 1962.

Dembo, Tamara; Leviton, Gloria L.; and Wright, Beatrice A. "Adjustment to Misfortune—A Problem of Social Psychological Rehabilitation." *Artificial Limbs* 3 (1956):4–62.

*de Tocqueville, Alexis. *Democracy in America* (1835–1840). New York: Harper & Row, 1966.

Deutsch, A. *The Shame of the States.* New York: Harcourt Brace, 1948.

*Dewey, J., and Bentley, A. F. *Knowing and the Known.* Boston: Beacon Press, 1949.

Dobzhansky, T. *Mankind Evolving.* New Haven: Yale University Press, 1962.

Dolson, M. T. "Where Women Stand in Administration." *The Modern Hospital* 108 (1967):100–105.

Dubin, R. *The World of Work; Industrial Society and Human Relations.* Englewood Cliffs, N.J.: Prentice-Hall, 1958.

Dunbar, F. *Emotions and Bodily Changes.* New York: Columbia University Press, 1954.

Elkin, A. P. *The Australian Aborigines.* Sidney: Angus & Robertson, 1938.

Elkin, F. "The Soldier's Language." *American Journal of Sociology* 51 (1946):414–422.

Engel, G. L. "Studies of Ulcerative Colitis, II." *American Journal of Medicine* 16 (1954).

Engel, G. L. "Studies of Ulcerative Colitis, III." *American Journal of Medicine* 19 (1955).

Engels, F. *The Origin of the Family, Private Property and the State (1884).* Chicago: Chas. H. Kerr, 1902.

Erikson, E. H. "Growth and Crises of the Healthy Personality." In *Symposium on the Healthy Personality,* edited by M. J. E. Senn. New York: Josiah Macy Foundation, 1950.

Erikson, Erik H. "Identity and the Life Cycle." *Psychological Issues* 1 (Monogr. No. 1) (1959).

*Erikson, Erik H. *Childhood and Society,* 2d ed. New York: Norton, 1963.

Eysenck, H. J. *The Scientific Study of Personality.* London: Routledge & Kegan Paul, 1952.

Falger, P. R. "Changes in Work Load as a Potential Risk Constellation for Myocardial Infarction." Tilberg, Netherlands: *Tijdschrift voor Psychologie* 7 (1979):96–114.

Ferenczi, S. "Sunday Neuroses" (1918). In *Further Contributions to the Theory and Technique of Psycho-analysis,* edited by S. Ferenczi. 2d ed. New York: Basic Books, 1950.

Ferree, C. E., and Rand, Gertrude. "Care Needed in Lighting." *Personnel Journal* 14 (1936):323–326.

Fishman, S. "Amputation." In *Psychogical Practices with the Physically Disabled* edited by J. F. Garrett and Edna S. Levine. New York: Columbia University Press, 1962.

Flanagan, J. C., et al. *Design for a Study of American Youth.* Boston: Houghton Mifflin, 1962.

Flanders, R. B. "Employment Patterns for the 1970s." *Occupational Outlook Quarterly* 14 (1970):2–6.

Foote, N. N., and Cottrell, L. S., Jr. *Identity and Interpersonal Competence.* Chicago: University of Chicago, Press, 1955.

*Forde, C. D. *Habitat, Economy and Society.* London: Methuen, 1934.

Fordyce, W. E. "Behavioral Methods in Rehabilitation. In *Rehabilitation Psychology,* edited by W. S. Neff. Washington, D.C.: American Psychological Association, 1971.

Fordyce, W. E. "A Behavioral Perspective in Rehabilitation." In *The Sociology of Physical Disability,* edited by G. L. Albrecht. London: Feffer and Simons, 1976.

Form, W. H., and Miller, D. C. *Industry, Labor, and Community.* New York: Harper & Row, 1960.

Foucault, M. *Madness and Civilization.* New York: Pantheon, 1965.

Frankfort, H. *The Birth of Civilization in the Near East.* London: Williams and Norgate, 1951.

*Freeman, H. D., and Simmons, O. G. *The Mental Patient Comes Home.* New York: Wiley, 1963.

French, J. R. P., and Kahn, R. L. "A Programmatic Approach to Studying the Industrial Environment and Mental Health." *Journal of Social Issues* 18 (1962):1–47.

Freud, S. "The Poet and Day-Dreaming." In *Collected Papers.* Vol. IV. London: Hogarth Press, 1948.

*Freud, S. "Civilization and Its Discontents." *Standard Edition of the Complete Psychological Works.* First published in German, 1930. London: Hogarth Press, 1953.

*Friedmann, G. *Industrial Society.* New York: The Free Press, 1955.

Fromm, E. *Man for Himself.* New York: Farrar and Rinehart, 1948.

*Fromm, E. *The Sane Society.* New York: Rinehart, 1955.

Gagné, R. M., ed. *Psychological Principles in System Development.* New York: Holt, Rinehart and Winston, 1962.

*Garrett, J. F., and Levine, Edna S. *Psychological Practices with the Physically Disabled.* New York: Columbia University Press, 1962.

Gechman, A. S., and Winer, Y. "Job Involvement and Satisfaction as Related to Mental Health and Personal Time Devoted to Work. *Journal of Applied Psychology* 60 (1975):521–523.

Gellerman, S. W. *Motivation and Productivity.* New York: American Management Association, 1963.

Gellman, W. "Roots of Prejudice Against the Handicapped." *Journal of Rehabilitation* 25 (1959):4–6.

*Gellman, W. G.; Gendel, H.; Glaser, N. M.; Friedman, S. B.; and Neff, W. S. *Adjusting People to Work.* Chicago: Jewish Vocational Service, 1957.

Ghiselli, E. E. *The Validity of Occupational Attitude Tests.* New York: Wiley, 1966.

Gilbreth, F. B. *Bricklaying System.* New York: Clark, 1909.

Gilbreth, F. B. *Motion Study.* New York: Van Nostrand, 1911.

Ginsberg, S. W. "The Mental Health Movement and Its Theoretical Assumptions." In *Community Programs for Mental Health,* edited by R. Kotinsky and H. Witmer. Cambridge, Mass. Harvard University Press, 1955.

*Ginzberg, E.; Ginsburg,; Axelrod, and Herma, *Occupational Choice: An Approach to a General Theory.* New York: Columbia University Press, 1951.

Glueck, N. *The Other Side of the Jordan.* New Haven: American School of Oriental Research, 1940.

Goffman, E. *Asylums.* New York: Doubleday (Anchor Books), 1961.

Goldberger, L., and Breznitz, S., eds. *Handbook of Stress: Theoretical and Clinical Aspects.* New York: The Free Press, 1983.

Goldman, A. R. "Wanting to Leave or Stay in a Mental Hospital: Incidental Correlates." *Journal of Clinical Psychology* 21 (1965):317–322.

Goldman, L. "Tests and Counseling: The Marriage that Failed." *Measurement and Evaluation in Guidance* 4 (1972):213–220.

Goldstein, K. *Human Nature in the Light of Psychopathology.* Boston, Mass.: Harvard University Press, 1940.

Goodman, P. "Youth in Organized Society." *Commentary* 29 (1960):95–107.

Goodman, P. *People or Personnel.* New York: Random House, 1965.

Gordon, E. W. "Vocational Guidance: Disadvantaged and Minority Populations." In *Vocational Guidance and Human Development,* edited by E. L. Herr. Boston: Houghton Mifflin, 1974.

Gorenstein, E. E. "Debating Mental Illness: Implications for Science, Medicine and Social Policy. *American Psychologist* 39 (1984):50–56.

Greenblatt, M., Levinson, D. J., and Williams, R. H. eds. *The Patient and the Mental Hospital.* Glencoe, Ill.: The Free Press, 1957.

Grinker, R. *Anxiety and Stress.* New York: McGraw-Hill, 1955.

Grinstein, A. *The Index of Psychoanalytic Writings.* 5 vols. New York: International Universities Press, 1960.

Grob, G. *Mental Institutions in America: Social Policy to 1965.* New York: The Free Press, 1973.

Gross, E. *Work and Society.* New York: Crowell, 1958.

Gross, E. "The Worker and Society." In *Man in a World at Work,* edited by H. Borow. Boston: Houghton Mifflin, 1964.

Group for the Advancement of Psychiatry. "The Chronic Mental Patient in the Community." Circular letter, undated.

Guion, R. M. *Personnel Testing.* New York: McGraw-Hill, 1965.

Gurel, L. *Preliminary Results of PEP II Study of Vocational Restoration.* Washington, D.C.: VA Program Evaluation Staff of the Psychiatry, Neurology and Psychology Service, 1963 (processed).

Hacker, F. J. "The Concept of Normality and Its Practical Significance." *American Journal of Orthopsychiatry* 16 (1945):47–64.

Haire, M. "Psychological Problems Relevant to Business and Industry." *Psychological Bulletin* 56 (1959):169–194.

Haire, M., ed. *Modern Organizational Theory.* New York: Wiley, 1959.

Hamilton, K. W. *Counseling the Handicapped in the Rehabilitation Process.* New York: Ronald Press, 1950.

Harrington, M. *The Other America.* New York: Macmillan, 1962.

Harris, A. S. "The Second Sex in Academe." *Bulletin, American Association of University Professors* (Fall 1970):283–295.

Harrison, R. V. "Job Stress in Person–Environment Misfit." Paper presented to 84th Annual Convention of the American Psychological Association, Washington, D.C., 1976.

Harrison, R. V. Person–Environment Fit and Job Stress. In *Stress at Work*, edited by C. L. Cooper and R. Payne. New York: Wiley, 1978.

Hartmann, H. "Psychoanalysis and the Concept of Health." *International Journal of Psychoanalysis* 20 (1939):308–321.

Hartmann, H. "On Rational and Irrational Action." In *Psychoanalysis and the Social Sciences*, edited by G. Roheim. New York: International Universities Press, 1947.

Hartmann, H. *Ego Psychology and the Problem of Adaptation*. New York: International Universities Press, 1958.

Havighurst, R. J. "Stages of Vocational Development." In *Vocational Behavior: Readings in Theory and Research*, edited by D. G. Zytowski. New York: Holt, Rinehart and Winston, 1968.

Haynes, S. G., and Kannel, W. B. "The Relationship of Psychosocial Factors to Coronary Heart Disease in the Framingham Study." *American Journal of Epidemiology* 107 (1978):362–402 and 111 (1980):37–58.

*Hendrick, I. "Instinct and the Ego during Infancy." *Psychoanalytic Quarterly* 11 (1942):33–58.

*Hendrick, I. "The Discussion of the Instinct to Master." *Psychoanalytic Quarterly* 12 (1943):561–565. (a)

*Hendrick, I. "Work and the Pleasure Principle." *Psychoanalytic Quarterly* 12 (1943):311–329. (b)

Herr, E. L. *Decision-Making and Vocational Development*. Guidance Monograph Series. Boston: Houghton Mifflin, 1970.

Herr, E. L. *Vocational Guidance and Human Development*. Boston: Houghton Mifflin, 1974.

Herrnstein, R. J. "I.Q." *The Atlantic Monthly* 228 (September 1971):43–64.

Hershenson, D. B. "Work Adjustment, Disability and the Three R's of Vocational Rehabilitation: A Conceptual Model." *Rehabilitation Counseling Bulletin* 25 (1981):91–97.

*Herskovitz, M. J. *Economic Anthropology*. New York: Knopf, 1952.

Herzberg, F. *Mental Health in Industry*. Pittsburgh: Psychological Services of Pittsburgh, 1955.

*Herzberg, F.; Mausner, B.; Paterson, R. O.; and Capwell, Dora F. *Job Attitudes: Review of Research and Opinion*. Pittsburgh: Psychological Services of Pittsburgh, 1957.

Herzberg, F.; Mausner, B.; and Snyderman, Barbara B. *The Motivation to Work*. 2d ed. New York: Wiley, 1959.

Holland, J. L. "Some Explorations of a Theory of Vocational Choice." *Psychological Monographs* 76 (26, Whole No. 545) (1962).

Holland, J. L. "Explorations of a Theory of Vocational Choice and Achievement." *Psychological Reports* 12 (1963):547–594.

Holland, J. L. *Making Vocational Choices: A Theory of Careers*. Englewood Cliffs, N.J.: Prentice-Hall, 1973.

Hollingshead, A. B., and Redlich, F., *Social Class and Mental Illness*. New York: Wiley, 1958.

Holt, R. B. "Occupational Stress." In *Handbook of Stress*, edited by I. Goldberger and S. Breznitz. New York: The Free Press, 1983.

Honingfeld, G., and Gillis, R. "The Role of Institutionalization in the Natural History of Schizophrenia." *Central Neuropsychiatric Record Library*, Report No. 64. Perry Point, Md.: 1966.

Hoppock, R. *Job Satisfaction*. New York: Harper, 1935.

House, J. S.; McMichael, A. J.; Wells, S. A.; Kaplan, B. H.; and Landerman, L. R. "Occupational Stress and Health among Factory Workers." *Journal of Health and Social Behavior* 20 (1979):139–160.

*Hughes, E. C. *Men and Their Work.* Glencoe, Ill.: The Free Press, 1958.

Hughes, E. C. "The Study of Occupations." In *Sociology Today,* edited by R. K. Merton *et al.* New York: Basic Books, 1959.

Hughes, E. C. "The Professions in Society." *Canadian Journal of Economics and Political Science* 26 (1960):54–61.

*Huizinga, Johan. *Homo Ludens: A Study of the Play-Element in Culture.* New York: Beacon Press, 1955.

Industrial Fatigue Research Board Reports. No. 1, 1919; No. 19, 1922; No. 39, 1927; No. 51, 1928.

Inkeles, Alex, and Levinson, D. J. "National Character: The Study of Modal Personality and Sociocultural Systems." In *Handbook of Social Psychology,* Vol. II, edited by G. Lindzey. Cambridge, Mass.: Addison-Wesley, 1954.

Institute for the Crippled and Disabled. *TOWER: Testing, Orientation and Work Evaluation in Rehabilitation.* New York: Institute, 1959.

Institute for the Crippled and Disabled. *The Job Sample in Vocational Evaluation.* Final Report of Research Project. Washington, D.C.: Social and Rehabilitation Service, 1968.

Ivancevish, J. M., and Matteson, M. T. *Stress and Work: A Managerial Perspective.* Glenview, Ill.: Scott, Foreman, 1980.

Jahoda, M. *Current Conceptions of Mental Health.* New York: Basic Books, 1958.

Jahoda, M. "The Meaning of Psychological Health." *Social Casework* 34 (1953):349–354.

Jahoda, M. "Toward a Social Psychology of Mental Health. In *Symposium on the Health Personality,* edited by M. J. E. Senn. 1979. New York: Josiah Macy Foundation: 1950.

Jahoda, M. "The impact of unemployment in the 1930s and 1970s." *Bulletin of the British Psychological Society,* 32 (1979):309–314.

Janowitz, M. *The Professional Soldier.* Glencoe, Ill.: The Free Press, 1960.

Jencks, C. *Inequality: A Reassessment of the Effect of Family and Schooling in America.* New York: Basic Books, 1972.

Jenkins, C. D., "Psychological and Social Precursors of Coronary Disease." *New England Journal of Medicine* 284 (1971):244–255.

Jenkins, C. D. "Recent Evidence Supporting Psychologic and Social Factors for Coronary Disease." *New England Journal of Medicine* 294 (1976):1033–38.

Jenkins, C. D., Rosenman, R. H., and Freedman, M. "Replicability of Rating the Coronary-Prone Behavior Pattern." *British Journal of Preventive and Social Medicine* 22 (1968):16–22.

Jensen, A. R. "Estimation of the Limits of Heritability of Traits by Comparison of Monozygotic and Dizygotic Twins." *Proceedings of the National Academy of Science* 58 (1967):149–156.

Jensen, A. R. "How Much Can We Boost IQ and Scholastic Achievement?" *Harvard Educational Review* 39 (1969):1–123.

Jensen, A. R. "IQs of Identical Twins Reared Apart." *Behavior Genetics* 1 (1970):133–146.

Johnson, D. F. "Education of Adult Workers in 1975." *Monthly Labor Review* 91 (1968):10–13.

Joint Commission on Mental Illness and Health. *Action for Mental Health.* New York: Basic Books, 1961.

Jones, K. *A History of Mental Health Services.* Boston: Routledge and Kegan Paul, 1972.

Jones, M. *The Therapeutic Community.* New York: Basic Books, 1953.

Jordaan, J. P., and Heyde, N. B. *Vocational Maturity during the High School Years.* New York: Teachers College Press, 1979.

Kahn, R. L. "The Meaning of Work: Interpretation and Proposals for Measurement." In *The Human Meaning of Social Change,* edited by A. A. Campbell and P. E. Converse. New York: Basic Books, 1972.

Kahn, R. L. "Workers and Jobs: Goodness of Fit. Paper presented at a *Workshop on the Role of Work in Psychiatric Treatment,* sponsored by the Work and Mental Health Section, U.S. Department of Health and Health Services. Washington, D.C., September 1983.

Kaley, M. M. "Attitudes Toward the Dual Role of the Married Professional Woman." *The American Psychologist* 26 (1971):301–306.

Kardiner, Abram. *The Individual and His Society.* New York: Columbia University Press, 1939.

Kasl, S. V. "Epidemiological Contributions to the Study of Work Stress." In *Stress at Work,* edited by C. L. Cooper and R. Payne. New York: Wiley, 1978.

Kasl, S. V., and Cobb, S. "Variability and Stress Effects among Men Experiencing Job Loss. In *Handbook of Stress,* edited by L. Goldberger and S. Breznitz. New York: The Free Press, 1983.

Katz, D., Maccoby, N., and Morse, N. C. *Productivity, Supervision, and Morale in an Office Situation.* Ann Arbor, Mich.: Survey Research Center, University of Michigan, 1950.

Katzell, R. A., Yankelovich, D., Fein, M., Oornati, O., and Nash, A. *Work, Productivity, and Job Satisfaction.* New York: Psychological Corporation, 1975.

Kessler-Harris, A. *Out to Work: A History of Wage-Earning Women in the United States.* New York: Oxford University Press, 1982.

Kirkpatrick, J. J., Ewen, R. B., Barrett, R. S., and Katzell, R. A. *Differential Selection among Applicants from Different Socioeconomic or Ethnic Backgrounds.* Final report submitted to the Ford Foundation. Mimeograph. New York: New York University, (May 1967).

Klineberg, O. *Negro Intelligence and Selective Migration.* New York: Columbia University Press, 1935.

Knight, J. A., and Baird, V. C. "Mental Health in Industrial Practice." *Journal of Occupational Medicine* 3 (1961):365–368, 412–416, 463–466.

Knox, J. B. *The Sociology of Industrial Relations.* New York: Random House, 1956.

Korman, A. K. "Self-esteem as a Moderator of the Relationship between Self-perceived Abilities and Vocational Choice." *Journal of Applied Psychology* 51 (1967):65–67.

*Kornhauser, A. *Mental Health of the Industrial Worker.* New York: Wiley, 1965.

Kramer, M., Pollack, S. E., and Redick, R. W. *Mental Disorder/Suicide.* Cambridge, Mass.: Harvard Univeristy Press, 1972.

Kris, E. "The Psychology of Caricature." *International Journal of Psychoanalysis,* 17 (1936).

Kuhn, T. *Structure of Scientific Revolutions.* Chicago: University of Chicago Press, 1970.

*Kutner, B., Fanshell, D., Togo, A. M., and Langner, T. H. *Five Hundred Over Sixty.* New York: Russell Sage Foundation, 1956.

*Lantos, Barbara. "Work and the Instincts." *International Journal of Psycho-Analysis* 24 (1943):114–119.

*Lantos, Barbara. "Metapsychological Considerations on the Concept of Work." *International Journal of Psycho-Analysis* 33 (1952):439–443.

Lawshe, C. H. *Principles of Personnel Testing.* New York: McGraw-Hill, 1948.

Levinson, H. *Emotional Health in the World of Work.* New York: Harper & Row, 1964.

Lifton, W. M. *Working with Groups: Process and Individual Growth.* New York: Wiley, 1961.

Likert, R. *New Patterns of Management.* New York: McGraw-Hill, 1961.

Lindner, R. *Must you conform?* New York: Rinehart, 1956.

*Linton, R. *The Tree of Culture.* New York: Knopf, 1955.

Lofquist, L., and Dawis, R. V. *Adjustment to Work.* New York: Appleton Century Crofts, 1969.

Lubbock, John. *The Origin of Civilization.* London: Longmans, Green, 1870.

McClelland, D. C. *The Achieving Society.* New York: Van Nostrand, 1961.

McClelland, D. C., Atkinson, J. W., Clark, R. A., and Lowell, E. I. *The Achievement Motive.* New York: Appleton-Century, 1953.

McCormick, E. J. *Human Engineering.* New York: McGraw-Hill, 1957.

McDougall, W. *Outline of Psychology.* New York: Scribner's, 1923.

McGrath, J. E. "A Conceptual Formulation for Research on Stress." In *Social and Psychological Factors in Stress,* edited by J. E. McGrath. New York: Holt, Rinehart, & Winston, 1970.

McGregor, D. *The Human Side of Enterprise.* New York: McGraw-Hill, 1960.

McLean, A., ed. *To Work is Human: Mental Health and the Business Community.* New York: Macmillan, 1967.

McLean, A. (ed.) *Occupational Mental Health.* Springfield, Ill: Thomas, 1974

McLean, A. *Work Stress.* Reading, Mass.: Addison-Wesley, 1979.

McMichael, A. J. "Personality, Behavioral and Situational Modifiers of Work Stressors." In *Stress at Work,* edited by C. L. Cooper and R. Payne. New York: Wiley, 1978.

Marcuse, H. *One Dimensional Man,* Boston: Beacon Press, 1964.

Marr, J. H. "Behavioral Analysis of Work Problems. In *Vocational Adjustment of Disabled Persons,* edited by B. Bolton. Baltimore, Md.: University Park Press, 1982.

Marshall, Elizabeth. *Warrior Herdsman.* New York: Knopf, 1965.

Marx, Karl. *Capital,* vol. 1. Chicago: Chas. H. Kerr, 1887.

*Marx, Karl. "Marx–Engels Gesamtausgabe." In *Karl Marx: Selected Writings in Sociology and Social Philosophy.* Translated by T. B. Bottomore and edited by T. B. Bottomore and M. Rubel. Vol. 1. New York: McGraw-Hill, 1964.

Maslow. A. H. "Self-Actualizing People: A Study of Psychological Health." *Personality Symposia,* 1950, 1, 16.

Matthaei, J. A. *An Economic History of Women in America.* New York: Schocken Books, 1982.

Mayman, M. "The Diagnosis of Mental Health." Menninger Foundation, unpublished, 1955.

*Mayo, E. *The Human Problems of an Industrial Civilization.* New York: Macmillan, 1933.

Meissner, M. *Technology and the Worker.* San Francisco: Chandler, 1969.

Meissner, M. "The Long Arm of the Job: A Study of Work and Leisure." *Industrial Relations* 10 (1971):239–260.

Menninger, Karl. "Work as Sublimation." *Bulletin of the Menninger Clinic* 6 (1942):170–182.

Merton, R. K. *Social Theory and Social Structure.* Rev. ed. Glencoe, Ill.: The Free Press, 1957.

Miller, C. H. "Carrier Development Theory in Perspective." In *Vocational Guidance and Human Development,* edited by E. L. Herr. Boston: Houghton Mifflin, 1974.

Miller, D. C., and Form, W. H. *Industrial Sociology: An Introduction to the Sociology of Work Relations.* New York: Harper & Row, 1957.

Morgan, L. H. *Ancient Society.* Chicago: Chas. H. Kerr, 1887.

Mumford, L. *The Condition of Man.* New York: Harcourt, Brace, 1944.

Murray, H. *Explorations in Personality.* New York: Oxford University Press, 1938.

Musil, A. *The Manners and Customs of the Rawala Bedouin.* New York: Czech Academy of Sciences and Arts, 1928.

National Opinion Research Center. "Jobs and Occupations: A Popular Evaluation." *Opinion News* 9 (1947):3–13.

Neff, W. S. "Socio-Economic Status and Intelligence: A Critical Survey." *Psychological Bulletin* 35 (1938):727–757.

Neff, W. S. "The Rehabilitation Workshop as a Therapeutic Medium." *Journal of Jewish Communal Service* 36 (1959):225–231.

Neff, W. S. *A Study of the Factors Involved in the Rehabilitation of Vocationally Disadvantaged Mental Patients.* A research proposal submitted to the Vocational Rehabilitation Administration. New York: Institute for the Crippled and Disabled, 1962.

Neff, W. S. "Psychoanalytic Conceptions of the Meaning of Work." *Psychiatry* 28 (1965):323–333.

Neff, W. S. "Problems of Work Evaluation." *Personnel and Guidance Journal* 44 (1966):682–688.

Neff, W. S. *Changes in the Meaning of Work during Psychiatric Rehabilitation.* Final Report, RD 1603-P. Washington, D.C.: Social and Rehabilitation Service, 1968.

Neff, W. S., and Koltuv, M. "Toleration for Psychiatric Rehabilitation as a Function of Coping Style." *Journal of Counseling Psychology* 31 (1967):364–370.

Neulinger, J. *The Psychology of Leisure.* Springfield, Ill.: Thomas, 1974.

*Nisbet, R. A. *The Sociological Tradition.* New York: Basic Books, 1966.

Oberndorf, C. P. "Psychopathology of Work." *Bulletin of the Menninger Clinic.* 15 (1951):77–84.

O'Hara, R. P. "Roots of Careers." *Elementary School Journal* 62 (1962):277–280.

Oltman, R. M. *Campus 1970—Where Do Women Stand?* Research report of a survey on women in academe. Washington, D.C.: American Association of University Women, 1970.

Opler, M. E. *An Apache Life-way.* Chicago: University of Chicago Press, 1941.

Osipow, S. H. *Theories of Career Development.* New York: Appleton-Century-Crofts, 1968.

O'Toole, J., ed. *Work and the Quality of Life.* Cambridge, Mass.: MIT Press, 1974.

Parsons, T. *The Social System.* Glencoe, Ill.: The Free Press, 1951.

Patterson, C. H. "Self-clarification and the Helping Relationship." In *Man in a World at Work,* edited by H. Borow. Boston: Houghton Mifflin, 1964.

Paul, G. L., and Lentz, R. L. *Psychosocial Treatment of Chronic Mental Patients.* Cambridge, Mass.: Harvard University Press, 1977.

*Piaget, J. *Play, Dreams, and Imitation in Childhood.* New York: Norton, 1951.

Piaget, J. *The Construction of Reality in the Child.* New York: Basic Books, 1937/ 1954.

Piaget, J. *The Language and Thought of the Child.* New York: World (Meridian Books), 1955.

Prediger, D. L. "The Role of Assessment in Career Guidance." In *Vocational Guidance and Human Development,* edited by E. L. Herr. Boston: Houghton Mifflin, 1974.

President's Task Force on Women's Rights and Responsibilities. *A Matter of Simple Justice.* Washington, D.C.: U.S. Government Printing Office, 1970.

Pruyser, P. W. "Work—curse or blessing? A psychoanalytic systematization." *Bulletin of the Menninger Clinic,* 44, (1980):59–73.

Pucel, D. J.; Nelson, H. F.; and Mohamed, D. A. *The Ability of Standardized Test Instruments to Predict Training Success and Employment Success.* Minneapolis: University of Minnesota, 1972.

Rapaport, D. "The Psychoanalytic Theory of Thinking." *International Journal of Psycho-Analysis* 30 (1950):1–10.

Raskin, N. J. "Visual Disability." In *Psychological Practices with the Physically Disabled,* edited by J. F. Garrett and E. S. Levine. New York: Columbia University Press, 1962.

Riesman, D.; Glazer, N.; and Danny, R. *The Lonely Crowd.* New Haven: Yale University Press, 1950.

Roe, Anne. *The Making of a Scientist.* New York: Dodd, Mead, 1953.

Roe, Anne. *The Psychology of Occupations.* New York: Wiley, 1956.

Roe, Anne. "Personality Structure and Occupational Behavior." In *Man in a World at Work,* edited by H. Borow. Boston: Houghton Mifflin, 1964.

*Roe, Anne, and Siegelman, M. *The Origin of Interests.* Washington, D.C.: American Personnel and Guidance Association, 1964.

*Roethlisberger, F. J., and Dickson, W. J. *Management and the Worker.* Cambridge, Mass.: Harvard University Press, 1939.

Rogers, C. R. *Counseling and Psychotherapy.* Boston: Houghton Mifflin, 1942.

Rogers, C. R. "A Theory of Therapy, Personality, and Interpersonal Relationships, as Developed in the Client-centered Framework." In *Psychology: A Study of Science,* vol. 3, edited by S. Koch. New York: McGraw-Hill, 1959.

Ronan, W. W., Cobb, J. M., Garrett, T. L., Lazzeri, J. D., Mosser, D. R., and Racine, A. E. "Occupational Level and Mental Health." *Journal of Occupational Behavior* 5 (1974):157–160.

Rosenman, R. H., Friedman, M., Strauss, R., Wurm, M., Kositchek, R., Hahn, W., and Werthessen, N. T. "Predictive Study of Coronary Heart Disease: The Western Collaborative Group Study." *Journal of the American Medical Association* 189 (1964):15–22.

Rosenman, R. H., Friedman, M., Strauss, R., et al. "Coronary Heart Disease in the Western Collaborative Group Study: A Follow-Up Experience of 4½ Years." *Journal of Chronic Disease* 23 (1970):173–190.

Rosenman, R. M., Brand, R. J., Jenkins, C. D., Friedman, M., Strauss, R., and Wurm, M. Coronary Heart Disease in the Western Collaborative Group Study: Final Follow-up Expeience of 8½ Years." *Journal of the American Medical Association* 233 (1975):872–877.

Rusk, Howard A., and Taylor, E. J. *Living with a Disability.* Garden City, N.J.: Blakiston Press, 1953.

Sawhill, Isabel. *Perspectives on Women and Work in America.* Report of a special task force to the Secretary of Health, Education and Welfare. Cambridge, Mass.: MIT Press, 1973.

Schneider, E. U. *Industrial Sociology, the Social Relations of Industry and the Community.* New York: McGraw-Hill, 1957.

*Seligman, B. B. *Most Notorious Victory: Man in an Age of Automation.* New York: The Free Press, 1966.

Selye, H. *The Stress of Life.* New York: McGraw-Hill, 1956.

Service, E. R. *Primitive Social Organization.* New York: Random House, 1962.

Sheppard, H. L., and Herrick, N. *Where Have All The Robots Gone?* New York: The Free Press, 1972.

Siller, J., with Ferguson, Linda; Vann, D. H.; and Holland, B. *Structure of Attitudes toward the Physically Handicapped.* Draft of final report, Contract No. RD-1276, Veterans Rehabilitation Administration, August 1967.

Singer, S. L., and Stefflre, B. "Sex Differences in Job Values and Desires." *Personnel and Guidance Journal* 32 (1954):483–484.

Skinner, B. F. *Science and Human Behavior.* New York: Macmillan, 1953.

Skinner, B. F. *About Behaviorism.* New York: Knopf, 1974.

Skodak, M., and Skeels, H. M. "A Final Follow-Up of 100 Adopted Children." *The Pedagogical Seminary and Journal of Genetic Psychology* 75 (1949), 85–125.

Smigel, E. O.; Monane, J.; Wood, R. B.; and Nye, Barbara R. "Occupational Sociology: A Re-examination." *Sociology and Social Research* 47 (1963):472–477.

Smuts, Robert W. *Women and Work in America.* New York: Columbia University Press, 1959.

Sonnenfeld, J. "Clarifying Critical Confusion in the Hawthorne Hysteria." *American Psychologist* 37 (1982):1397–1401.

Special Task Force, Department of Health, Education and Welfare. *Work in America.* Cambridge, Mass.: MIT Press, 1973.

Srole, L.; Langner, T. H.; Michael, S. T.; Opler, M. K.; and Rennie, T. A. C. *Mental Health in the Metropolis: The Midtown Manhattan Study.* New York: McGraw-Hill, 1962.

Stanton, A. H., and Schwartz, M. S. *The Mental Hospital.* New York: Basic Books, 1954.

Stenning, D. J. *Savannah Nomads.* London: Oxford University Press, 1959.

*Steward, J. H. *Theory of Culture Change.* Urbana, Ill.: University of Illinois Press, 1955.

Stogdill, R. M. *Individual Behavior and Group Achievement.* New York: Oxford University Press, 1959.

Stone, L. J., and Church, J. *Childhood and Adolescence.* 2d ed. New York: Random House, 1968.

Strauss, G. "Is There a Blue-Collar Revolt against Work?" In *Work and the Quality of Life,* edited by J. O'Toole. Cambridge Mass.: MIT Press, 1974.

Strauss, J. S. "The Course of Psychiatric Disorder: A Model for Understanding Treatment." Paper presented to the Annual Meeting of the American Psychiatric Association, 1983.

Strauss, J. S., and Carpenter, W. T. "The Prediction of Outcome in Schizophrenia." *Archives of General Psychiatry* 31 (1974):37–42.

Strong, E. K., Jr. *Vocational Interests of Men and Women.* Stanford, Calif.: Stanford University Press, 1943.

Strong, E. K., Jr. *Vocational Interests 18 Years after College.* Minneapolis: University of Minnesota Press, 1955.

Sullivan, H. S. *Conceptions of Modern Psychiatry.* 2d ed. New York: Norton, 1953.

Super, D. E. *Appraising Vocational Fitness by Means of Psychological Tests.* New York: Harper & Row, 1949.

Super, D. E. "A Theory of Vocational Development." *American Psychologist* 8 (1953):185–190.

*Super, D. E. *The Psychology of Careers: An Introduction to Vocational Development.* New York: Harper & Row, 1957.

Super, D. E. "The Critical Ninth-Grade: Vocational Choice or Vocational Exploration." *Personnel and Guidance Journal* 39 (1960):106–109.

Super, D. E. ed. *Measuring Vocational Maturity for Counseling and Evaluation.* Washington, D.C.: American Personnel and Guidance Association, 1974.

Super, D. E., and Bohn, M. J. *Occupational Psychology.* Monterey, Calif.: Brooks-Cole, 1970.

Super, D. E., and Overstreet, P. L. *The Vocational Maturity of Ninth-Grade Boys.* New York: Bureau of Publications, Teachers College, Columbia University, 1960.

Super, D. E., Crites, J. O., Hummel, R. C., Maser, H. P., Overstreet, P. L., and Warnath, C. F. *Vocational Development: A Framework for Research.* New York: Teachers College Press, 1957.

*Super, D. E., Starishevsky, R., Matlin, N., and Jordaan, J. P. *Career Development: Self-Concept Theory.* Princeton, N.J.: College Entrance Examination Board, 1963.

Super, D. E., Starishevsky, R., Matlin, K., and Jordaan, J. P. *Career Development: Self-Concept Theory.* New York: College Entrance Board, 1967.

Susser, M. "Causes of Peptic Ulcer: A Selective Epidemiological Review." *Journal of Chronic Disease* 20 (1967):435–456.

Swanton, J. R. *The Indian Tribes of North America.* Washington, D.C.: The Smithsonian Institution, 1952.

Szasz, T. *The Myth of Mental Illness.* New York: Hoeber-Harper, 1961.

Szasz, T. *Law, Liberty and Psychiatry.* New York: Macmillan, 1963.

Szasz, T. *The Age of Madness.* Garden City, N.J.: Anchor Press, 1973.

Tawney, R. H. *Religion and the Rise of Capitalism.* New York: Harcourt, Brace, 1926.

*Taylor, F. W. *The Principles of Scientific Management.* New York: Harper, 1911.

Terkel, Studs. *Working.* New York: Pantheon Books, 1974.

Thorndike, R. L. "The Prediction of Vocational Success." *The Vocational Guidance Quarterly* 11 (1963):179–187.

Tiedeman, D. V., and Miller, A. L. "Technology and Guidance: The Challenge to More Elastic Existence amid Accelerating Obsolescence." In *Vocational Guidance and Human Development,* edited by E. L. Herr. Boston: Houghton Mifflin, 1974.

Tiedeman, D. V., O'Hara, R. P., and Baruch, R. W. *Career Development: Choice and Adjustment.* Princeton, N.J.: College Entrance Examination Board, 1963.

Tiedeman, D. V., and Willis, M. B., eds. *Career Education and the Technology of Career Development.* Palo Alto, Calif.: American Institutes of Research, 1972.

Tilgher, A. *Work: What It Has Meant to Men through the Ages.* New York: Harcourt, Brace, 1930.

Tyler, L. E. "The Relationship of Interests to Abilities and Reputation among First Grade Children." *Educational Psychology Measurement* 11 (1951):255–264.

Tyler, L. E. "The Development of Vocational Interests: I. The Organization of Likes and Dislikes in Ten-Year-Old Children." *Journal of Genetic Psychology* 86 (1955):33–34.

Tyler, L. E. "The Development of Career Interests in Girls." *Genetic Psychology Monographs* 70 (1964):203–212.

Tyler, E. B. *Primitive Culture.* 2d ed. New York: Holt, 1887.

U.S. Department of Health, Education, and Welfare, Special Task Force. *Work in America.* Cambridge, Mass.: MIT Press, 1973.

U.S. Department of Labor. *Dictionary of Occupational Titles.* Washington, D.C.: U.S. Employment Service, 1949.

U.S. Department of Labor, Bureau of Employment Security. *Estimates of Worker Trait Requirements for 4000 Jobs as Defined in the Dictionary of Occupational Titles.* Washington, D.C.: U.S. Government Printing Office, 1956.

U.S. Department of Labor. *U.S. Manpower in the 1970s: Opportunities and Challenge.* Washington, D.C.: U.S. Government Printing Office, 1970.

U.S. Office of Strategic Services. *Assessment of Men.* New York: Rinehart, 1948.

*Vroom, Victor H. *Work and Motivation.* New York: Wiley, 1964.

Washington State Department of Health. *Conference on Research and Evaluation of Mental Health Programs.* Seattle, Wash.: Washington State Department of Public Health, 1951.

Watson, W. *Flint Implements: An Account of Stone Age Techniques and Cultures.* London: British Museum, 1950.

Weber, M. *The Protestant Ethic and the Spirit of Capitalism.* London: Allen and Unwin, 1930.

Weiner, H. *Psychology and Human Disease.* New York: Elsevier, 1977.

Weinstein, E. A., and Kahn, R. L. *Denial of Illness.* Springfield, Ill.: Chas. C. Thomas, 1955.

Wells, J. A. "Differences in Sources of Social Support in Conditioning and Effect of Perceived Stress on Health." Paper presented to Annual Meeting of the Southern Sociological Association, Georgia, 1977.

Werner, H. *The Comparative Psychology of Mental Development.* Chicago: Follett, 1948.

Westermarck, E. A. *The History of Human Marriage.* 5th ed. London: Macmillan, 1889/1921.

Wheelis, A. *The Quest for Identity.* New York: Norton, 1953.

White, J. J. "Women in the Law." *Michigan Law Review* 65 (1967):1051–1122.

White, Robert W. "Motivation Reconsidered: The Concept of Competence." *Psychological Review* 60 (1959):297–333.

*White, Robert W. "Ego and Reality in Psychoanalytic Theory." *Psychological Issues,* vol. 3 (Whole No. 11). New York: International Universities Press, 1963.

Whitehouse, F. A. "Cardiovascular Disability." In *Psychological Practices with the Physically Disabled,* edited by J. F. Garrett and Edna S. Levine. New York: Columbia University Press, 1962.

Whyte, W. F. *Human Relations in the Restaurant Industry.* New York: McGraw-Hill, 1948.

Whyte, W. F. *Men at Work.* Homewood, Ill.: Irwin, 1961.

Whyte, W. H., Jr. *The Organization Man.* New York: Simon & Schuster, 1956.

Wiener, N. *Cybernetics.* 2d ed. Cambridge, Mass.: MIT Press, 1961.

Wilensky, H. L. "Human Relations in the Workplace: An Appraisal of Some Associations." In *Aging and Leisure,* edited by R. W. Kleemeier. New York: Harper & Row, 1957.

Wilensky, H. L. "Life Cycle, Work Situation and Participation in Formal Associations." In *Aging and Leisure,* edited by R. W. Kleemeier. New York: Oxford University Press, 1961.

*Wilensky, H. L. "Varieties of Work Experience." In *Man in a World at Work,* edited by H. Borow. Boston: Houghton Mifflin, 1964.

Wing, J. K.; Bennett, D. H.; and Denham, J. *The Industrial Rehabilitation of Long-Stay Schizophrenic Patients.* London: Medical Research Council Memo No. 42, HMSO, 1962.

Wing, J. K., and Brown, G. W. *Institutionalization and Schizophrenia.* Cambridge, England: Cambridge University Press, 1970.

Wishner, J. "A Concept of Efficiency in Psychological Health." *Psychological Review* 62 (1955).

Wittkower, E. D., and Cleghorn, R. A., eds. *Recent Developments in Psychosomatic Medicine*. Philadelphia: Lippincott, 1954.

Women's Bureau, U.S. Department of Labor. *1969 Handbook on Women Workers*. Washington, D.C., 1969.

Woodson, W. E. *Human Engineering Guide for Equipment Designers*. Berkeley, Calif: University of California Press, 1954.

Wooley, C. L. *The Sumarians*. Oxford: Clarendon Press, 1928.

*Wright, Beatrice A. *Physical Disability—A Psychological Approach*. New York: Harper & Row, 1960.

Wylie, Ruth. *The Self-Concept*. Lincoln: University of Nebraska Press, 1961.

Yolles, S. A. "Mental Health at Work." In *To Work is Human: Mental Health and the Business Community*, edited by A. McLean. New York: Macmillan, 1967.

Yuker, H. E., Block, J. R., and Campbell, W. J. *A Scale to Measure Attitudes toward the Disabled Person*. New York: Human Resources Foundation, 1960.

Zaccaria, J. *Theories of Occupational Choice and Development*. Guidance Monograph Series. Boston: Houghton Mifflin, 1970.

NAME INDEX

SUBJECT INDEX

A

Achievement, concept of, 92, 162ff, 305ff
Activity, need for, 148–149
Adolescence, 157, 162
Aggression, 90, 92–93, 95, 148
Agriculture, 25, 27ff, 38, 43–45, 58–59, 134, 150–151
Alienation, 52ff
American Orthopsychiatric Association, 303
Animal laborens, 34
Anomie, 58
Anormalization, concept, 292
Anxiety, 220ff, 225ff
Aptitudes, 105ff, 111
Aptitude testing, 171ff, 176, 185
Army Alpha, the, 171
Aryans, 32
Assembly-line workers, 301
Assessment, of work behavior, 169ff
Attitudes
    toward authority, 129–130, 141, 163, 165–166, 129ff, 221–222
    toward peers, 130–131, 136, 166, 167, 221–222
    toward work, 25, 113ff, 161, 178ff, 303ff
Automation, 298ff

B

Bahutu, 32
Barbarism, 32
Bedouin, 32–33
Behavior, 9ff, 12, 73ff, 125
Behaviorism, 9
Benedictine Order, 36
Berdache, 28
Binet, 171

Blue-collar worker

Blue-collar worker, 39, 62ff, 67, 80, 125, 133, 297
Boredom, 148–150

C

Calvinism, 37
Capitalism, 20–22, 36
Careers, 105ff, 115, 160–161
Center for Occupational Mental Health, 228
Child development, 157ff, 288, 293, 303, 305–306, 314–315
Civilization, 23
Client-centered counseling, 191
Clinical psychology, 89, 189, 193–195
Community mental health, 243ff
Competence, 160
Competition, 130–131, 166
Cooperation, 130–131, 166
Coping, 75
Coping Scale, 225ff
Counseling Psychology, 188, 211ff
Crafts, 41–42, 54ff
Craftsman, 27, 34, 36, 42–43, 56, 297, 302
Creativity
    need for, 152–153
    relation to production, 152
Cultural relativism, 98
Culture, 54, 73, 96, 101, 131ff, 164, 311, 312, 314–315
Custom, 131–132

D

Demands, of work, 122ff, 139, 166, 314–315
Denial of illness, 292
Department of Health, Education and Welfare, U.S., 5, 61, 201, 238, 241, 245, 251